13

DIETRICH FISCHER-DIESKAU

Dietrich Fischer-Dieskau Mastersinger

A Documented Study

KENNETH S. WHITTON

OSWALD WOLFF
London

FOR MARJORY, KIRSTY and KENNETH

Es sei, wie es wolle,
Es war doch so schön!

© 1981 Oswald Wolff (Publishers) Ltd., London

British Library Cataloguing in Publication Data

Whitton, Kenneth S.
 Dietrich Fischer-Dieskau
 1. Fischer-Dieskau, Dietrich
 2. Singers, German
 I. Title
 784.3′0092′4   ML420.F

ISBN 0–85496–405–3

Set by Input Typesetting Ltd., London
Printed in the United States of America

Contents

Introduction and Acknowledgements

For over thirty years, the art of Dietrich Fischer-Dieskau has played a major rôle in my own life and career. A Germanist by profession, I have found the greatest inspiration for my work and writings from the imaginative insights that this great artist has given me, not only into the settings of German poems that we know as *Lieder*, but also into other musical genres. He has illuminated for me, as for many others, the worlds of European music and literature.

Having had the good fortune to meet Dietrich Fischer-Dieskau in the early years of his career (1949–1950), I have been able to share the triumphs of his remarkable life and to discuss them with him, in Britain, Germany and elsewhere, on many occasions.

On 7 June 1951, Fischer-Dieskau made his first appearance in Great Britain when he sang in Frederick Delius' *A Mass of Life* at Sir Thomas Beecham's invitation at the Albert Hall. The present book is not intended to be a 'biography', but is a tribute to his massive achievements over the last thirty years. Fischer-Dieskau, still only fifty-six, is singing as well as ever, as his 1979 recording of Schubert's *Winterreise* with Daniel Barenboim emphatically proves, and a definitive biography is, I trust, a task for a far distant day. This 'Documented Study' attempts to put his career since his début in 1947 into perspective by documenting his achievements and delineating those aspects of his art which make him, not only unique, but, in the opinion of most good judges, a musical phenomenon. The study is set against the background of the re-building of war-shattered Germany for whom the singer has been such a distinguished cultural ambassador to the musical centres of the new Europe and far beyond.

Thus, the book is in the nature of an 'interim report', as the business world might say, by a contemporary who possesses or has heard every Fischer-Dieskau record made and has seen him on stage and concert-platform all over Europe over the last thirty years, and has been able to correspond with him and to visit him in his homes in Germany over this long period. It attempts – and with such a rich and varied career it can *only* attempt – to document his stage and concert appearances and his recordings by examining his work in the three main musical areas: oratorio, opera and the solo song. Chapter Six looks finally at some further 'Aspects of Dietrich Fischer-Dieskau' which may surprise some readers who think of Fischer-Dieskau only as a singer.

It is clearly impossible to thank adequately all the people who have helped me in the writing of this book: Dietrich Fischer-Dieskau himself, and his secretary, Diether Warneck, have made available to me documents, diaries, letters and photographs without number. Some of this material has reached me via the Secretary of the recently-formed Dietrich Fischer-Dieskau Gesellschaft in Munich, Herr F. Axel Mehrle, who afforded me every possible assistance during my research work in Munich and Berlin. I am eternally grateful too to Gerald Moore for the interest that he has taken in the work and for his generous Foreword – nor could I omit my thanks to his charming wife Enid for her hospitality during my visit to their lovely cottage in Buckinghamshire.

To all the distinguished musicians, critics, friends and colleagues who have patiently answered my questions, I owe a deep debt of gratitude: if I mention in particular Dame Janet Baker, Leonard Bernstein, Frau Lotte Buckmann, Jörg Demus, Gottfried von Einem, Mathias Fischer-Dieskau, the Earl of Harewood, Dr Ernest Hirschbach, Professor Hans Hotter, Herbert von Karajan, William Mann, Herr Karl-Heinz Meyer, (the Rektor of the Beucke-Oberschule in Berlin-Zehlendorf), Gerald Moore, Alec Robertson, Wolfgang Sawallisch, Desmond Shawe-Taylor and Sir Georg Solti, there are many, many more to whom I have spoken and written about Dietrich Fischer-Dieskau over the years. I am also pleased to acknowledge that the excerpts from the letters of Benjamin Britten are © 1980 by The Britten Estate and are reproduced by kind permission of his Executors.

During this time, too, I have had the privilege of being able to lecture to universities and music societies in Britain and abroad on 'The Art of Dietrich Fischer-Dieskau'; indeed, some of the material in this book was first presented in lecture form. I am grateful to the libraries of various British and German universities for procuring material for me and should like to thank, in particular, Mr Derek Bell, the Music Librarian of the City of Bradford Library, for his co-operation in the latter stages of the work.

It is a particular pleasure to thank a young music scholar, Philip Crookes, for his skilful and enthusiastic assistance with the preparation of the music examples, Andrew Ford, Fellow in Music at the University of Bradford, for valuable suggestions, and my colleagues at Bradford, Professor Stephen Holt and Professor Roger Tilford, for their interest. Dr Maurice Wright is owed a special debt of gratitude for his labours in the preparation of the first complete discography of Fischer-Dieskau's over five hundred recordings.

Finally, I must thank my publisher, Mrs Ilse R. Wolff, who commissioned the work and whose enthusiasm for Fischer-Dieskau's art almost equals my own; Dietrich and Julia Fischer-Dieskau, for their hospitality in their homes in Berlin and Munich; and my wife Marjory who – fortunately for us both! – has shared my admiration and respect for this great artist over the last thirty years.

Kenneth S. Whitton
Leeds and Bradford
August 1980

Foreword by Gerald Moore

No written word can describe the quality of a voice, especially of a voice, as this is the case, which responds with unrivalled technique and discriminative colour to the singer's inspiration, but it can give a strong image of this singer's motivation, of the depth of understanding and the poetry in his soul which give that voice impulse. Kenneth Whitton has achieved this daunting task because of his profound knowledge of the *Lied*, the field of opera, the human voice, and his friendship with Dietrich Fischer-Dieskau.

Fischer-Dieskau's first recordings in London were *Die Schöne Müllerin* and though he was then in his early twenties, the claim that he was one of the greatest interpretative artists that Germany had ever produced was soon substantiated by all associated with him in the studio and by the finished records. Sure enough, this prodigy was not cast in the same mould as most of his famous predecessors. He was, even then, the complete musician and a fluent pianist, as much absorbed in the pianoforte's contribution to the song as his partner at the keyboard, and he recognised that the projection of a song's mood – narrative – picture – was not only the exclusive responsibility of the voice. This was very gratifying to the accompanist who was fortunate enough to be playing for him.

What makes him unique? The answer deserves a book and no one is capable of giving us more enlightenment than the author of this volume. To pin-point one salient feature of the singer's genius, it can be stated categorically that he is no *routinier*. To plant his feet in the same footprints, step by step, along a path he has made before is not in his nature. His conception is ever green, so that a repetition amounts to an act of composition. He would not seek to 'improve' on Schubert or Schumann, Wolf or Brahms, on the contrary, his respect for them is so profound that in rehearsal he would approach a well-loved *Lied* as if it were fresh to him. Plodding uniformity, mandatory bondage to the metronome, are anathema to him; rhythm, lissom and alive, is his golden rule. As every artist of authority should, he embraces a freedom that is subject to discipline of form and taste.

In short, Fischer-Dieskau believes in *tempo rubato* and uses it with unparalleled finesse. It follows that each bar is not mathematically the same length as its neighbour, it is subservient to the phrase which may extend over several bars: the crucial moment of this phrase is sought. It is, in other words, a high point, not necessarily significant by being a top note in the vocal line, rather it may be a subtle turn in the melody begging to be stressed, or a poignant change of harmony in the accompaniment, or, again, a vital word in the lyric. Once decided upon, this high point can be projected gently and persuasively or driven home with emphasis, as occasion requires; more important still, it can be given *time*. *Rubato*, this life-force or main spring, is a most recondite affair and it is precariously balanced; mishandled, it can reduce a passage of chaste beauty into sickly sentimentality, it can distort an elegant phrase, turn nobility to vulgarity. Fischer-Dieskau wields it with such control and sensitivity that he gives wings to the music's urge and leaves the listener, be he never so enlightened, transported without knowing the cause.

When I reflect on my years of association with this man, it is mostly our rehearsals that come to mind, for these were moments of joy and flights of imagination involving hard, deep concentration, with ideas bursting into flame. Bursts of laughter too were in evidence, for this singer behind the scenes is not the austere recitalist of the public platform. I found the man as inspiring as the artist, for the voice is part of the man. That is what this book is about.

I am convinced that Dr Kenneth Whitton has written a work which is destined to become historic, for it unfolds for the benefit of posterity the measure of this extraordinary artist, Dietrich Fischer-Dieskau.

Gerald Moore.

CHAPTER ONE

The Making of a Master

A musical Colossus, Dietrich Fischer-Dieskau has bestridden with equal success the worlds of the art-song, opera and oratorio since his first public appearances in 1947, and has become, in addition, the most-recorded artist of the age.

The singer was born Albert Dietrich Fischer on 28 May 1925 in No. 24 Burggrafenstrasse in Zehlendorf, a middle-class suburb of south-west Berlin. The district was heavily bombed in the latter days of the Second World War and the parental house has vanished. The street, now renamed Beuckestrasse, still boasts however the school founded by the singer's father, then known as Dr Albert Fischer, a classical scholar with an unusual breadth of interests who had also founded two other schools in the district. Formerly the Zehlendorfer Gymnasium (Grammar or High School), the school, (now named the Beucke-Oberschule), is a *Realschule* whose headmaster, Herr Karl-Heinz Meyer, takes legitimate pride in its seventy-fifth anniversary in 1981. The School Hall, with its fine Grecian marble columns, is reached through the impressive portal with the gnomic lines: 'Nur dem Ernst, den keine Mühe bleichet/ Rauscht der Wahrheit tiefversteckter Born' (Truth will only be attained by those who are not deterred by difficulties), a quotation from Friedrich Schiller's poem *Das Ideal und das Leben*, written in 1795 at the height of the German classical movement.

A former pupil of the school, Dr Ernest Hirschbach, now living in Two Mountains, Quebec, remembers how Dr Fischer tried to countervail the oppressively over-academic tendencies of the day and, while continuing to stress the importance of the classical languages, as well as of the German language and its literature, introduced other activities, particularly music, into the curriculum. Dr Hirschbach believed that Dr Fischer was regarded as a 'radical' in those days (circa 1920–1928), since he tried much more than most Grammar School headmasters to *understand* his pupils. He introduced a school newspaper, a *Landheim* (a week-end retreat in the mountains, the *Riesengebirge*), and encouraged annual hikes for staff and pupils. But, above all, he encouraged pupils to play, understand, listen to and even compose music. Fischer-Dieskau, who remembers his father for his undoctrinaire approach to education, told me once that his father's father resolutely refused to allow the young Albert to become a musician, rejecting the profession as a 'brotlose Kunst' (literally, a 'breadless art'!)

Dr Albert Fischer was born on 1 April 1865 in Althaldensleben near Magdeburg in north Germany and married, firstly, Elisabeth Puder (1874–1917), by whom he had a son Joachim (born 28 November 1896) and a daughter, both of whom are now dead, and, secondly, Theodora (Dora) Klingelhöffer (1884–1966) by whom he had three sons, Klaus (born 1921), Martin (born 1923) and Dietrich (the singer) (born 1925).

The wife of the former headmaster of the Schadow School, the neighbouring school to Dr Fischer's, Frau Lotte Buckmann, recalls Dr Fischer as a short, solemn, but very scholarly and musical gentleman. She remembers too the great pleasure that the *Gemeinde* (parish) of Zehlendorf felt when Dr Fischer's operetta *Sesenheim* was first produced in the Theater des Westens in the Kantstrasse in Berlin in the early 1920's. The theme of the work was the turbulent love-affair between Germany's most famous poet, Johann Wolfgang von Goethe (1749–1832), and the naive country lass Friederike Brion, during one of Goethe's visits to the village of Sesenheim while he was studying in 1770–1771 at the nearby university of Strassburg. If the theme was treated in a more professional and commercially more successful way by Franz Lehár (*Friederike* 1928), Fischer-Dieskau is eager to give his father credit for having encouraged music-making in Zehlendorf, particularly by his founding of a successful concert-series which brought great names such as Richard Strauss, Emmy Destinn, Franz von Vecsey, Claire Dux, Frieda Hempel, Emilie Herzog and many others to the little suburb. These concerts were Fischer-Dieskau's introduction to great music, just as his father's library, with its well-thumbed and annotated Cotta edition of Goethe's works, was his introduction to great literature.

In 1937 Dr Fischer decided to preserve his mother's maiden name and added, by due process of law, the 'Dieskau' to his own. This re-established a musical connection which, it is fanciful to think, might have quickened the singer's interest, since Emma Fischer (*née* von Dieskau) (1835–1908) was a direct descendant of that Kammerherr Carl Heinrich von Dieskau for whom Johann Sebastian Bach wrote his secular cantata *Mer hahn en neue Oberkeet* (We've got a new squire), the so-called *Bauernkantate* (Peasant Cantata), first performed on 30 August 1742. On that day, von Dieskau was invested with the lands of Klein-Zschocher and Knauthain near Leipzig after the signing of the Treaty of Berlin in July 1742. The text slily tries to suggest that the villagers of Klein-Zschocher might have their taxes reduced by their new squire and it ends with the rousing adulatory chorus: 'Es lebe Dieskau und sein Haus' (Long live Dieskau and his kin); Fischer-Dieskau has sung this cantata on many occasions, but his savouring of the name Dieskau on the 1961 recording is a joy to hear.

Although the artist has no longer many close or active connections with Zehlendorf, the family name is preserved at the entrance to a small path off the Königstrasse leading past the Paul Mebes park. The path is named the 'Fischer-Dieskau-Weg' and the metal plaque reads: 'Dr Albert Fischer-Dieskau, Geheimer Studienrat, Begründer (i.e. founder) des Zehlendorfer Gymnasiums, 1865–1937', while Dr Fischer-Dieskau, his mother and his two wives, lie buried in the curiously-named 'Onkel Tom' cemetery in Zehlendorf.

It is interesting to imagine the reception that would have been given to Dr Fischer's operetta in the Theater des Westens in the 1920's. That was, of course, the period directly following the catastrophic defeat of Germany in the First World War and the founding of the ill-fated Weimar Republic in 1919, and also the time of the cruel inflation of January 1923 when one pre-war gold Reichsmark could have bought two thousand five hundred paper marks. An operetta by a Grammar School Headmaster in his fifties seems a strange bed-fellow for the works of Kurt Weill, Paul Dessau, Ernst Křenek and the other composers of the Expressionist and *Neue Sachlichkeit* (New Objectivity) movements, the brash, vulgar, emotional background to which was so well portrayed in films like

Cabaret and in books such as Peter Gay's *Weimar Culture*, in English, and *Die Kultur der Weimarer Republik* (1978) by Jost Hermand and Frank Trommler, in German.

Of course, there was another side to Berlin in the 1920's. Bruno Walter wrote that it was 'as if all the eminent artistic forces were shining forth once more, imparting to the last festive symposium of the minds a many-hued brilliance before the night of barbarism closed in'. (*Theme and Variations*, 1946). This, Walter reminds us, was the time when Furtwängler was conducting the Philharmonic concerts, the State Opera was premièring Alban Berg's *Wozzeck* (1925), conducted by Erich Kleiber, the Kroll Opera was under the direction of Otto Klemperer and the Municipal Opera under Walter himself. I too was born in 1925 and vividly remember my parents' description of these often bitter years, dominated in Britain, of course, by the General Strike of 1926.

Dr Albert Fischer(-Dieskau) was sixty when his third son, Albert Dietrich, was born; the singer has often recalled – with some wonderment – to me that Hugo Wolf was only five years older than his father. Although Fischer-Dieskau's grandfather had published a book on church hymns (with the title *Hymnologie*), there is no professional musical training in the Fischer-Dieskau family. The father was a professional philologist and a self-taught musician, while the mother was a talented, but amateur, pianist who had always wanted to be a singer. The singer's earliest musical memories are of sitting beneath his father's grand piano on Sundays listening to the latter's skilful chorale improvisations and of attending the concerts and theatrical performances in the school hall, initiated and organised by his father. Thus, we have no *Wunderkind* story here, no Mozart, no Menuhin.

When I asked Fischer-Dieskau to try to describe himself as a young boy, he answered: 'Shy, clumsy, obedient and uninterested in sport'. The last words interested me, since I remembered that his father had demonstrated *his* wide range of sympathies by founing, apart from the concerts, the Zehlendorf Tennis Club (the 'Zehlendorfer Wespen', the Zehlendorf Wasps)in 1911 and also – in 1912– the first school rowing club on the Wannsee, a large lake in south-west Berlin.

When he was five, Fischer-Dieskau was sent to a small primary school for boys only in Berlin-Lichterfelde, but was nine before he started to take piano lessons. He swears that the first musical work to make an impression on him was the Wedding March from Wagner's *Lohengrin*, which he thinks he heard on the radio when he was about six years old. Later, when he began work on one of his youthful passions, his puppet-theatre, he produced Weber's *Der Freischütz* with the help of gramophone records, (another early passion), and figures cut out of the *Neuruppiner Bilderbogen*.

His piano lessons led indirectly to the second great artistic influence in his life: painting and drawing. Encouraged by Friedrich Seyer who was the father of his first piano teacher, Joachim Seyer-Stephan, and who often illustrated fairy tales such as *The Arabian Nights*, the young Fischer-Dieskau began to draw and paint. It was many years before he was brave enough to try his hand at oils, but today in his two beautiful houses, in the Lindenallee in Berlin-Charlottenburg and in Berg just outside Munich, there hang the many testimonies to his skill and interest. As he often says, 'It helps to release the tensions and strains of my profession', a view shared by many musicians, including Tito Gobbi.

When Fischer-Dieskau was asked in 1961 to name the picture which had meant most to him at that time, he nominated Paul Klee's last picture *Ohne Titel* (No Title) of 1940, with the remark that he was much more inhibited about venturing into the world of modern art than that of modern music and blamed the shuttered world of Hitlerian Germany for his ignorance. His own oil-paintings are very 'modern', 'non-representational' and lively, expressing a vibrant love of primary colours and unusual shapes. He confesses to an insatiable curiosity in *all* paintings and to having no favourites, although Max Ernst, Wilhelm Leibl, Claude Monet, Gustave Courbet and the 'unknown' works of Pablo Picasso crop up in conversation.

The singer's secondary schooldays and formative years were spent, of course, in the shadow of the 'Thousand Year Reich', Hitler's Germany (1933–1945). The dictator came to power on 30 January 1933 when the singer was seven; his memories of these years are extremely vivid.

His parents were apolitical. He describes his father as 'kaiser-treu, aber national-liberal' in the First World War, that is, a supporter of the German Kaiser, but in a liberal way. The father had not served in the war because of his post as a teacher, although

the son Joachim (Fischer-Dieskau's half-brother) was a lieutenant
in the field. Like most young Germans, Fischer-Dieskau had to
join the *Hitler-Jugend* (Hitler Youth movement). Hardly the stuff
of which Nazi heroes were fashioned, the 'shy, clumsy' boy made
little of the Spartan-like discipline of the early 30's in Germany,
and remembers with vivid bitterness the exhaustion he experienced
after having carried torches through Berlin's Olympic Stadium in
an eight-hour stint, and the unashamed warlike nature of their
activities. In school, too, the Nazi ideology made itself felt;
although Fischer-Dieskau remembers that most of the pupils disliked the régime and often disturbed the Latin classes in particular
with their anti-Nazi questions, he remembers too the disturbing
anti-Semitism of the religion classes and the militariness of the
drill-practice in the games hours, and above all, the *Turnen*, gym-
nastics, the Nazi sport *par excellence*.

By this time of course, his father had retired from schoolteaching
and had nothing to do with his former school. He was also able to
devote more of his time to his three sons. The mother too, a keen
pianist who had introduced the young Dieter to the piano, was
able to take the children to concerts in that culture-rich Berlin that
I have mentioned. Fischer-Dieskau's first operatic experience in
the theatre was Wagner's *Lohengrin*. 'The splendour of the Knight's
swan-shield and all the rest made me realise for the first time that
I wanted to be a singer', he wrote. 'And even if I never had the
chance to try out the golden curls (which I used to think were
genuine) on my own head, then I did at least manage to earn a
living a third of a tone lower down among the baritones!'

His father's retirement and the leisure that it gave him to write
also had an influence on the growing boy. His father received a
postcard one day from his eight-year old son on holiday which
proudly proclaimed that he had started a novel entitled *My garden*
and that he had already covered fourteen sides of his school note-
book. This work of art vanished in the flames of war-torn Berlin,
but Fischer-Dieskau recalls a few sentences: 'I wanted to get married, so I telephoned all over the place until I found a wife. Then
I told her that we were going to the Registry Office first thing in
the morning'. The theme does not sound particularly promising!

If there is anything in the line from Schiller's play *Wallensteins
Tod* (The Death of Wallenstein), 'Und in dem Heute wandelt

schon das Morgen' (And tomorrow is already seen in today. . .),
it might seem as if most of Fischer-Dieskau's present professional
and leisure interests were already foreshadowed in these early
years: singing *per se*, opera, painting, writing. One outstanding
exception remains to be mentioned: conducting. When Fischer-
Dieskau made his début as a conductor with the Camerata Academica of Salzburg in the Stadtsaal in Innsbruck on 16 October
1973, it was in fact the fulfillment of a long-cherished ambition.
Like many a lover of music, he has always conducted to his gramophone records, and his imagination was set racing at the sight of
the silvery-locked conductor at his first orchestral concert when he
was eleven. It was a Liszt programme and included the *Faust
Symphony* and Konrad Hansen in piano works. Earlier dreams of
becoming President of the Reichstag – or even of becoming an
engine-driver! – faded before this inspiring spectacle. Of such are
dreams made – and to a few is given the opportunity of realising
them.

Although 1973 was his 'official' professional début, the singer
recalls with some embarrassment his 'unofficial' début. His parents were 'taking the waters' in the east German spa of Flinsberg,
when a competition for conductors was announced. Then twelve
years old, Fischer-Dieskau decided to enter and to conduct the
overture to Weber's *Der Freischütz* (which he knew so well, of
course). The leader of the orchestra felt however that it would be
easier for the young lad if they played a waltz – and chose *The
Blue Danube*. That seemed to suit a twelve-year old in a sailor's suit
rather better! Unfortunately it was not in the 'conductor's' repertoire, and, although he entered into the spirit of the occasion,
standing on a chair and waving the bâton about merrily, he
misunderstood a friendly horn-player's warning that a rest was
coming and promptly conducted the orchestra through the awful
stillness. Thus ended – for the time being anyway – a promising
career.

Fischer-Dieskau's early years were therefore very normal. His
elder brother Klaus, born on 2 January 1921, had also showed
musical leanings, and these emerged later when he too became a
professional musician, an organist, composer and conductor of the
Hugo-Distler-Chor, which he had formed in Berlin. The middle

boy, Martin, was born handicapped. We shall hear more of him shortly.

After beginning piano lessons with Joachim Seyer-Stephan at nine years öld, Fischer-Dieskau became proficient enough to accompany school friends playing clarinet and flute. His voice was now beginning to develop however and had been noticed by his teacher in his primary school. It was a good boy's alto voice, and after he had played piano solos at school concerts – he recalls playing Mozart's C minor Fantasia, for example – he was asked to undertake solo vocal rôles as well as being allowed to conduct the school orchestra in, for example, the *Sanctus* from the E flat major Schubert Mass.

His visits to concerts with his parents and the many records in his house had bred a keen interest in the great singers of the past as well as in those singers whom he had had an opportunity to hear in Berlin, particularly Emmi Leisner (1885–1958) whom he worshipped. Leisner, a fine expressive contralto is perhaps best known in this country for her recording with Friedrich Schorr of the Fricka-Wotan duet from Act II of *Die Walküre* on DB 1720–1. She had a rich powerful voice, still singing strongly on records issued in 1933 when she was 48. Fischer-Dieskau's interest in the *Lieder* of Max Reger also stems from this friendship. Spurred to emulate her, he began to study a German song – the first time he remembers doing so consciously – Brahms' *Wie bist du, meine Königin*. This early love for Brahms coincided with the breaking of his voice, at about fifteen – a very gentle break, Fischer-Dieskau recalls, which did not necessitate any interruption to his school studies, most of his singing being done anyway in rooms far away from any possible listeners. The contrast between Fischer-Dieskau at fifteen singing Brahms in an empty room, and Fischer-Dieskau forty years later singing the same song to audiences of up to three thousand and more, has a certain piquancy, I think.

With the invasion of Poland on 3 September 1939, Hitler had unleashed the Second World War; those who lived through the period will remember vividly the first two phases: the 'phoney war' up to the Fall of France and the Dunkirk retreat in 1940, and then the unbroken run of Nazi victories up to Rommel's defeats in Africa in 1943. Until big-city bombing began in 1942, life in Berlin, as life elsewhere, proceeded fairly naturally; people went about their daily business, children to school, their parents to work. Fischer-Dieskau was fourteen at the outbreak of the war and, as we have seen, his education had not been interfered with. Teachers now began to disappear into the armed forces however, which eventually resulted in temporary examination arrangements for school leavers. The *Abitur*, the German school leaving certificate, normally taken in ten (or more) subjects, was substituted by the so-called 'Not-Abitur' (Emergency Leaving Certificate); Fischer-Dieskau took only the oral part of this examination in 1942, which occasioned another curious link with Johann Sebastian Bach. His music teacher, presuming that Fischer-Dieskau, above all people, would know Bach's *Peasant Cantata*, chose for his pupil's oral *Abitur*-theme 'Parallels to Bach's *Phöbus und Pan*', since one of Pan's arias (*Zu Tanze, zu Sprunge*) in the latter work is identical with the bass aria *Dein Wachstum sei feste* in the 1742 cantata.

After his father's death on 30 August 1937 at the age of 72, the young Dieter had come much more under the influence of his artistic mother who was to survive her husband by some thirty years. (She died in Berlin on 5 September 1966). The singer had been no great scholar in his early years of school; his teachers had somehow failed to waken that intellectual curiosity which so manifested itself in later life, and, apart perhaps from his work in German, music, drawing and English ('but with no opportunities to speak, of course'!), he had gained little from his school studies. For as long as I have known him, he has maintained that he could never imagine himself as a teacher and that he had no wish to write an instructional book or to hold master-classes. His views were curiously similar indeed to those of his friend, Sir Geraint Evans, who told John Higgins of *The Times*, 'I would rather produce an opera than train young singers; the voice is a terribly fragile instrument and I am frightened to death of giving people the wrong lessons', (20 January 1973). Yet, although Fischer-Dieskau is critical of some of the teaching being given at the present in a few of Germany's music academies, he naturally acknowledges that every student of music needs a good teacher; he himself continually reminds listeners of the debt he owes to his own teachers. But when he received the Ernst-von-Siemens Music Prize in the Bavarian *Akademie der Schönen Künste* in Munich on 11 April 1980, he surprised most listeners when he announced that he would

donate the prize of 150,000 Swiss francs (c. £40,000) to the founding of a bursary scheme for gifted young singers. 'When I eventually have fewer international commitments', he said, 'I should like
to teach', specifying that he would like to give young singers training in the wider aspects of vocal technique, namely concert and
stage practice. Jörg Demus, the Austrian concert pianist and one
of Fischer-Dieskau's most distinguished accompanists, would certainly be pleased with that announcement. Some time ago he wrote
to me: 'Had I as a pianist been confronted with such an over-
life-size figure as a predecessor, then it would have been my most
burning desire to study and analyse his talents and to make them
my own. But we still hear singers who have not mastered their art
intellectually, who declaim in a weak or even false manner, who
phrase in short breaths, who, in a word, sing badly – and are *still*
praised'. And he added that he hoped that Fischer-Dieskau would
– in his later years – turn to teaching to help eradicate these faults.

Fischer-Dieskau was also a late reader; only after much enjoyment of those most popular of German children's books, the American Western adventures of Karl May and Friedrich Gerstäcker,
and the rather sickly stories of Johanna Spyri (of 'Heidi' fame),
did he come to the great works of German literature, of 'Goethe,
Schiller, Kleist and Keller', to quote him. It is true, however, that
because of his father's co-founding of the *Theater der Höheren Schulen*
(Theatre for Grammar Schools) in Berlin, he had been able to see
many of the great classical plays and actors eg. Heinrich George
in Goethe's *Götz von Berlichingen*, Ludwig Wüllner in *King Lear*,
and Eugen Klöpfer in Schiller's *Wilhelm Tell*.

His mother, (whose own mother had been a well-known pianist
just old enough to have seen Greig conduct), encouraged him to
play her favourite Schumann, Chopin and Brahms, while from his
father, who preferred operatic music, he had learned a great deal
about Wagner and Richard Strauss. (Dr. Fischer thought Verdi
rather too naive ['simpel']).

These home interests, along with the intensive musical life of the
school, allowed a suggestion made by Emmi Leisner to fall on
fertile soil; she did not want to teach him herself, she said, but
recommended that he should study with Georg A. Walter, an old
Zehlendorfer, who had had a fine reputation as a Bach tenor,
particularly as the Evangelist in the Passions. Fischer-Dieskau was

sixteen at the time and although he had had dreams of becoming a *Heldentenor* – especially after his *Lohengrin* experience! – it was soon clear that his voice had broken to a high lyric baritone as is so often the case with deep boys' voices. Walter worked through all the Bach cantatas with his willing pupil and quite clearly prepared the ground for that intimate and almost personal relationship with Bach which Fischer-Dieskau seems to enjoy. They worked on his *coloratura*, those fiendishly difficult ornaments, figurations, runs, trills, and the like, which terrify so many singers of Bach and which one takes for granted in Fischer-Dieskau's performances.

But even Fischer-Dieskau looks back more with horror than with pride on a performance given at one of Walter's pupils' concerts when he sang Hans Sachs' *Schlussansprache* from *Die Meistersinger* – at seventeen. As he says, 'it was really rather a stupid thing to try with so young a voice'. Who knows how that experience determined him never to sing Sachs again until he felt himself to be ready? And that was not until he was nearly fifty-one, at the Deutsche Oper in Berlin, on 12 February 1976.

It will be seen therefore that the singer already had a considerable active and passive repertoire behind him by 1942–1943; he had made a thorough study of Bach's cantatas, he had begun to investigate the art of *Lieder*-singing, above all at Emmi Leisner's *Liederabende*, and had been fortunate enough to have been able to see and hear operas such as *Parsifal* (with Franz Völker and Rudolf Bockelmann), *Fidelio* (with Frida Leider), *Ariadne* (with, firstly, Erna Berger, and then Elisabeth Schwarzkopf as Zerbinetta) and the *Marriage of Figaro*. He was therefore hardly the average 'fresher' when he began his studies at Berlin's Academy of Music in 1942. This was evident when, on 31 January 1943, he undertook an engagement which even now sets the senses racing – his first *Winterreise*! He sang it in the Gemeindehaus in Zehlendorf and it turned out to be a singular evening. Accompanied by a female colleague, he followed the piano trio of the first half of the concert before an audience of some 150. The duo had decided to omit two of the 'most difficult songs', as he put it to me – No. 8 *Rückblick* and No. 9 *Irrlicht* – and they had barely got under way when the wail of sirens heralded one of the heaviest Berlin air-raids yet experienced. After a three hours' wait in the air-raid shelters, the singer remembers with some legitimate pride that *all* the audience returned to hear his, by his own confession, rather sentimental ('schmachtend') rendering of the Schubert cycle.

Among his first teachers at the Academy was the senior professor, Hermann Weissenborn, to whom the singer to this day pays touching homage. Till the professor's death in 1956, he went to see him at least twice a week, in order, as he told me, 'to have my voice controlled'. From Professor Weissenborn, a pupil of Johannes Messchaert and the great Raimund von zur Mühlen, Fischer-Dieskau learned above all his breathing technique (the Garcia method),* how to shape vowels, and how to interpret all types of music. (Weissenborn was the teacher of other well-known artists, among them, the late Gerhard Stolze, Marga Höffgen, Elisabeth Höngen and Donald Bell).

His beginner's studies with Hermann Weissenborn lasted barely a semester (three months), but they laid the foundations both of Fischer-Dieskau's later technical mastery of the vocal repertoire and also of his attitude to his art. The tiny music professor insisted that perfection was the goal, and perfection was only attained by hard and constant work – and once *at*tained, it had to be *maintained*. And each artist has to achieve this by himself, which is why Fischer-Dieskau loves to quote a Weissenborn maxim: 'You can help a pupil into the saddle, but he has to ride by himself'. One of Fischer-Dieskau's most endearing characteristics is his modesty, his belief that he can never stop learning. All his colleagues pay tribute to this trait. Dame Janet Baker, in a charming little letter to me, wrote that 'the most touching thing about him is his vulnerability. This large man with an unequalled reputation can still be hurt by what others say about him, can still be grateful for the kind word'. (One of his friends told me that the 'smallest room' in his house in Berlin was once papered with adverse critical reviews!)

By 1943, it had become obvious to those concerned with the conduct of the war (on both sides) that the 'Grand Alliance' of the United States, Britain and the Soviet Union now held the upper

---

*After Manuel Garcia (1805–1906), the inventor of the 'laryngoscope', which allowed singers to watch their vocal chords 'in action', as it were. He taught at the R.A.M. from 1848 to 1895.

hand. That year, the German *Wehrmacht* suffered over one and a half million casualties and, as John Toland writes in his book *Adolf Hitler* (1976), 'it was so difficult to find replacements that the conscription law exempting the youngest or only son of a family was suspended and fifty-year old men veterans of the First World War were deemed eligible for service'.

It was therefore unlikely that a young singer like Fischer-Dieskau would escape conscription, no matter who spoke for him. Professor Weissenborn's attempts to help him are to be found in a letter from Berlin-Wilmersdorf of 12 October 1943. He wrote:

'Mr Dietrich Fischer-Dieskau has an extraordinary vocal and musical talent. His unusually beautiful baritone voice has a rare charm, is full of expression and has an extensive range. He interprets *Lieder* and arias with expressive intensity and has proved himself to be a creative artist of great musicality.

To further Fischer-Dieskau's remarkable talents in any way possible is a high priority and is in keeping with our Führer's instruction that the development of our young artists should be maintained and promoted'.

There was however no reaction in 1943 from a leadership which, in private, had just proceeded to the 'Final Solution' of the Jewish 'problem' in the Warsaw ghetto on 9 April 1943, which, in retrospect, can be seen as the first confession of the certainty of defeat, after the costly failure to take Stalingrad in January 1943.

Leaving behind, not only his studies but also a young fellow-student for whom he had formed a deep affection, Irmgard Poppen, a student of the cello, Fischer-Dieskau was called up in late 1943 and was posted firstly to an Army veterinary unit in Fürstenwalde, east of Berlin, because of a blood-vessel disorder. He was then immediately ordered with his unit to help save a trainload of one hundred and fifty sickly horses from a Soviet attack at Zitomir, west of Kiev. The singer gives a delightful description of how he used to sing into the ears of his unruly horses as he brushed them down.

Whether he sang *Winterreise* to them he cannot remember, but I possess an interesting account of his second public performance of the cycle. During a spell of leave in early 1944, he paid a visit to his old Academy of Music in Berlin and an anonymous student recorded the event in student's prose:

> We are sitting in the Great Hall of the Academy of Music for a lecture on *The Art of the Lied*, obligatory for all students studying singing, although most find the subject pretty boring since they are all dreaming of a brilliant career as opera stars. . .
> We've 'done' Schubert and are finishing off with his *Winterreise*. Prof. Kusterer is at the piano explaining and demonstrating; he talks about the text, the musical setting and other things, all that a singer has to know to interpret a Schubert *Lied*. Suddenly he asks if any student would like to sing a *Lied*. A young man stands up and walks calmly to the piano. We look at each other in astonishment: A newcomer! Thin, tall, in a uniform which seems to fit nowhere! We are doubly amazed that it is a young *man* – we have very few male students now. 'He's probably got study leave', someone whispers. Professor Kusterer and 'the newcomer' agree on the *Lied* and begin.
>
> The first song from *Winterreise* goes: 'I came as a stranger and I depart as a stranger' (Fremd bin ich eingezogen. . .). We listen. And are again amazed. The young soldier with the almost childish face has a voice that is quite unbelievable. His almost tangible sort of musicality transmits itself to us immediately. Amazing!
>
> The song finishes. The Professor turns the pages of the score, looks up at the young man – he nods and sings on. And *how* he sings. Suddenly we are experiencing in fascinating intensity, with an immediacy that pierces the soul, the torture of unrequited love – we are lost in the ice and the snow, experiencing hope, despair, defiance, pity, the tragic fate of a lonely soul.
>
> The lecture hour is long since past, but no one realises it – again and again the door opens and other students tiptoe in – and listen. It is almost as if the news had been spirited round the Academy: 'Someone is singing *Winterreise*: Come and listen!' Anyway, the Great Hall is packed – there is not an empty seat. 'The newcomer' sings on, one *Lied* after the other, with modest, confident self-assurance.
>
> And suddenly we are all aware of something that cannot be

expressed in words – we are unbelievably moved – we dimly perceive that a star is being born. 'Strange old man, will you go with me? Will you play your organ to my songs?' The last notes die away. The Professor's hands drop from the piano. Utter silence! Then he looks up at the singer. 'What's your name, young man?'. . .'Dietrich Fischer-Dieskau'.

Fischer-Dieskau was then posted for infantry training to Perleberg, and in late spring 1944, was detailed for his first real mission, into the Soviet Union. Near Leipzig however, the company was diverted to Italy where it ran into a heavy air attack causing many casualties and where Lance-corporal (Private First-Class) Fischer-Dieskau spent the remainder of the war in the neighbourhood of Pisa and Bologna. Most of his days and nights were spent in shell-holes – but he is proud that he never fired on a human being. He told me that the six compulsory rounds that had to be fired each day were fired into the air at night.

Yet there were compensations. His musical talents were already known and he was now and then driven on the rations lorry over heavily-shelled roads to Bologna where he performed solo in front of the Nazi General in command. 'After saying my "Heil Hitler!"', he told me, 'I had to sing the *Erlkönig*!'

Fischer-Dieskau suffered all the traumas of impending defeat as he and his comrades had to listen each night to the voice of Thomas Mann's son, Klaus, tempting the German soldiers to desert and join the Allied cause. (Although Fischer-Dieskau himself was 'deeply moved and worried' by Thomas Mann's message to the German nation after the end of the war in 1945, I witnessed the author's unfriendly reception from his former countrymen and -women when he returned to Frankfurt from his exile in California in 1949 to receive the Goethe Prize. The reception doubtless determined him to settle in Kilchberg in Zürich where he died in 1955).

On 5 May 1945, three days before VE Day (the end of the war in Europe), Fischer-Dieskau was captured by the Americans after he and his comrades had halted on their flight to repair the roof of a peasant's cottage in the Po valley. There followed two years' imprisonment.

I myself have little doubt that Fischer-Dieskau's experiences, both in war and in prison camp, have contributed greatly to his development as a man and as an artist. Far from being the distant, austere, almost Olympian figure that some music journalists have tried to make of him, Fischer-Dieskau is a charming, approachable, although undeniably shy man who, with his bubbling laugh, has a great talent for attracting friendship and loyalty. These years in a prison-of-war camp taught him the value of friendship, the meaning of 'humanity' and 'tolerance' and the value of art as a means of raising one's eyes from the ground to allow one to look up at the stars. This study will attempt to show how he has striven to place his great art at the disposal of all men and women of all countries, to help, in some small way, to make good the terrible injustices of Man's inhumanity to Man.

He wrote to me once about his feelings as a German after the war: '. . .mainly shame, for a long time, even during my first European tours, when there was still dislike of Germans which I understood only too well. I had early wanted to change everything to do with Germany since I had heard from relations and my step-brother (Joachim, who was working in the Ministry of Labour) the complaints and reproaches and the desire to end this madness. So it didn't need Thomas Mann's appeal to the Germans to be read in POW camps to open my eyes. In any case, the Nazis had allowed my handicapped brother Martin to starve to death in the 'sanatorium' to which they had transported him. From the 'Crystal Night' (the infamous *Kristallnacht* of 10 November 1938 when 814 Jewish shop-windows, 171 homes and 191 synagogues were destroyed and burned and thirty-six Jews murdered. KSW) to Goebbels' speeches in the Olympia Stadium, there was hardly any event which did not arouse an instinctive, and later, a conscious revulsion in me. . .'

The positive side to his period in the POW camp is seen in his command of, and feeling for the Italian language. He was eventually able to speak to local peasants and workers as he helped to construct buildings in the Appenines, enjoying their chestnut tarts at the same time! He never claims to be fluent in spoken Italian, 'but can get about when I have to!'

It was in prisoner-of-war camp, too, that he was able better to judge the effect of 'classical' music on the ordinary, perhaps not too well-educated man. Fischer-Dieskau was prevailed upon (by the American recreation officer) to act as a 'cultural adviser'. He sang *Lieder* without scores – either without accompaniment or to hastily-improvised ones – gave recitations of poetry, and even copied out the *Schöne Müllerin* from memory, as well as playing piano duets (of the original four-handed version of Brahms' Haydn variations, op. 56b of 1873, for instance). He was often sent round the various camps on lorries with a piano, a pianist who had worked with Leipzig Radio and a page-turner and, although it is probable that the soldiers preferred his renderings of the arias from Eduard Künnecke's 1921 operetta *Der Vetter aus Dingsda* (The Cousin from Nowhere) to his art-songs, he still receives letters from old 'Landser' (infantrymen) who recall his efforts with pleasure. The singer used to stage the works himself in a barracks with seating for a thousand people! (One should add here that Gustav Adolf Trumpff, a musicologist who eventually settled in Darmstadt, remembers introducing Fischer-Dieskau to Wolf's *Italienisches Liederbuch*, bought for two packets of cigarettes in Pisa, and performing Heinrich Schütz's *Christmas Oratorio*, with Fischer-Dieskau singing all the parts – including the soprano – at a Christmas concert in 1945).

It was difficult in these circumstances to hear good music or to experience life outside the camp. Fischer-Dieskau's one effort to steal out to see the cathedral in Pisa ended in arrest by the American M.P.'s and an eight-day confinement 'with bread and water'. He only heard one opera during the whole period – a very provincial performance in Bologna. Yet, looking back on these days, on the strange cultural life, on the music he studied and sang, the baritone is certain that it was here that he learned his profession – but also about human nature, its strengths and weaknesses, essential knowledge for any portrayer of stage-rôles. Here too, he learned a great deal of his future repertoire in relative peace and quiet, how to face a public, how to act, how to build a programme of songs for a critical audience – and much else besides. As he says: All this replaced the traditional tours of the provinces for him and enabled him to seize the great chance that came his way in 1948.

*   *   *   *   *

Before that chance appeared, however, came his dramatic return to Germany in 1947, where he arrived on the last hospital train from Pisa in Göppingen, (now in Baden-Württemberg in south-west Germany), dressed only in pyjamas, to be greeted by that former student, Irmgard Poppen, to whom he was now engaged. Defeated Germany had by that time been divided into four zones, Soviet in the east, American in the south, British in the north and a small French zone in the south-west. Inter-zonal rail passes were hard to come by, and Fischer-Dieskau chuckles when he remembers how he dodged the passport officials by creeping along the train as it crossed from the American into the French zone.

Irmgard Poppen's home was in Freiburg in the Black Forest, while her uncle, Professor Hermann Meinhard Poppen, an erst-while pupil of Max Reger, was Music Director in nearby Heidelberg; thus the young singer found plenty of encouragement to continue his studies. It was in Baden-Württemberg indeed that he took the first small step towards the glittering prizes when he met an urgent request for a replacement for a sick baritone in Brahms' *German Requiem* in Badenweiler in September 1947. With the experienced soprano, Tilla Briem, as his partner, and with the Freiburg Bach Choir directed by Theo Egel, Fischer-Dieskau, without rehearsal, gave a performance described as 'outstanding' and 'highly meritorious', which brought him to the notice of, among others, Professor Elsa Schiller, the then director of the Music Department of *RIAS* (*R*adio *im* *a*merikanischen *S*ektor), the radio station in the American sector of Berlin. Fischer-Dieskau had already attempted the, at that time, difficult task of crossing the American-Soviet zonal border and had got as far as Hanover before being turned back. Only with the help of an 'Anforderung' (a request for his return) from the Academy of Music and Professor Weissenborn, was he able to get back to his mother's house in the Schützallee in Berlin and to take up his studies again. These were, however, to prove to be very fleeting, and he has always thought of himself as, in essence, an autodidact.

Professor Elsa Schiller (1897–1974), later, (from 1952–1965), the director of Deutsche Grammophon's recorded classical repertory, remained one of Fischer-Dieskau's staunchest champions. A Jewess in the Roman Catholic faith who had endured the purgatory of the concentration camp at Theresienstadt, Elsa Schiller immediately recognised the quality and the immense human appeal of

Fischer-Dieskau's voice and character, and engaged him for his first broadcast *Winterreise* in *RIAS*. This broadcast in December 1947, repeated on numerous occasions, either *in toto*, as separate *Lieder*, or for schools programmes, brought Fischer-Dieskau's name to the wide general public

South-west Germany knew him already; after the Brahms' success, he sang the rôle of Jesus in Bach's *St Matthew Passion* in Konstanz, singing the bass arias as well when his colleague fell ill. But not even an offer from Gustav Scheck, the Director of the Freiburg Academy of Music, to stay on as a lecturer in music, could keep him from Berlin. The decision proved to be a wise one. Germany's appalling losses in the war, (one estimate is four million dead), had resulted not only in serious social, economic and political problems – in 1967, twenty years after the war, there were still three million more women than men in West Germany, almost all over forty. It had torn great gaps in its cultural life, too. It was therefore not difficult for a gifted young male singer to find work. Guided by Professor Weissenborn, Fischer-Dieskau began to extend his repertoire and his professional engagements. Professor H. H. Stuckenschmidt, now the music critic of the *Frankfurter Allgemeine Zeitung*, recalled (in 1970) his first Fischer-Dieskau concert on a January evening in 1948 in the hall of the Gertrauden Schule, a girls' school in Berlin-Dahlem. The twenty-two year old thin, gangling baritone sang Schumann and Wolf; the next day in the *Neue Zeitung*, Stuckenschmidt wrote of the 'gold in the unusually beautiful sound of his baritone voice'.

Now, in April 1948, the singer began to keep what I call his 'musical diary', a record of every engagement undertaken. The first entry is a series of broadcasts (for *RIAS*) on 18 and 25 April and 2 May of Wolf's *Italienisches Liederbuch* with Marie-Louise Mansfeld (soprano) and Walter Welsch (piano). There followed performances of Bach's Cantata No. 82 *Ich habe genug*, with the Karl Ristenpart Orchestra, Brahms' *Vier ernste Gesänge* (with Ludwig Hoffmann at the piano) (which he had first sung in the University of Freiburg in 1947), and, on 6/7 May 1948, his first operatic rôle, the bass part of Colas, the village sooth-sayer, in the twelve-year old Mozart's *Bastien und Bastienne* (K 50), what Charles Osborne, in his *The Complete Operas of Mozart* (1978), has described as 'an unambitious little one-act pastorale interspersed with songs which are hardly grand enough to be called arias'. Undemanding though the arias are (for example, the two verses of 'Befraget mich ein zartes Kind um sein zukünft'ges Glück' (If a gentle child asked me to prophesy the future)), it marks Fischer-Dieskau's first foray into opera – and in a Mozart opera at that!

He had turned down an offer from Ernst Legal, the *Intendant* of the Berlin State Opera, in order to concentrate on his oratorio singing, for, after his *Winterreise*, *RIAS* was keen to use this exceptional new singer. With the Karl Ristenpart chamber orchestra, he now embarked on recordings of some forty of the Bach cantatas. Partnered usually by that most reliable of Bach tenors, Helmut Krebs, Fischer-Dieskau sang most of the bass parts. These recordings, repeated, like *Winterreise*, all over Germany and eventually all over Europe, established the twenty-three year old singer as a star of the future. They were my own introduction to his voice and I can well remember with what impatience I awaited the heralded appearance of his first 78 r.p.m. recordings.

Most great artists can look back on one event in his life which gave him and those who wished him well confidence in his ability to continue with his career, in the certainty that he had it within himself to make good. Fischer-Dieskau has no doubt that his 'Sternstunde', his fateful hour, came in autumn 1948, when he met Heinz Tietjen who had that summer been appointed *Intendant* of the Berlin *Städtische Oper* (the Municipal Opera) in the Kantstrasse. Tietjen, sixty-seven years old, who, as former *Generalintendant* of the Prussian State Theatres up till 1945, had had some little difficulty with the 'denazification' procedure, and was not finally 'cleared' until 1947, was, like most other *Intendanten*, desperately short of good male singers – and particularly of a lyric baritone. Fischer-Dieskau was invited to an audition, firstly to sing, in German, Renato's aria *Eri tu che macchiavi quell'anima* from Act III of Verdi's *Un ballo in maschera* on the stage, and then, alone with Tietjen in a separate room, a few *Lieder* (including Schubert's *Doppelgänger* and *Am Meer* from the *Schwanengesang*). Then came those fateful words, which Fischer-Dieskau has never forgotten: 'In vier Wochen werden Sie den Posa in unserer neuen Inszenierung des *Don Carlos* von Verdi singen' (You'll be singing Posa in our new production of Verdi's *Don Carlos* in four weeks' time)!

Fischer-Dieskau told me how his knees went weak and his mouth dry; apart from the *Vetter aus Dingsda* in the POW camp and Colas on the radio, he had no theatrical experience whatsoever, but it was a pleasing coincidence that the *Städtische Oper* was the former *Theater des Westens* where his father's operetta had been performed in the 20's. (On 30 December 1978, with great ceremony, the house was restored as a theatre for lighter music, under its former name *Theater des Westens*, a stone's throw from the Kurfürstendamm).

As operagoers know only too well, and as John Steane proves very conclusively in his fine book *The Grand Tradition* (1974), a voice is not enough nowadays to make an opera star. Apart from the great emotions, the loving, the laughing and the dying, a singer must be able to stand up, sit down, drink, fence, even smoke, all with complete naturalness. Despite the mellifluence of the voice, it is doubtful whether the reported wooden-ness of some of the great names of the past would be acceptable nowadays on the world's opera stages. And Fischer-Dieskau had an added problem – his height. Although his frame has filled out somewhat in the intervening years, he was still nearly six feet three in 1948, which brought further difficulties for a beginner learning stagecraft.

Despite Tietjen's assurance of offers of help, the singer found that he had largely to teach himself, although, first Josef Greindl, the bass singing King Philip II, and then the conductor, the thirty-three year old Hungarian Ferenc Fricsay, went out of their way to help him. Greindl even gave him private coaching, remarking quizzically, 'Well, after all, I can hardly play you off the stage now, can I?' Fischer-Dieskau remembers too with gratitude the help given by friends like Hans Erich Riebensahm and Leo Blech, who taught him so much about his art, and by constructive critics like H. H. Stuckenschmidt and Werner Oehlmann, among others.

In 1948, Verdi's opera was very topical, based as it is, of course, on Friedrich Schiller's play *Don Carlos* (1787) with its strongly-delineated conflict, between, firstly, the headstrong Don Carlos and his father King Philip, and, secondly, the young prince and the older, more restrained but idealistic Marquis Posa, the Maltese Knight, the upholder of political freedom against the monarchical dictator Philip. The great line in the original German play, 'Sire, Geben Sie Gedankenfreiheit' (Act III, Scene 10) (Sire, give them freedom of thought!) had the proper ring for a truth-starved German audience in the years after the war.

The blend of youthful good looks, imposing presence and lyrical voice brought Fischer-Dieskau a tremendous ovation on that first night, 18 November 1948. At the end of the death-scene aria in Act IV, Fischer-Dieskau's voice 'broke' on the last words 'Ich sterbe' (I'm dying), but in Wolf-Eberhard von Lewinski's words, this was no 'crude naturalism, but rather the artistic rounding-off of a characterisation where Death was the crown of life'. (Don Carlos was sung at the première by Boris Greverus, later by Rudolf Schock, the direction was by Julius Kapp, and the sets by Josef Fenneker). Fischer-Dieskau treasures a letter from Professor Elsa Schiller written on 18 November *1968*, in which this 'staunch champion' reminded him of his great triumph of twenty years earlier. 'Today', she wrote, 'I should like to thank you from the bottom of my heart that you have fulfilled everything – indeed more – that you promised then. How many wonderful, unforgettable evenings have you given us since!'

Yet it was undoubtedly the inspiration that the twenty-three year old baritone received from Ferenc Fricsay that has remained in his memory as he looks back on his early days. He remembers auditioning again in front of Fricsay, who was clad in a leather coat against the rigours of a post-war, coal-less Berlin winter. Correcting Fischer-Dieskau here and there in his own harsh tenor voice, he summed up finally: 'I didn't expect to find an Italian baritone in Berlin'. But Fricsay was not just a conductor; he took a passionate interest in the whole dramatic concept, and strove to marry his own musical ideas of the work with the dramaturgical concepts of the director. He showed enormous patience with the young beginner, explaining to him those tiny details so important in performances – how to lay his hand on the dagger, how to make his cloak swing as he leaves the stage, everything that makes up a stage characterisation. Later in life, Fischer-Dieskau had cause to be grateful to this man and to wonder '. . .if my operatic début would have led to such a successful career on the stage, had it taken place under a less fortunate star, and without his (Fricsay's) sympathetic direction'. Since then, he has often compared Fricsay's 'iron patience' with an orchestra to that of Toscanini; on the conductor's tragically early death at the age of forty-eight in 1963,

he wrote a moving letter to the *Salzburger Nachrichten* on 9 March,
in which he reminded readers that, *inter alia*, it was Fricsay who
had first convinced him and others that Gluck's *Orfeo could* be sung
by a male voice. 'He knew how to communicate his enthusiastic
love of discovery to his artists', wrote the singer, '. . .I have known
no other conductor who could correspond in a more vibrant, empathetic and artistic way with his singers', and the secret of Fricsay's
method lay almost certainly in a phrase in a letter to Fischer-
Dieskau written on 6 July 1959. 'We never finish learning in our
profession and the wonderful thing is that we shall always – to our
dying day – be amazed at everything that has happened to us up
to now – for when one can discover nothing new in music, then we
are dead'.

   Thus, 1948 can fairly be called the beginning of Fischer-
Dieskau's career. He gave thirty-nine concerts in that year, mainly
in north Germany, and often in *RIAS* broadcasts. There were many
different accompanists: Walter Welsch, Ludwig Hoffmann, Joachim Seyer-Stephan (his early piano teacher), Rudolf Wille, to
name a few, and conductors like Karl Ristenpart and Karl Forster,
(the latter directing an exciting Brahms' *Requiem* with Gerda Lammers on 7 November.).

   The pianist Leo Stein had accompanied Fischer-Dieskau on his
first 78 r.p.m. record – Carl Loewe's *Tom der Reimer* (op. 135), a
setting of the old Scottish ballad which appears in Theodor Fon-
tane's charming book *Jenseits der Tweed*, backed by *Die Uhr* (op.
123/3) – recorded for Electrola* on 2 June 1948. In the light of
Fischer-Dieskau's later championing of the unfashionable Carl
Loewe (1796–1869), it was a brave and somehow typical choice
for his first record. Those who have a copy of the record will find
that they have a very pleasant nest-egg for their old age!

   Talking with Fischer-Dieskau on this period of his life brings
back vividly these cold, cheerless, *Angst*-ridden days. Politically, it
had become clear that there was little chance of ideological agreement between what were now recognised as the two great super-
powers, the USA and the USSR. The Americans, still fairly naive
about matters European (these were pre-Korea, pre-Vietnam,

*Electrola is the German branch of EMI/HMV.

pre-Watergate days), prevailed upon the more realistic British and French politicians not to create another Versailles and to help the shattered Germans back to their feet again. Thus, after the bitter political quarrels of 1947–1948 had developed into a non-military 'Cold·War', West Europeans realised that a split was inevitable, and that an Iron Curtain (a phrase coined, ironically enough, by Dr Goebbels!) was about to fall on the continent. The currency reform of 20 June 1948 eventually led to the founding of the two separate German states in 1949.

The singer lived through these traumatic days in Berlin. Although a beginner in professional life, he was, of course, a man with a good deal of experience of 'Life', of human suffering and of material deprivation behind him. He told me however that he had never once imagined that he would be killed in the war – despite the fact that of his *Abitur* class of 1942, only three survived. Only those who saw and experienced Germany in these immediate post-war years can have any idea of what it meant to try to hew out a career as a German artist. These young men and women had lived a cloistered, shuttered life in the Third Reich. Many European (and naturally all Jewish) works remained unknown to them, much modern, to the Nazis, decadent ('entartet') culture was a closed book. 1945–1949 was thus a time of discovery, of Kafka, James Joyce, T. S. Eliot in literature; of Picasso and Klee in art, of Bruckner and Mahler, Stravinsky and Shostakovich in music. It is not surprising that Fischer-Dieskau remembers the period as an exciting one for a young German musician.

Because of his acquaintance with gramophone records of the pre-war years, Fischer-Dieskau was fairly *au fait* with the repertoire and style of earlier singers. Among his favourites were Gerhard Hüsch, Walther Ludwig, Hans Hotter, Heinrich Schlusnus, Emmi Leisner, Elisabeth Schumann, Erna Berger, Elisabeth Schwarz-kopf, Maria Ivogün and Karl Erb, while among his favourite records were the 1927 Gigli-de Luca duet *Solenne in quest'ora* from Verdi's *La forza del destino*, the Rethberg-Gigli-Pinza trio from Verdi's *Attila*, Melchior's recording of Siegfried's *Narration and Death* in *Götterdämmerung*, Hotter's Brahms' *Lieder*, Gigli's *Improvviso* from *Andrea Chénier* and Alexander Kipnis' wonderful 1927 record of the Good Friday music from *Parsifal*. Indeed, it is interesting that the artistic fastidiousness attributed by some to Fischer-

Dieskau, does not reveal itself in his choice of favourite music or artist. Gigli's swooning, and at times 'vulgar' *portamenti* can excite a Fischer-Dieskau too!

It could be said therefore that Fischer-Dieskau was the right man in the right place at the right time. I shall have more to say about his reception in various countries in later chapters, but it is fair to say that most critics found him a potentially great, fundamentally serious, but certainly, a 'Germanic' singer, with all that that prejudice-laden word meant in 1948–1950 or so. The singer ascribes this reputation for 'seriousness' mainly to the music that he had to sing in these days. He insists that he has always sung only what he has been asked to sing – and Brahms in particular was much requested in those chill post-war days. (His third professional recording – on DGG 17047 – was of Brahms' *Vier ernste Gesänge* accompanied by Hertha Klust, made on 20 September 1949). It is nevertheless true that German literature, more I believe that any other major literature, tends to deal with the darker side of life. Many reasons could be advanced for this: Germany's constant preoccupation with her own or other peoples' wars on her territory, and the resulting destruction and loss of life – one thinks of the Thirty Years' War of 1618–1648 among many others; German philosophy's struggle with *Sein* and *Schein*, the 'real' and the 'illusory', and the resultant frustration from the inability to integrate these; the great Romantic movement's major themes: *Sehnsucht* (longing), unrequited love, dreams and death, mirrored in the poems set by the Romantic *Lieder* composers from Schubert on. Many reasons indeed. And indeed it should be remembered that it was Franz Schubert himself who said: *Eine lustige Musik gibt es nicht* ('There is no such thing as cheerful music') – for him anyway.

Fischer-Dieskau found the German public of 1947–1950 hungry for two offerings above all: the twentieth-century music that had been denied them since 1933, and an art-form that would raise them above their drab day-to-day existence. As Friedrich Luft, the Berlin critic, wrote at the time: 'Art is necessary, particularly in times of want'. Fischer-Dieskau believes that his own immediate success was due not just to the voice, not to his virtuosity, not to his musicality, not even to his fine stage appearance, but, above all, to his sensitivity, and to the involvement of his whole being in his performances – it is the sense of complete involvement in the song or the rôle which seizes an audience's attention. As he sings *Die schöne Müllerin*, and despite his aristocratic bearing and immaculate tails, he becomes the humble love-lorn lad; his Lear in Aribert Reimann's 1979 opera was just so dramatic because the audience felt, physically, the mad King's personal grief.

The appalling physical conditions of Berlin in 1948, the ruins, the hunger, the terrible, sweet smell of death in the air, conditions which endured well into the fifties incidentally, also aided the development of his career, since the public was keen to seize on any hope or chance of betterment – and great art, created, formed and shaped in a happier past, held out this hope to it.

In February 1949, Fischer-Dieskau married his fellow-student from the Academy of Music, Irmgard Poppen, in Freiburg in Breisgau, and it was while she was attending a summer school given by her cello teacher, Enrico Mainardi, in Salzburg in the summer of that year, that Fischer-Dieskau's next momentous meeting took place. It was in the house of the Director of the Summer Academy of the Mozarteum, Professor Eberhard Preussner, that he was introduced to the conductor, Wilhelm Furtwängler who, with a single word of greeting (viz. 'Furtwängler!') turned to the piano and struck the opening notes of Brahms' *Vier ernste Gesänge*. Despite the seeming frostiness of the greeting and the equally terse 'Ich danke Ihnen' (Thank you) after Fischer-Dieskau had sung the songs, the meeting led to a firm friendship, almost worship on the younger man's part, and to his first appearance at the Salzburg Festival. The never-to-be-forgotten, now legendary performance of Mahler's *Lieder eines fahrenden Gesellen* at the 11 am concert in the Festspielhaus on 19 August 1951, with the Vienna Philharmonic Orchestra, led Furtwängler, then already sixty-five years old, to confess to the young singer that his performance had finally converted him to Mahler's music.

Fischer-Dieskau was not of course the only German singer to be heard in these years. I well remember the excitement engendered in my home town of Edinburgh by the appearance of the enchanting Elisabeth Schumann (then sixty-three years old) in 1948; Richard Tauber (1892–1948), Karl Erb (1877–1958), Heinrich Schlusnus (1888–1952), Heinrich Rehkemper (1894–1949), the great bass Paul Bender (1875–1947) of the older singers, and Hans

Hotter, Elisabeth Schwarzkopf, Hilde Güden among others, were either still performing or were of recent fond memory. Yet as Fischer-Dieskau's reputation grew, it became clear that he was offering the public something different; an outstanding vocal technique, unbelievable breath-control, unimagined depths of interpretation indeed – but what else? He told me once: 'I didn't want to sing these pot-pourri programmes'. (He actually calls them *Feld-, Wald- und Wiesenprogramme*, literally, 'field, wood and meadow programmes'!). 'I had to fight to avoid them', and he said elsewhere: 'I discovered the significance of cyclical programmes in symphony concerts. A symphony with its different movements and therefore range of emotions holds a listener's attention more than a series of smaller compositions. So, just as in a Chopin recital pieces that belong together should be grouped together, so too should *Lieder* be grouped together so that a listener can stay with a composer or a theme for a little longer. He will then always listen more attentively. We would also learn to appreciate a composer's versatility better if his different *Lieder* were made into one programme. I believe that this is the future of the *Liederabend*'. Thus his programmes would present a single composer or a single poet or a single period, and would *not* feature a Handel group, a Schubert/Schumann group, a few Verdi/Puccini arias, and, finally, a group of 'modern' French/American/British composers. Among the illustrations is the programme of a Fischer-Dieskau concert that I attended as a student in Bonn on 11 March 1950; a Schubert-Schumann programme, based, however, on the poems of Heinrich Heine. Although the point will be raised again later, it may be said here that most singers have felt themselves unable to follow Fischer-Dieskau's precepts, and, perhaps because of the demands of the 'A & R' men in the record industry, the recital programme of the eighties looks not unlike one of those suggested by Harry Plunket Greene in his 1913 book *Interpretation in Song*! ('In the miscellaneous programme, change of *Composer* is advisable for change's sake'!)

Fischer-Dieskau's modest first fee of three hundred West Marks, (about £25 in the strong British currency of those days), was soon multiplied as his fame spread. After the Bonn concert of 11 March 1950, a friend wrote to Professor Poppen, Irmgard Fischer-Dieskau's uncle: '. . .this artist is truly a phenomenon. There were people in the audience who were saying that 'you only hear something like this once in a hundred years', and, 'I could listen to this singer all night'. Concert, operatic and recording offers flowed in. In 1950, there were thirty-three stage appearances and fifteen recordings, performances crowned in that year by the award of Berlin's *Kunstpreis für Musik* (Art Prize for Music) for 'the most promising singer of the year'.

On 7 June 1951, Britain welcomed him for the first time when Sir Thomas Beecham invited him to sing the baritone rôle in Delius' *A Mass of Life*, a 1905 setting of Nietzsche's words, in the Albert Hall in London. Monica Sinclair, Sylvia Fisher and David Lloyd sang too with Beecham's Royal Philharmonic Orchestra. *The Times* wrote of the performance:

'Herr Fischer-Dieskau has a high baritone of ringing nobility and a remarkable range of colour through all its registers; he sings, as the best Germans do, on his consonants, but more than that, he threw immense conviction into his enunciation of the German text, so as to touch poetry in Zarathustra's soliloquy at midnight'. (8 June 1951)

(Fischer-Dieskau remained unconvinced however about the musical worth of Delius' work when I discussed it with him in Berlin a year or so ago. 'Rather too much for the text – and not quite to our taste today' he said.)

The performance led to an invitation to take tea with Sir Thomas and his wife Betty at the Ritz. Sir Thomas introduced his new find to his wife as 'the most perfect foreign speaker of English he had ever met'. 'Go on, Herr Fischer-Dieskau', he said, 'say my name in English'. There was polite consternation all round, Fischer-Dieskau told me, when he gave the word 'Thōmas' the long German 'o'! (Montague Haltrecht in his book on Sir David Webster, *The Quiet Showman*, records that Sir Thomas later put forward Fischer-Dieskau's name as a possible Hans Sachs for the Covent Garden *Die Meistersinger* of 1950–1951, but nothing came of it).

In October of the same year, 1951, another portentous meeting took place: 'My first meeting with Fischer-Dieskau was at the Wigmore Hall. . .I think it was at a recital by Seefried or Schwarzkopf. . .I met him in the artists' room afterwards and didn't set eyes on him again until we met in the studios to record – I don't think we rehearsed even, except, of course, before each song,', Gerald Moore told me when I visited him. The 'King of Accompanists', as Fischer-Dieskau describes him in his book on Schubert, wrote in *his* book *Am I too loud?* that after fifty years of accompanying the greatest singers in the world, 'this man, Fischer-Dieskau, has taken me deeper into the hearts of Schubert, Schumann, Wolf, Brahms than I have ever been before'. They recorded for the first time together between 2 and 7 October 1951 in the EMI studios in London: Schubert's *Schöne Müllerin, Du bist die Ruh, Erlkönig, Nacht und Träume, Ständchen* and the six Heine-Lieder from the *Schwanengesang*; then Schumann's *Mondnacht, Die Lotosblume, Du bist wie eine Blume* and *Die beiden Grenadiere*, and, finally, Beethoven's song-cycle *An die ferne Geliebte*. The welcome given to these recordings, when they were issued as 78 r.p.m.'s, was multiplied a hundredfold at Fischer-Dieskau's first appearance at the Edinburgh Festival in 1952, when he sang *Winterreise* with Gerald Moore in the Freemasons' Hall on 31 August, followed by a performance of his beloved *Vier ernste Gesänge* of Brahms with Sir John Barbirolli's Hallé Orchestra in the Usher Hall on 4 September, an occasion, Fischer-Dieskau told me, made even more frightening by the knowledge that Kathleen Ferrier was in the audience. He has never forgotten her spontaneous congratulations in the artists' room later.

Irmgard, his wife, had continued her professional career as a cellist, but, on 10 February 1951, her career was interrupted when she gave birth to their first son, Mathias, in Berlin. It proved an idyllically happy marriage, vouched for by another happy couple, Gerald and Enid Moore, who spoke so fondly of 'Dieter' and 'Irmel' when I visited them at their cottage in Buckinghamshire. Gerald recalled with great joy too that first *Schöne Müllerin* in the Kingsway Hall in London on 31 January 1952 and the *Winterreise* in the following October, when Fischer-Dieskau, completely immersed in the music, walked off the wrong side of the platform!

The Times of 4 February had found that Fischer-Dieskau's interpretations were more intelligent than emotional, and he allowed Schubert to speak through him by reason of the sheer accuracy of his singing which was a joy to the ear; 'the notes are hit squarely in tune whatever the intervals, the rhythm is never disturbed, the articulation never careless and the voice is beautifully placed. . .'

When Fischer-Dieskau and Gerald Moore performed *Winterreise* in the Festival Hall as the first of the Philharmonic *Lieder* recitals on Sunday afternoon, 12 October, of that year, the same newspaper wrote:

> 'The cycle overwhelms the listener even in a mediocre interpretation; when voice, poetic and musical imagination are matched, as they are in Mr Dieskau's (*sic*) singing, the effect comes near to stunning the emotional centres. . .'

Concerts like these (thirty-three in 1952 and fifty-eight in 1953), and ensuing recordings (fifteen in 1952 and sixteen in 1953), brought Fischer-Dieskau international acclaim. He himself attributes his international 'breakthrough' to that first *Schöne Müllerin* recording with Gerald Moore, eventually issued in January 1952 as *DB 21388–95*. His itineraries begin to take the now familiar shape from that year on. The Protean nature of his art was early visible too; his musical diary displays a bewildering variety of parts and places: that same year 1952 brought these 'first' experiences for him: 25 February, his first *Schöne Müllerin* with that sensitive equal to Gerald Moore, the Austrian pianist Jörg Demus, in the Mozartsaal in Vienna. (Jörg Demus recalls that 'he was the captain, I was the helmsman on our journey'!). Then on 1 April, the first concert with Günther Weissenborn (Schubert-Schumann) in the Zeughaus in Veuss; in June 1952 that legendary recording of Wagner's *Tristan und Isolde* under Furtwängler's bâton, with Fischer-Dieskau as Kurwenal, Kirsten Flagstad as Isolde, Ludwig Suthaus as Tristan and Josef Greindl as King Mark, recorded in the Kingsway Hall in London, followed in the same month by Fischer-Dieskau's first, and arguably still best, version of Mahler's *Lieder eines fahrenden Gesellen* with Wilhelm Furtwängler and the Philharmonia Orchestra. Next came his first Jokanaan in Richard Strauss' opera *Salome*, first in Berlin under Heinz Tietjen and Artur Rother, and then under Joseph Keilberth at the Prinzregententheater in Munich in August 1952 (with Christel Goltz and Elisabeth Höngen), and in October, his first recording of Hans Pfitzner's 1917 opera *Palestrina*, conducted by Richard Kraus, in which he sang the *Charakterbariton* rôle of Morone to Hans Hotter's magisterial Borromeo and Helmut Krebs' Palestrina.

Thus, it seems to me that by 1952 the years of apprenticeship were past; the singer had now to set out on his 'journeying' to perfect his art as a singer. It has always struck me as odd that we translate Mahler's *Lieder eines fahrenden Gesellen* as *Songs of a Wayfarer*. The medieval German *Geselle* was a 'journeyman', who, having served as an 'apprentice' (*Lehrling*), now set out to travel from town to town for seven years, before returning to his native heath to prepare for his admission as a 'master' (*Meister*). Fischer-Dieskau, too, now had to set out on his 'wanderings' from country to country, to perfect his art, and to gain the accolade of 'Meister'.

*   *   *   *   *

The founding of the Federal Republic of Germany in Beethoven's birthplace, the 'provisional' capital of Bonn am Rhein, on 7 September 1949, was the mark of the confidence of the Western powers in their ability to rehabilitate and re-educate those Germans who had been brought up in the perverted world of Nazism. As a twenty-four year old ex-RAF student of German literature at the University of Bonn, I witnessed at first hand the vast programmes of 'Entnazifizierung und Umerziehung', (denazification and re-education), which were set in motion at the time, while the Germans themselves, under the leadership of Dr Konrad Adenauer of the Catholic Christian Democratic Union, strove to put their various houses, political, social, economic and cultural, back in order. 'Kultur', especially the German version, was not however everyone's cup of tea in the late 1940's. (Of course, Hermann Göring, too, had been known to quote the line from Hanns Johst's 1931 play *Schlageter*: 'Wenn ich Kultur höre. . ., entsichere ich meinen Browning' (When I hear the word *Kultur*. . ., I release the safety-catch of my Browning)). Nevertheless, the nation's determination to restore its cultural life with all possible speed, was impressive. It had already been demonstrated most vividly, when only ten days after the declaration of the end of the war in Europe on 'VE Day', (8 May 1945), the orchestra of the Municipal Opera in Berlin had given the first post-war concert in the Radio House in the Masurenallee, conducted by Leopold Ludwig – Overture to *The Marriage of Figaro*, and Tchaikovsky's Fifth Symphony to finish with! On 7 September 1945, the renamed 'Max Reinhardts Deutsches Theater' opened with a performance of *Nathan der Weise*, a play about a wise and tolerant Jew, by Gotthold Ephraim Less-ing, while in Vienna, Oscar Fritz Schuh's production of *The Marriage of Figaro* had opened in the Volksoper on 1 May 1945, with Irmgard Seefried and Elisabeth Höngen in the cast conducted by Anton Paulik.

I myself was fortunate enough to be present at one of the many celebrations for the 'Bach-Jahr' in June 1950, the 200th anniversary of the composer's death, when, in the Peterskirche in undamaged Heidelberg in the American Zone, 'Dieter(sic) Fischer-Dieskau' sang the bass arias in the *St John Passion* on 8 June under the direction of his wife's uncle, Professor Poppen. Despite privations of the bitterest sort, artistic life in general was early restored, creating a tradition of concern for the arts which was to flourish in economically more secure times – it was calculated in 1963 that the Federal Republic of Germany paid out forty times more on theatre subsidies than Great Britain. In 1978, the Arts in West Germany received a subsidy of £7 per head; in Britain, 50p.

In the sister art of literature, the first post-war generation of German writers (*circa* 1947–1955) had mirrored the deep concern of the population to banish all traces of Fascism from their country. These, the so-called 'Kahlschlägler' (literally 'clearers of the undergrowth'), tried to come to terms with the legacy of bitterness and shame by removing all vestiges of Nazi vocabulary from the German language. Novels and plays of writers like Wolfgang Borchert (1921–1947), Heinrich Böll (born 1917), who was to win the Nobel Prize in later years, and Alfred Andersch (1914–1980), circled round the theme of the 'Bewältigung der Vergangenheit', the 'overcoming of the past'. Significantly however, it was two Swiss writers, Max Frisch (born 1911) and Friedrich Dürrenmatt (born 1921), who quickly established themselves as the leading writers in German. It was clearly felt that *their* German was untainted.

Yet, in music, it seemed to me anyway that the attempt was made consciously to *re-create* the past – but the past of the so-called 'heilen Welt', the sane world. Thus the works of the great Germanic masters, Bach, Haydn, Mozart, Beethoven, Schubert, Schumann and Brahms were played to show that Germany *could* hold her head up in the comity of nations as a cultural force.

Although Fischer-Dieskau had been made keenly aware of Germany's degradation, it seems that he was not conscious at the time of any profound differences arising from the more stable conditions prevailing after 1949–1950. 'Creative artists', he wrote to me on this theme, 'can never worry about politics or living conditions. They can only be concerned with themselves and the work that they are called upon to do'. If that may seem at first sight to be a selfish statement, it will emerge from the later chapters of this study that it is in fact Fischer-Dieskau's artistic *credo*: he has been granted his unique gifts to interpret the works of the great composers to his own age, although, of course, he does not see himself as in any way a missionary!

Although, in recent years, his visits to Great Britain have been restricted to London and Edinburgh, in 1953 he made several appearances in some unlikely places. Herman Reutter, the composer, accompanied him in the Sheldonian Theatre in Oxford on 12 March, and, two days later, in the Whitlam Hall in Belfast, in a programme of Goethe *Lieder* by Beethoven, Schubert and Wolf, while, on 26 and 28 August, the singer made a surprising appearance at the Dartington Hall Summer School in Totnes when he sang Beethoven *Lieder* and *Winterreise* to (now Sir) William Glock's accompaniment. There were fifty-eight concerts that year, held in Austria, Britain, Holland, Iceland and Denmark, plus the now obligatory 'German tours', (in May that year), with the Wolf *Spanisches* and *Italienisches Liederbuch* accompanied by Günther Weissenborn. Later he sang Beethoven *Lieder* with the accompanist to his first public *Schöne Müllerin* (in the Titania Palast, Berlin, on 29 June 1949), Hertha Klust.

Other shores beckoned now; perhaps *Winterreise* was not such a surprising choice for the ex-soldier's return to Italy. Accompanied by Giorgio Favaretto, he sang the cycle in the Teatro alla Pergola in Florence on 16 January 1954, and again in the Teatro Eliseo in Rome on 18 January, and stunned the Italian audiences with the 'sheer beauty of the instrument'. He went on to sing Mahler, Wolf and Schumann in Perugia and Milan.

By 1955, Fischer-Dieskau was established as the leading German baritone. There was, of course, 'competition': Hermann Prey and Eberhard Wächter in Germany and Austria, Gérard Souzay in France, and when Fischer-Dieskau's first *Winterreise* recording was issued in November 1955, he was inevitably compared with his great predecessor Hans Hotter. Alec Robertson, the doyen of *The*

Gramophone critics, freely admitted that it was his *own* age that led him to prefer the older singer, since 'Hans Hotter presents a picture of a weary, disillusioned man, Fischer-Dieskau one of a man vigorous enough to snap his fingers at fate, and rather in revolt against life than disillusioned'. The singer, however, believes that his interpretation takes into account not only the respective ages of the German poet (twenty-nine, when the first twelve poems were published in 1823) and the Austrian composer (thirty in 1827), but also 'the revolutionary nature of the verses'. The recording made with Gerald Moore for Electrola in Germany in January 1955 (along with Carl Loewe's *Erlkönig* and Wolf's *Der Tambour, Der Feuerreiter* and *Storchenbotschaft*) which were issued on an E.P. in August 1955) will be discussed more fully in the chapter on the *Lied*. Since I have just mentioned Hans Hotter, however, it might not be out of place here to put this great artist's appreciation of Fischer-Dieskau on record. Professor Hotter wrote to me in 1979:

'. . .here we had, in a unique symbiosis, extreme musicality, intense artistic sensibility and an intelligence based on great learning, which, with his extraordinary and technically perfectly controlled vocal qualities, created the premisses for a career in the interpretation of *Lieder* which made him known all over the world. His very personal way of singing *Lieder* will be authoritative for budding interpreters of the *Lied* for a very long time to come'.

Fischer-Dieskau made his first appearance with (now Sir) Georg Solti and the Frankfurt Museumsorchester in the Grosses Haus in Frankfurt in another legendary *Lieder eines fahrenden Gesellen* on 14 February 1955; this was followed by a further two 'firsts': his first visit to Paris, to the Salle Gaveau, where, on 23 February, he was accompanied by his Austrian accompanist Jörg Demus, in his now favourite Schubert (six Heine-*Lieder*) and Schumann (*Dichterliebe*) programme, and then, in April 1955, came his first visit to the United States of America and Canada. He 'opened' in Cincinnati, Ohio, on 15 April 1955 with Bach's *Kreuzstabkantate* (BWV 56) and Brahms' *Deutsches Requiem* with the Cincinnati Symphony Orchestra conducted by Thomas Johnson. After this concert, Mary Leighton wrote prophetically in *Musical America*: 'Mr Fischer-Dieskau's voice was remarkably sonorous, his singing masterful in matter of diction, phrasing, breath control and profundity of interpretation. He impressed me as a singer of the first magnitude'.

The tour then took him to St Paul, Toronto, Montreal, Ottawa, Washington, and finally, a *Winterreise* with Gerald Moore in the Town Hall, New York on 2 May. Apart from the first orchestral concert in Cincinnati, he only gave *Lieder* recitals on this visit, accompanied by Gerald Moore, who reminded me that it was on this tour that Fischer-Dieskau made almost the only serious mistake that Gerald could remember his making in their fifteen years of recitals together; he missed an entry, but, added Gerald, 'it was because he had swallowed a hair' – and he went on in his inimitable way to tell me of the tenor at Covent Garden who swallowed his false moustache! Indeed, I might add here that the overriding impression that Gerald Moore gives of his partnership with Fischer-Dieskau is of – joy: the sheer pleasure that both men had in their mutual achievement. This emerges very clearly from the delightful chapter on the singer in Gerald Moore's book of memories *Am I too loud?* (1962)

Speaking to Michael Marcus of *Records and Recordings* in November 1959, Fischer-Dieskau mentioned that he had had only one request to appear in opera in Britain so far – to sing *Don Giovanni*, in English! 'That did not seem to me to be quite right', he added. It is sometimes forgotten how little the British public knew of his operatic work (and the American public even less) until he made his début under Georg Solti in Richard Strauss' *Arabella* at Covent Garden on 29 January 1965. As late as 1966, indeed, Harold Rosenthal could write: 'It might come as a surprise to English and American readers of this book (*Great Singers of Today*) that Fischer-Dieskau is admired as much as an opera singer in Germany and Austria as he is as a lieder (sic) singer in England and America'. Yet after his 1948 debut as Marquis Posa, Fischer-Dieskau had sung Marcel in Puccini's *La Bohème* (directed by Hans Stüwe and conducted by Hans Lenzer), the Landgraf in Liszt's *Die heilige Elisabeth* (Julius Kapp/Leo Blech), and Wolfram in Wagner's *Tannhäuser* (Heinz Tietjen/Leopold Ludwig) in Berlin in 1949. Then in 1950, Don Fernando in Beethoven's *Fidelio* (Tietjen/Ferenc Fricsay), Valentin in Gounod's *Faust* (Georg Reinhardt/Artur Rother) and Ottokar in Weber's *Der Freischütz* (Tietjen/Rother), all in Berlin. In 1951 came the premiere of Winfried Zillig's *Troilus und*

Cressida (Werner Kelch/Leopold Ludwig) in Berlin (with Elisabeth Grümmer), and, in 1952, the first Jokanaan in Strauss' *Salome* (Tietjen/Rother). A notable 'breakthrough' was his first *Don Giovanni* (sung in German) under Werner Kelch and Karl Böhm at the Städtische Oper in Berlin in 1953, a personal triumph, since it had seemed unlikely to some that the aristocratic, serious, almost austere, but certainly lonely *Lieder* singer could ever be transformed into the demonic, erotic, gregarious Don. Lord Harewood, who was on the Board of Covent Garden at this time, told me that he had gone to see the Berlin *Don Giovanni* and had found Fischer-Dieskau's 'possibly the most brilliant Don Giovanni I had then ever seen or indeed have since. It was stunningly articulated, (I still think he did it better in German than in Italian), and dazzlingly acted, played as the most successful and brilliant undergraduate of the year'. (He had gone to Berlin incidentally, to try to persuade Fischer-Dieskau to sing the title rôle in Benjamin Britten's 1951 opera *Billy Budd*, but was unable to get him to do it).

All these were followed by his first appearance at Bayreuth in 1954 – a magnificent Wolfram in *Tannhäuser*, and later as the Herald in *Lohengrin*, under Wolfgang Wagner and Eugen Jochum, and then in 1955 by one of the first of his many pioneering services to the operatic stage: the revival of Ferruccio Busoni's 1925 masterpiece *Doktor Faust* in the Städtische Oper in Berlin directed by Wolf Völker and conducted by Richard Kraus, a rôle that the singer was to make his own and to record in 1969. In that same year, 1955, he was to sing his first full Amfortas in a *Parsifal* in Berlin (Völker/Rother) and in Bayreuth under Hans Knappertsbusch. This, with Wolfram, are the two Wagnerian rôles that, he feels, lie really *perfectly* for his voice.

Fischer Dieskau has often remarked to me that he can only be 'happy' when his human and artistic needs are being completely fulfilled. I believe that this was most strikingly the case during the years when he was building up his great reputation. His second son, Mar in. was born on 17 June 1954, and his wife Irmgard had shared almost all of his artistic triumphs, as well as participating in many of his successful recordings. My own favourite recording, long since deleted, alas, was the record of *Duets* in various languages, made for Electrola with Victoria de los Angeles in December 1960, partnered by Irmgard (cello), Gerald Moore and Eduard Drolc (violin).

National and international honours came his way too; in 1955 he received the *Golden Orpheus* of the city of Mantua in Italy, awarded each year to 'the five best singers of the year'. (Fischer-Dieskau jokes that no baritone award was made for 1956!) In 1956, he was appointed a Member of the *Akademie der Künste* (Academy of Fine Arts) in Berlin and of the German Section of the International Music Council. In 1957 came Honorary Membership of the Gustav Mahler Society and one of the highest national honours of the Federal Republic, the *Bundesverdienstkreuz, I. Klasse* (The Federal Cross of Merit, First Class). Then in 1959 a prized honour: the title of *Bayrischer Kammersänger* from the *Land* of Bavaria; the Edison Prize came in 1960, Honorary Membership of the Vienna Konzerthaus Society and the Mozart Medal in 1962. Possibly the highest distinction for him as a Berliner was the conferring of the title of *Kammersänger* from his native Berlin in 1963. To all of these awards and honours must be added, of course, the numerous *Grands Prix du Disque*, after the first award in 1955.

He was now recognised as one of the world's leading and most trustworthy singers, in the sense that his performances, whether on the concert platform, on stage or on record, never fell below an extremely high level. Legends began to grow around him; one circulated by a leading music critic led me to a passage at arms with him. In March 1963, Desmond Shawe-Taylor, a brilliant and usually reliable music critic, gave voice to his own prejudices about Dietrich Fischer-Dieskau which had been noticeable since his early pieces in *The Gramophone* as far back as October 1953. In *The Sunday Times* for 17 March, in an article entitled *The importance of not being earnest*, which dealt with Fischer-Dieskau's concert with Gerald Moore in the Festival Hall on 11 March 1963, and in our ensuing correspondence, Mr Shawe-Taylor felt that the German baritone was rather more solemn than some of his great predecessors, comparing his style with that of Elena Gerhardt and Lotte Lehmann who, he claimed, displayed a 'life-enhancing spirit' and a 'sense of infectious contact'. As is well known, Mr Shawe-Taylor is one of the most perceptive critics of vocal music in Britain or America;

his love and knowledge of *Lieder* prove that he is not a prisoner of that generation which, perhaps understandably, grew up inimical to German culture. My argument was that Fischer-Dieskau's 'seriousness' was not 'teutonischer Ernst' (Teutonic seriousness), but 'genuine' seriousness, a complete involvement in the spirit of the *Lied* being sung – an object lesson in interpretation. Mr Shawe-Taylor acknowledged that he had not met the singer, and certainly his view contrasted greatly with those of friends and colleagues like Gerald Moore and Janet Baker who knew him well and valued his sense of humour. Gerald Moore once said to me indeed that Fischer-Dieskau's concerts were always spontaneous and fresh, that 'his unfolding of a song seems to be evergreen', and that rehearsals were occasions of great joy.

Mr Shawe-Taylor wrote a generous review of that concert, nevertheless, and mentioned that he had heard that the singer had not been in the best of health (which was correct); he *did* change his views in later years. It is strange, however, that such misunderstandings arise, and one wonders how much the Anglo-Saxon view of Schubert in particular, and the German *Lied* in general, has been influenced by a book which has become the 'Bible' for the English-speaking lover of Schubert: Richard Capell's *Schubert's Songs*, originally published in 1928? But the *Daily Telegraph*'s critic's book betrays the date of its writing in its prejudiced view of German literature and the German language. Fischer-Dieskau himself had to take issue with Capell over the latter's interpretation of a number of *Lieder* (e.g. *Vor meiner Wiege* (D 927) and *Der Winterabend* (D 938)), while the journalist's own knowledge of German literature seems rather inadequate in places. He wrote, for example: 'Between the misty middle-ages and the generation before Schubert's own, there were virtually no German poets. The sixteenth and seventeenth centuries were blank' (page 7) – yet only blank, perhaps, for those who do not read German? Again, his stricture on the German language – 'The German language strikes the stranger as uncouth and repellent. . .' (page 55) – does seem to bear the stamp of post-First World War prejudices.

One wonders indeed how many would agree with that last criticism after hearing Fischer-Dieskau's crystal-clear pronunciation of some of the loveliest words in *any* language: *kühl*, *Wonne*, *sanft*, *Liebe*, for example? Indeed, I believe that not the least of

Fischer-Dieskau's many ambassadorial services to his language and his country has been the 'use' to which he has been 'put' in the teaching of German abroad. Many apart from myself, I am sure, have used his records as models of German diction, either for students of singing, or of the German language. In fact, I know of one teacher who starts his adult beginner's study of the language with Fischer-Dieskau's Goethe settings, *Erlkönig*, *Meeresstille* and *Über allen Gipfeln*! His extraordinarily beautiful pointing of words has led many to an awareness of the true meaning of a certain phrase for the first time; I am certain that the fine German diction one hears nowadays from great foreign singers like Sir Peter Pears, Dame Janet Baker, Frederica von Stade, Elly Ameling, Benjamin Luxon and others, must, in some measure at least, be due to the lead given by this artist. It is particularly in this area that Fischer-Dieskau seems to me to have the edge over the great pre-war *Lieder* singers, such as Janssen, Rehkemper and Schlusnus. Through the clarity of his diction, and of course the intensity of his interpretations, Fischer-Dieskau '*realises* the phrase' more often than they did, to use John Steane's perceptive remark.

It was naturally inevitable that controversy should rage over this exciting new singer as he was compared with past and present favourites, just as it raged over Caruso and Gigli or over Callas and Tebaldi. In the December 1955 issue of *The Gramophone*, Alec Robertson, a champion (but also a critic) of Fischer-Dieskau since the early 1952 records, defended himself against the charge of 'undiscriminating adulation' of Fischer-Dieskau levelled by a Welsh reader. Robertson quoted some of his own more critical observations and continued: 'I admit that a sense of humour is not his strong point; but it is not fair to say that he infused no humour into his singing of Wolf's *Der Tambour* or *Storchenbotschaft*'. This criticism of a 'lack of a sense of humour' was a cliché in those early days, and was of course closely linked to the then prevalent, British, post-war view of the pedantic, narrow-minded, 'heavy' Teuton popularised in war-epics and some 'higher', often pro-French, literary criticism. The leavening and opening-up of Federal German society in the 1960's, however, the replacement of 'Teutonic' *mores* with 'Anglo-Saxon', the attack on old-fashioned German paternalistic authoritarianism (spectacularly visible in the student *événements* of May 1968), the effect of the 'Sexwelle', (the sex-wave), which has affected all strata of Federal German society and is indicative, among others, of that society's new attitude to women, to family life and to religion – all these have changed, or *should* have changed our stereotyped view of 'Germany'.*

In an article I wrote on Fischer-Dieskau in the journal *Modern Languages* in 1962, I said that Fischer-Dieskau had a 'devastating sense of humour', and added that 'he would be a poor Berliner without it!' Humour is not, of course, a feature of the predominantly serious world of the German *Lied*, and it is quite understandable that, since British and American audiences had had little or no opportunity to see him on the stage, they could not be aware of this most appealing side of his character. In Germany and Austria however, during this period 1955–1963, he was becoming increasingly famous for the depths of his operatic characterisations. During the Mozart bi-centenary celebrations in 1956, he had sung his first Salzburg Count Almaviva (in Mozart's *Le nozze di Figaro*) in Oscar Fritz Schuh's production in the Festspielhaus. Flanked by Elisabeth Schwarzkopf, Irmgard Seefried, Erich Kunz, Christa Ludwig, Murray Dickie, Oskar Czerwenka, and under Karl Böhm's bâton, Fischer-Dieskau was praised for the infectious, albeit bitter humour with which he invested that ironic, broken character; again, in the summer of 1958, his first Salzburg portrayal of Richard Strauss' bluff, melancholic, yet also humorous Mandryka (in *Arabella* with Otto Edelmann, Lisa della Casa and Anneliese Rothenberger, directed by Rudolf Hartmann under Joseph Keilberth), was taken to be almost a model for the rôle.

His Falstaff, first sung in German at the Städtische Oper in Berlin in 1957 (under Carl Ebert and Alberto Erede) was to become one of his great comic interpretations, while, although he has never sung the rôle on the stage, his Papageno in the famous 1955 DG recording of Mozart's *Die Zauberflöte* under Ferenc Fricsay, astounded some critics unaware of his comic gifts. 'Fischer-Dieskau is easily the best Papageno since Hüsch', wrote the *EMI Monthly*

---

*One interesting theory to explain this prejudice is the early 20th century British intellectual belief that the post-Roman, pre-Norman Anglo-Saxon age was one of 'non-culture', of barbarian desolation – the 'Dark Ages'. The discovery at Sutton Hoo of a treasure of Anglo-Saxon artistry in 1967 put paid to that notion – but two World Wars left their mark.

Letter in March 1956, 'and is evidently not as devoid of humour as his lieder (sic) recitals sometimes suggest. . .'

This brilliant period, as he 'journeyed' from success to success, saw also his third (1955), fourth (1957) and fifth (1959) appearances at the Edinburgh Festival, his second (1956), third (1958) and fourth (1960) tours of the United States, and, in October 1963, his first tour of Japan with the new Deutsche Oper in Berlin and its productions of *Fidelio* and *Le nozze di Figaro*, conducted by Karl Böhm. Nor would British readers forget the uplifting experience of the première of Benjamin Britten's *War Requiem* written for Fischer-Dieskau (as the German protagonist), Peter Pears and Galina Vishnevskaya, (although Heather Harper sang the rôle), in Coventry Cathedral on 30 May 1962. In a sense, this performance, the token of reconciliation for the destruction of Coventry by German bombers in 1940, could be said to have brought to an end the post-war Anglo-German estrangement, and I am sure that it was no coincidence that Fischer-Dieskau was chosen as the artistic ambassador of the new bond of friendship.

But this happy and successful period of his life was to come to a tragic close with the death of his wife Irmgard after giving birth to their third son, Manuel, on 15 December 1963. Fischer-Dieskau is a very self-sufficient man and artist, but I have always believed that the agonising experience of the death of his handicapped brother in 1944, his grim war service, and the death of his young wife, were all shattering experiences which have left their mark on his poignant portrayals of human sorrow and grief on stage and concert platform. His Amfortas, Wozzeck and Lear are all characters in mental torment, wracked by personal grief; those who have seen or heard Fischer-Dieskau in these rôles have been unbearably moved by their truth to life. Such truthfulness informs the even more intense and dramatic world of the *Lied*: in *Winterreise*, the *Abschied* from Mahler's *Das Lied von der Erde*, Brahms' *Vier ernste Gesänge*, all depictions of the human spirit in travail.

A *Lieder* singer's re-marriage would hardly merit headlines in the British press; in a country like West Germany, where every town of any size has not only an opera house, but also a concert hall, and where, in 1975, the arts received a subsidy of DM 924 million (about £230,000,000), the lives of opera stars, producers and conductors produce headlines reserved in Britain for soccer or cricket stars. Fischer-Dieskau's marriage to the famous film-star Ruth Leuwerik on 11 September 1965 in Zürich brought banner headlines in the gossip journal *Stern* for that week: 'Millions know their names. . .' they proclaimed. Ruth Leuwerik was thirty-nine and celebrated particularly for her rôle as the Baroness Trapp in the German original of what later became Julie Andrews' hit musical *The Sound of Music*.

The marriage was not a success and was dissolved in August 1967. The singer then married Christina Pugell, the twenty-four-year-old only daughter of an Austrian émigré, a professor of singing in New York, on 7 October 1968 in Berlin, but the couple separated in 1974. Since 1978, he has been married to Julia Varady, the Hungarian/Romanian soprano, who has herself already gained a world-wide reputation as an operatic singer.

*   *   *   *   *

It was about this time too that Fischer-Dieskau began seriously to examine the Italian and Wagnerian repertoire. His performances in these works will be discussed in Chapter III, but it might be worth-while at this stage to examine some of the critical assessments of these performances. These vary of course from country to country; the British for example have always been rather suspicious about German baritones in Italian opera. Although we as a nation are not ourselves noted for our gift of tongues – and the British pronunciation of, say, Latin, with its triphthongised vowels, can raise eyebrows abroad – we will criticise the German for his 'strange' or 'provincial' Italian. ('Kvando' or 'kvesto' is the favourite slap-stick). Curiously enough, this criticism only seems to hold good for Italian Grand Opera since Glyndebourne and Edinburgh Mozart productions always have non-Italian speakers in the casts. Indeed in Edinburgh's famous *Nozze di Figaro* in 1975, we had German, English, Welsh, Spanish, Romanian, Swedish, Scottish and French singers in the cast – and an Israeli conductor, Daniel Barenboim! Germans have tended to accept their own people singing Italian and find Fischer-Dieskau a natural 'Italian' baritone – although they tend to prefer Italian opera sung in German – while many Italians have been quick to praise the singer's 'gusto' and would say that although his accent is not perfect, he does manage to achieve that elusive *italianità*, that feeling for the Italian style. Opinions are bound to differ, of course; Fischer-Dieskau takes issue, however, with those who think that he sings a Verdi aria like a Schubert *Lied* and enjoys reminding such people of the often over-looked similarity between those two great melodic composers.

John Steane's penetrating assessment of Fischer-Dieskau's art includes a generous mead of praise for his work in Italian opera and he asks rhetorically if the singer has ever sung anything without shedding some light on it? I myself have always believed that it was his bringing of his great interpretative gifts to bear on the sometimes undervalued libretti of certain Italian operas that constituted Fischer-Dieskau's greatest contribution to the genre. Certainly Leonard Bernstein felt this when he wrote to me about their collaboration in Verdi's *Falstaff* in the widely-acclaimed production in the Vienna State Opera in March 1966; he found their partnership 'a wonderful experience'.

Some years ago, Fischer-Dieskau said simply to me: 'I admire Wagner and sing him now and then; I love Verdi and sing him often'. That seems to me to sum up the singer's attitude to the two great operatic composers admirably. The baritone has of course written and spoken about Wagner, the Wagner 'cult' and the Wagnerian operas on many occasions; he is of the opinion that not many Wagnerian rôles suit his particular voice since he is in essence a lyric and not a *Heldenbariton* – and yet. . .and yet. . .Those who know and cherish his recorded performances as Kurwenal in *Tristan und Isolde*, Telramund in *Lohengrin*, the Dutchman in *Der fliegende Holländer* and, of course, as Wotan in the 1968 Karajan recording of *Das Rheingold* for DG, would not be without them. Nevertheless, Wolfram von Eschenbach in *Tannhäuser* and the grieving king Amfortas in *Parsifal* are the two parts that lie perfectly for his voice and in which he has gained greatest acclaim from his public.

It is interesting, therefore, that Fischer-Dieskau has an unchallenged reputation in so many twentieth-century works which, in fact, demand a *Heldenbariton* voice. One thinks of Dr Schön in Alban Berg's *Lulu*, the name-part in Ferruccio Busoni's *Doktor Faust*, Borromeo in Hans Pfitzner's *Palestrina* and, above all perhaps, King Lear in Aribert Reimann's 1979 opera *Lear*, a part written specially for Fischer-Dieskau. In these and other 'modern' rôles, he has shown the amazingly wide range of his vocal and interpretative genius, and, at the same time, encouraged a perhaps timid public to listen to him in works which might otherwise have been neglected.

It would be wellnigh impossible, and possibly even counter-productive, to attempt to chart here the various stages in the singer's career, as the 'Master-singer' that he had now undoubtedly become, from these early 1960's to the present day. His career and its many achievements will be discussed in the chapters which follow. A final word, then, on Dietrich Fischer-Dieskau, the man, as I have known him for nearly thirty years.

He is a private man, above all, well guarded by his private secretary, my good friend, Diether Warneck, to whom I have been so indebted for additions to my own archive since he took over the post in 1959 from Fischer-Dieskau's first secretary, Franz Offer-manns, who had been with him since 1954 and left to become manager of an orchestra.

Fischer-Dieskau has two homes; one, the old villa in the Lin-denallee by the busy Theodor-Heuss-Platz in the Charlottenburg district of West Berlin, and a magnificent new house, planned by himself, in a beautiful lakeside setting just outside Munich. (De-spite the new Munich home and his many artistic connections with the Bavarian capital, Fischer-Dieskau seems to me however to have remained the Berliner who proudly announced to a Berlin journalist in 1960: 'I should like to stay in Berlin till I breathe my last!')

Both houses are massive enough to suit the sheer size of the man: six-feet-three, broad, soldier-straight, hair graying at the temples. He has clear blue eyes, aided now by distinguished rimless gold spectacles, and a winning boyish smile, which can crease his whole face when he is really amused. The houses are lined with books, the Munich one particularly also with his own paintings, many of them lit from above by wall-lights. He has an extensive collection of cuttings about musicians and composers, and enjoys inviting a few close friends to listen to records of composers while watching slides of their historical and geographical ambiences. Fischer-Dieskau believes that every musician should take the trouble to find out as much as possible about the period in which the writer, poet or composer lived, in order to be able to place the song or the opera in its proper context.

For such a powerful singing voice, Fischer-Dieskau's speaking voice has an almost light tenorial quality. He speaks as he moves on stage, quickly and decisively, with a good *Bühnenaussprache* (literally 'stage pronunciation', and the German language's only equivalent to BBC English). His English, with a British rather than an American accent, is fluent without being perfect. We normally speak in German together, but, like most Germans nowadays, he loves to insert the odd word of English, a language of which he is very fond.

His shyness with journalists often leads him into smoking, and one usually finds him with a cigarette in his hand after a concert as well. Despite the legend that he is difficult to track down, there must be thousands of people all over the world who have been charmed to have him sign their programmes so readily after an exhausting concert (albeit with the famous illegible signature!)

The unremitting round of concerts, recordings, operatic performances and writing have been made possible by three factors: insatiable artistic curiosity – a constant desire to learn something new – reasonably good health, and, as he puts it himself, 'Zeiteinteilung' (literally, division of time), a rational dividing up of the time available for the various activities. At fifty-six, he is a man with a sense of achievement. There are of course many aspects of modern life and culture which depress him deeply, but his new life with Julia Varady has given him a fresh interest in the younger generation of singers and musicians who look up to him for advice and encouragement, since, despite thirty hard years in the profession, the voice is as good as ever it was – and there can be no doubt that there has been no other artist in the history of music who has achieved so much in so many fields. There is certainly no artist who has recorded so much. His testament is there for ever. The gramophone record firm Electrola/EMI recognised this when they presented him with the rare 'Electrola-Ring' on 17 November 1970. Professor H. H. Stuckenschmidt's *laudatio* underlined Fischer-Dieskau's many-sided talents and achievements and looked forward to a similarly rich future.

The careers of his two elder sons have given him great pleasure too. Mathias, (born in 1951), is now a stage-designer in Berlin, while Martin, (born in 1954), after music training in Berlin, followed one of his father's careers and became conductor of his own orchestra, the *Junges Ensemble für Musiktheater* in West Berlin. He had previously won the *Deutsche Musikrat* prize as the most promising conductor in 1976. Neither son has seemed either discouraged or embarrassed by his father's fame, but has been content to 'do his own thing'. The two sons even combined their talents in July 1975 when they produced Antonio Salieri's rarely-heard opera *Prima la musica, poi le parole* (First the music, then the words) with their *Junges Ensemble* in the beautiful rococo theatre in Drottningholm near Stockholm.

The youngest son Manuel, (born in 1963), shows much promise as a cellist, having won not only the Berlin young cellist award, but also the Federal German prize 'Jugend musiziert' (Young musicians); as a result, he has been chosen to play in the European Community Youth Orchestra. The reader might recall that the cello was his mother's instrument, too.

When on his fiftieth birthday the baritone accepted the Deutsche Grammophon company's highest award, the Golden Gramophone, in honour of his long and distinguished service to the firm, his short and simple speech of thanks reminded his audience that his eldest son, when asked on his first day at school what his father was, replied: 'He plays records!' More will be said in Chapter VI of his two new careers, authorship and conducting; his books, *Texte deutscher Lieder* (1968), *Auf den Spuren der Schubert-Lieder* (1971) and *Wagner und Nietzsche* (1974), and his conducting commitments since his début in Innsbruck in 1973, have woven fresh material into the incredibly rich tapestry of his life. This scholarly work has gained recognition in many quarters: he was elected Honorary President of the International Schubert Society, and on 21 June 1978 received the honorary degree of Doctor of Music from the University of Oxford, sharing the platform with another distinguished musician, his good friend, Herbert von Karajan. As the Public Orator, Mr John Griffiths, said in his Latin oration: '. . .quid plura? In re musica Proteus est, non homo', which, being translated, means: 'Why say more? In music he is Proteus personified, no mere mortal'. Fischer-Dieskau told me that he hugely enjoyed the archaic ceremony (particularly the 'Dietrichum Fischer-Dieskau') and the procession with his seven fellow doctorands. He told me too how horrified he had been to see his wife, Julia Varady, deep in conversation with the Oxford University Chancellor, Sir Harold Macmillan, after the ceremony. Despite the fact that Julia's English was non-existent, the two were chatting more excitedly than all the others, he added with some pride!

Many more honours have come his way since – a second honorary doctorate from the Sorbonne in Paris in 1980, for example – but the time has now come to look in more detail at the career that has made him 'probably the best-known baritone in the western world'.

Dietrich Fischer-Dieskau... personal

1 The path named after the singer's father, Dr Albert Fischer-Dieskau, in Berlin-Zehlendorf
2 The singer's mother, oil painting by Dietrich Fischer-Dieskau, 1965

3 Frau Theodora Fischer-Dieskau, 1884-1966
4 Dr Albert Fischer-Dieskau, 1865-1937
5 Dietrich Fischer-Dieskau, 4 years old, 1929

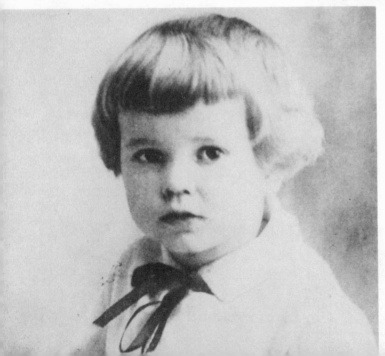

6 Letter from Professor Hermann Weissenborn
  requesting exemption from military service
  for Fischer-Dieskau, 1943
7 Fischer-Dieskau as a soldier, 1944
8 At the time of his first radio recordings for
  RIAS, Berlin, 1948
9 An early rehearsal, 1948

10 With his first wife, Irmgard Poppen, who died in 1963
11 With his first son, Mathias, born 1951
12 A favourite programme, Bonn, 1950
13 In 1958

14 'Yours in friendship, Dieter Fischer-Dieskau',
from a letter to the author

CHAPTER TWO

Oratorios and Sacred Music

There is a charming story of Dr Albert Schweitzer being inter-
viewed in his hospital in Lambaréné in Africa by a keen and
pressing young American journalist. Tiring of the questioning, the
Doctor rammed his battered trilby on his head and made for his
hut where he was found later relaxing, listening to a record of
Fischer-Dieskau singing Bach. He found in his singing, the Doctor
said, 'a devotion to Bach and a radiant gravity' akin to his own.

Although I know that the singer would deny it, I cannot but
think that the family connection with Johann Sebastian Bach, has
led to a particular affinity between the two musicians. But it is also
true that both the singer's meditative temperament, and the challenge of the technical difficulties in Bach's music, demanded a
response to the work of the eighteenth-century German master.
Further, in the Germany of late 1945, there was an upsurge of
religious feeling after the twelve years of atheistic 'brown barbarism'; churches, Catholic and Protestant alike, were filled to over-
flowing. I can well remember one midnight Mass celebrated in the
war-damaged Bonn Minster filled with women in black, praying
for the souls of those killed in the war. The Bach of the Passions
found ready listeners, particularly in Communist-beleaguered Berlin, that 'island in the red sea'.

Bach's cantatas were among the first works that the young
Fischer-Dieskau recorded with Karl Ristenpart and his orchestra
in Berlin in the early years of his career, and he was to record
many of them many times over, most recently with Karl Richter
and his Munich Bach Orchestra.

What makes Fischer-Dieskau such a fine singer of Bach? It is
not, as some have suggested, his 'deep religious feelings'. He is not
a deeply religious man. 'There are many ways to become blessed',

he will say with a rueful smile. Religion is to him only one facet of life with which an artist must come to terms. Although Fischer-Dieskau likes to express himself *qua* philosopher, he rarely speaks or writes of composers in that sentimental fashion beloved by music journalists e.g. 'When Bach speaks, it is in the language of the angels; when Mozart speaks, God listens'.

Fischer-Dieskau is a practical artist who responds to words and music which deal honestly with the human condition; he has told me how much he enjoys interpreting music, whether religious, operatic or *Lieder*, which deals with *human beings*. Bach's enormous corpus of vocal music, with its technical challenges, (as severe as any in vocal music), its opportunities for dramatic acting with the voice, and, in the Passions, for ensemble singing or teamwork, as if on a stage, satisfies this need.

The baritone sings Bach only rarely now in public; in 1977 there was a *Christmas Oratorio* for *RIAS* in Berlin, in 1978 no Bach at all, in 1979 only the Easter *St Matthew Passion* with Karl Richter in Munich. (At that performance, his wife, Julia Varady, deputised for the indisposed British soprano, Margaret Price). In 1980, there were a few performances of Bach cantatas in New York. The reason for this comparative neglect of Bach is sad but interesting: 'There are few conductors around', Fischer-Dieskau says, 'who conduct Bach as I think he should be conducted'. He feels that Bach's great works belong in a church, since it has become increasingly common in West Germany to perform the Passions, (particularly the *St Matthew Passion* at Easter time), in a concert hall – with a request for no applause, 'because of the liturgical significance'. It may well be that we shall eventually see Fischer-Dieskau conducting his own Bach.

The features of his Bach style are his smooth *legato*, the finely-spun *mezza voce* singing, and the dramatic handling of the words. He is not the first singer, of course, to find inspiration in the Biblical texts, nor is it surprising that listeners have found his interpretations 'religious'. I must admit that I feel nearer to the spirit of the Gospels in a Fischer-Dieskau Bach recital than in many a dreary modern church service. I feel this particularly when listening to what I believe (and the singer himself agrees) is one of his finest recordings – the Electrola *Bach: Cantata Arias* with the Berlin Philharmonic Orchestra conducted by Karl Forster. It was recorded in February 1958 at a time when he was singing a good deal of Bach. (The DG *St Matthew Passion* with the Munich Bach Orchestra under Karl Richter, in which he sang the bass arias, was recorded in the August of the same year).

The recitatives and arias on the record come from Cantatas 8, 13, 73, 157, 158 and 159; for twenty years now this record has been the model by which I measure present-day Bach singers. And not I alone. In *The Gramophone* for August 1959, Alec Robertson wrote: 'Everything on this disc, Bach's music, Fischer-Dieskau's singing, the playing of the solo instruments and the orchestra, the choir (of St Hedwig's Cathedral, Berlin, KSW) and the recording, conspires to make this one of the most beautiful discs I have ever had to review'.

Of all the excerpts on this record, I am sure that the most moving is the aria 'Es ist vollbracht' from Cantata No. 159 *Sehet, wir geh'n hinauf gen Jerusalem* (Behold we go up to Jerusalem), for Quinquagesima, the Sunday before Lent. This solo cantata can be seen as a pendant to the *St Matthew Passion*, and the final bass aria to Christ's last words breathes the same spirit of quiet but profound devotion. To *obtain* this spirit, the singer must not allow technical difficulties to obtrude, and it is in Fischer-Dieskau's overcoming of the sheer *technical* difficulties of the vocal writing that the glory of this recording resides. A. E. F. Dickinson avers in *The Art of J. S. Bach* that Bach is a far from unvocal writer: 'He only appears so to those who cannot appreciate a contrapuntal scheme or (who) lack that sense of long phrases which instrumentalists cultivate more as a matter of course than singers'. That is at least a debatable point. It is certainly true however that the 'sense of long phrases' is a peculiar gift of Fischer-Dieskau's, indeed, it is central to his art, in *Lied* and aria, as well as in Bach singing.

'Es ist vollbracht, das Leid ist alle' (It is finished) begins with a plaintive oboe melody, (beautifully played by Lothar Koch), while the voice enters after eight bars. (Ex. 1). Over plangent strings, and supported throughout by the oboe obbligato, the voice of the dying Christ bids farewell to the world: 'Welt, gute Nacht' (World, good night). The 'Nacht' of the last reprise has to be sustained until, softly, the voice repeats twice 'Es ist vollbracht', and the oboe and strings close with a repeat of the introductory bars, a wonderfully effective device.

Ex. 1

That is one important aspect of Fischer-Dieskau's Bach singing: impressive, emotional, *legato* production. Another is technical agility: this is seen to best advantage in an excerpt from Cantata No. 8 *Liebster Gott, wann werd' ich sterben?* (Dearest God, when shall I die?) Death is a common theme in the literature of the German peoples, but the Lutheran Bach's approach to Death was often far from solemn. This Cantata, written for the sixteenth Sunday after Trinity and on the theme of the raising of the widow's son, speaks of Death as a release; the bass aria 'Doch weichet, ihr tollen, vergeblichen Sorgen' (Depart, you senseless, futile worries) has a joyous springy 12/8 rhythm which demands agility, both of voice production and of declamation, and includes runs of frightening length on the words 'weichet', 'tollen' and 'Sorgen', as well as long-held notes on the word 'Sorgen' (worries), at one place for three bars. Equally demanding is the flute obbligato, (played on this record by Aurèle Nicolet), since it provides the moving joy while the voice rests on these long-held notes. The performance of the two artists is an exhilarating experience.

Although Fischer-Dieskau has recorded and performed many times two of Bach's solo cantatas viz, *Ich will den Kreuzstab gerne tragen* (I shall willingly bear the cross) (BWV No. 56) and *Ich habe genug* (It is enough) (BWV No. 82), with that heavenly central section 'Schlummert ein, ihr matten Augen' (Slumber now, you weary eyes), I have always preferred his first recording made in the Jesus-Christus-Kirche in Berlin-Dahlem in June 1951, with the Karl Ristenpart Chamber Orchestra for the DG Archive Production series. In the first cantata, the rocking *recitativo* 'Mein Wandel auf der Welt ist einer Schiffahrt gleich' (My journey on earth is like a sea-voyage), followed by the spirited and sprightly aria 'Endlich, endlich wird mein Joch wieder von mir weichen müssen' (At last my yoke will have to be taken from me), with a fearsome run on the word 'weichen' (Ex. 2) display the full wonder of this voice, while in *Ich habe genug*, the gentle, almost operatic-like *cantilena* of 'Schlummert ein' melts into a beautiful conclusion on 'Süssen Frieden, stille Ruh' (Sweet peace and quiet rest), with a slow trill on the first 'stille', reminding us of Albert Schweitzer's 'rule' for Bach instrumentalists: 'The better the player, the slower he can play Bach'. In addition, Fischer-Dieskau's perfectly-formed *Umlaut* in 'süssen' and the liquid German 'll's' in 'stille' add to the music's breath of peace. This is followed by the final florid aria, 'Ich freue mich auf meinen Tod' (I look forward to my death), where Fischer-Dieskau gives an example of an art as good as lost among modern singers in the lower registers – the ability to sing a full trill at speed – on the word 'eingefunden' (taken place).

Ex. 2

Both cantatas call for bass singers of exceptional compass, and yet I find an actual bass voice too heavy and unresponsive to do these arias justice. (Dame Janet Baker's 1967 contralto version, on the other hand, seems a little too insubstantial). The runs on 'Ich freue mich' in No. 82 can sound elephantine without the feeling of freedom afforded by the lighter, baritonal quality. It did mean, of course, that Fischer-Dieskau transposed the low G's at the end of the first *arioso* (on 'Ich habe genug') an octave higher.

It is however in the great Passions that the public, particularly in Germany, will have been able to hear, see and admire Fischer-Dieskau, the Bach singer. From these early appearances during the Bach Year of 1950 – at the Bach Festival in Göttingen and in Heidelberg – Fischer-Dieskau has become a distinguished interpreter of the central rôle of the suffering Redeemer. One need not accept Schweitzer's, now rather discredited, symbolical interpretation of the Passions ('about twenty to twenty-five root themes') too literally to feel that Fischer-Dieskau invests the Biblical text with a deeper symbolical meaning than most singers. Nor would it be heretical to suggest that it takes a really great singer to bring to life some of the bass arias in, say, the *St Matthew Passion* – as he did in the 1958 recording. In 'Mache dich, mein Herze, rein' (Make thee clean, my heart, from sin) for example, Fischer-Dieskau lifts the heart at the musical 'lift' on the word 'dich' (thee) (Ex. 3).

Ex. 3

ma - che dich mein Her - ze   rein.

Fischer-Dieskau has taken part in five major recordings of the *St Matthew Passion*: firstly, as Christ, in an April 1949 Vox recording under Fritz Lehmann, in the 1958 DG recording already mentioned, then as Christ for Electrola, in January 1961 under Otto Klemperer; again in January 1972, for DG under Herbert von Karajan, and in August 1979, for DG, under Karl Richter. He has also taken part in many radio and television recordings, as well as on his first appearances at Karajan's Easter Festival in Salzburg on 26, 28 and 31 March 1972.

Nevertheless, the singer has told me that he has never taken part in a 'perfect' performance of the Passion – not even those famous evenings, firstly under van Beinum in Amsterdam, then four days later under Wilhelm Furtwängler in Vienna in April 1954, shortly before the latter's death near Heidelberg on 30 November. The Munich performance at Easter 1979, for example, under Karl Richter, held all the familiar vocal magic, yet I, at least, felt that it lacked the atmosphere that a church performance would have imparted. The work is, after all, a true religious *drama* and belongs in its own setting, the 'stage' of the church. C. S. Terry recalled a contemporary conversation after the first perform-ance: One old widow said: 'God help us! 'tis surely an opera-comedy!' (In *Bach: A Biography*, 1928). I am certain that Fischer-Dieskau, the actor to his finger-tips, misses just this setting. Curi-ously enough, the dramatic atmosphere *is* present in some of the recordings, particularly, I feel, in the 1972 Karajan performance (held by some critics, one must admit, to smack too much of '19th century Bach'). But Geoffrey Crankshaw in *Records and Recordings* in November 1973 believed that 'Fischer-Dieskau's Jesus must surely be regarded as beyond compare'. The singer is profoundly moving at the 'Nehmet, esset, das ist mein Leib' (Take, eat, this is my body) section – superb vocal acting – and particularly so at the great cry 'Eli, Eli, lama asabthani' (My God, my God, why hast Thou forsaken me?), where, by making a slight pause between 'asab-' and '-thani', the baritone achieves a dramatic and moving effect.

Fischer-Dieskau's 1960 Electrola recording of the *Bauernkantate* ('Mer hahn en neue Oberkeet') (BWV 212) (*The Peasant Cantata*), with the Berlin Philharmonic Orchestra conducted by Karl For-ster, which contains that famous eulogy of his distant relation, the new Chamberlain, Carl Heinrich von Dieskau, is a hilarious affair. One has to relish the sheer delight that the singer puts into the pronunciation of the six-times repeated word 'Tudelsack' (the bag-pipe, *der Dudelsack* in modern German), in the last duet with Lisa Otto: 'Wir gehn nun, wo der Tudelsack. . .' (Let's go to where the bagpipes are playing. . .) (Ex. 4) – and also, a few bars earlier, when the pair sing the eulogy to the patron: 'Es lebe Dieskau und

sein Haus' (Long live Dieskau and his kin) – how the baritone
savours the long '-ie' sound in *Dieskau!*

Ex. 4

Wir   gehn nun, wo   der   Tu - del - sack, der   Tu-del Tu-del Tu-del Tu-del-

Tu-del Tu-del-sack in   un - srer   Schen-ke   brummt.

The five volumes of Deutsche Grammophon's Archiv Produktion
of sixty-four Bach cantatas, starting with the publication of the
Advent and Christmas cantatas in 1972, with the Munich Bach
Orchestra conducted by Karl Richter, were completed in 1979,
although some of the works were recorded as far back as 1969.

Richter had three regular soloists for the series: Edith Mathis,
Peter Schreier and Dietrich Fischer-Dieskau, but called on several
other distinguished singers, particularly for Volume 1. I agree with
Paul Hume of *The Washington Post* that this was a 'volume of
indescribable wonders', and it was here, I believe, that Fischer-
Dieskau's Bach singing was heard at its mellifluous best. These
works encompass some of Bach's finest musical inspirations and
the Discography will show how devoted a servant Fischer-Dieskau
has been to Bach over the years. Not all these arias lie well for the
voice: pity the bass singer who has to cope with that aria from
Cantata No. 178 *Wo Gott, der Herr, nicht bei uns hält* – even a
Fischer-Dieskau must quail at the thought of the passage 'Gleich-
wie die wilden Meereswellen/mit Ungestüm ein Schiff zerschellen'
(As the wild waves of the sea violently shatter a ship)! Yet in that
same volume (No. 5) what beauty there is in No. 70 *Wachet, betet,
seid bereit allezeit.*

In that Volume 1, however, after his beautiful *Ächzend und
erbärmlich Weinen* from Cantata No. 13 *Meine Seufzer, meine Tränen,*
the last side of the set contained that great solo cantata, No. 82,
Ich habe genug. While *Ächzend und erbärmlich Weinen* is one of those

Bach arias which needs a great voice, I feel, to sustain the interest, *Ich habe genug* is a miracle of melodious inspiration. It is unlikely that many readers will be able to hear Fischer-Dieskau's 1951 performance of the work – which is, I believe, still his finest – but I cannot think that many would be disappointed with this latest version. He brought to the slow section *Schlummert ein, ihr matten Augen* all the experienced *Lieder* singer's feeling for words and sounds, and his joyous *Ich freue mich auf meinen Tod* was as light and as flexible in the runs as in the earlier performance. The voice has darkened over the years, inevitably of course, and it seemed fitting therefore that he should go down to the low G (on Ich *habe* genug) in this version. Of all his Bach performances, Fischer-Dieskau's *Ich habe genug* is the nearest to perfection.

As might well be expected, Fischer-Dieskau was also in demand for Bach works such as the *Easter* and *Christmas Oratorios* and for the few bass arias in the *B minor Mass* which he recorded in February 1961 with Karl Richter for Deutsche Grammophon. There have not been all that many performances of these works with Fischer-Dieskau during his career, but, in truth, they do not contain many really interesting arias for him. His singing of *Et in spiritum sanctum* from the B minor Mass however was as distinguished as could be wished for.*

Mention was made in Chapter One of Fischer-Dieskau's performance in the American POW camp of Heinrich Schütz's *Christmas Oratorio*; he has continued to enjoy singing Schütz and sang a good many of the vocal works under Alfred Langenbeck in the 1950's. These recordings are now in the Fischer-Dieskau Archive in Munich. He also recorded in February 1961 a 'family' perform-

---

*George Frideric Handel (or Georg Friedrich Händel to Germans) has not bulked large in Fischer-Dieskau's oratorio repertoire. There was a *Judas Maccabeus* under Ferenc Fricsay in 1959 (in which he sang the contralto arias as well!), a *Salomo* (Solomon) under Günther Weissenborn at the Göttingen Handel Festival on 19 June 1970 and a *Saul* (with Julia Varady) in the Stadthalle in Göttingen on 26 June 1975. He has also recorded a few cantatas (e.g. *Cuopre tal volta il cielo* and *Dalla guerra amorosa* with Edith Picht-Axenfeld (harpsichord), his first wife Irmgard Poppen on the cello, Aurèle Nicolet (flute) and Lothar Koch (oboe) in February 1960). Anglo-Saxon readers will probably know that *Messiah*, a Christmas rite in Great Britain and America, has no such significance in German-speaking countries. (For Fischer-Dieskau's performances in Handel's operas, see pp. 105–107).

ance of Schütz's *St Matthew Passion* for DG with the Hugo-Distler-Chor conducted by his brother Klaus, who had founded the choir.

For a time, Fischer-Dieskau showed an interest too in the music of Georg Philipp Telemann, now generally regarded as a peer of J. S. Bach's. The dramatic Epiphany cantata *Ihr Völker, hört, was Gott aufs neue spricht* (Hear, o ye people, what God says again) (for baritone, flute and continuo) performed at the Royal Festival Hall on 29 October 1971, magnificently accompanied by Jean-Pierre Rampal (flute) and Robert Veyron-Lacroix (harpsichord), then recorded for Electrola a few days later, set the singer a Bach-like challenge. The two arias and the long recitative ('Die Finsternis entweicht') (Darkness vanishes) require stupendous breath-control, (cf. at 'die Herrlichkeit Gottes *erscheinet* der Welt') (Let the glory of God appear to the world), trills and genuine baroque decorations, (on 'Erheitert die Seelen') (Let all the souls rejoice). Fischer-Dieskau is also fond of the same composer's tragi-comic *Kanarienvogelkantate* (1737) on the death of his pet canary. Accompanied, among others, by his wife Irmgard on cello, his 1962 Electrola recording displayed all his dramatic as well as his comic gifts. The delectable final aria 'Mein Canarine, gute Nacht!' (Good night, my dear canary!) has a truly haunting melody which was enhanced by the singer's melting *mezza voce*. As Conrad Wilson pointed out in *The Scotsman* of 9 September 1972, it could be a fairly feeble musical joke. Performed with relish, as it was by Fischer-Dieskau at that Edinburgh Festival, it 'crowned the concert'.

Let us now leave the Baroque period, the century of 'fugal polyphony', to quote Hans Joachim Moser, to turn to Fischer-Dieskau's work with the composers of oratorio and sacred music in the homophonic Classical Age of Haydn, Mozart and Beethoven. We leave too the age of florid ornamentation, of Lutheran exhortatory declamation, and, perhaps most importantly, we leave a composer 'whose writing for the voice', Francis Toye said, 'nearly always betrays an instrumental bias', and whose 'ornamentations often (seem) tortuous and awkward – the reverse of grateful to a singer' – perhaps too sweeping a judgement for those like the late

Benjamin Britten, who told me in 1966 that he regarded Bach's *B Minor Mass* along with Schubert's *Winterreise* as 'the twin peaks of Western culture'.

The sacred music of Franz Josef Haydn is a far remove from the stern Protestant world of the north German masters. His Austrian Catholicism expressed itself in a simpler, more naive way and Fischer-Dieskau sees in the spontaneity of the response of the three Viennese masters to *words* the birth of the *Kunstlied*, the art song. It was not until April 1959 that the baritone worked on Haydn's music in any detail, when he recorded eighteen *Lieder* with Gerald Moore for Electrola. Indeed, he had been more identified with a modern *Creation* (Wolfgang Fortner's 1955 work) than with Haydn's.

The DG recording of Haydn's *Die Schöpfung* (The Creation) (1798) with the Berlin Philharmonic Orchestra under Herbert von Karajan, is a sad memory for the singer, since it reminds him of the death – at only thirty-six years of age – of another good friend: Fritz Wunderlich, for me the finest Germanic tenor that I have heard, blessedly free from those vocal constrictions which make so unattractive the voices of some pre-war German tenors. There is surely no finer testament to any singer than Wunderlich's exquisite 'Dies Bildnis ist bezaubernd schön' in the June 1964 DG recording of Mozart's *Die Zauberflöte* under Karl Böhm. (q.v.) The smoothness of the *legato* repeats of the final words 'Ewig wäre sie dann mein' (She would be mine for ever) remains a minor miracle (Ex. 5.). Fischer-Dieskau's moving letter in September 1966,

Ex. 5

Und e - - wig   wä - re sie dann mein,   e - wig
wä - re sie dann mein, e - wig wä - re sie dann mein.

shortly after Wunderlich's death in a fall in Heidelberg on 17 September, deserves to be quoted here in full as some measure of the artist's sympathy with, and admiration for a fellow musician:

'A voice has ceased to sing. Its owner was a short-lived master of his art, on the way to the pinnacle of his fame. The news came like a thunderbolt; we heard it without being able to grasp its significance. Fritz Wunderlich was in a class of his own. Only a few weeks ago, when we met to record scenes from *La Traviata* and *Zar und Zimmermann* (10 and 12 September 1966, KSW), how incomparable was this tenor voice, how, with all its sweetness, it still possessed a majestic power. He was the one hope and fulfillment of a vocal genre which, for some time, had been waiting for someone like him. His silence is therefore all the more painful, all the more tangible. The flame of his love of life, of his joy in living, burned bright. There were hardly any technical difficulties for him, his talent had been given the opportunity to mature and had been able to develop over many musical fields. So this was not only a richly-endowed voice, but also one imbued with the sheer love of singing.

We shall not miss his art only – but also the intelligent absence of sentimentality in his character, his cheerful nature and his willingness to help others in need. His records will remain as a reflection of his personality.'

In the recording of *The Creation* released in 1969, Wunderlich sang Uriel's three arias in Parts I and II, and, after his tragic death, the recitatives were added, sung by Werner Krenn whose voice has a timbre not unlike that of Wunderlich – but lacking the latter's artistry, I felt. This artistry was displayed at its best in the aria *Mit Würd' und Hoheit angetan* (In native worth and honour clad), that splendid paean of praise to eighteenth century Man, 'Herr und König der Natur', (Lord and King of Nature).

Fischer-Dieskau sang the rôle of Adam in Part III of the work. 'Papa Haydn' wrote many heart-warming melodies, but surely none more beautiful than the gentle elegiac praise of the Lord and His goodness in the great Eva and Adam duet. Fischer-Dieskau's great voice is scaled down to the merest whisper as, accompanied by a divine oboe (and later by the chorus), he and the soprano Gundula Janowitz sing 'Von Deiner Güt', o Herr und Gott/Ist Erd' und Himmel voll' (Earth and Heaven are full of Thy goodness, o Lord our God). I have seen people moved to tears at the beauty of this interpretation and willing to believe that, as the

seventy-five year old Haydn is reported to have said at a performance in Vienna on 27 March 1808, this music 'kommt von dort'
(comes from there), pointing up to Heaven.

I always feel that we come down to earth in more senses than
one in the passages which follow that duet, where Haydn's librettist, Baron Gottfried van Swieten, who also wrote the libretto for
The Seasons (1801), makes a very bourgeois, almost *Biedermeier*-ish
pair out of the divine lovers, when he bids them remember the
dangers of 'falschen Wahn' (false vanity). Fischer-Dieskau has to
sing those passages more as a father than as a lover with a hint of
the *paterfamilias*; the age of 'Women's Lib' was not yet upon us!

Gerald Moore's retirement from concert work, celebrated at that
remarkable Farewell Concert organised by Walter Legge in the
Royal Festival Hall in London on 20 February 1967, when
Fischer-Dieskau was joined by Victoria de los Angeles and Elisa-
beth Schwarzkopf (Gerald's 'three pets') to pay tribute to their
colleague, meant that Fischer-Dieskau now had to find a new
British accompanist. (Contrary to the belief of some people in
Great Britain, Fischer-Dieskau *has* had other accompanists!)

Although Gerald Moore was soon to make mock of the word
'retirement' by launching into that remarkable recording marathon
of all the male Schubert *Lieder* with Fischer-Dieskau, (and indeed
he also left for his farewell American tour with Fischer-Dieskau
only three weeks after the Farewell Concert in London), the singer
was soon to find a new 'British' partner in the Argentine-born,
London-based Israeli musician, Daniel Barenboim (born 15
November 1942), who first performed a *Winterreise* with Fischer-
Dieskau at the Royal Festival Hall on 17 August 1969. Barenboim's
name will occur frequently in this study from now on and tribute
will be paid to his many-sided talents. He and Fischer-Dieskau are
well met indeed. It was their collaboration in an exciting version
of Mozart's unfinished *Requiem Mass*, recorded in London in July
1971, which first merited comment. The Electrola recording was
made during the early days of the illness of Barenboim's wife, the
gifted cellist, Jacqueline du Pré, and Fischer-Dieskau is full of
admiration for Barenboim's bearing at the time.

There is always a problem for a baritone singing bass parts in eighteenth-century music. Fischer-Dieskau wrote me some little time ago that his vocal range was still what it had always been viz. 'depending on the musical context, from bottom E to top A'. Those who know all his recordings will be well aware that he has sung through nearly three octaves during his long career, taking tenor and bass notes in his stride. After the solemn two-bar trombone introduction in the *Requiem*, the bass begins the third section of the Mass with 'Tuba mirum spargens sonum' (The trumpet scattering a wondrous sound). A low G on *sepulchra* has to be negotiated, then the singer is faced with the succeeding *omnes, ante* and *thronum* in the phrase *coget omnes ante thronum* (will gather all before the throne), comfortable notes for a deep bass voice only. The baritone negotiated them very satisfactorily, however, and there was general agreement among the *cognoscenti* that his contribution, (limited though it is), to the ensembles which followed was extremely distinguished, particularly in No. XI, the ethereal *Benedictus qui venit in nomine Domini* (Blessed is he that cometh in the name of the Lord) with its fine trills on the word *Domini*. (This section is largely the work of Mozart's pupil, Franz Xavier Süssmayr, who completed the Mass after Mozart's death on 4 December 1791 at the pitifully early age of thirty-five. Curiously enough, in the year of the Barenboim recording (1971), the Eulenburg firm in Germany issued a new version of the Mass edited by Franz Beyer. This version, which simplifies Süssmayr's orchestration, was recorded by Neville Marriner and the Academy of St Martin-in-the-Fields and released in 1977. I must say that I still prefer the Barenboim recording.)

Fischer-Dieskau has not sung Mozart's *Requiem Mass* often in public, but *has* sung the small bass rôle towards the end of Mozart's C minor Mass (*The Great Mass*) (K. 427), most recently with the Munich Philharmonic Orchestra under Gary Bertini on 31 January 1979. He also sang in the *Coronation Mass* (No. 16 in C major) (K. 317) recording in July 1976 for Electrola in Munich, with the Bavarian Radio Symphony Orchestra under Eugen Jochum.

The last of the great eighteenth century Viennese masters is, of course, Ludwig van Beethoven. Fischer-Dieskau's championing of Beethoven's *Lieder* will be dealt with fully in Chapter Five. Here

I should like to look at other vocal works of his with which Fischer-Dieskau has been associated.

Beethoven's own statement, 'Ich schreibe ungern Lieder' (I don't like writing songs) has often been taken to mean that he did not like writing for the voice *per se*. It is certainly true that he was a child of his age and would probably not have disagreed with the title of the opera by Mozart's great rival Antonio Salieri, *Prima la musica, poi le parole* (First the music, then the words). Although Fischer-Dieskau said to me that he was doubtful whether Mozart really believed that his own comment viz. that the text had to be a 'dutiful daughter' of the music, was valid for all his own compositions, it is undeniably true that the post-Beethoven corpus of music is more concerned with the voice than were its predecessors. Even a casual look at Beethoven's *oeuvre* would nevertheless give the lie to any statement that he 'didn't write for the voice'. Whether he wrote *well* or *sympathetically* for the voice, is another matter. As George Bernard Shaw wrote of the last movement of the Ninth Symphony in a concert review:

> '. . .the strain was inhuman; and the florid variation beat both the choir and the principals, since it required smooth vocal execution as well as mere pluck, which quality the choir shewed as they held on desperately to high A after high A'. (8 March 1893).

(The high A's of which Shaw wrote are sustained for twelve bars!)

It is now customary for recording companies to muster a glittering star-quartet for the fourth movement of that *Choral Symphony* (No. 9 in D minor, opus 125 of 1824) the setting of Friedrich Schiller's poem *An die Freude* (To Joy) (1785). The Ode's original title was *An die Freiheit* (To Freedom), and it is clear from his letters that Beethoven knew that Joy was here a synonym for Freedom. The movement, which begins with a bridge passage reviewing themes of the preceding movements, is Beethoven's *credo*, his eighteenth-century belief in the ideals of the Brotherhood of Man, Tolerance and Humanity, and the great melody became the anthem of the 'Two Germanies' at sporting functions, such as the Olympic Games, as long as the German Democratic Republic in the east was still *de facto* and not *de jure*. It has mystical significance for many Austrians and Germans, (as indeed has Beethoven's only opera *Fidelio*), since both works speak of a nobler Germany than they have known, and of an age when German culture was universally respected.

One must add however that most good judges would share J. W. N. Sullivan's opinion that 'it (the fourth movement) is nevertheless felt as an inadequate culmination of the spiritual process portrayed in the first three movements', (in his *Beethoven* (1927)), and we are fairly certain that Beethoven himself felt this too. Beethoven's 'one instance of (a) failure, in a major work, to rise to the height of his great argument', is often attributed to the intrusion of the human voice. Listening to an inadequate performance of the work tends to make one agree.

After an orchestral discord at the end of the bridge passage mentioned above, the baritone solo enters with 'Freunde, nicht diese Töne, sondern lasst uns angenehmere anstimmen und freudenvollere' (Friends, not these sounds. Let us sing more pleasant and more joyful songs). These words were Beethoven's own. Fischer-Dieskau's spirited attack on the opening word 'Freunde', and his broad interpretation of the great melody which follows, earned him widespread praise from the critics of the DG recording made in January 1958, with the Berlin Philharmonic Orchestra under Ference Fricsay, the first stereo version of the work. Trevor Harvey was moved to write that he had never heard the section better done (in *The Gramophone*, May 1959). As in all his ensemble singing, Fischer-Dieskau seemed to provide here too that firm underpinning to quartets that all the great basses and baritones of the past have supplied – I am thinking here of the greatest of them all – Giuseppe de Luca. Fischer-Dieskau told me once that he had almost every record that de Luca had made.

Although I feel that Fischer-Dieskau's particular gift of bringing texts magically to life is often squandered on some of the unpoetical libretti of eighteenth-century works and that some of the music lies ungratefully for the bass voice, it can be said that, where the music lay well for the singer, and where the texts were worthy of his gift for pure enunciation, as, for example, in many of the Bach cantata arias, then we have performances from him which can be taken as models. Yet even in these sometimes wooden libretti, we meet the problem which will become central to our discussion of this great singer's art, what Germans call the 'Wort-Ton' argument: the relationship of the words to the music. Fischer-Dieskau noted this once in connection with the music that we have been discussing:

'An unaccompanied Evangelist recitative in a Heinrich Schütz work, based on the words alone and inimical to the Latin litany of the Mass, has to be interpreted with much more emphasis on the language, than a Bach aria, in which the textual weight lies on a few key words and the interpretation is carried by the melody, the ornamentations and the coloratura'.

As we move into the nineteenth century proper to discuss the oratorios and sacred music of its composers, this matter will loom large.

*   *   *   *   *

Both in German-speaking countries and in Great Britain the nineteenth century wears a rather sentimental face; under the name of 'Victorian' in Britain, 'Biedermeier' and later 'Wilhelmi-nisch' in Germany, the age bequeathed a reputation for spurious-ness, for false religiosity, and later, for hypocrisy, as the sexual sins of the fathers became known to the children! The German word *Kitsch* which Duden, the 'Bible' of German language studies, de-fines as 'something artistically worthless, exaggeratedly sentimen-tal and tasteless', is often used to describe nineteenth-century art productions, particularly of religious provenance. Unfortunately, many of their descendants are still to be found in gift-shops in Bavaria or Austria.

It is also true, as Professor Ronald Taylor wrote, that 'the moral associative distinction between religious and secular is a pheno-menon of the nineteenth and twentieth centuries', (reminding us, incidentally, that seventeen numbers of Bach's *Christmas Oratorio* were borrowed from his own secular cantatas).*

The 'poetic revolution' in Germany from, say, 1770 onwards, that sudden burgeoning of literary masterpieces, will be a proper subject for our chapter on the *Lied*, but its effect on the writing of sacred music or oratorios should be noted here. A move away from

*In *German Music* in *Germany: A companion to German Studies* (1972).

'pure' instrumental music (played in a group) in general, can be seen, consonant with the move away from eighteenth-century 'commonalty', the striving for Brotherhood and Universality of the Age of the Enlightenment, (*Aufklärung* in German), towards the Romantic concepts of individualism and self-awareness and – expression, the search for, as the German Romantic writer, Friedrich von Hardenberg (called 'Novalis'), put it, the 'way inwards': 'Nach Innen geht der geheimnisvolle Weg', he wrote.

In his book *Wagner und Nietzsche*, Fischer-Dieskau touches on this question in the early pages. Having established that, with the coming of Romanticism, poetry became the dominant factor in music, he goes on:

> 'The love of the mysterious was then transformed into Christian mysticism, music apotheosized the Catholicism of feelings. It could conjure up spirits, and, by rebelling against the dominance of pure Reason, the music of the Romantics became a protest-movement'.

The blend of the afore-mentioned *Kitsch* and that 'Christian mysticism' of which the singer wrote, seems to me to be found *a fortiori* in the sacred music of Felix Mendelssohn-Bartholdy. Strenuous efforts have been made recently to 'rehabilitate' the Berlin-born Jewish composer who had once been accused, particularly by some critics in the United States, of being 'a Jewish snob trying to pass into Christian society with religious scores as his passport', (Paul Rosenfeld).

As is well known, Mendelssohn's music was particularly popular with Queen Victoria and her German-born husband, Prince Albert; *Elijah* (op. 70) (1846) is felt to be an 'English' work, like Handel's *Messiah*, part of the British established (and establishment!) tradition, and it may well be Fischer-Dieskau's regard for Britain and the British which has led him not only to perform in *Elijah* and *St Paul* (op. 36) (1836), but also, as we shall see, to resurrect many of Mendelssohn's fine but almost forgotten *Lieder* in a 1970 Electrola recording.

I myself have never been able to warm to Mendelssohn's 'sacred music'. When I hear his oratorios, I picture to myself large corseted sopranos, contraltos with voices 'as dark as a fruit jelly', to quote Philip Hope-Wallace, tenors with waxed moustaches and plastered-down black hair, singing in front of large choirs in hired dress-suits in huge north of England halls decorated in pink and blue plaster work, with admonitions such as *Labor omnia vincit* or *Honour thy father and thy mother* scrolled on the walls. My view is not a common one, however, and Mendelssohn's *Elijah* continues to be second in popularity only to Handel's *Messiah* in Britain and America, although it is not very much sought-after in Germany.

Fischer-Dieskau's first appearance in a Mendelssohn work was in an *Elijah* at the Royal Festival Hall in London on 30 June 1968, with Gwyneth Jones, Janet Baker and Nicolai Gedda, and the New Philharmonia Orchestra and Choir under Rafael Frühbeck de Burgos. (The work was then recorded for Electrola in the Kingsway Hall, London in the early days of July, shortly before Fischer-Dieskau went on to record Verdi's *Otello* with Gwyneth Jones). On 25 and 26 March 1971, he appeared in *St Paul (Paulus* in German), (again under Rafael Frühbeck de Burgos), in the Rheinhalle in Düsseldorf where the work was first performed in 1836, and then recorded the work there for Electrola in October 1976, again with Frühbeck de Burgos, but this time with the excellent Düsseldorf Symphony Orchestra.

Although one may have doubts about Mendelssohn's music in general, it is not difficult to admire some of the great solos in *Elijah,* even the 'over-sweet' arias such as *O, rest in the Lord* (for contralto). Fischer-Dieskau had reached what I have called his 'Mastersinger' period when he recorded the work, and had been performing in Italian and Wagnerian opera, which enabled him to bring a wealth of developed dramatic technique to the music. This in turn enabled him to invest Mendelssohn's Old Testament prophet with the right measure of dignity and fearsomeness. As Frühbeck de Burgos said at the time: 'Dietrich Fischer-Dieskau really makes Elijah a living credible being which is precisely how Mendelssohn wanted him to be portrayed'. Mendelssohn himself wrote to his librettist Julius Schubring: '. . .with such a subject as Elijah. . .the dramatic quality must predominate. . .the people must be introduced speaking and acting in a true-to-life fashion. . .' (6 December 1838); and Philip Hope-Wallace remarked that his grandparents' generation were *spiritually* on their knees when Charles Santley sang Elijah. For them, he *was* the prophet.

The first *Elijah,* (*Elias* to the Germans), was heard at the Bir-

mingham Festival in 1846. Fischer-Dieskau's Elijah is as black and
as fearsome as any Old Testament prophet; he rages and burns
indeed in 'Is not his word like a fire?', but then produces the most
honeyed tone for the recitative 'I journey hence to the wilderness',
before the lovely aria, (with cello obbligato), 'It is enough, o Lord,
now take my life', a memory for Fischer-Dieskau of the *Es ist
vollbracht* aria from Bach's *St John Passion*. The gentle crescendo on
'better', in the phrase 'I am not better than my fathers' (Ex. 6.) is
wonderfully controlled, painting Elijah's humility and typifying
the singer's subtle handling of the English text. Like Nicolai

Ex. 6

I am not   bet - ter, I am not bet - ter than my fa - thers!

Gedda, the tenor in the recording, he shows a complete familiarity
with every nuance of the language, stumbling only over the 'a'
vowel (on 'have', for example), a sound which few Germans can
command. Desmond Shawe-Taylor felt that Fischer-Dieskau now
and again allowed 'a too openly dramatic and declamatory note
to obtrude', but granted the nobility of his lyrical singing (in *The
Gramophone*, January 1969). I think myself that the work needs just
this injection of (musical) drama.

It took a Fischer-Dieskau to enable one listener to hear *Elijah*
with a new pair of ears, but not even his great art could win me
over to *St Paul*, an Electrola recording made in October 1976, but
not released until 1978. Even Frühbeck de Burgos' 'operatic' reading of the score could not conceal its *Kitsch*-ness, I felt. We know
that Wagner thought highly of the work, although he grew to
dislike Mendelssohn intensely later and to indulge in some of the
worst Wagnerian anti-semitic antics on the subject. (But he wrote
to Mendelssohn once: 'I am proud to belong to the nation which
produced you and your *Paulus*').
   As in the *Elijah* recording, Fischer-Dieskau tries desperately
hard to make the 'second founder of Christianity' a 'living credible
being' too, by dramatising the appropriate parts of Schubring's
libretto, but, apart from the fine *allegro maestoso* section of Paul's

second aria, No. 18 'Herr, tue meine Lippen auf, dass mein Mund deinen Ruhm verkündige' (Then open Thou my lips, O Lord), I did not feel that this was a work 'which is witness to the most flourishing condition of our art', as Wagner described it. Most of the reviewers of the 1978 release took the view that 'it was worth reviving but. . .', and agreed that it would need an artist of the calibre of a Fischer-Dieskau to make a public performance worthwhile. (It had been revived for the Berlin Festival of 1972 with Fischer-Dieskau, Gerti Zeumer, Marga Höffgen and Werner Hollweg, with the choir of the Deutsche Oper and the Berlin Radio Symphony Orchestra under Lorin Maazel, and was well received as a 'forgotten treasure' (*Der Tagesspiegel*, Berlin, 3 October 1972)).

In his book *Wagner und Nietzsche*, Dietrich Fischer-Dieskau quotes Nietzsche's remark that Johannes Brahms was the only one qualified to be called 'the North German musician', the 'spokesman for the North German soul', and even in his own life-time, Brahms' sparse asceticism and his 'colourless' orchestral palette were contrasted unfavourably with the richer tones and hues of other composers and particularly, of his great contemporary Richard Wagner. From the 1870's and on, opinion was sharply divided into supporters of one composer or the other. 'Aimez-vous Brahms?' indeed! Most, it is fair to say (like Hugo Wolf in Austria, G. B. Shaw in Britain and Romain Rolland in France), were in the camp of Wagner, and even Bernard Jacobson, in his *The Music of Johannes Brahms* (as late as 1977), feels that he has to admit that 'the Brahmsian victory is not yet complete', and to show that 'Brahms is a composer undervalued, not merely in general, but even by many of his admirers'. If he is more accepted in his own country, there are nevertheless doubters there too, as Hans Gàl's book on the composer *Johannes Brahms* (1961)) makes abundantly clear.

Yet to the man-in-the-German-street, one work of Brahms has become the institution that Handel's *Messiah* has become in Great Britain: *Ein deutsches Requiem* (opus 45) (1868), which can be heard in most parts of Germany on All Souls' Day and All Saints' Day (1 and 2 November). Brahms himself wrote from Vienna to his dear friend Clara Schumann in October 1879: 'I have to conduct my Requiem on Sunday here in the Court Opera. . .Before it, the overture to Mendelssohn's Athalia, and, after it, the Eroica. Actually, the Director just wanted Brahms, but I made up this better programme. November 1 and 2 are All Souls' and All Saints' Days where everybody visits the graves, and, in the evenings, just wants to hear either 'Müller und sein Kind' or a requiem'.

It could well have been the combination of 'German' and 'Requiem' which made the work so popular in the immediate post-1945 period in Germany. The German public, after twelve years of incessant nationalistic propaganda, still thought 'deutsch', while the catastrophic loss of life during the war made a requiem a profoundly moving and comforting experience. Brahms' comment that 'everybody visits the graves' on All Saints' Day held for the post-war years – and indeed holds for today as well. There were as many women in black at a performance of the *Requiem* with Fischer-Dieskau which I attended in Baden-Baden in November 1970, as there had been at my first German experience of the work in Cologne in November 1949.

As a young German who had himself been through the rigours of the war, Fischer-Dieskau could not but be influenced by the *gravitas* of this work, when he was asked to substitute for the baritone soloist in Badenweiler in south-west Germany in September 1947, although it is another Brahms' work, the *Vier ernste Gesänge* of 1896, which 'lies closest' to his heart.

In contrast to the period immediately after the First World War, there was no flight into escapism after 1945. The horrors of war, the rubble and the all-pervading smell of death, were much more apparent to the bomb-scarred inhabitants of German cities. A requiem which began 'Selig sind die, die Leid tragen/denn sie sollen getröstet werden', (Blessed are they that mourn: for they shall be comforted (Matthew V, 4)), but then triumphantly affirms 'Tod, wo ist dein Stachel? Hölle, wo ist dein Sieg?' (O death, where is they sting? O grave, where is thy victory? (I Corinthians XV, 55)), could console and uplift at the same time.

This is how Fischer-Dieskau experienced the work when he performed it for the first time to a larger audience in the Marienkirche in Berlin on 7 November 1948 with Gerda Lammers, the choir of St Hedwig's Cathedral, Berlin and the Staatskapelle conducted by Karl Forster, and next (and more notably) in the Grosser Konzerthaussaal in Vienna on 24 and 25 January 1951 in a

famous performance with Irmgard Seefried, the Vienna Singaka-
demie and the Vienna Symphony Orchestra under Wilhelm Furtwängler. It was this performance which Rudolf Kempe took as
his model when he conducted Fischer-Dieskau's first recording in
the Jesus-Christus-Kirche in Berlin-Dahlem on 29 June 1955. 'If
I could do it only half as beautifully as Furtwängler did it in
Vienna', Fischer-Dieskau remembers him saying, 'then I would be
happy', a remark which the singer felt placed Kempe in a rare
class – a modest conductor!

That Electrola recording with Elisabeth Grümmer, the choir of
St Hedwig's Cathedral and the Berlin Philharmonic Orchestra was
the second post-war recording – Fritz Lehmann had recorded it
for DG earlier in 1955. The baritone's beautiful performance was
highly praised, particularly in his own country, where one reviewer
wrote of a 'Schorr re-born'!

It was the second Electrola version, with Elisabeth Schwarzkopf
and the Philharmonia Chorus and Orchestra under Otto Klemperer, which was described as 'sensational'. It was recorded in
January 1961, shortly before the performance in the Royal Festival
Hall with the same forces in March 1961 – a performance still
spoken of in hushed terms by one old colleague of mine!

Of the seven sections of the *Requiem*, four are for choir alone –
which led once to a charming comment from an American reviewer
of a Fischer-Dieskau performance in Chicago in January 1973:
'. . .but what was Fischer-Dieskau doing in all this? Although the
work requires a baritone soloist, nothing is more frustrating than
spending the greater part of an evening seeing Fischer-Dieskau but
not hearing him. . .surely he could have had a song or two of his
own before the Brahms?'. The baritone's solos with choir, viz. No.
III 'Herr, lehre doch mich, dass ein Ende mit mir haben muss'
(Lord, make me to know mine end), and No. VI 'Denn wir haben
hier keine bleibende Stadt' (For here we have no continuing city),
seem to have been written for the Fischer-Dieskavian vocal timbre;
they need weight of tone, but also, (at the opening of No. III for
example), a quiet firmness depicting humility and resignation
(Ex. 7.). I myself prefer the more *pianissimo* approach of the Kempe
version, but Fischer-Dieskau has the knack of making the interpretation of *his* part fit the overall conception: he does so here.

There is no Mendelssohnian odour of sanctimoniousness in this

Ex. 7

work; the singers do not *need* to dramatise, but can let the music speak for itself. Performances often stand and fall therefore on the conductor's choice of tempi; it was Daniel Barenboim's choice of rather slow tempi which involved him in some critical controversy, firstly in the performance with Fischer-Dieskau, Sheila Armstrong and the BBC Orchestra and Chorus in the Royal Festival Hall on 15 March 1972, then again at the Edinburgh Festival on 29 and 30 August (this time with Edith Mathis, the Edinburgh Festival Chorus and the London Philharmonic Orchestra), and, finally, in the DG recording with the same forces, recorded in Edinburgh in September 1972. Gillian Widdicombe in the *Financial Times* found this performance 'incredibly glutinous, painstakingly slow' and felt that the earlier Klemperer recording had brought out all the dignity of the work through its 'simplicity and inscrutable steadiness' (1 February 1973). None however faulted Fischer-Dieskau's performance; Geoffrey Crankshaw (in *Records and Recordings* for January 1973) wrote indeed: 'I doubt whether anyone has invested the opening phrases of the third movement with such majestic authority and his wonderful change of tone at 'Ach wie gar nichts'' (sind alle Menschen ᴋsᴡ) (Verily every man at his best state is altogether vanity) has to be heard to be believed'.

The Brahms' *Requiem* has therefore been a regular feature in Fischer-Dieskau's repertoire, and he has sung the work under all the great conductors. I shall never forget the performance with Bruno Walter at the 1953 Edinburgh Festival, and the reader might remember that he chose this work – with Bach's *Kreuzstabkantate* – for his USA début in Cincinnati on 15 April 1955.

In 1972 he went on to take part in a much-lauded performance at the Berliner Festwochen (the Berlin Festival) on 23 and 24

September (with Gundula Janowitz and the Berlin Philharmonic Orchestra under Herbert von Karajan). After performing the work at the 1978 Edinburgh Festival (under Carlo Maria Giulini) on 25 and 26 August, he included it in his 1980 American tour, singing in Detroit (on 26 April), New York (16 May) and Washington (17 May), under the bâton of Antal Dorati. It is clearly one of his favourite works.

French praise for Fischer-Dieskau's art can be readily found in music journals and newspapers. (It was a French newspaper indeed that described his voice as 'the most phonogenic of the century'!) He has been a welcome guest in the country (at, for example, the *Festival en Touraine* in Tours) since his first appearance at the Salle Gaveau in Paris in February 1955, and one would like to think that he has contributed more than a little to the establishment of friendly relations between the two countries who had (arguably) been feuding since the death of Charlemagne (or Karl der Grosse!) in AD 814. When Dr Konrad Adenauer and General de Gaulle took the lead in establishing the European Economic Community on 1 January 1958 (– it had been created by the signing of the Treaty of Rome on 25 March 1957) – a thousand years of enmity had been, (they hoped), put aside.

Fischer-Dieskau's love of France and French culture is profound. He told me that he would dearly love to include some more French works in his recital programmes and he has tried to do so in recent years. His French accent, like his English and Italian, satisfies all but the most fastidious listener, so that an un-French sound like his first 'soud*ain*' in Liszt's setting of Victor Hugo's *O, quand je dors* tends to come as a shock! But, as always, he is sensitive to every nuance of this language, too.

A French work of sacred music that has always given the singer great pleasure is the *Requiem* (op. 48) (1887) of Gabriel Fauré. This *messe* is both 'petite' and 'solennelle', lasting barely sixty minutes in performance and set to the words of the traditional Latin Mass in seven sections.

Here too, as in the Brahms' work, the baritone has only two solos, both, however, much shorter than in the German requiem. In the *Offertory*, he sings the *Hostias et preces tibi, Domine, laudis offerimus* (With our prayers, o Lord, we offer a sacrifice of praise), and in the *Libera me*, the first section up to 'When thou shalt come to judge the world by fire', (*dum veneris judicare saeculum per ignem*).

Fauré's is a gentle work, quite unlike the heaven-storming masterpieces· of Bach or Verdi, and it allowed Fischer-Dieskau to display that aspect of his vocal art for which he had become particularly famous at that period of his career, his *mezza voce* singing. The Fauré score rarely rises above a *mezzoforte*, and Fischer-Dieskau caresses the Latin text in the first recording that he made, issued in the (then new) 'Angel' format in 1963. The work was recorded for Electrola in the church of Saint-Roch in Paris in May 1962, with Victoria de los Angeles, the Elisabeth Brasseur Chorale and the Paris Conservatoire Orchestra under the Belgian conductor, André Cluytens. Fischer-Dieskau's wonderfully *spiritual* performance – I am thinking particularly of that long-held 'memoriam facimus' in the *Offertory* – merited its plaudits. The French critics were quick to compare it favourably with the Gérard Souzay version, of 1960. The second recording seemed to me to lack that inward spiritual quality, in general. That was with Daniel Barenboim and the Orchestre de Paris, with Sheila Armstrong and the Edinburgh Festival Chorus. They performed the work in the Théâtre des Champs-Elysées on 31 January and 1 and 2 February 1974, and then recorded it there for Electrola. A French critic wrote lyrically about the Paris performance: 'Fischer-Dieskau is a star fixed to an immutable talent. I know no other singer who so regularly attains perfection', (*France-Soir*, 1 February 1974).*

The oblique reference above to a 'Petite Messe solennelle' will have prepared readers perhaps for a mention of Rossini's work under that title. Gioacchino Rossini called the work 'the last mortal sin' of his old age; it is a strange operatic setting of the Latin Mass (in eight parts) for four voices, a double quartet as chorus, harmonium and two pianos. Wolfgang Sawallisch, the then Director

*(Shortly before this, on 24/25 January, Fischer-Dieskau had sung the Christ in the rarely-heard César Franck oratorio *Les Béatitudes* (1879) in the Herkulessaal in Munich under Rafael Kubelik. The Münchner Merkur spoke of the 'extraordinary ovation' given to this 'unusual work').

of the Bavarian State Opera, a former concert-pianist and a long-standing friend and colleague of Fischer-Dieskau's, took time off from the Munich Festival in 1972 to lead a distinguished cast out to the lovely Baumburg Monastery chapel in Chiemgau, not far from Munich, to perform (and record) this work, for the first time in Germany, in this, its original (1863) version, on 15 July. In a letter to me, Sawallisch spoke warmly of his twenty-five years' association with 'Fi-Di', (as Fischer-Dieskau is affectionately known to his colleagues), stressing the pleasure that he as a conductor had had from Fischer-Dieskau's 'ravishing musicality' and his profound knowledge of the 'style' of the music being performed.

In the Ariola/Eurodisc recording released in 1973, Fischer-Dieskau has one solo only, the *Quoniam tu solus sanctus* (For Thou alone art holy), but he obviously enjoyed the 'operatic' flavour of the unison passages. The aria, accompanied by Wolfgang Sawallisch at the piano, has a bass coloration taking the singer down (on a trill) to the low A on 'Jesu Christe'; in the beautiful reprise of the opening words, Fischer-Dieskau's *legato* singing was heard at its sweetest, while the alternative top E at the conclusion – on the word *Christe* – was taken with ringing confidence.

The German public (and later, the reviewers) waxed lyrical over the performances of Kari Lövaas (soprano), Brigitte Fassbaender (contralto) and Peter Schreier (tenor) – indeed the first performance was such a success that it had to be repeated on 16 July. Johannes Justus (in the *Münchner Merkur* of 18 July 1972) felt that listeners had had 'Paradise opened to them', as Rossini had prayed that God would do for him in his letter attached to the score. (The same ensemble performed the work at the Lucerne Festival on 30/31 August 1973 and again at the Munich Festival on 8 July 1974, a good example of that rare bird, a classical 'hit').

A word finally about a work that not many singers have taken the trouble to discover: Liszt's enormously long and rarely-performed *Christus* (1866). One of the most accurate descriptions of Liszt's 'sacred music' that I have read is the succinct summary in the *Penguin Dictionary of Music* edited by Robert Illing, viz. it is 'incongruous in the extreme'! He refers no doubt to the Weimarian abbé's many unpriestly liaisons. Robert Collett in the symposium entitled *Franz Liszt* (1970) would call such a view a 'major critical blunder', for he feels that the orchestral writing in this work is 'the summit of Liszt's orchestral technique'.

Fischer-Dieskau had studied Liszt's *Lieder* with Jörg Demus in November 1961 (for their DG recording), and he sang both the baritone and the bass parts in the *Christus* under Antal Dorati in Berlin in March 1962. Twelve years were to pass before he sang it again, this time in Nuremberg, under Ljubomir Romansky in June 1974. French critics reviewed the work favourably when Fischer-Dieskau sang it under Rafael Kubelik in Paris in June 1977. His singing of this neglected work is just one more example of his tireless involvement in music of all styles and ages.

It will be obvious that 'sacred music' also exists outside oratorio; Wagnerian religiosity (as in *Parsifal* and *Tannhäuser*), and settings of religious poems by Schubert and many others will be dealt with later. The works that I have mentioned, ranging from the merely sanctimoniousness to the genuinely deeply religious, find in Fischer-Dieskau an ideal interpreter. It is as if someone had removed the Victorian varnish from an old painting, or the gaudy colouring from a delicate medieval wood-carving. The honesty of his artistry allows us to judge the work for itself, untouched and unvarnished. 'The truth of a musical utterance, in whatever new, unusual form it might be couched, will eventually assert its own triumphant rights', is a Carl Maria von Weber remark often quoted by the singer.

*   *   *   *   *

When Viscount Grey of Fallodon proclaimed on the eve of the First World War (3 August 1914) that the lamps were going out all over Europe, he accurately prophesied the end of the nineteenth century and the Victorian Age for Great Britain; for Germany, the defeat in 1918 meant the end of authoritarian, monarchical government and the promise of a dawn of democratic republican rule with the establishment of the Weimar Constitution in the town of Goethe and Schiller on 11 August 1919. That it proved a false dawn, that the day belonged to the reactionary, albeit 'National *Socialist* German *Labour* (or *Workers*) Party' of Adolf Hitler, has conditioned German history for the remainder of the twentieth century. No German has been allowed to forget the Nazi blood-curse; as Heinrich Böll, the German Nobel Prize winner for literature of 1972, wrote in a short story *Die Botschaft* (The Message) in 1953: 'Then I knew that the war would never be over, never as long as a single wound inflicted by it continues to bleed'. Although the wounds inflicted by and on the Germans continue to bleed in the 1980's ('Holocaust'!), and will do so, I suspect and fear, until the generation responsible for the blood-letting has died away, strenuous efforts have been made in all fields of activity, political, economic and cultural, to 'conquer the past' (*Bewältigung der Vergangenheit*, in German), and to forge links of friendship with old enemies.

If it was a German philosopher, Friedrich Nietzsche, who made his Zarathustra (in *Also sprach Zarathustra* (Thus spake Zarathustra)) proclaim: 'Gott ist tot' (God is dead), (and few would deny the loosening of the hold of institutionalised religion on the twentieth century), composers of music, that 'universal language', have produced their own pleas for reconciliation in works written both within and outside the Christian tradition.

Fischer-Dieskau had become a good friend of the late Lord Britten and his colleague Peter Pears, even before his first appearance (in June 1965) at the Aldeburgh Festival, to sing Brahms' *Die schöne Magelone* with Sviatoslav Richter. Benjamin Britten had conceived his *War Requiem* (op. 66) (1962) as an extension of his favourite theme of 'innocence outraged and ruined', (to quote William Plomer), a condemnation of the folly and stupidity of war, and yet, like the poetry of Wilfred Owen, which he combined with the Latin *Missa pro Defunctis* (Mass for the dead) in his libretto, also a plea for pity and reconciliation. In his letter to Fischer-Dieskau (of 16 February 1961) asking the singer, 'with great temerity', to sing the baritone part, Britten wrote: 'These magnificent poems, full of the hate of destruction, are a kind of commentary on the Mass', and added that his settings 'will need singing with the utmost beauty, intensity and sincerity'. The plea was symbolised, firstly, in the choice of soloists: a Russian, Galina Vishnevskaya, a German, Fischer-Dieskau, and a Briton, Peter Pears, and secondly, in the choice of venue, the rebuilt Coventry Cathedral, destroyed by German bombers in 1940 and restored with the help of German money and young German volunteer labour.

Because of indisposition, Galina Vishnevskaya had to be replaced by the British soprano, Heather Harper, at the first performance on 30 May 1962; the enormous forces included the Melos Ensemble, the Birmingham University Choir and the Liverpool Philharmonic Orchestra, conducted by Meredith Davies and Britten himself. I was not the only one who would have preferred Miss Harper's radiant voice in the part on the Decca recording eventually made in the Kingsway Hall in London in January 1963, with the London Bach Choir, the Melos Ensemble and the London Symphony Orchestra conducted by Britten.

Fischer-Dieskau found the whole experience 'tief erschütternd' (deeply moving), he told me, and one need not really ask why. His own part, written for his vocal timbre, fits him, both musically and temperamentally, like a glove; musically, in that it exploits all his strengths – his perfect English enunciation, his *legato* and *mezza voce* singing, his dramatic power; temperamentally, in that the theme touched him personally, as a German who had been a soldier and who had himself seen the folly and stupidity of war at first-hand, and who was now journeying all over the world with an art-form which knew no national boundaries.

Much has been written on the *War Requiem*, but I know of no finer tribute than Alec Robertson's eloquent review in *The Gramophone* for May 1963. I too cannot listen to Peter Pears' and Fischer-Dieskau's duet 'It seemed that out of battle I escaped' (Owen's poem *Strange Meeting*) save through tears. Fischer-Dieskau's command of the English language enables him to make the line, 'I am the enemy you killed,' unbearably moving – as is the beginning of the conclusion of the work where the tenor and baritone voices lead off into 'Let us sleep now'. On 17 August 1962, Britten wrote to Fischer-Dieskau that the Coventry performance was 'one of the great artistic experiences of [my] life', and that he was so touched by the baritone's 'complete understanding of what [I] was trying to say in this work'.

As often happens on the death of a great artist, Britten's work is undergoing a revaluation; one must add that German musicians have never accepted the *Requiem*, *qua* music that is, quite as readily as their British counterparts. The reviews of a performance in the Munich Nationaltheater on 12 November 1973 (perhaps in place of the Brahms' *Requiem*?) with Heather Harper, Robert Tear and

Fischer-Dieskau (under Wolfgang Sawallisch), were not untypical of German musical opinion; one saw the text itself, (translated, incidentally, by Ludwig Landgraf* and Fischer-Dieskau himself), as being in parts almost blasphemous, while the music, with its reminiscences of Berlioz (and 'many other' European composers), seemed 'second-hand'; another reviewer held the *Requiem* to be mere 'Stimmungsmache' (i.e. a work written to produce a particular, here religious, emotion) and claimed that he had sat for ninety minutes before 'an artistic lie'. I cannot share such views.

Nor can Fischer-Dieskau who has performed in the work frequently, most notably under Karajan (with Wilma Lipp and John van Kesteren) in the Berlin Philharmonie in March 1964, in Amsterdam under Bernard Haitink and Britten (with Vishnevskaya and Pears), in June 1964, and in the Austrian première with Margaret Tynes, Georges Maran and the Bavarian Radio Orchestra under Istvan Kertesz and Britten in Vienna in October 1964. Then there were the memorable performances in the Albert Hall in London, with Heather Harper and Peter Pears (under Wilhelm Pitz) on 16 January 1966, and with Galina Vishnevskaya and Peter Pears conducted by Carlo Maria Giulini and Britten at the 1968 Edinburgh Festival. His latest performance in the work was in Tokyo (under Sawallisch) on 7 May 1979.

To quote from the score, Britten's *Cantata Misericordium* (op. 69) was 'composed for and first performed at the solemn ceremony on the Commemoration Day of the centenary of the Red Cross, Geneva, September 1st 1963', with Fischer-Dieskau, Peter Pears and the Orchestra de la Suisse Romande conducted by Ernest Ansermet. It is a short work lasting some twenty minutes, a dramatised version of the parable of the Good Samaritan, once again on the theme of pity and tolerance. It played no great part in Fischer-Dieskau's repertoire after the early performances, and I must say that I find his rôle (*Viator*, the Traveller) less rewarding than Peter Pears' Samaritan, although the Traveller's dramatic cry after being attacked 'Subveni, ah, subveni; ne patere me mori' (Help, o help me, do not let me die), lies perfectly for Fischer-Dieskau's voice.

The Stravinsky-like score lacks, however, Britten's great gift for melody; it does seem to be indeed what the composer called it in

---

*The *nom-de-plume* of Britten's great friend and patron, Prince Ludwig of Hesse.

a letter to Fischer-Dieskau on 12 June 1963: a 'direct and simple' work for an 'international non-musical occasion'. It was recorded in London for Decca on 13 December 1963 with the London Symphony Orchestra, just after a performance of the *War Requiem* in the Royal Festival Hall. The two soloists performed it again in Blythburgh Church near Aldeburgh on 26 June 1965, and also at the 1968 Edinburgh Festival.

The only other twentieth-century British composer represented in Fischer-Dieskau's present repertoire is Sir Michael Tippett; before the 1966 Albert Hall *War Requiem* mentioned above, Fischer-Dieskau had sung the baritone solo in the first perform- ance, on 12 January 1966, of Tippett's *The Vision of St Augustine* in the Royal Festival Hall. I did not hear the singer in this short work (– it lasts fifteen minutes –) and he has not yet recorded it – but John Shirley-Quirk's excellent interpretation of the mystical, yet all-too-human monk on the 1972 RCA recording (under Sir Michael) allows us to imagine what Fischer-Dieskau must have made of this very difficult music. He has not sung the work again since the German première under Tippett in Berlin on 5 October 1966 and told me that he finds it 'problematical', but a work to be taken seriously. It is, I am told, Sir Michael's own favourite composition.

I shall have more to say about Fischer-Dieskau's attitude to the music of the twentieth century in later chapters, but it is well known that he has never failed to support the work of living composers, even although he has more than superficial worries about the state of music in our century. 'If music wants to maintain its place in our cultural life', he said to Wolf-Eberhard von Le- winski in September 1974, 'it will have to keep the word 'singa- bility' in mind – in the metaphorical sense, that is, I am not thinking about its application to the voice. Yet I don't know what there is left to discover. That has been our worry since the begin- ning of the century – that musicians – and their instruments – have exhausted their possibilities, and we now have to look around for new sounds and new instruments. I believe that it is the *mind* which decides these things, so that new music will have to come from there, from the *content*, and not so much from experiments with instruments'. That is one side of the coin; the other is that he regrets that so many concertgoers simply want to hear what he calls 'cultural treasures from the museums', that is, the 'music of the masters'.

Fischer-Dieskau's commitment to 'modern' music has meant the assumption of an entirely different musical personality and a different vocal technique. The effortless stream of beautiful tone needed for most nineteenth-century music is rarely demanded in the modern idiom where emphasis is laid more on separate and single phrases. It is striking therefore to note how many twentieth-century works coming into our category of 'sacred music' were included in his repertoire in the earliest days of his career: Herbert Trantow (a fellow prisoner in Italy), had his new *Berliner Weihnachtskantate* (Berlin Christmas Cantata) performed by Fischer-Dieskau in December 1948; there was Max Reger's *Der Einsiedler* (The Hermit) (1912–1916) in July 1949; Carl Orff's *Carmina burana* (1936) in January 1950 (which was recorded incidentally for DG under Eugen Jochum in October 1967 with Fischer-Dieskau as a hilarious Abbot!); Paul Hindemith's *Requiem* to Walt Whitman's *Ode on Lincoln* ('When lilacs last in the dooryard bloom'd) (1946), and the same composer's *Apparebit repentina dies* in February and May 1950 respectively; Walton's *Belshazzar's Feast* (1931) in German under Karl Rankl in March 1950 (and at the 1955 Edinburgh Festival under Sir Malcolm Sargent); Fischer-Dieskau's brother Klaus' cantata *Komm, Trost der Nacht* in March 1951; Hindemith's cantata *Das Unaufhörliche* (1930) (The Unceasing) in May 1951; Bartók's *Cantata profana* (1934) in September 1951; Hermann Reutter's *Weihnachtskantilene* in December 1952, and finally, a work which he was later to perform regularly, Wolfgang Fortner's *The Creation* (premièred in Basel on 18 February 1955), to poems by the American negro James Weldon Johnson and recorded for DG under Hans Schmidt-Isserstedt in 1957.

Although it would be clearly impossible to mention every twentieth-century work performed by the singer, he himself, I know, would regret the omission of Igor Stravinsky's *Abraham and Isaac*, premièred in Jerusalem in 1964, of which Fischer-Dieskau gave the European première with the Berlin Philharmonic Orchestra under the Stravinsky disciple, Robert Craft, in the Philharmonie in Berlin on 22 September 1964, while there is an April

1967 CBS recording in the Archive with Stravinsky himself conducting. Nor should we forget another great 'modern', Witold
Lutoslawksi (born 1913), the Polish composer, who conducted the
Berlin Philharmonic Orchestra in the first performance of his *Les
espaces·du sommeil*, written for Fischer-Dieskau, in Berlin on 12 April
1978.

The kind reader will pardon the list of works; it was intended
to show that Fischer-Dieskau's interest in 'modern music' is no
new development brought on, one might think, by the 'contempt'
bred by the 'familiarity' of the standard repertoire, a surfeit of
Bach, Schubert and Wagner – but is rather proof of a live and
steady involvement with, and an insatiable curiosity about, the
music and the composers of his own century. As Gerald Moore
said jokingly to me: 'Music is the air that Fischer-Dieskau breathes;
he would suffocate without music' – a comic but pardonable
hyperbole! But when, as late as August 1959, Arthur Jacobs, a
perceptive British musician, could write: 'We do not (despite his
participation in the complete recording of *Capriccio* and the DGG
Musica nova) associate him (i.e. Fischer-Dieskau) with 20th century
music. . .' (in *The Gramophone*), Britain's isolation from the contemporary continental music scene was all too evident!

Mention should be made finally of four contemporary composers
who have either written works for Fischer-Dieskau or had them
performed regularly by him: Karl Amadeus Hartmann (1905–
1963), Gottfried von Einem (born 1918), Aribert Reimann (born
1936) and Hans Werner Henze (born 1926).

Hartmann's *Gesangsszene* (1963), written for Fischer-Dieskau, but
which the composer did not live to complete, demands all the vocal
power at the baritone's command, since he has to ride over a
massive orchestral part and yet also express quiet and peaceful
resignation. The closing section has to be spoken since the music
to it was not written; critics remarked at the time what a fine
speaking voice Fischer-Dieskau had – the text is from Giraudoux'
Sodome et Gomorrhe – and the last words 'Es ist ein Ende der Welt!
Das traurigste von allen' (This is one end to the world, the saddest
of all), were spoken with 'true Shakespearean pathos', which made
some wonder if we might yet see Fischer-Dieskau in spoken drama.
The singer gave the first performance of the work in Frankfurt

(under Dean Dixon) on 12 November 1964, and a memorable one at the 1968 Edinburgh Festival under Rafael Kubelik.*

Gottfried von Einem, the Swiss-Austrian composer, will figure in our later chapters on the opera and the *Lied*; I just mention here his *An die Nachgeborenen* (To those born afterwards), of which Fischer-Dieskau gave the first performance (with Julia Hamari and conducted by Carlo Maria Giulini) in the United Nations' Assembly Hall in New York on 24 October 1975 (and it was recorded by DG on 17 November 1975), and of which the composer wrote to him gratefully on 22 November: 'There's another climate as soon as you sing'!

In recent years, one of Fischer-Dieskau's most regular collaborators has been his fellow-Berliner, Aribert Reimann, a pupil of Boris Blacher. Not only has Reimann composed song-cycles, oratorios and, in 1979, the great opera *Lear* for Fischer-Dieskau, he has also accompanied him at the piano at many *Lieder* recitals. Here I must mention Reimann's *Requiem* of which the baritone gave the first performance in Landau in the Rhine-Palatinate (not far from Karlsruhe) as part of the town's 700th anniversary celebrations on 2 June 1974.

The work, entitled *Wolkenloses Christfest* (A cloudless Christmas), is a setting of poems by Otfried Büthe, a Frankfurt poet. It is curious in that it is written for the lower registers of both voice and instruments; Fischer-Dieskau's baritone is accompanied by ten cellos and six basses, plus an array of percussion instruments. (The orchestra was that of the Saarland Radio conducted by Hans Zender). The composer's strong sense of drama is seen in the, at times, brutal music (which clearly leads to his Lear opera), and the aggressive setting of Büthe's often anti-clerical poems which have contemporary significance cf. one portion of the text: 'Kruzifixus advenit und Napalm – aber wir feiern die Ankunft der Feuerpause zwischen unseren bethleheminischen Morden' (The crucifix arrives and napalm – but we are celebrating the arrival of the cease-fire between our murders in Bethlehem). Fischer-Dieskau sang the work in the Royal Festival Hall in London on 3 March 1977 (again under Hans Zender) with the New Philharmonia

*See Discography p. 323

Orchestra – Siegfried Palm played the impressive cello solos on both occasions.

Finally, Hans Werner Henze: Henze was a pupil of Wolfgang Fortner in Heidelberg in 1947 and is arguably the most talented (and the best known) of contemporary German composers; he is certainly the most prolific. His opera *Elegy for young lovers* written to a libretto by W. H. Auden and Chester Kallman, composed for Fischer-Dieskau, was given its first performance in Schwetzingen on 20 May 1961. On 24 April 1963, Fischer-Dieskau (under Henze's direction and with Elisabeth Söderström, Kerstin Meyer and Peter Pears) gave the first performance of the cantata *Novae de infinito laudes* (New praises on the infinite) in the Teatro la Fenice in Venice. (Henze was living in Italy). The six-part work, based on the writings of Giordano Bruno who was burned as a heretic by the Inquisition in 1600, has passages of great tonal, almost classical, beauty mingled with fiendishly difficult sections with a more contemporary sound. It is a work which Fischer-Dieskau enjoys singing, but reviews would seem to indicate that it will never be a widely-accepted concert-hall favourite.

Although Henze followed that with another work for Fischer-Dieskau, a concert version of his 1951 radio-cantata *Der Landarzt* (The country doctor) (a setting of Franz Kafka's ghoulish short story) in 1964, the work which linked the baritone's name most closely to Henze and which caused great controversy was *Das Floss der Medusa* (The raft of the frigate Meduse) which *was* to have been performed in Hamburg's 'Planten un Blomen' (Botanical Gardens) Hall on 9 December 1968 at the height of the students' riots in Europe. Henze was already well known for his anti-'fascist', pro-left-wing sympathies – ('I have been composing for the depressed masses. . .') – and there were many left-wing students in the audience who had come to protest against the USA's involvement in Vietnam. Before the performance began, a student hung a large poster of Che Guevara (to whom the work is dedicated) on the rostrum rail, presumably knowing of Henze's admiration for the Cuban revolutionary leader. When the chorus (the *RIAS* choir from West Berlin), the soloists, Edda Moser (soprano), Fischer-Dieskau and Charles Régnier (speaker), the orchestra (the North German Radio Symphony Orchestra) and Henze appeared, bedlam broke loose. The *RIAS* choir began to chant: 'We shall not sing under the Red Flag', (which had appeared on the platform along with North Vietnam's black flag), and left the platform. Scuffles broke out, the police intervened none too gently and Henze came back to the platform to announce that police action had prevented a performance – and led a chant of 'Ho-Ho-Ho, Ho-Chi-Minh', the student war-cry of the day. The audience dispersed – some no doubt to listen to the recording of the dress rehearsal which NDR (The North German Radio) had fortunately made earlier.

When I asked Fischer-Dieskau about the débâcle, he said:

'All I know is what I saw: the Red Flag beside the conductor, a West Berlin choir on the stage who wanted to sing, shouting students in the audience, clumsy and rather violent uniformed police. . .after a quarter of an hour's useless standing around waiting to begin, the choir got up and left. As a West Berliner, I felt solidarity with them, so I went too, tired of all the ado about nothing. But I still think that the work is first-class, full of tension – absolutely representative of the justified unrest of the young people of 1968'.

That recording was eventually released by DG in April 1970 to much praise. Fischer-Dieskau's rôle as the mulatto Jean-Charles, cast adrift on 2 July 1816 by the officers of the wrecked French frigate, with 149 soldiers and crew members on a raft which was picked up twelve days later with only fifteen survivors, is as powerful as Théodore Géricault's famous Louvre painting of the incident (*Le radeau de la Méduse* (1819)).

Of all the twentieth-century composers whose works he has sung, perhaps it is Henze who most nearly meets Fischer-Dieskau's demand for 'singability'. Agreeing that Henze has become more 'conservative' with the passing of the years, Fischer-Dieskau remarked once that the composer had discovered that 'the road you walk needs support from the ground'. Certainly Henze's concern for 'beautiful sounds' is everywhere apparent in his vocal music. Indeed, he said once that it was after he had studied Italian opera that he became aware of how much stronger the physical presence of music is in a singer than in an instrument. That might well account for his desire to write music for Dietrich Fischer-Dieskau.

The 'radiant gravity' that Albert Schweitzer found in Fischer-Dieskau's singing of Bach can be found everywhere in his singing of sacred music. If the singer is some way removed from that boy celebrant in church who wanted to become a Lutheran clergyman, and from the prisoner-of-war nearly converted by zealous Roman Catholic missionaries who delighted so much in his singing, he is still emotionally affected by great sacred music. 'It is the thought of someone sacrificing himself for others that is so moving', he murmured to me in Berlin when we were discussing his singing of the great Bach Passions.

His empathetic involvement in this music too is of a piece with his intense characterisations of operatic rôles and great *Lieder* cycles – all bear witness to his artistic honesty and integrity.

CHAPTER THREE

Opera and Dramatic Music

By the mid-1960's, Fischer-Dieskau's repertoire and commitments had grown almost beyond belief; from that period on, there are on average fifty to seventy engagements per year and, of course, in the case of an operatic engagement, that could mean two to five appearances. About five to ten recordings per year were also made, each taking up to three days for preparation, rehearsal and performance.

His seemingly inexhaustible energy and insatiable thirst for new, and often very difficult, musical experiences, as well as for the established classical works, gave him a reputation for versatility and performances of high standing second to none. It will have already been noticed that a good time often elapsed between the making and the issue of a record; the question was often asked why record companies insisted on releasing sometimes two or even three Fischer-Dieskau recordings in one month. It set a pretty problem for the not-too-affluent record collector, and led one journalist to suggest jokingly that we should establish a list of the 'hundred best Fischer-Dieskau records of the year'. The singer himself has always said however that he sings what and where he is asked to, and that he will go on doing so as long as the public want and ask him to, and it is abundantly clear that the public has never been able to get enough 'Fischer-Dieskau'.

Offers were now reaching the artist from all over the world; since his first tour of 1955, he has visited the major cities in the United States fifteen times (up to August 1980). The large proportion of Americans of Germanic stock no doubt appreciated his beautifully enunciated diction and his repertoire of the beloved German *Lieder*, and their children now stream into his sold-out concerts. Yet it is strange that he has not yet appeared in opera there, apart from a few concert performances. The critics are as one in admiring his handsome masculine figure on the concert platform. 'Tall and perennially boyish-looking, he is a sort of Germanic Ivy League type', wrote *The Examiner* of San Francisco in April 1974. So, why has he not sung at the Met? The singer told me that when he could or might have sung there, nobody asked him – and when they asked him, he was busy elsewhere. Harold C. Schonberg added his plea in the *Baltimore Sun* in December 1974: 'Can't Fischer-Dieskau be captured for the Met., if only on the fly?'

There have been six wonderfully successful tours of Japan since that first epoch-making *Fidelio* with the Deutsche Oper of Berlin in Tokyo in late 1963. The Japanese are now among his most enthusiastic audiences, and the Federal German Government has not ignored Fischer-Dieskau's contribution to the forging of cultural links there. Nor can I forget his faithful attendance at the Edinburgh Festival – since 1952 he has appeared at thirteen Festivals in a bewildering variety of works – oratorio, *Lied* and opera – some accompanied by the magnificent Edinburgh Festival Chorus. In my conversations with him, he often says how much he appreciates Edinburgh, a 'small big town' which has a true Festival atmosphere. London, on the other hand, frightened him at first by its sheer size. Scenically, too, the Scottish capital city gives him a rare pleasure and he has captured some of these scenes in his paintings. Hanging in his house in Munich is a painting of one of his favourite views in Edinburgh – looking over the Dean Bridge towards the city. The work is titled 'Douglas Gardens'.

In June 1971 came the first very important visit with Daniel Barenboim to Tel Aviv in Israel, the first German singer to appear there since the war. He sang Mahler's *Lieder eines fahrenden Gesellen* with Barenboim and the Israel Philharmonic Orchestra, *Winterreise* and some Beethoven *Lieder* accompanied by Barenboim. Of all his 'ambassadorial' visits abroad, none had such profound cultural consequences as this one, and his subsequent visits in 1973, 1974 and 1976. It must not be forgotten that the music of Wagner and Richard Strauss, for example, is still banned in Israel, and that it was only in 1970 that the fourth movement of Beethoven's *Choral Symphony* had been sung in German for the first time in the new state. Wolfgang Lewy, the principal horn player in the Israel orchestra, had been trying to get Fischer-Dieskau to Israel since 1967, but admitted that the time had never seemed quite ripe. Fischer-Dieskau's *Winterreise* with Barenboim in Tel Aviv on 22 June 1971 was a revelation to the Israelis, sung, as one man said afterwards, 'free from sentimentality'. Another said: 'I didn't think it possible that a human being could sing with such concentration, such musicality, such earnestness – and I hadn't even heard his name before!'

Fischer-Dieskau himself found the visit an enormous strain:

'I came out on to the stage', he said to Klaus Geitel of *Die Welt*, 'and saw as usual an indistinct mass in the background; the faces in the first six rows were all turned up at me, expectant, but perhaps also embarrassed. Although they were silent, these faces spoke to me; and I understood that language straightaway. They were the faces that I miss in my audiences in Germany, and, of course, I know that I and my whole generation will never forget the reason for that. Although belonging to strangers, they were well-known faces, easy to place: Frankfurt, Berlin, Baden-Baden. But other names pushed these place-names aside. Fearful names. And even without knowing these, it is not really easy to sing Schubert. In this case, however. . .'

When, contrary to his usual custom, he and his wife (Christina Pugell) attended a reception given by the German Ambassador, Jesco von Puttkamer, for over two hundred guests in the Tel-Aviv Hilton, his shy, modest bearing won him many more friends and admirers.

His one visit to the USSR to sing Wolf and Schubert with Sviatoslav Richter in October 1977 remained in his mind, he told me, largely because the Soviet authorities cleared the Hermitage in Leningrad to allow the singer to look around the magnificent gallery in peace! (A second visit to the Soviet Union planned for October 1980 – also with Richter – was cancelled because of 'administrative difficulties').

His visits to other countries of the eastern bloc – Poland, Czechoslovakia and Hungary in 1973 for example – were also enormous successes, but none greater than the most delicate visit of all, particularly for a West Berliner: his concert in the Komische Oper in East Berlin on 16 April 1978. As anyone who has visited the 'socialist' countries of Eastern Europe could testify, there are no more 'bourgeois' audiences to be found anywhere in the world. The safe 'cultural treasures' of the eighteenth and nineteenth centuries are their staple musical diet. However Fischer-Dieskau gave them a *Liederabend*, accompanied by Aribert Reimann, of Schoenberg, Berg and Webern!

The award in 1974 of the Federal Republic of Germany's highest honour, the *Grosses Verdienstkreuz des Bundesverdienstordens* (The Grand Cross of Merit) signified his country's awareness of his tireless work as an ambassador of music over so many years. When presenting the medal on 12 September, Klaus Schütz, the then Mayor of West Berlin, said: 'People say of this singer that he is the most important artist that German music has produced since the war. I should like to add to him: You have given the art-song a new dimension. You have also helped contemporary music to gain a foothold. You have performed superbly in opera. And, in addition to all that, you have given us all a great deal of happiness'.

But it was the granting of Honorary Membership of the Deutsche Oper in Berlin in 1978 – for thirty years' distinguished service – that allows us the *entrée* proper to the theme of this chapter – Fischer-Dieskau in opera – for the reader will recall that Fischer-Dieskau made his début at the Berlin Städtische Oper (Municipal Opera) in the Kantstrasse (the former Theater des Westens) on 18 November 1948 when he sang Marquis Posa in the Heinz Tietjen-Ferenc Fricsay production of Verdi's *Don Carlos*. Since that date, he has been in constant demand for operatic rôles throughout Germany and Austria, and for numerous guest appearances in other countries.

In this chapter, I should like to document Fischer-Dieskau's massive achievements in the fields of opera and dramatic music generally. He has ranged as widely here as in any other musical field, from eighteenth-century baroque opera through the nineteenth-century Italian and German repertoire to his distinguished involvement in the music of our own times. Since, as we know, he has made only a few guest appearances in Great Britain, (and then mainly in London and Edinburgh), and since Americans and Canadians have only seen him in concert performances of operatic works, the music lover in these countries will have heard him only in recorded accounts of his many operatic rôles. He or she will bear in mind, in addition, that, particularly in the 1950's and 1960's, the singer was dividing his time fairly evenly between appearances on the concert platform in *Lieder* recitals, and appearances in very varied rôles in opera houses in a number of towns and countries.

To begin then almost at the beginning of operatic history: and with a familiar controversy – what voice should sing Gluck's *Orfeo*? I think that it must be very difficult for British people ever to forget the sad but beautiful sight of the late and much-loved contralto, Kathleen Ferrier, singing the rôle in her first and what proved to be, alas, her last performances at Covent Garden in February 1953. It is well known that Gluck wrote the music for an alto *castrato*, Gaetano Guadagni, for the Vienna première (in Italian) in 1762, and that he then re-wrote it for a high tenor, an *haute contre*, for the Paris performance in French twelve years later. There are those who, (like the late Ernest Newman), hear the 'trumpet' of the heroic only in the *castrato*'s (or modern female equivalent's) tone; there are others who feel, as Ferenc Fricsay did, that the psychology of the rôle asks for the deeper man's voice; although Emmi Leisner, Fischer-Dieskau's idol of his early years, had been the Orfeo in Jacques-Lacroze's celebrated production at Hellerau near Dresden, Fischer-Dieskau was convinced by Fricsay of the *necessity* of having a male singer in the leading rôle, and it was under Fricsay indeed that he recorded it for DG in a German version (*Orpheus und Eurydike*) with Maria Stader, Rita Streich and the *RIAS* Symphony Orchestra in September 1956; a year later, there was another performance in the Berlin Academy of Music, also under Fricsay.

Martin Cooper in his *Gluck* (1935) has given the 'establishment' reason for having either a *castrato* or a contralto Orfeo:

'Orpheus is not simply a husband sobbing on his wife's grave; had he been no more than that, the change from contralto to tenor would have been unquestionably an improvement. But he is a symbol, like all symbols imprecise, of the artist and of the power of music able to conquer death, but conquered in its turn by human passion'.

It is claimed that the transposition down an octave for the baritone leads to a loss of tone in the lower register.

It is a difficult question. Fischer-Dieskau's performance of 'Ach, ich habe sie verloren' (*Che farò senza Euridice?*), backed with 'Welch reiner Himmel' (*Che puro ciel*) and issued in November 1959 as an E.P. (Extended Play) record (ELP 30405) was a winner, but I much preferred his second recording of the original Vienna version made for DG in August 1967 and released in 1969. Karl Richter conducted the Munich Bach Orchestra. I happen to dislike all transvestite performances and therefore must admit that I prefer a man to sing a male rôle from a purely practical or aesthetic point of view – although Nicolai Gedda's May 1958 tenor version was rather a strain for performer and listener alike. In the same month, Risë Stevens' version was reviewed in the *EMI Monthly Letter* thus:

'At the risk of appearing Philistine, we take our courage in both hands and roundly assert that the part of Orphée sung by a woman is an anathema, an abomination and a malpractice. Gluck wrote the part originally for a male alto and then re-wrote it for a tenor. No doubt many people will assert that a female mezzo-soprano is the vocal equivalent of a male alto, but this is not the case. Miss Risë Stevens' voice. . .is far too feminine and bosomy for any male singer however alto. We are inclined to think, (in our crude commonsense way), that the reasonable solution is to use a high baritone and the nearest to this is in Fischer-Dieskau's performance, where one at least feels that Orphée is a manly man'.

I think that these would be my sentiments too; there are no doubt some baritones who would have to reach for the lower notes, but Fischer-Dieskau negotiates all of them with no sense of strain, and he sings the two major arias, not only with warmth, but also with poise and grace, particularly the lovely line, 'sono il mio solo, il mio diletto Eliso' (You are my only, my blissful Elysium) in *Che puro ciel* in Act II. Fischer-Dieskau also obeys Gluck's reported instruction to Guadagni to shout Eurydice's name 'as if you had suffered a real loss' in the *Che farò!**

In June 1972, Fischer-Dieskau sang Agamemnon in Gluck's *Iphigenie in Aulis* (in German) for a Eurodisc recording with the Munich Radio Orchestra under Kurt Eichhorn. The version used was Wagner's 'thorough-going revision of the score' in which he had tried 'to make the various phases of the development of the plot more comprehensible without interrupting it with unnecessary vocal ornamentation'. Although the work has Gluck's revised (1775) ending (i.e. Iphigeneia is sent to Tauris as a priestess), few reviewers in Britain or America or elsewhere seemed to approve of this version. Fischer-Dieskau received excellent notices however – Stanley Sadie in *The Gramophone* for December 1976 found him to be 'an Agamemnon both fiery and lyrical' – but the recording did not stay very long in our catalogues.

Fischer-Dieskau's professional colleagues continually praise his ability to master all styles of music; Jörg Demus wrote me that it was Fischer-Dieskau's ability to move *naturally* from the lyrical to the dramatic which made him such an outstanding artist and this is clearly what makes him such an exciting singer to watch – and to hear. Perhaps, however, there is not the full scope in baroque opera for a singer with such a range of talents, nor is there such a wide variety of music suitable for his voice to be found in the eighteenth century as in the nineteenth or twentieth. *He* certainly has little time for the arguments about *Orfeo*, believing that all three voices (contralto, tenor or baritone) can do justice to the beautiful music.

Such was the case too with his recording (with Irmgard Seefried) of the Caesar and Cleopatra arias from Handel's *Giulio Cesare* (1724), made in April 1960 for DG with the Berlin Radio Symphony Orchestra conducted by Karl Böhm. The recording, made in a large church, has always pleased the singer, but again there was discussion about the type of voice that should sing the rôle of Caesar. As we know, Handel wrote it for a male alto (Francesco

*One could never deny, however, the artistic merit of a Kathleen Ferrier or a Janet Baker stage performance. It is fairly certain too that Orfeo is one of the three or four rôles that Fischer-Dieskau would never undertake on stage. Nevertheless, he has given quite a few concert performances of the work, notably for the American Opera Society, in Carnegie Hall in April 1967, with Elisabeth Schwarzkopf, Lucia Popp and Marilyn Tyler, under Junel Perlea, shortly before the DG recording mentioned above.

Bernardini Senesino) and there were some critics, Desmond Shawe-Taylor among them, who were of the opinion that 'these florid arias are bound to lie awkwardly' for a baritone (*The Gramophone*, April 1961), although I could hear little that was awkward in Fischer-Dieskau's smooth singing of the lovely E major arietta on Cleopatra's beauty *Non è si vago e bello il fior nel prato* (There is no other (so desirous and beautiful) flower in the meadow), with its perfectly-produced trill later on *prato* and the finely-controlled run on *vago* (Ex. 8.). What a pity that there were not more ornamentations!

Later, the singer took part in a recording of the complete opera for Deutsche Grammophon, in April 1969, with Karl Richter and his Munich Bach Orchestra. Partnered here by the Cleopatra of Tatiana Troyanos, Fischer-Dieskau presented a Caesar vigorous and ardent, passionate and lyrical. Indeed the *Non è si vago* in this recording was felt by some to be almost (too) Schubertian. I could see what was meant, but I could also see that it matched the singer's general interpretation of Caesar as a simple man in love. What was admired here above all was Fischer-Dieskau's superlative breath-control in the long Handelian runs, and his ability to give at times a *crescendo* on the last notes of a phrase where other singers would long since have been out of breath! G. A. Trumpff, while regretting the loss of Handelian brilliance by the transposition to the lower voice, found the singer's interpretation 'a miracle of empathy', revealing Caesar's 'intellectuality, tolerance and humanity', (in *Neue Zeitschrift für Musik*, May 1971).

Earlier, in January 1966, Fischer-Dieskau had recorded Handel's opera-cum-'cantata à 2' *Apollo e Dafne* (1708) for DG. A

section of the Berlin Philharmonic Orchestra under Günther Weissenborn accompanied the baritone and the mellifluous Agnes Giebel. Here the singer was simply at his 'superb best', as Roger Fiske
reported; his phrasing in the final lament, the scene *Mie piante
correte* (Pursue my steps), and the beautiful aria *Cara pianta co'miei
pianti. . .* (Dearest plant, with my sorrows. . .), had one staggering
phrase at the conclusion, at 'Sommi eroi coronerò' where the
baritone took the florid phrase in one breath to end on a superb
trill on 'coronerò'. I thought that this work, perched on that
uneasy border between cantata and opera, was shown to be a
masterpiece in the performances of two great singers – I should
not like to be without Agnes Giebel's version of the wonderful aria
Felicissima quest'alma (Blessed is the soul) (No. 5) with Karl Steins'
curling oboe accompaniment.

The Deutsche Grammophon record of ten arias from Handel's
operas with the Müncher Kammerorchester conducted by Hans
Stadlmair (made in August 1977) allowed us to imagine the baritone in other Handelian operatic rôles. Apart from the vigorous
lower voice arias from *Saul* and *Samson*, most of the others were
originally written for *castrato* and had to be transposed down an
octave which, as with the *Caesar* arias, led to some loss of brilliance.
Fischer-Dieskau's version of the celebrated and perhaps too well-
known *Ombra mai fu* ('Handel's Largo') was as cultivated and
sensitive as one would wish and expect, with a melting 'soave piu'
to conclude, but he told me that he was not too happy about the
technical aspects of this recording. He certainly seemed to me to
have been recorded too close to the microphone on occasion.

It is fairly clear that the singer does not find too many operas
of outstanding musical interest in this period. He lavishes great
care on those works that he is called upon to perform – as always –
but I feel that he sings them more out of a sense of 'duty' than
otherwise!

This might be the most suitable moment to mention Beethoven's
only opera *Fidelio* (1805) before we turn to the great operas of
Mozart. Fischer-Dieskau has sung two of the male rôles in this
work, the evil prison governor, Don Pizarro, and the righteous
Minister of State, Don Fernando. Neither is a major part – but I

find that *Fidelio* is an opera that needs a 'star cast' to be entirely successful. Fischer-Dieskau's experience of the latter rôle goes back to the earliest days of his work with Heinz Tietjen and Ferenc Fricsay in Berlin where, in 1950, he sang the part of the freedom-giving *deus ex machina*, the Minister of State, dressed in the white costume which Otto Klemperer had made into a tradition there. As in the introduction to the final movement of the Ninth Symphony, the Minister's words 'Es sucht der Bruder seine Brüder/Und kann er helfen, hilft er gern' (A brother seeks his brothers and he will help them wherever he can), express that eighteenth-century longing for brotherhood and freedom which has made *Fidelio* an institution in post-war Germany and Austria.

Fischer-Dieskau's first recorded rôle, however, was Don Pizarro, the black-hearted, totalitarian prison governor. He made it for Deutsche Grammophon with Fricsay and the Bavarian State Opera Orchestra in Munich in June 1957. It is a glorious recording, marred, alas, by the dialogue having been given to actors to speak rather than to the singers. For those who understand German, however, what a relief it is nevertheless to have the dialogue properly *acted* instead of 'hammed', as in the Klemperer version of 1962. The reviewer who wrote of that recording that 'the extensive dialogue is spoken (thank goodness) *with deep feeling*' (my italics), could surely have had little or no German? *Fidelio* is only half an opera without this dialogue properly spoken – which holds for *Die Zauberflöte* as well, I believe. The beautiful singing in the Klemperer version seems to me to be, in part anyway, vitiated by the 'stagey' dialogue.

The second recording, with Fischer-Dieskau as Don Fernando, made twenty years later, with Leonard Bernstein conducting the Vienna Philharmonic Orchestra, underlines my point about dialogue. The DG recording made in the Grosser Musikverein in Vienna in 1977 contains the most naturally-spoken dialogue of any recording that I know – the singers were specially coached for the occasion by Otto Schenk!

Bernstein, who believes that Fischer-Dieskau is one of the few musicians who, as he put it to me, 'can make sounds that come close to your heart', chose his Minister of State wisely. Here, Fischer-Dieskau is as benevolent as he was malevolent in the first recording. Bernstein, who has worked closely with the singer in other musical fields, brought the very best out of him: his melting request to Leonore to undo Florestan's chains: 'Euch ziemt es, ganz ihn zu befrei'n', (*You* must release him), leads the quartet smoothly in to the ecstatic conjugal finale. When listening to this section, I have to recall the Munich critic who, after a disappointing *Fidelio* at one festival, wrote: ' "Ha! Der Minister!" cries Pizarro after Leonore has put the pistol to his chest. "Ha! Fischer-Dieskau!" thinks the audience, relieved and expectant'!

Although Maynard Solomon, in his excellent Beethoven book, castigates the Fidelio plot and libretto as 'stagnant in its action, cumbersome in its dramatic development and awkward in its blending of styles', the opera does seem somehow to 'work' on the stage when the voices are great enough. Fischer-Dieskau found this particularly during that epoch-making 'cultural-cum-political' visit of the newly-founded Deutsche Oper to Japan during October and November 1963, when the company performed *Fidelio* and *Le nozze di Figaro* in Tokyo's massive new Nissei Theatre under the bâton of Karl Böhm and in front of many dignitaries, including the President of the Federal Republic.

The preceding pages have covered Fischer-Dieskau's major commitments in baroque and eighteenth-century opera to date. Edward Dent wrote once that 'what charms a modern audience in Gluck is the illusion of classical dignity; they are ideal museum pieces, for they give the modern listener the impression of a purely imaginary ancient Greece, populated, not by human beings, but by statues of white marble', (in *The New Musical Companion*, 1954). But the Fischer-Dieskau that I enjoy most in opera is certainly not Fischer-Dieskau as 'a statue of white marble', but that Fischer-Dieskau caught up in the web of human passions where he in turn can employ his unique vocal and histrionic abilities to ensnare the listener or watcher. Such rôles, characters with as much 'Saft und Blut' as possible, characters full of 'juice and blood', as he puts it, are not encountered in the eighteenth century until Vienna becomes the centre of the musical world and brings forth the operas of Wolfgang Amadeus Mozart.

* * * * *

One probably need not go as far as Miss Brigid Brophy in her fascinating but rather turgid book *Mozart the Dramatist* (1964), to prove that Mozart was Beethoven's superior in the field of opera (or anywhere else). Her dislike of what she calls 'Beethovenolatry', (in J. W. N. Sullivan's celebrated book in particular), leads her to the opposite extreme. The 'touchy' problem of where to 'place' Mozart admits of only one solution, she writes: 'He stands on the very pinnacle of Parnassus'. Many would agree with her.

In her discussion of Don Giovanni, Miss Brophy is surprised that Mozart made him a baritone; she is nearly certain that 'a Verdi would have made such a celebrated lover a tenor'! But William Mann in his *The Operas of Mozart* (1977) reminds her and us that, 'as always for Mozart, the singers determined the nature of the music,' and that Luigi Bassi, the baritone who had sung Count Almaviva, was also available for Don Giovanni.

In April 1964, Fischer-Dieskau wrote an appreciation of Ferenc Fricsay who had died, aged only 48, in 1963, and who had guided him in his first recording of *Don Giovanni* in 1958. The singer recalls that the preparations for the performance which opened the new Deutsche Oper in Berlin in September 1961 had not gone all that smoothly – there had been disagreements between Fricsay and the director, Carl Ebert, and Fischer-Dieskau had had to go his own way, find his own interpretation without, of course, disturbing the arranged ensembles. This is how he described his characterisation of the Don: 'Restrained passion, a steady intensification of despair at his flight from his own self, and finally some measure of greatness, as he fights to retain his own personality before the demons drag him down to Hell' – all that lay, he felt, in Fricsay's handling of the score as well.

He had sung the rôle for the first time in 1953 in Berlin under Werner Kelch and Karl Böhm, and Lord Harewood was so impressed by that performance that he thought that it was the most brilliant Don Giovanni that he had ever seen; that performance was in German, of course – Lord Harewood believed that Fischer-Dieskau was actually more incisive in the German version, highlights from which can be heard on a DG record made in February 1963, conducted by Hans Löwlein. According to reports from German friends, Fischer-Dieskau played that Don as an erotic charmer, a 'conqueror of women's hearts', wrote one, which presented a pretty paradox to those who had seen him only as a dignified and perhaps rather *un*-erotic Lieder singer in tails on a concert platform. But something of that eroticism remains, I believe, in the Fricsay DG recording made in September 1958, in Italian.

It was Søren Kierkegaard who praised the 'immediate erotic' of Mozart's musical expression, and I am sure that it would take a stronger woman than a stage Zerlina to resist this Don's wooing, especially at the recitative before their *duettino Là ci darem la mano* (Give me your hand) (No. 7). As Fischer-Dieskau caresses the words 'e là, gioiello mio, ci sposeremo' (and there we'll wed, my little jewel), one senses what advantages the *Lieder* singer has in opera; textual nuances like these often go for nothing, as the opera singer seeks to make his 'beautiful sound' (Ex. 9.). The despairing

Ex. 9 *Don Giovanni*

e là, gio - iel - lo mi - o, ci spo-se - re - mo

Don that Fischer-Dieskau mentioned, is heard in what the Germans call the *Champagne Aria*, (from a bad translation of *vino* as 'der Champagner'), *Finch'han dal vino calda la testa*, which is sung with enormous verve and sexual vitality – a true character-sketch of the man – but which ends on an almost hectic laugh betraying Giovanni's uncertainty. His final scene, 'Che strazio! ohimé! che smania! che inferno!. . .che terror! . . .', as the Don smells the avenging fires of hell, ends on the 'Ah!', (or 'No'!) 'occasionally sung on the A natural, an octave higher than written, by baritones who have the range for it', writes Charles Osborne in *The Complete Operas of Mozart* (1978) and he goes on '– Dietrich Fischer-Dieskau for instance – and who can blame them?'

All in all, it is an electrifying performance, ranging from the erotic through the lyrical to the dramatic. Italian reviewers found themselves comparing him with 'the great voices of the past', although they did not go quite as far as the critic in *Records and Recordings* for November 1959. After praising the baritone's 'remarkable psychological insight', he concluded: 'If this reads as an unqualified "rave", it is meant to, for I seriously consider the German baritone's Don unsurpassable and, everything considered, the greatest performance of any complete operatic rôle ever recorded'.

Fischer-Dieskau's second complete *Don Giovanni* for Deutsche Grammophon was recorded nine years later, appropriately enough in Prague, where the opera had had its première one hundred and eighty years earlier, in 1787. Despite the promising cast, I could not warm to the February/March 1967 recording – the orchestra in particular, the Prague National Theatre Orchestra under Karl Böhm, played without Mozartian sparkle, while Birgit Nilsson was miscast, I thought, as Donna Anna. 'All silk', however would be an apt description for the Fischer-Dieskau lovely serenade to Donna Elvira's maid, *Deh, vieni alla finestra, o mio tesoro* (Come to the window, my treasure), although the conductor's slow tempi for the *duettino* with Zerlina made that seductive and erotic moment rather workaday.

However, the singer's overall interpretation was as thoughtful as ever, even if I did miss the sense of inevitability that marked his first version of this 'dramma giocoso'. Still, I am certain that any opera audience would have settled for a Don with these vocal and theatrical gifts.

Friedrich Luft, the distinguished Berlin theatre critic, wrote once of Fischer-Dieskau: 'A new light shines in the theatre when he steps on to the stage' – and I felt this almost physically at his first entrance in *Le nozze di Figaro* at the Edinburgh Festival in 1975. I had been with him shortly before the performance, discussing my work on his Schubert book, and remember him calling the King's Theatre in Edinburgh 'etwas primitiv' (a little primitive) – but his aristocratic figure in its eighteenth-century coat and wig lit up the whole, rather old-fashioned theatre. He had sung the role of Count Almaviva many times before, of course, since his first appearance in it in Salzburg in the 1956 Mozart bi-centenary production under Karl Böhm. It remains one of his favourite parts, since it enables him to build up a paradoxical, tragicomic, flesh-and-blood character – aristocrat, lover, philanderer, and, finally, deceiver deceived. Like all great actors, Fischer-Dieskau is 'in the action' all the time, reacting as in life to the developing situation, not above a bit of 'comic business', such as playfully slapping Susanna's bottom, (as Mozart was said to have nipped his Zerlina's), or fooling about with the tool box in Act Two.

He had sung the part earlier in 1956 in Berlin and in a guest performance with the Städtische Oper at the Théâtre des Champs Elysées in Paris on 27 April, but Oscar Fritz Schuh's 1956 production was the beginning of a long and successful association with Salzburg and with great artists such as Karl Böhm, Carl Ebert, Günther Rennert, Gustav Rudolf Sellner, and the stage designers, Caspar Neher and Teo Otto. His singing of these Mozartian rôles from 1953 onwards seemed to me to have had an effect on his whole *persona*. Apart from giving him the 'courage' to use full voice in the concert hall – and that is what Fischer-Dieskau believes that it did – the *élan* and gaiety of these operas, the opportunities for team-work and large-scale characterisation development, not only increased his already keen insight into human strengths and foibles, but also brought into play that element of his character rarely seen on the concert platform – his acute sense of humour.

'Musical himself, he is the cause of musicality in those who sing with him (to paraphrase Falstaff)', wrote Philip Hope-Wallace. 'His Italian is excellent and the degree of haughtiness and arrogance in the characterisation is nicely calculated – I believe without overdone hectoring or boorishness, though not all critics agree. Listen to *Vedrò mentr'io sospiro* or the third act duet with Susanna and see if you do not endorse my view'. Thus one of the senior critics in *The Gramophone* for February 1962 on Fischer-Dieskau's first complete DG recording of the opera (September 1960), with Ferenc Fricsay and the Radio Symphony Orchestra of Berlin. The cast was largely a German one, but even the odd 'kvesto' did not worry Mr Hope-Wallace too much here! Fischer-Dieskau was regarded as simply 'the best Count of the day'. He has since recorded the opera twice more in complete versions, for DG under Karl Böhm in March 1968, and again with that superb Edinburgh cast (Geraint Evans, Heather Harper, Teresa Berganza, Judith Blegen and Birgit Finnilä, under Daniel Barenboim, for Electrola in August 1976. (He also filmed the rôle at Shepperton Studios in June 1976, in a performance conducted by Karl Böhm and directed by Jean-Pierre Ponnelle, with the delectable Kiri te Kanawa, Mirella Freni, Maria Ewing, John van Kesteren and Hermann Prey).

An interesting aside on Fischer-Dieskau's interpretation of the rôle came from Sir Geraint Evans who produced the Edinburgh *Marriage of Figaro*. Sir Geraint said that his own way of playing Figaro changed after 'a conversation with Dietrich in Salzburg' in 1972 after working with the producer Gustav Rudolf Sellner. Fischer-Dieskau suggested that the climax of the opera came just before the finale of Act Three when Figaro turns on the Count with: 'Perchè nò? Io non impugno mai quel che non so' (Why not? I never dispute what I don't know). This, Fischer-Dieskau suggested, was the first time that the Count had been challenged by a servant – thus it had to be played as the beginning of a revolution. 'And that has shaped my Figaro ever since', added Sir Geraint.*

Fischer-Dieskau has played Don Giovanni and the Count with great distinction in many productions; audiences for *Die Zauberflöte* have only seen him, however, in the small but impressive part of *Der Sprecher* (The Speaker, or the Orator, as some translators have it), a 'serious bass' in the cast list, and never as Papageno, the bird catcher. The reason is simple: His six-feet three frame would look silly, he feels, clad in Papageno's bird feathers! On record, however, his Papageno ranks as one of the great comic creations. Emanuel Schikaneder's libretto is full of the wittiest and cleverest word-plays which seemingly pass by non-German speaking critics who 'cannot wait for the music to start again', as one wrote. With Fischer-Dieskau in the rôle, Papageno is a clown of the first water. The famous 'Pa-Pa-Pa' duet with his Papagena, Lisa Otto, became a best-seller in July 1957 and introduced the lighter Fischer-Dieskau to those audiences who had seen him only in concerts of 'serious' *Lieder*.

Professor Jacques Chailley's detailed survey of the Masonic elements in his *La flûte enchantée, opera maçonnique*, (1968) has certainly

---

*A good example of Fischer-Dieskau's scholarly and, at the same time, pioneering attitude to his art was his October 1969 Decca recording of Christopher Raeburn's discovery in Florence of a revised version of the Count's Act Three recitative and aria 'Hai già vinta la causa... Vedrò mentr'io sospiro' (We've won our case...Must I see my servant made happy while I am left to sigh?) (No. 17). Mozart's new Almaviva, Francesco Albertarelli, must have been a high baritone for this 'revised *allegro assai* of startling virtuosity', as William Mann suggests in *The Operas of Mozart* (1977), since the aria is festooned with high G's and D's, particularly near the conclusion, and on 'e giubilar mi fa'. This 1789 version had probably not been performed since the eighteenth century.

helped us to understand a good deal of the symbolism behind the opera, and I for one am sure that one cannot fully appreciate the serious content of the work without such an understanding. Joscelyn Godwin's fascinating article *The layers of meaning in The Magic Flute* (in the *Musical Quarterly* for October 1979) mentions no fewer than three full-length books devoted to the topic;* he writes that the books 'concur in one important respect: they all find the libretto sensible, consistent and full of meaning', and of course we know that Goethe was moved enough by it to consider writing a sequel to the opera.

But Papageno's rôle is, I believe, that of the true clown; he must balance the solemnity and the comic and try to achieve what Wilson Knight called the 'sublime incongruity'. Fischer-Dieskau plays the bird-catcher's 'mock tragedy' with a wonderfully light touch. When Papageno, believing that he has lost his beloved Papagena for ever, contemplates suicide, Mozart takes him into his 'tragic' key of G minor for 'Nun wohlan, es bleibt dabei. . .weil mich nichts zurücke hält, gute Nacht, du falsche Welt. . .' (All right then, what must be, must be, since there is nothing to keep me here, good night, false world!) (Ex. 10.). Fischer-Dieskau is extraordinarily moving here, even although we know that the tragedy is indeed 'mock'.

Ex. 10

*One of the best is E. M. Batley's *A Preface to The Magic Flute* (Dobson, 1969)

There are three *Zauberflöte* recordings, two with Fischer-Dieskau as Papageno, and one as The Speaker: the first one, recorded for DG in June 1955 with Ferenc Fricsay and the RIAS Symphony Orchestra, showed many for the first time the *Lieder* singer unbuttoned, as it were; the second Papageno recording, under Karl Böhm and Gustav Rudolf Sellner, made in June 1964 with the Berlin Philharmonic Orchestra (likewise for DG) led Edward Greenfield to comment that it was difficult to believe that 'ten taxing years had passed' since the first recording, for the voice was if anything 'lighter and better focussed' than before.

Fischer-Dieskau had many competitors in the part of the vivacious bird-catcher, but he has held his position out in front in my opinion mainly because of the wealth of characterisation he puts into the rôle; even when he is singing through sealed lips, he manages to portray the rather simple but lovable Papageno, while he is a fine anchor-man in the duets with Lisa Otto.

Fischer-Dieskau's third *Zauberflöte* recording (as The Speaker) was made for Decca under (Sir) Georg Solti and the Vienna Philharmonic Orchestra in October 1969 with Hermann Prey as the Papageno; Pilar Lorengar, Cristina Deutekom, Stuart Burrows and Martti Talvela completed the superb cast. Curiously enough, as The Speaker, Fischer-Dieskau does give himself an air of reverential authoritarianism. Yet again, even this simple rôle is somehow looked at afresh, interpreted, not just sung. Listen to his sonorous 'sobald dich führt der Freundschaft Hand ins Heiligtum zum ew'gen Band' (The hand of friendship will lead you to embrace the sacred bond in our sanctum), as he tells Tamino what mysteries await him. (And what a wonderful Tamino Stuart Burrows gave us in this recording! It was as if Wunderlich had been re-born).

The hallmark of the Fischer-Dieskau Mozart style is – elegance: elegance of deportment, elegance of dress, elegance of gesture, above all, of course, elegance of voice. Nowhere was this more clearly demonstrated than at one of his (and the cast's) greatest triumphs, the Salzburg production of *Così fan tutte* in 1972. Rarely has there been such a unanimous chorus of praise for a production, for Karl Böhm's conducting, Ita Maximovna's sets and, above all, for Günther Rennert's masterful direction. As actors and singers the main vocal quartet could scarcely have been bettered: Gundula Janowitz as Fiordiligi, Brigitte Fassbaender as Dorabella, Hermann Prey as Guglielmo and Peter Schreier as Ferrando, (a circus turn in their 'Albanian' disguise). Reri Grist was the perfect Mozartian soubrette as Despina – which left the Don Alfonso. The 'headmaster' of this *scuola degli amanti* is of course a *basso buffo* rôle, a cynic for whom 'la donna è mobile' – but even a cynic must have a sense of style. Fischer-Dieskau played him as a wise old sceptic aware of human weaknesses and foibles, a loveable puppet-master of his players.

Stanley Newman, writing in the American periodical *Cue* about the Salzburg *Così fan tutte*, suggested that 'to experience Fischer-Dieskau's total performance as Don Alfonso in *Così* is to see a whole new side of this amazing artist and is alone almost worth the trip', while Elizabeth Forbes in *The Financial Times* said that he was the ideal interpreter, 'physically dominating the stage by his height and musically underpinning the ensembles with his firm, secure singing'.

Fischer-Dieskau recorded the opera under Eugen Jochum and the Berlin Philharmonic Orchestra in December 1962, a good, workmanlike performance, but hardly one to waft that 'air' which, according to Hippolyte Taine on Mozart, 'is so soft that one has only to breathe it in order to be happy'.*

So what of Fischer-Dieskau as a Mozart singer? It is clear that public, collegial and critical acclaim alike have placed him in the very front rank; it could not be denied that regular appearances at Salzburg are regarded as *the* accolade for Mozart singers. He occupies that position by dint, first and foremost, of the beauty of the timbre of his voice and, secondly, of the artistry of his interpretations. When one considers the extraordinary range of his performances and recordings over so many years and has taken the trouble to see and to hear them, then one must come to the conclusion

---

*In September 1975, (then again in August 1976), he recorded a rather similar rôle, that of the elderly merchant Geronimo in Domenico Cimarosa's *Il matrimonio segreto* (1792) in which his actual wife, Julia Varady, sings the soprano part of Elisetta, his elder daughter. Cimarosa was admired above Mozart in his day, but the music and, above all, the libretto with its tiresome repetitions, seems to me (although not to Emperor Leopold II!) to fall short of Mozart, at least of the Mozart of *Così fan tutte*. The comparison is nevertheless interesting and, one feels, must have been made by the singer when recording the rôles.

that in Dietrich Fischer-Dieskau, we have one of the finest
Mozartian singers of our times.

*   *   *   *   *

J. B. Steane spends a considerable portion of his interesting
section on Fischer-Dieskau in his book *The Grand Tradition* discussing the singer as a Verdian baritone, and I shall be referring to his
work shortly. When I present record programmes on this theme,
I generally begin with excerpts from the Electrola record which
(I still think), gives the best impression of what Fischer-Dieskau
sounds like in the operas of Giuseppe Verdi. (It is also one of the
singer's own favourite records). Made in June 1959, accompanied
by the Berlin Philharmonic Orchestra conducted by Alberto Erede,
it was issued in Great Britain as ALP 1825 (later ASD 407) in
March 1961 – and cost 39/9 = £2!

When they heard it, older Germans recalled with moist eyes
their pre-war idol, Heinrich Schlusnus, who was also a very fine
Verdian baritone, while British reviewers expressed generous
appreciation of the superb sense of 'line'. With excerpts from *Il
Trovatore*, *Rigoletto*, *Les vêpres siciliennes*, *Don Carlos*, *Un ballo in maschera* and *Falstaff*, Fischer-Dieskau anticipated most of the Verdian
rôles that he was to sing in later years.

The questions of national style and national language are closely
allied. I remember a time when only a Beecham could play Delius
(born in Bradford, Yorkshire, of German parents), and only the
Vienna Philharmonic could play Johann Strauss. Air travel, pack-
age tours, records and cassettes from all over the globe, jet-setting
stars singing in up to half-a-dozen different languages, or in one
'Euro-language', 'have changed all that'. The Americans are proud
to have their Wagnerian singers in most of the leading German
opera-houses, Gérard Souzay, the French baritone, has a deserved
reputation as a singer of German *Lieder*, Dame Janet Baker is
welcomed throughout the world, and there are now few composers
felt to be the property of one country alone (– Elgar still perhaps?).

Fischer-Dieskau is none too happy about singers who sing in
languages which they do not understand. He feels that they cannot
express what he calls the 'Duktus und Gusto' (roughly the 'feeling
and taste') of such a language. (Fischer-Dieskau, who has an
immense reputation as a singer-linguist, has taken this precept

almost as far as it can go, one would think, by recording Bartók's
Duke Bluebeard's Castle in the original Hungarian, accompanied by
his wife Julia Varady, a native speaker of the language (q.v.)).

The teaching of modern languages is now so improved that we
can expect artists to sing in the original language – and audiences
to understand at least more than they used to. Perhaps then the
days of 'Your tiny hand is frozen', 'Fairest daughter of the graces',
'Lovely maid in the moonlight' and 'Softly awakes my heart' will
remain but a memory for those of us who still possess those nostalgic 78's of Webster Booth, Joan Cross, Dennis Noble and Heddle
Nash, 'with an orchestra conducted by Warwick Braithwaite'! All
leading singers must certainly now command German, Italian and
French, and perhaps Russian and Spanish as well.

This is not a digression, because it is Fischer-Dieskau's command and knowledge of Italian which makes his Verdi singing so
remarkable. It has already been remarked that someone thought
that he sang a Verdi aria like a Schubert *Lied* – but Fischer-
Dieskau himself never tires of pointing out the similarity between
a Schubert *Lied* (like *Der Fluss* (D 693), for example) and Verdian
cantilena. His singing of *Il balen del suo sorriso* from Act II of *Il
Trovatore* (on the record mentioned above), which was criticised in
this vein, has all the smoothness of legato needed for the other
genre. In conversation, however, Fischer-Dieskau pointed out that
he had only followed Verdi's own markings in the aria!

The close links between German-speaking countries and Italy
are not always appreciated outside Germany. Apart from the more
distant historical connections, such as Barbarossa, the Hohenstau-
fen King's occupation of Lombardy, and the Habsburg's Italian
connections securing the position of the Italian language at court,
the more recent Axis relationship between Mussolini and Hitler
had brought the two nations together again. After Johann Wolfgang von Goethe had made his *Italian Journey* in 1786–8, it was the
fashion for Italian manners and the Italian language to be regarded
as *chic*; to this day, Italy and things Italian hold a special place in
the German psyche. Italian tenors are always popular on radio
and television programmes; they stand for *bel canto* (= 'pure tone,
exact phrasing'), swooning *mezza voce* à la Tito Schipa or Benia-
mino Gigli, smooth *legato* – in a word, for 'romance'. And it was

after all in the Germany of the 1920's that the great Verdian revival began – with *Macbeth* in Dresden in April 1928.

Fischer-Dieskau made his début in opera in Verdi's *Don Carlos* on 18 November 1948. Ferenc Fricsay, the conductor, could hardly believe his good fortune in finding 'an Italian baritone in Berlin'. *He* never had any doubts about Fischer-Dieskau's *italianità*. It was under Fricsay that Fischer-Dieskau learned the Verdian repertoire and adopted his own attitude towards a composer whom, he told me once, he loved 'from A to Z'. '*Furor* and *cantabile* are not the whole Verdi', he said in 1963. 'People forget, and not just in Italy, how carefully Verdi planned his characters, what clear, definite instructions, often supported with p's and pp's, he gave'.*

The singer's reputation as a Verdian baritone might well rest on his interpretation of four major rôles: the eponymous *Rigoletto*, *Macbeth* and *Falstaff*, and the villainous Iago in *Otello*. We shall never see a Fischer-Dieskau Rigoletto on stage, however – 'the hunchback jester is not compatible with a six-feet-three frame', Fischer-Dieskau has always said – although there have been many offers. His first interpretation is captured in the DG recording of 'highlights' which he made in April 1962. This was a performance in German, conducted by Horst Stein, with the Berlin Philharmonic Orchestra. Two years later, in July 1964, he was invited to record the opera in La Scala, Milan under Rafael Kubelik. Opposite him were a rather shrill Renata Scotto, Carlo Bergonzi, Fiorenza Cossotto and Ivo Vinco. I myself rank this among the finest recordings he has made, and of the opera altogether. I have compared the Fischer-Dieskau and the Tito Gobbi (1956) versions again and again – and Fischer-Dieskau wins each time. The reason lies, I believe, in his extraordinary ability to *colour* words and phrases. (I choose the word 'colour' deliberately, since in his fascinating interview with Harold Rosenthal for the British Institute of Recorded Sound held in the Queen Elizabeth Hall in London on 5 March 1979, Gobbi mentioned that he used a 'palette' to colour his voice too. His colour for Rigoletto, for example, was blue-violet, and for Figaro, orange-yellow!)

*cf. 'There is in Verdi, as in no other composer before him, a superabundance of dynamic markings'. Rudolf Celletti: *On Verdi's Vocal Writing* in *The Verdi Companion* (W. W. Morton 1979)

Let me give a few examples out of scores of Fischer-Dieskau's sensitivity to words: When, in Act I, Rigoletto mocks Monterone for protecting his daughter's honour, Fischer-Dieskau makes two delicious trills on 'qual vi piglia or *delirio* a tutte *l'ore.* . . . (What madness makes you keep on complaining every hour about your daughter's honour?) which convey to perfection the hunchback's vicarious lechery and which few other baritones attempt, although they are in the score (Ex. 11). Again, in Act II when *he* is being

Ex. 11

mocked by the courtiers, Ceprano turns to him with 'Ch'hai di nuovo, buffon?' (What's new, Fool?) – Fischer-Dieskau throws the phrase back at the Count by comically over-stressing the 'buffon' – and finally in the great duet with Gilda his daughter at the end of Act II, the baritone makes something unearthly out of 'Ah, piangi, fanciulla' (Weep my child), as Gilda tells him of her guilt. Small things in themselves, but *in toto* they build up into a most satisfying interpretation of the doomed jester; Conrad Osborne certainly, in the American periodical *Hi-Fi*, found him 'in the rôle every step of the way'; the interpretation 'made my hair stand on end', he wrote! Cedric Wallis, the British critic, after mentioning the 'golden opulence' of some of the legendary Italian baritones, summed up: 'I think on balance that this is a very fine Rigoletto indeed'.

The Fischer-Dieskau Rigoletto interpretation is based, as all his work is based, on a desire to be as faithful as possible to the composer's intentions. Argue with him on a point of interpretation, and in the twinkling of an eye you will be presented with the score to show how the interpretation is justified! *And* he insists that it was the interpretation that interested Verdi most. 'Just read what he said about the rehearsals for *Aida*', Fischer-Dieskau urges, and he quotes: 'The voice alone, however beautiful, is not enough. The so-called perfection of the vocal art is of little concern to me: I love having the rôles sung as I want them', and Fischer-Dieskau adds that Verdi always became annoyed when the *characterisation* was lacking in the singing. His own gift for characterisation, his ability to make a character come to life through his colouring of the words, is nowhere better illustrated than in the hunchback's venomous attack on the courtiers who have abducted his daughter (in Act II): 'Cortigiani, vil razza dannata' (Vile and cursed race of courtiers). After the explosive opening bars, the jester has literally to change his tune and, on his knees, plead with the Duke's men to return his 'impagabil tesor' (his treasure beyond price). With cello obbligato, Fischer-Dieskau launches out on the heartbreaking *cantilena* 'Ebben, piango! Marullo' (Yes, I am weeping, Marullo).

I really do not believe that any modern baritone has sung this aria more convincingly, and I play it to all who doubt that a non-Italian can sing Verdi – *and* he sings a top E flat on 'difende l'onor' (defends her honour)! Thus I should agree with the reviewer who wrote in *Records and Recordings*: 'I can only say that I could not hope ever to hear a finer assumption of Rigoletto than this'.

Because of the unfortunate vocal inadequacies of his Lady Macbeth (Elena Souliotis) in his Decca recording (made in August 1970 in London), Fischer-Dieskau's own portrayal of one of his (and Verdi's) favourite rôles, Macbeth, has tended to be overlooked. He had scored a great success at Salzburg in Oscar Fritz Schuh's production in 1964 and 1965; with Grace Bumbry as Lady Macbeth, the performances were conducted by Wolfgang Sawallisch. Fischer-Dieskau's blonde wig contrasted strongly with the dark 'Scotch mist' of the production, but none will forget his emotionless 'Tutto è finito' when he came out of Duncan's room, after the committing of the bloody deed.

The recording (of the 1865 revised version) with the London Philharmonic Orchestra under that superb Verdi conductor, Lamberto Gardelli, is, on the whole, very fine. One does not see or hear *Macbeth* in either version all that often and forgets how dramatic and tuneful an opera it is, but even although Verdi himself did not want a Lady Macbeth 'who just sings prettily', she *does* need to sing in tune – and not only in 'La luce langue' in Act II.

Fischer-Dieskau interprets Macbeth sensitively as a disillusioned, reflective man, whose 'flighty purpose never is o'ertook unless the deed go with it'. Very impressive as he is in the great dramatic passages (e.g. in the Apparition Scene in Act III), only in a few places did I seem to hear his true Verdian *bel canto* – at the close of the work, for example, where Macbeth rues his fate in the beautiful passage 'Pietà, rispetto, amore, conforto a'dì cadenti' (Pity, honour, love, the comfort of advancing years) with its fine cadenza on 'nenia' in 'sol la bestemmia, ahi lasso! la nenia tua sarà!' (Curses alone, alas, shall be your funeral dirge!) (Ex. 12.)

Ex. 12

sol . . . la bes-tem-mia, ahi lasso! la ne — — — — — nia, la nenia tua sa -

- rà.

Fischer-Dieskau felt that it was a great pity that EMI's earlier plans to have Maria Callas partner him did not come to fruition, for the singer finds this opera the one above all in which he senses 'the full spectrum of Verdi's possibilities'.* (For true Scots, of course, Macbeth hovers on the verge of 'comic opera', with Birnam Wood arbitrarily transplanted to the Border country, and the hearty choruses sounding much more like the marching songs of the *Risorgimento* than the chant of Macduff's tattered, tartaned, 'unrough youths'!)

Again and again, one hears and reads of the value of Fischer-Dieskau as a collaborative artist who is a tower of strength in ensemble singing. I believe that that in itself is a measure of the man's greatness when one considers his reputation as a solo *Lieder*-singer. Wolfgang Sawallisch, the director of the Bavarian

---

*Callas' curious aversion to the rôle of Lady Macbeth is documented by Arianna Stassinopoulos in her rather over-written book: *Maria: Beyond the Callas Legend* (Weidenfeld and Nicholson) 1980, pp. 94–95.

State Opera, who has worked with the singer in German and Italian opera (and as an accompanist) for nearly thirty years, wrote me of Fischer-Dieskau's 'strong personality on the stage where he tries to be, not 'Fi-Di' (his own nickname but, curiously enough – as 'Fidi' – that of Wagner's son, Siegfried as well!), but to live himself into the role'. He added that 'Fi-Di' was a joy to any conductor because of his sheer musicality. That, allied to his 'vast intelligence' and 'fine and subtle acting talent', had endeared him too to Leonard Bernstein, the American conductor told me.

It is not generally realised in other countries perhaps that Germans grow up with Shakespeare much as we do ourselves, since they possess a series of superb translations – the best being, I still believe, the Schlegel-Tieck versions done between 1797 and 1810, that is, at the height of the Romantic Movement. As J. G. Robertson remarked in his *History of German Literature*, August Wilhelm Schlegel (1767–1845) 'made Shakespeare a national poet of the German people'. For this reason, Germans like Fischer-Dieskau would get to know Shakespeare even during the dark days of the Nazi era. Shakespeare is played in Germany very much as Fischer-Dieskau would want it – characters full of passion and fire, full of 'juice and blood', as he says – and with comedy. I would reiterate how rarely we in the Anglo-Saxon countries have been able to appreciate Fischer-Dieskau, the full-blooded comic actor. His fat, ebullient Falstaff astonished audiences who had not seen him in comic rôles. A slight hint had been given on that 1959 record mentioned above: his 'Ehi! paggio' (to Robin in Act I – the 'Honour' aria, that 'smiling sister of the *Credo* of Iago'), and the great 'Ehi! Taverniere!' monologue at the beginning of Act III (with the *crescendo* on 'E il trillo invade il mondo!!!' (And the trill invades the world)), showed his ability to interpret the rôle, which he had first encountered as far back as 1951 when he recorded the part of Ford in the Falstaff-Ford duet from Act II with Josef Metternich for *RIAS* in a performance conducted by Fricsay. By the time he appeared on the stage of the Vienna State Opera for that famous performance with Leonard Bernstein (on 14 March 1966), he had sung the rôle many times, mainly in German, it is true. His German début, in 1957, had been the result of some coercion on the part of Carl Ebert; he himself had doubted whether his voice would suit the part. The public wondered more about the difficult task of transforming the suave, aristocratic-looking *Lieder* singer into the pot-bellied knight! Under the bâton of Alberto Erede, Fischer-Dieskau scored an enormous success to be repeated many, many times over. His Falstaff does, in fact, retain something of the aristocratic flavour; we are reminded that the old rogue is (or was) *Sir* John – indeed, the whole delightful irony would go for nought were that to be forgotten. As Sir John says himself at the end, despite all his defeats, he is the true creative spirit of the opera – 'l'arguzia mia crea l'arguzia degl' altri'!

As we shall see shortly, certain London critics criticised Fischer-Dieskau's Falstaff; Vienna, on the other hand, lauded it to the skies: '. . .he sang with all the delicacy of phrasing one is accustomed to expect from him, but with a volume of tone and strength of timbre for which we were quite unprepared', wrote *The Times* Special Correspondent from Vienna. The cast included Ilva Ligabue, Hilde Rössl-Majdan, Graziella Sciutti, Regina Resnik, Erich Kunz, Gerhard Stolze, Murray Dickie, Juan Oncina and Rolando Panerai. What the performance *did* have was verve and drive – and plenty of them! Luchino Visconti's début as a producer ensured that, and Bernstein whipped the Vienna Philharmonic Orchestra into a frenzy at times. Bernstein praised the orchestra highly in an interview with the Munich *Abendzeitung* on 9 March during the rehearsals, and said of Fischer-Dieskau: 'I've never known such a flexible Falstaff. He has a masterly command of the dramatic as well as of the lyrical passages', and he wrote to me later that the subsequent recording ranked as his favourite Fischer-Dieskau performance.

The Decca recording was made during the six performances of the Vienna run and it gained almost unanimous critical approval – the highest coming, I thought, from Alec Robertson in *The Gramophone* (February 1967) when he wrote, 'and in terms of A. C. Bradley's essay (on King Henry's rejection of Falstaff KSW), and of Elgar's view of Falstaff, Fischer-Dieskau's interpretation, a miracle of art concealing art, is for me the most satisfying that we have had', while Desmond Shawe-Taylor acknowledged the 'splendid performance', cavilling at only a few details, and an Italian reviewer did not hesitate to compare his interpretation with that of the 'Falstaff of the century', Mariano Stabile.

The recording was issued in Great Britain in January 1967. We had just seen Fischer-Dieskau in five highly-acclaimed performances as Mandryka in Richard Strauss' *Arabella* at Covent Garden, and I shall be referring to this triumph shortly. It was therefore with enormous anticipation that London opera-goers awaited the rise of the curtain on the opening night of his first *Falstaff* on 10 February 1967. The cast included Josephine Veasey, Louise Bosabalian, Elizabeth Robson, John Shaw and John Wakefield and was conducted by Edward Downes. The audience had no doubt of the success of the evening – journalistic opinions varied however, at least about the first night. Stanley Sadie of *The Times*, in a review headed 'A Falstaff of insight by Fischer-Dieskau', wrote that 'when he strolled into Alice's boudoir in all his absurd finery and sang his phrase to her lute, there was no buffoonery; this was a man of charm and of character, a real seducer, if by now a superannuated one'! *The Observer* writer, Peter Heyworth, however, seemed to have reservations; granting that much of Fischer-Dieskau's singing was 'as distinguished as one might expect', he went on to complain that there was far too much 'stage business' – 'Hardly a bar is left unadorned', he wrote regretfully – other writers, such as John Warrack of *The Sunday Times*, agreed.

The result of it all earns a curious mention in Montague Haltrecht's book (*The Quiet Showman*) on Sir David Webster, the former General Administrator of Covent Garden. Averring that artists had, in the main, been happy to return to the Garden, 'as long as the press didn't misbehave', he added, 'as they had once more when Fischer-Dieskau sang Falstaff. *He* wasn't coming back'. And of course, he didn't – and has not returned since, at any rate, not in opera. He *did* sing a Celebrity Recital Schumann programme, quite by chance on 10 February *1980*, accompanied by Wolfgang Sawallisch to a packed audience in the opera house – and found the acoustics very dry, he told me!

The bone of contention in London was Fischer-Dieskau's interpretation of Shakespearean humour, for Boito's libretto, as Francis Toye has suggested (in his book *Verdi, His Life and Works*) is quintessentially Shakespearean, although he went on to say that *he* found the opera 'brilliant, graceful, witty, rather than funny'. This production, originally Zeffirelli's, certainly saw it as 'funny'; in Germany, Shakespearean humour is played very broadly, with much emphasis on slapstick and, in recent years, in the wake of the 'Sex Wave', with a good deal of lasciviousness. Perhaps Fischer-Dieskau, sensitive as he is to cultural climates, felt this, for he certainly stressed Sir John's sexual playfulness. John Warrack was one who disliked the broad humour. He much appreciated Fischer-Dieskau's 'affecting' playing, but, he went on: 'Jollity sits much less easily on him.' It could be pointed out, of course, that these 'faults', (if faults indeed they were), should really have been laid at the door of the producer, who no doubt inspired the pinching of bottoms and the sicking-up of sack and other 'vulgarisms'. First nights can, of course, be uncertain arbiters of taste and the later performances were much more positively reviewed. It all seemed a great pity, for Falstaff is one of the singer's favourite Verdian parts: 'Sir John, the wise rogue and good-natured drunk', he says, 'is the quintessence, the clearest realisation, of everything that Verdi was striving to achieve'.

It must be added, too, that this account must appear incomprehensible to those who were present at the extraordinary scenes after Fischer-Dieskau's *Falstaff* in Munich in July 1974, for example, and subsequent performances elsewhere. 'His comedy is as full as his doublet', wrote Karl-Heinz Ruppel in the *Süddeutsche Zeitung*, reminding the reader of Fischer-Dieskau's great breakthrough as a comic actor with his first *Falstaff* under Carl Ebert in Berlin in 1957. Is it just possible then that we are out of step in this country? Could we be looking for the Shakespearean Falstaff rather than the Verdian? Certainly continental writers have said that those British critics were disappointed with the Fischer-Dieskau Falstaff because they expected another 'Sir Geraint'-interpretation, whereas the German baritone gave them the Falstaff applauded and expected in Berlin, Munich, Salzburg, Vienna and Milan!

Unjustified criticism will always rankle with a sensitive artist and Fischer-Dieskau is no exception. He talks only unwillingly about the Falstaff episode and simply reminds his conversational partner that it was only in Britain that he had had criticisms – which a reading of his notices will confirm.

It was almost certain that he would have followed up his *Falstaff* with another Shakespearean stage triumph – his first Iago in Verdi's *Otello*. He had prepared the rôle of the 'honest ancient', Iago, for a Gustav Rudolf Sellner production at the Deutsche Oper in Berlin, but, in a stage fall in December 1967, he broke a bone in his foot and had to be replaced by Guiseppe Taddei. He has not yet sung the rôle on stage, but recorded it for Electrola in August 1968 with Sir John Barbirolli and the New Philharmonia Orchestra. Gwyneth Jones sang Desdemona and James McCracken Otello. Nearly seventy at the time, Sir John retained fond memories of the occasion. He recalled how he and Fischer-Dieskau had discussed the rôle in detail a full year before the recording: 'How beautifully he sang Iago's Dream', Sir John said. I thought it a beautiful performance too – particularly in those passages where the famous Fischer-Dieskau *mezza voce* was allowed to 'voice-act' the insinuating black-hearted white man's intrigues as in *Éra la notte, Cassio dormia* (It was night, Cassio was asleep) at the end of Act Two. That wonderful line in Cassio's alleged dream 'Desdemona soave! Il nostro amor s'asconda' (Sweet Desdemona! Let us hide our love) is surely great Verdi singing by any standards? (Ex. 13.)

Ex. 13

All the great Iagos of the past, Ruffo, Granforte, Amato et al, have excelled in *one* passage: the thrilling close to Act Two where Otello and Iago raise their hands to heaven and vow vengeance on Cassio: 'Si, pel ciel marmoreo giuro' (I swear by yond marble heavens). This duo does not extinguish memories of these great artists, but Fischer-Dieskau's performance is astoundingly powerful and always tuneful baritone singing in the true Verdian manner. Again, in the 'apotheosis of melodramatic villainy', the *Credo*, with the fine high F on 'dal germe della culla' (from the germ of the cradle) descending to the sinister 'al verme dell'avel' (to the worm of the grave), Fischer-Dieskau paints a picture of blackest evil. (Exx. 14/14a.).

Some reviewers criticised Fischer-Dieskau's singing of the drinking scene in Act One, where his 'beva con me' 's (drink with me)

Ex. 14

dal   ger — — — —   me   del - la   cul - la

Ex. 14a

al   ver - me   del - l'a - vel

were said to be rather rough – but is it not meant to be a 'rough' scene? Iago is trying to get Cassio drunk after all – and in a not very subtle way. And if a few passages *are* rough or 'blustery', are we not amply recompensed by jewels of subtle interpretation, such as the full virile trill on *seno* in Act Two in 'vivida piaga le squarcia il *seno*' (A vivid wound upon its bosom'), and, a few bars farther on, the wonderfully expressive repeated 'vigilate' 's (observe her) to Otello as Desdemona approaches? The truth is that there have never been perfect operatic performances, either on stage or on record – Fischer-Dieskau's highly intelligent interpretations, based firmly on what the composer wrote, stand, in my opinion, comparison with any. . .

And there have been many: space would not permit a full discussion of them all, but the reader should perhaps be aware of the wealth of practical stage and recording-studio experience that Fischer-Dieskau brings to the singing of Verdian rôles. His is not a 'part-time' involvement, time taken off the more important task of giving Schubert recitals, as some might think.

He took part for example in the complete Decca recording of *Don Carlos* in June 1965 with the Covent Garden Orchestra conducted by Sir Georg Solti with this marvellous cast: Renata Tebaldi, Grace Bumbry, Carlo Bergonzi, Nicolai Ghiaurov and Martti Talvela. John Higgins in *The Times* (7 August 1971) praised Fischer-Dieskau's bringing-out of the 'visionary side of Posa', (which he had missed in Sherill Milne's earlier performance), while Mr Shawe-Taylor admired his 'pure and essentially Italian style in Posa's last aria in Act Four "Per me giunto è il di supremo",' (For me the final day has come KSW) (*The Gramophone*, April 1966).

In June 1968, there came another complete Verdi recording for
Decca, of *La Traviata* with Pilar Lorengar and Giacomo Aragal,
with the Deutsche Oper Orchestra, Berlin, under Lorin Maazel,
in a 'repertoire' Berlin performance. Some even thought that
Fischer-Dieskau's *père* Germont was his best Verdian performance, his 'Di Provenza il mar,' (plus the rarely-performed *cabaletta*
'No, non udrai'), being sung 'with a natural feeling for Italian
melody', wrote John Steane in *The Grand Tradition*.

It will be appreciated, too, that apart from these 'star' performances, he has taken part (since 1948) in countless regular repertory
performances of these operas in Berlin and Munich, as well as
singing Don Carlo di Vargas in *La forza del destino*, Montfort in *Les
vêpres siciliennes* and Renato in *Un ballo in maschera*, (which he sang
indeed for the first time under Fritz Busch in a Cologne (NWDR)
broadcast (in German) on 15 February 1951 – and about which
he tells a nice story. During the rehearsals, he sang a wrong note.
Busch looked at him with his twinkling eyes and said: 'Junge,
komponier' nich'!' (Laddie, don't compose!) Busch died that same
year, 1951. The recording was mentioned in the New York
German-language paper *Aufbau* (on 19 February 1971) as being
available from the Fritz Busch Society in the United States.).

'In *bel canto* singing', Fischer-Dieskau said to me, 'the breath
must be expelled steadily, so that as little air as possible emerges
with the sound. You must be able to sing without extinguishing a
candle held in front of you'. But Fischer-Dieskau's *bel canto* is much,
much more than 'beautiful sounds' or 'beautiful singing'; behind
the sound lies the sense, the feeling, not only for the beauty of the
music, but for the meaning of the language, too. This 'intelligent'
approach is perhaps not everyone's cup of tea, not for those who
like their Verdi red-blooded and naive – *Aida* in the Baths of
Caracalla at night, for example – but can it be denied that
Fischer-Dieskau's treatment of the really great Verdian libretti
(*Otello* and *Falstaff*, perhaps) would not have delighted the composer who wanted to give Boito's verses 'the most true and significant accents possible'? Many would agree with the German
critic Werner Oehlmann in his short monograph on Fischer-
Dieskau, where he wrote that the singer has overcome national
boundaries here; he is 'Italian in the *cantilenas*, in the dramatic

urgency of the recitatives, German in the mysterious inwardness, in the heavy burden of the dark, murderous emotions', and, in so being, he has given a new dimension to Verdi performances.

* * * * *

One of the most interesting, and in some ways disturbing, paradoxes of intellectual life in Great Britain is our national attitude to Richard Wagner; on the one hand, the powerful advocacy of his works by the 'perfect Wagnerites' like Bernard Shaw and Ernest Newman still echoes in the writings of journalists such as Bernard Levin in *The Times* – the 'deep E flat major chord' at the beginning of the *Rheingold* prelude is regularly praised as one of the wonders of the musical world; on the other, the rejection of his works and all that they stand for by people from the same stratum of society, but who see in Wagner a symbol of that nationalistic, orgiastic Germany against which 'we fought' in two bitter wars. That Hitler loved Wagner's music can never be forgotten – or forgiven, it seems. Many remembered Hitler's axiom: 'Those who want to understand National Socialist Germany must know Wagner', and when *Die Walküre* was allowed to be produced again in the Prinzregententheater in Munich on 29 April 1947, a wreath was laid at the theatre with the inscription: 'Congratulations on your denazification'!

Fischer-Dieskau holds equally ambivalent views: he too recoiled from the over-exposure of Wagnerian Pan-Germanic grandiloquence and, although he enjoys singing some Wagner rôles, he is disturbed by the 'exaggerated theatrical pathos' in many of the operas. During an interview (perhaps significantly in Israel) in 1971, he said bluntly: 'I don't like Wagner. Whatever I do, I cannot like the unpleasant creature that he was. . .' (In *Maariw* on 22 June 1971).

The reader might recall that it was a performance of *Lohengrin* which first awakened an interest in opera in the young Fischer-Dieskau and he was to see and hear a good deal of Wagner in his younger days. Since his first Berlin *Tannhäuser* in 1949, he has sung Wagner fairly regularly on record, though comparatively rarely on stage.

His book on the Wagner-Nietzsche relationship made fairly clear that his sympathies lay with the philosopher rather than with the

composer; yet one is left in little doubt when talking to Fischer-
Dieskau that he regards Wagner as an absolutely crucial element
in the fashioning of the music of our own times. 'One cannot
imagine it without him', he says, and he will talk with uninhibited
enthusiasm about the Wagner rôles that he has undertaken. These
are many: apart from Wolfram in *Tannhäuser*, there were Kurwenal in *Tristan und Isolde*, the Dutchman in *Der fliegende Holländer*,
Telramund in *Lohengrin*, Gunther in *Götterdämmerung*, Wotan in
Das Rheingold, Amfortas in *Parsifal* and, in 1976, his first Hans
Sachs in *Die Meistersinger von Nürnberg*. I believe that he is just a
little disappointed at not having been invited back to sing at
Bayreuth since his 1961 Wolfram and feels that there surely must
have been some rôle that he could have sung in these twenty
years! But no one has invited him. (An interesting account of
Fischer-Dieskau's Bayreuth appearances can be found in Penelope
Turing's book *New Bayreuth* (1969)).

It is nevertheless true that, as he has maintained on many
occasions, there are only a few Wagner rôles that suit his vocal
timbre. Although he did eventually sing it both on stage and in a
recording, Wotan in *Das Rheingold* was a rôle that he had originally
rejected as quite unsuitable for himself – he thought of it as unsuitable as that of Baron Ochs in Strauss' *Der Rosenkavalier*. In an
interview in *Der Spiegel* in 1964, he said of the rôle of Hans Sachs
too: 'I've studied the rôle privately, of course, but I don't want to
ruin my voice with this dangerous part. I'm not a *Heldenbariton* of
the purest sort and, apart from that, there really are more interesting things to do', and he said to me that he would wait until he
was fifty before he sang it – and, in fact, he sang it for the first
time in March 1976, two months before his fifty-first birthday!

The two rôles which said and meant most to him in his early
days as a Wagner singer were Wolfram von Eschenbach in *Tannhäuser* and Amfortas in *Parsifal*, (the original of which was written,
of course, by the historical Wolfram). The reasons are clear; Wolfram is a ballad-singer, and Wagner's music for him lies perfectly
for a lyric baritone like Fischer-Dieskau, while the libretto fits the
singer's lyrical-meditative temperament admirably. Amfortas, on
the other hand, the grief-laden King, is one of those characters of
strong human emotions whom Fischer-Dieskau loves to portray.

I am certain that he finds both rôles more 'credible' than some other Wagnerian parts.

His first *Tannhäuser* with Heinz Tietjen and Leopold Ludwig in Berlin on 6 December 1949 was followed by a performance in the Neues Funkhaus in Cologne in March 1951 under Richard Kraus and one in Munich with the great tenor, Max Lorenz, on 11 July 1951. Heinz Tiessen, the composer, wrote to Fischer-Dieskau about that first *Tannhäuser*: 'Earlier I had always had the impression that Wolfram wasn't admiring, but wanted to *be* admired. There is nothing of that in your interpretation. And that is, I believe, the deeper root of your great talent', while another composer-friend, Wolfgang Fortner, wrote to him in 1954 that, had *he* been Elisabeth, he would have never fallen in love with Tannhäuser, but would have followed Wolfram 'on the path of virtue'! Fischer-Dieskau has sung the rôle many times since, including a famous first appearance at Bayreuth with Ramón Vinay, Gré Brouwen-stijn, Josef Greindl and Josef Traxel, in 1954. It was in Bayreuth in 1954 that Andrew Porter remembers 'his heart turning over', when Fischer-Dieskau asked Tannhäuser not to leave Elisabeth: 'Bleib bei Elisabeth!' The singer has always earned plaudits for the intensity of his acting and singing of this rôle, the loyal, elegiac Wolfram, partner to the more impulsive, passionate Tannhäuser.

He repeated his Bayreuth triumph in 1955, and again, (but for the last time, to date), in 1961, even though he was then recovering from a heavy cold.

His first recording for Electrola (of the 1861 Paris version) with Franz Konwitschny and the Deutsche Staatsoper Orchestra in October 1960, saw him in the company of Elisabeth Grümmer, Marianne Schech, the young Fritz Wunderlich and Hans Hopf – and in opposition to one of the pre-war German idols, Heinrich Schlusnus, whose Wolfram was on a rival DG (1950) recording. Most critics gave the palm to the thirty-five year old Fischer-Dieskau, largely because of Schlusnus' unsteady tone and spread-ing notes. (He was, of course, sixty-two at the time his record was made). It is an interesting comparison, since, as Dr Hugh Garten rightly notes in *Wagner, the Dramatist* (1977): '*Tannhäuser* is Wag-ner's first consciously German opera' – and here was the Berlin singer matched with a long Germanic tradition. I know from German friends that this performance convinced many that here was the true heir of that long tradition.* What impressed them most was the lack of sentimentality in his portrayal of a potentially sickly, even boring character; he even improved on this achievement in his second recording (for DG) in Berlin in November 1968 (under Otto Gerdes with the Deutsche Oper Orchestra), with Birgit Nilsson, who sang both Elisabeth and Venus, Wolfgang Windgassen and Horst R. Laubenthal, in the original Dresden (1845) version. Fischer-Dieskau was quoted as saying of this performance that 'much that was new and which had so far gone unnoticed was discovered for this recording', and readers will now realise how typical that remark is of his general attitude to music. As Gerald Moore has said: 'His conception is evergreen'.

Alec Robertson, always a master of words, wrote of the singer's 1968 Wolfram: 'Wolfram is the truly noble character in the opera, worth a bushel of Tannhäusers, and his nobility and compassion are fully brought out by this great artist' (*The Gramophone*, January 1970), and he praised above all his 'absolutely exquisite' rendering of the *Star of Eve* aria (*O du, mein holder Abendstern*). Fischer-Dieskau's is certainly a fascinating interpretation which includes one small item which surprised and even 'annoyed' some early reviewers (eg. Shawe-Taylor in *The Gramophone* for April 1962) – his unusual turn on the word 'Engel' in the phrase 'ein sel'ger Engel dort zu werden'. (Ex. 15.) Fischer-Dieskau sings the turn on

Ex. 15

*An interesting sidelight illuminates the point. In 1968, the popular German magazine *Stern* carried out a poll to determine *inter alia* which artist (in any medium) attracted its readers most. The 'top ten' were: 1. Rudolf Schock (the pre-war German tenor); 2. Pablo Picasso; 3. Herbert von Karajan; 4. Heinz Rühmann (a comedian); 5. Peter Alexander (a popular singer); 6. Hanns Lothar; 7. O. W. Fischer (a classical actor); 8. Fischer-Dieskau; 9. Günter Grass (the celebrated novelist); 10. Gerhart Hauptmann (a long-established playwright who died in 1946). After these came Bertolt Brecht, the Beatles, Sammy Davis Jr., Hermann Prey . . .and Kafka!

the *lower* note, i.e. in the inverted form. He assured me that he had this on the authority of Cosima Wagner herself (*via* Heinz Tietjen), and that it was a 'device often found in Bach's writing for the voice'. He recorded it this way too (in 1956) on an EP record (E 50041) with the Philharmonic Orchestra, conducted by Wilhelm Schüchter.

Hugh Garten points out in the interesting book already mentioned that Tannhäuser's death-wish (*O Göttin, woll' es fassen/ Mich drängt es hin zum Tod*) (O goddess, understand, it is driving me on to death), relates him not only to the Flying Dutchman and Tristan, but also to Amfortas in *Parsifal*, Wagner's last opera, in which Fischer-Dieskau first sang on 16 April 1949, in a concert performance of Act III, with Hans Beirer and Wilhelm Schirp, conducted by Leopold Ludwig, and then again under Hans Knappertsbusch at Bayreuth, in 1955 and 1956, the latter performance being recorded live by *Cetra*.

Fischer-Dieskau's Amfortas is a shattering experience on the stage – all of his great ability to understand and to portray suffering mankind is poured into this 'intensified Tristan', as Wagner thought of him. Amfortas, hounded by his surrender to carnal love, (and in Wolfram's original poem he is pierced through the testicles, not through the side, as in Wagner), 'suffers' throughout the opera, indeed in some productions he lies on a bed until his 'redemption through the redeemer' in the last scene. Fischer-Dieskau remarked to me on one occasion that modern directors make him move around the stage too much to allow him to interpret adequately this 'tortured, suffering' music which takes so much out of a performer in any case.

Christopher Raeburn, the recording manager for Decca's *Parsifal*, wrote that Fischer-Dieskau gave Amfortas 'a new dimension', while Deryck Cooke found his 'an interpretation of the most remarkable intensity'. He realised that the singer's subdued interpretation was trying to express this very 'death-wish' of which I wrote above. Instead of forcing the anguish of the character as some other singers had done, Fischer-Dieskau let the lyrical music speak for itself.

The Decca recording was made on December 1971, (although

not released in Great Britain until April 1973), with Sir Georg Solti conducting the Vienna Philharmonic Orchestra. The cast was: Christa Ludwig, René Kollo, Gottlob Frick (who had come out of his retirement at sixty-six!), Hans Hotter (as Titurel) and Britain's Robert Tear, in the part of the First Grail Knight. By common critical consent, it was regarded as being the finest achievement to that date by the Decca team, indeed it still remains the choice of most Wagnerians. It was therefore no surprise that Fischer-Dieskau was awarded the *Grand Prix* of the French Ministry of Culture for his Amfortas – the 'highest award for a vocal record' – in December 1973.

The modern generation tends to treat *Parsifal* with rather less solemnity than did Wagner's who saw it as the 'Bühnenweihfestspiel' (*lit.* Sacred Dedication Festival Play) that the Master demanded, although even Bernard Shaw, it might be remembered, felt some qualms about 'the elaborate make-believe of Holy Communion, culminating in the descent of a stuffed dove through a flood of electric radiance' (7 August 1889)! Nevertheless, it is still performed in some places in Germany at Easter, without applause, as a religious festival. However, when the Munich National Theatre staged it for the first time in twenty years (in April 1973), Dietrich Haugk and Günther Rennert flew in the face of all conventions and produced a '*Parsifal* im Jugendstil' (the art-style of the 1900's), which provoked applause and boos. But, even there, Fischer-Dieskau's Amfortas, (his first since the 1958 Bayreuth performance), was still the bearer of 'the suffering of all mankind', as Wagner had stipulated he should be.

The singer is refreshingly candid about Wagner's demands on his casts. He speaks for example of the Master's 'sadism' at keeping Hans Sachs on the stage for so long, and Amfortas is, of course, prostrate for a good part of the time in *Parsifal* – which led Samuel Longford, the inimitable critic of the old *Manchester Guardian*, to remark once: 'Amfortas? The only wise man here – he's brought his bed with him'!

But Amfortas makes great vocal demands too. Fischer-Dieskau quotes, (with some glee, I feel), the outraged comment of Wagner's first Amfortas, Theodor Reichmann, after Wagner had himself conducted the last scene: 'You can only do that once! Only the Master could force anyone to use so much breath and so much voice', and when I met Fischer-Dieskau on one occasion the day after a *Parsifal* performance, the strain of the performance could still be seen on his face.

One of Fischer-Dieskau's earliest rôles was one which relates psychologically to Amfortas: the Dutchman in *Der fliegende Hol-länder*. Although the singer, perhaps surprisingly, has never sung the rôle on stage, he made what I am sure is one of the best recordings of the part in February 1960. He had just sung two fine *Tannhäuser* performances (in Munich in August 1959 under Sir Georg Solti) and was obviously in his best Wagnerian form. This Electrola recording was made with Franz Konwitschny and the orchestra of the German State Opera in Berlin, (with which he then recorded the *Tannhäuser* mentioned above), with a rather shrill Marianne Schech as Senta, Rudolf Schock, Sieglinde Wagner, Fritz Wunderlich (as the Steersman) and Gottlob Frick. The recording crackles with vitality, (particularly in the choral passages), and Fischer-Dieskau's wonderfully sombre *Die Frist ist um* (My time has come) has an Amfortas-like doom about it. Nowhere I believe were Fischer-Dieskau's great gifts as a *Lieder* singer put to better use than in this recording. Again and again one draws in one's breath as he invests the familiar text with new life and meaning, as when, in Act Two, the Dutchman begins to tell Senta of the curse laid upon him: 'Wie aus der Ferne längst vergang'ner Zeiten' (As out of the mist of times long past), which Fischer-Dieskau sings in an almost unreal half-voice (Ex. 16.) John Steane

Ex. 16

mezza voce e con molto portamento

Wie   aus   der   Fer - ne   längst ver - gang'-ner   Zei - ten

remarked on this trait eighteen years later in July 1978 when Electrola issued a record 'Fischer-Dieskau sings Wagner' in which he sang *Die Frist ist um* again, this time with the Bavarian Radio Symphony Orchestra conducted by Rafael Kubelik. 'The Dutchman's seven years may well come round a time or two', he wrote, 'before we look upon his equal'. I too believe that Fischer-Dieskau is the finest Dutchman on record. (Desmond Shawe-Taylor had waxed lyrical about the earlier record: 'What a Wotan, what a Sachs he will one day be!' he wrote prophetically in *The Gramophone* of January 1961).

Among many magical moments, one of the finest is the Dutchman's narration of how he is doomed to wander the seas until the love of a 'good woman' will set him free. On 'bis eure letzte Welle sich bricht und euer letztes Nass versiegt' (till your last wave breaks and your seas dry up), the great voice whispers to a close on 'Nass', and then rises at the end to a fine unforced 'ist's getan'. Once again, we note the artistry of the move from the lyrical to the dramatic.

Praise for Fischer-Dieskau the Wagnerian lyric baritone had of course been voiced early – by no less an authority than Wilhelm Furtwängler who was possibly one of the first to sense Fischer-Dieskau's potential in Wagnerian rôles. The baritone enjoys telling the story of being talked into singing the part of Kurwenal in *Tristan und Isolde* which he recorded for Electrola in the Kingsway Hall in London in June 1952 with Kirsten Flagstad, Blanche Thebom and Ludwig Suthaus, with the Philharmonia Orchestra and the Covent Garden Chorus. As Fischer-Dieskau says, he only got to know Furtwängler when the great conductor's hearing was impaired, and when he felt that he would rather have been composing than conducting anyway. Fischer-Dieskau still feels that he was much too young for the Kurwenal rôle, (he was twenty-seven), and remembers how he sought to make his voice sound 'older' by darkening the vocal timbre. Furtwängler forbade that, telling him to follow his 'own sound' and to sing 'naturally'. 'A piece of advice like that stayed in the ears of the young beginner for the rest of his life', adds the singer.

The recording has, of course, become famous: Walter Legge's Philharmonia Orchestra had never played better, and Flagstad (then in her maturity at fifty-seven) had never sung better, while Ludwig Suthaus was an ardent Tristan. Kurwenal, Tristan's tutor, is, not unlike Wolfram, an elegiac servant, who comes into his own only in Act Three; Fischer-Dieskau's wonderful 'Erwachte er, wär's doch nur, um für immer zu verscheiden' (If he awoke, it would only be to leave us for ever) (Ex. 17.) as he watches over the unconscious Tristan under the lime-tree in Brittany, gave

Ex. 17

promise of a great career in Wagnerian opera yet, curiously enough, he has never sung the rôle again. Daniel Barenboim was much looking forward to conducting his first *Tristan* at the Deutsche Oper in Berlin in April 1980, with Fischer-Dieskau as Kurwenal, Spes Wenkhoff as Tristan and Catarina Ligendza as Isolde (under Götz Friedrich's new *Intendant*-ship), but all were disappointed when Fischer-Dieskau withdrew with a stomach complaint.*

His performance with Furtwängler led indirectly to his first appearance at Bayreuth in 1954, when, besides the Wolfram already mentioned, he sang the small part of the *Heerrufer* (The Herald) in *Lohengrin*; the singer said once that he was grateful to Wagner for having written *some* baritone parts free from that 'exaggerated theatrical pathos' which he so dislikes elsewhere in the *oeuvre*.

There are, however, not many of those; the lyric baritone has a fairly lean time on the whole in Wagner's operas since the soprano and the *Heldentenor* steal the limelight most of the time, as indeed soprano and tenor do in most nineteenth-century operas. Nevertheless, Wagner presents a challenge to an artist like Fischer-Dieskau, and he readily granted to me that his career would have been much less exciting without his Wagnerian ventures – which eventually led to his greatest Wagnerian achievement, his Hans Sachs in 1976. Before then, however, this remarkable singer added three additional and very varied rôles to his repertoire.

---

*Strangely enough, this occurred at a time when there had been discussion in the German press that Fischer-Dieskau himself might take over the *Intendant*-ship of the Deutsche Oper in Berlin.

He was invited, firstly, to sing the rôle of (Friedrich von) Telramund, the Count of Brabant, in the complete Electrola recording of *Lohengrin* under Rudolf Kempe made in late November/early December 1962. The cast included Elisabeth Grümmer, Christa Ludwig, Jess Thomas (surely one of the few operatic Ph.D's?) Gottlob Frick and the Vienna Philharmonic Orchestra. In this most romantic of operas, 'the voice is still the statue and the orchestra the pedestal', as Ernest Newman put it in his 1924 book *Wagner as man and artist* (reissued in 1963). I cannot find much interest in the rather wooden Telramund, but what there *is* in him, Fischer-Dieskau undoubtedly found; perhaps the best example of his amazing gift for breathing magic into stodge is in the Act Two duet where Telramund reproaches his wife Ortrud for enticing him to have Elsa accused of the murder of her brother Gottfried. Fischer-Dieskau and Christa Ludwig present an almost Macbeth-Lady Macbeth relationship, while the passionate music severely tests Fischer-Dieskau's high notes. He passes this examination with flying colours, I should say, as does Miss Ludwig – but then Telramund is unfortunately killed at the beginning of Act Three and the rest of the glory belongs to Lohengrin, the 'knight in shining armour' (. . .*in lichter Waffen Scheine!*)

Fischer-Dieskau next took part in the making of an 'epic': Decca's stupendously expensive production of *Götterdämmerung*, Part Four of the great cycle *Der Ring des Nibelungen* – the *Death of Siegfried*, as it was originally called. John Culshaw, (whose death in 1980 came as such a shock), the then Classical Artists' and Repertoire Manager of the company, gave a fascinating insight into the making of both the record and the BBC TV film which followed it in an article in the May 1965 issue of *The Gramophone*, out of which then sprang his interesting book *Ring Resounding* (1967) which registers the progress of the complete recording of *The Ring*, 'from 24 September 1958 to 19 November 1965'. Viewers of the BBC/Austrian TV film of the recording of *Götterdämmerung*, (shown on BBC2 on 16 May 1965), will perhaps remember it best for one superb un-Wagnerian scene in front of the microphones, when, just before the first take of the Immolation Scene in Act III, the TV stage hands led on Brünnhilde's horse, Grane, to the stupefaction of the statuesque Birgit Nilsson – who promptly let out a peal of refreshingly un-Wagnerian laughter!

This particular recording was made in Vienna from the early days of May to December 1964. Wolfgang Windgassen, then forty-nine, Claire Watson, Christa Ludwig and Gottlob Frick were the co-stars, with the Vienna Philharmonic Orchestra under Sir Georg Solti. Fischer-Dieskau sang the part of Gunther, the King.

As is well known, Wagner wrote the texts 'backwards', so to speak, starting with Part Four, the *Death of Siegfried*, in 1848, completing the full tetralogy in 1852. For a Germanist who studies the texts *qua* literature, they are a very mixed pleasure indeed! The continually long-winded, bombastic and archaic diction, the excruciating alliterations of the *Stabreime* ('. . . nach dem *w*unsch- und *w*ahnlos heiligsten *W*ahlland'), and jarring poetical conceits which left even the Thomas Mann of *Adel des Geistes* cold, are mixed with snatches of purest poetry. *Mutatis mutandis*, one could say the same for *Götterdämmerung* and its music. The opera runs for four hours, twenty-five minutes and takes up six records. Of all Wagner's operas, it is the one best fitted for what I think Edward Dent called the selection of 'bleeding chunks'.

John Culshaw reminds us of the central problem of the characterisation of Gunther: How noble should he be? and complains that most Gunthers are weaklings from the start, so that they are nonentities by Act Three. Fischer-Dieskau was, however, a King from the outset, and therefore his eventual decline became all the more terrible. His devotion to his sister Gutrune becomes an obsession; he grows more and more helpless and dejected and finally loses his self-control just before he learns the truth and is killed by Hagen (at 'Angst und Unheil greife dich immer') (Fear and disaster be your lot).

Such a rôle, (actually written for a 'lyric baritone') seemed tailor-made for Fischer-Dieskau's meditative and imaginative artistry. It was a most distinguished performance which, once again, let us see an old picture stripped of its brown varnish. Many felt indeed that this was the finest performance since Herbert Janssen's Covent Garden triumphs in the late thirties.

The singer did not continue his collaboration with the Decca team in their massive saga, but did return rather surprisingly to the world of *The Ring* when he recorded with Herbert von Karajan and the Berlin Philharmonic Orchestra the part of Wotan in *Das Rheingold*, the actual 'Prologue to the Trilogy'. I was surprised to hear of his decision to sing the rôle, for he had always said that it (with Baron Ochs, Hans Sachs and some of the Verdi rôles already mentioned), was one of those rôles that he would never sing or act because of his own vocal or physical limitations.

There are many fine passages in the opera for him; listen, for example, to the episode starting with Froh's 'Zur Burg führt die Brücke' at the end of the work, where Wotan sings to Fricka, 'Folge mir, Frau! In Walhall wohne mit mir!' Fischer-Dieskau negotiates the top D flats on 'Walhall' with marvellous skill, conveying the sense of deity in the character. (Ex. 18) Throughout the work indeed, it is his feeling for the text, his imaginative creation of the character *through* the words as well as the music, which distinguishes his performance.

Ex. 18

His part was recorded for DG over the New Year period from December 1967 to the January; I missed the thrills of Kirsten Flagstad in Josephine Veasey's performance and also the sonorous voice of Gustav Neidlinger who sang with Flagstad in the 1959 Decca set with Sir Georg Solti, but enjoyed the overall result. Herbert von Karajan wrote to Fischer-Dieskau after he had heard the first test record that 'your first version is so magnificent that it will take time for it to receive its full mead of praise. You have realised the style that I had in my mind to perfection – a symbol above all, but a symbol of deep humanity (and that is why it is so convincing) . . . a model of terseness and *bel canto* at the same time – and more – the character has been given, in addition, the fascination of a late Renaissance prince!'

It was on his return from singing Wotan at Karajan's Easter Festival in Salzburg in 1968 that Fischer-Dieskau's Mercedes, driven as usual by his secretary, Diether Warneck, was involved in a six-car pile-up near Holzkirchen on that dangerous Salzburg-Munich Autobahn on 16 April. Fischer-Dieskau sustained a broken collar-bone, an injury which made the national headlines, since it led to his withdrawal from all operatic engagements from April 1968 till his return in the Deutsche Oper *Falstaff*, conducted by Lorin Maazel and produced in 'the Nissei Theater in Tokyo on 27 March 1970. Although he returned to the German theatre as The Speaker in *Die Zauberflöte* under Rafael Kubelik in the Staatsoper in Munich only on 14 July 1970, he had recorded a great deal of opera during the enforced 'rest'. Some sensation-seeking 'critics' had taken the opportunity to claim that he had 'retired' from the operatic stage because his voice was failing. I wonder what they thought if they were in the audience for his 1976 Hans Sachs!

12 March 1976, shortly before his fifty-first birthday, was the day for his first Hans Sachs, in his 'own' Deutsche Oper in Berlin. I did not manage to attend the first night – I find first nights uncertain measures of quality – but saw the next performance on the 16th. It was a moving occasion as the Berlin audience greeted its favourite musical son who had given them nearly thirty years of outstanding musical memories in a wide range of parts, and non-German members of the audience who had not seen Fischer-Dieskau on the operatic stages of their own country were made aware of the massive reputation he has as an operatic baritone in German-speaking countries. His recordings, full, varied and stimulating though they are, do not give the measure of his outstanding abilities as an actor. One must see him on stage.

The production, which celebrated the 400th anniversary of Sachs' death, was by Peter Beauvais, and the beautiful Dürer-like sets by Jan Schublach, (which drew spontaneous applause), were an enormous success. Fischer-Dieskau looked every inch the wise old man of Nürnberg who, as Germanists knew only too well, cobbled verses as he cobbled shoes. Eugen Jochum conducted the 'house orchestra', and Gerti Zeumer, Gerd Brenneis, Ernst Krukowski, Ruth Hesse and Horst Laubenthal supported Fischer-Dieskau. In an interesting interview with Alan Blyth in *The Times* (16 November 1976) on the opera, Fischer-Dieskau said: 'As usual, Wagner didn't know when to finish a work. *Götterdämmerung* goes on too long; so does *Meistersinger*. Sach's part should end after the first speech on the Festwiese'. He went on to praise the part, however, since Sachs' philosophy and wit gave him almost endless opportunities for variety. He also mentioned to Blyth, as he had done to me, how effective was the move from comedy to tragedy in this opera (especially in Acts II and III). He found this rare in Wagner's works – 'Mime and Alberich are not, for my taste, comic figures – (they are) a little disgusting really!' Perhaps he had forgotten the *very* comical Kothner that he gave in Bayreuth under Cluytens in 1956 which had made people in Bayreuth long for his first Hans Sachs. Letters in his archive suggest 1961 indeed as the date of the first serious approach from Bayreuth for him to sing Sachs.

In my conversations with him about the rôle of Sachs, he continually mentioned how cruel Wagner was towards singers. 'I'm on the stage for five or six hours and only sing for two!' He found the rôle physically exhausting, although rewarding as 'a goal for all singers'. It was certainly one of the most complex that he had had to learn, and more difficult for him, a lyric baritone.

There were five performances in Berlin in that 1976 Berlin run which was much applauded by the German musical establishment. Fischer-Dieskau was a 'gentle fatherly friend with the odd outburst of spontaneous joviality or naïve irascibility – he then became meditatively lyrical, and finally came the ecstatic pathos', wrote *Die Zeit* on 26 March 1976. He sang the rôle again in Berlin in September 1976 and in September and November 1977, and then at the Munich and Berlin Festivals, in July and September 1979 respectively.

The Deutsche Grammophon recording of the opera, (made coincidentally with the Berlin performance), had many cast changes – and one most surprising one: Walther von Stolzing was sung by the great Verdian tenor, Placido Domingo. In the light of my previous remarks about Fischer-Dieskau as a Verdian baritone, I asked him his opinion about Verdian singers in German rôles. Assuring me that Domingo would not wish to undertake the rôle again, he reminded me nevertheless that Gigli, (whom he greatly admires), had once recorded the *Lohengrin* aria, *Nun sei bedankt, mein lieber Schwan*. I could only reply that I felt that the result was little better than the Italian tenor's attempt to sing *Lieder*, thinking of that tragic record (DA 1504) of *Il fior di loto* (Die Lotosblume!) of Schumann, recorded in June 1936!

I must admit that I found the *Meistersinger* recording much less enjoyable than the stage performance, perhaps because of the unidiomatic German of the Walther and also of the replacement Eva, Catarina Ligendza, particularly, in the famous quintet in Act Three. Fischer-Dieskau's own performance is masterly; some felt that he had hardly suggested the 'arm einfältigen Mann' (poor simple man) that Hans Sachs himself claimed he was in the opera – but a man of Fischer-Dieskau's learning would know that the remark was made ironically. The real Hans Sachs, as all students of German were aware, wrote literally thousands of *Meisterlieder* and numerous verse-dramas – he was a highly literate man with a sound knowledge of Latin and Greek. Fischer-Dieskau portrays just such a man, learned, warm-hearted, friendly, wise and tolerant – the incorporator indeed of the 'good' Germanic virtues of the Lutheran Reformation – his 'Was duftet doch der Flieder' (How strong is the scent of the lilac bush) from Act Two, warm and reflective, gives a good idea of his interpretation. If Fischer-Dieskau might feel somewhat uncomfortable at the close of the opera, where Sachs and the assembled company praise 'die heil'ge deutsche Kunst' (our sacred German art), it is because he probably feels, as he later claimed Friedrich Nietzsche felt, that this is a 'petty-German' (klein-deutsch), not a 'universal German' (welt-deutsch) attitude, that is, to worship a 'master from a provincial corner of Germany' is anachronistic in an age of European and world unification. (Paul Rosenfeld's article *The Nazis and Die Meistersinger* in *Musical Impressions* (op. cit.) does stress the point, however, that Wagner's Hans Sachs is a citizen of the 'free city' of Nuremberg. 'Deutsche Kunst' was to be an expression of 'the democratic unity of the nation').

Thus Fischer-Dieskau would agree that Wagner is an irreplaceable strand in the fabric of musical history; musically, his influence was enormous on all who followed him in Europe. His call, 'Kinder, macht Neues', (Children, do something different), had its effect on Richard Strauss, Bruckner, Mahler, even on Debussy; culturally, on the European symbolists like Dégas and Cézanne;

Alphonse Daudet wrote: 'We studied his characters as if Wotan held the secret of the world and Hans Sachs was the spokesman for free, natural and spontaneous art'; politically, with the baleful assistance of writers like his son-in-law, the Englishman, Houston Stewart Chamberlain, on the anti-democratic forces around Adolf Hitler, and, generally, as Ernest Newman wrote: '. . . he was one of those dynamically charged personalities, after whose passing the world can never be the same as it was before he came'.

Like his friend and neighbour Dr Fischer-Fabian, whose book *Die ersten Deutschen (The First Germans)* (1975) sought to explode the myth that the Germani were at all like Wagner's portrayal of them, Fischer-Dieskau has also spoken of the Wagner-cult with some scepticism: 'The discrepancy in Wagner's demands is between the need for sheer dumb physical strength and for intelligence of interpretation. Today, I think that singers tend to be more intelligent, but to lack the voice for Wagner. The two attributes seldom go together'. For him, Wagner is a *musical* phenomenon that no singer can ignore; the private life is for the biographer. Thus, Wagner meant a new field of artistic activity, a fresh challenge, and he is sure that, without Wagner, his career would have been much less interesting.

It might now be interesting to take a look at those other operatic works of the period that have attracted Fischer-Dieskau's attention. Some of these recordings and performances might have been passed over had it not been that Fischer-Dieskau's massive authority had restored a few of them to the recorded repertoire at least – much as his recordings of, say, Mendelssohn's or Liszt's *Lieder* have encouraged other artists to study and perform them.

As with his Verdi portrayals, Fischer-Dieskau anticipated some of these other rôles on a single DG record entitled 'Opera Recital' (LPM 18700) with the Berlin Radio Sinfonieorchester conducted by Ferenc Fricsay, made in April 1961. Excerpts from Bizet's *Carmen*, Gounod's *Faust* (or *Margarete*, as the Germans call it), Bizet's *Les pêcheurs de perles*, Verdi's *La forza del destino* (a very fine *Urna fatale del mio destino*), Rossini's *Wilhelm Tell*, Verdi's *La Traviata*, Giordano's *Andrea Chénier* (Gérard's monologue) and the

Prologue from Leoncavallo's *Pagliacci*, enabled the singer to present a complete picture of his art at that time. He is particularly interesting in the items from the French repertoire, from the superbly confident, ringing tones of Bizet's Escamillo via Gounod's melting Valentin's Farewell *(Avant de quitter ces lieux)* to Zurga's recitative and aria *L'orage s'est calmé* . . . from *Les pêcheurs de perles*. (He recorded the rôle of Zurga in this last opera for the West Berlin radio network in December 1950, with Rita Streich, in a performance conducted by Artur Rother). The finely-graded conclusion of the aria (at 'ah, pardonnez . . .') is an object lesson.

(William Tell's aria *Resta immobile* would recall to the singer his singularly successful visit to Milan from 15–20 April 1956, when he sang the role of Tell for RAI Milano with Anita Cerquetta and under Mario Rossi, who said after the performance: 'I'm going to send my Italian baritones to Berlin to learn how to sing!')

It is difficult to realise that, while Fischer-Dieskau was seen and heard all over the world in these amazingly successful *Lieder* recitals, he was still 'doing his job' as Principal Lyric Baritone of the Municipal Opera and, later, the Deutsche Oper in Berlin. That he sang the rôle of Enrico in Donizetti's *Lucia di Lammermoor* (with Maria Stader and Ernst Häfliger under Fricsay, in January 1953), and twenty years later, in 1973, could record the tiny rôle of Valentin in Gounod's *Faust* (with Edda Moser and Nicolai Gedda) shows that willingness to sing these smaller supporting repertory rôles which makes 'Fi-Di' such a respected and popular colleague.

His presence in otherwise insignificant works can often raise the standing of the whole work and its performance. His love for Schubert encouraged Electrola to record the rarely-performed *Singspiel Die Zwillingsbrüder* in which he sings the 'good-bad' roles of the brothers Friedrich and Franz, but not even his *Liebe, teure Muttererde* (My dear mother-earth, your child has returned), a lilting *Lied*-like aria which follows a beautifully-spoken little recitative, could make me want to see this rather dreary little piece. It was recorded in January 1975 with the Bavarian State Opera orchestra conducted by Wolfgang Sawallisch. Fischer-Dieskau also sang in Schubert's *Singspiel Der vierjährige Posten* with the Munich Radio Orchestra under Heinz Wallberg in August 1977, and then joined with Hermann Prey in a much-praised Electrola recording

of the same composer's most lyrical opera *Alfonso und Estrella* with
the Berlin State Orchestra under Otmar Suitner in 1979. The rest
of the cast, Edith Mathis, Peter Schreier, and Theo Adam certainly
did the little work proud! It was delightful to hear Fischer-Dieskau
and Prey together (as Troila and Mauregato) in the reconciliation
aria (no. 33) *Es ist die höchste Lust* (It is the greatest joy . . . to
forgive a friend with love)!

(In July and August 1978, the baritone sang the rôle of the
comic Kauz (for Electrola) in the one-act operetta that the
twenty-year old Mendelssohn had written for his parents' silver
wedding, *Die Heimkehr aus der Fremde* (*anglice* Son and Stranger).
His colleagues, who also spoke the rather extensive dialogue, were
Hanna Schwarz, Helen Donath, Peter Schreier and Benno Kusche,
with the Munich Radio Orchestra under Heinz Wallberg again,
and he followed that with a recording of Mendelssohn's *Die beiden
Pädagogen* – labours of love indeed!)

I mentioned above Schubert's attempts to write operas; in his
Schubert book (q.v.) Fischer-Dieskau writes sympathetically,
although hardly enthusiastically, about these works. I have hugely
enjoyed amateur performances of one which has had a revival
lately, the modest *Die Verschworenen* (The Conspirators), but it is
clear that the lyrical Schubert lacked the dramatic gift (and, as
the singer points out, a genial librettist). That cannot be said of
Schubert's 'successor' as 'King of the Lied', Robert Schumann; *his*
forays into the world of 'dramatic music', (if not of pure opera),
were by no means unsuccessful. Gerald Abrahams in *Schumann: A
Symposium* claims, indeed, that the three works for the theatre,
Manfred (1849), *Genoveva* (1850) and *Szenen aus Goethes Faust* (1853),
contain some of Schumann's finest music.

Fischer-Dieskau recorded the rôle of Siegfried in Schumann's
only opera, his reworking of *Genoveva*, a drama by Friedrich Hebbel, on the typical Romantic theme of the outraged wife, in an
Electrola (Leipzig) production in October 1976, with Peter
Schreier, Edda Moser and the Gewandhaus Orchestra under Kurt
Masur. Although Mr Abrahams mentions the historico-musical
interest of Schumann's 'thematic reminiscence', a fore-runner of
the Wagnerian *Leitmotiv*, only the overture of the opera remains in
the repertoire. The *Scenes from Faust*, however, although technically

an 'oratorio', are a very different matter. The superb 1972 Decca recording, which followed Benjamin Britten's equally superb Aldeburgh revival, first brought home the beauty of this work to many. In his letter to the singer about the preparations for the Aldeburgh performance on 8 June 1972, Britten mentions how 'his admiration and affection for it grow steadily'. Heather Harper, Jennifer Vyvyan, Peter Pears and Michael Rippon completed the Aldeburgh cast.

Ernest Newman had often remarked that Schumann's Faust was the real *German* Faust of Goethe; Fischer-Dieskau in Schumann's version made us realise how sweetly saccharined Gounod's French Faust really is! 'Fischer-Dieskau sang Faust with a range and certainty of expression – reflective, passionate, sardonic, visionary – beyond the reach of any other singer today', wrote Ronald Crichton in *Musical Times* of the June Aldeburgh performance. (He also sang the part of Doctor Marianus in Part Three).

The Decca recording, (made in September 1972), had, as main singers, Elisabeth Harwood, (replacing Heather Harper), Peter Pears and John Shirley-Quirk (replacing Michael Rippon), with the English Chamber Orchestra, the Wandsworth School Choir and the Aldeburgh Festival Singers under Benjamin Britten himself. Fischer-Dieskau's singing of Faust's monologue after his blinding in Part Two reminds us how much Schumann admired Wagner's *Tannhäuser*, and his wonderful Death Scene on Goethe's lines to the 'passing moment' 'Verweile doch, du bist so schön' (Stay awhile! You are so beautiful), when the lemurs seize Faust's body at Mephistopheles' behest, would surely have gladdened Goethe's not un-musical ear had he heard it. Fischer-Dieskau told me once, interestingly enough, that he would love to conduct this work to help 'bring it back to life'!

Goethe who finished his *Faust* (Part II) in 1832, a few weeks before his death, over sixty years after its first conception, had believed that the Mozart of *The Magic Flute* was the only composer capable of writing music for Faust. After Goethe's death, Faust became known as the 'Bible of modern man'; the nineteenth century placed it among the great works of literature, with Homer, Aristotle and Dante, which explains the regularity with which it, or Part I at any rate, was set to music.

As a well-read German, Fischer-Dieskau is naturally fascinated by, and attracted to such settings. We shall shortly be reading of his services to Ferruccio Busoni's *Doktor Faust* (1925). At this juncture, however, we turn to the Frenchman Hector Berlioz and his *La damnation de Faust* (1846). Although A. E. F. Dickinson, in his *The Music of Berlioz*, warns us against assuming that this Faust 'was meant to be an opera but was unfortunately diverted to the concert platform', the music undoubtedly has an operatic quality, infinitely superior, I believe, to Gounod's. Lord Harewood, I know, believes that the work is too dramatic for concert form and not dramatic enough for the opera house, and it is of course properly termed 'a dramatic legend'; nevertheless, Daniel Barenboim's 1978 recording for Deutsche Grammophon, with his Orchestre de Paris, is full of true operatic verve. (Listen to the *Hungarian March* as an example!) The defective French of some of the non-French speakers in the cast detracted from my enjoyment, but I was fascinated by Fischer-Dieskau's assumption of the role of Méphistophélès. 'Ingratiating, sinister and powerful' were terms properly used of his performance. The 'patter-song' quality of the *Sérénade*, ('Devant la maison de celui qui t'adore') (In front of the house of the one who loves you), is beautifully judged, and the critic who mentioned the 'un-French swelling-out' of the 'que' on 'que fais-tu' should listen to Gérard Souzay's almost identical interpretation!

Throughout, Fischer-Dieskau's remarkable ability to change the quality and power of his tone keeps one's attention riveted. The text is of course a nightmare for all who know and love Goethe's majestic verses – the French have an unhappy knack of sentimentalising everything 'romantic' – and Marguérite's (or Gretchen's) 'D'amour, l'ardente flamme' is a second-rate substitute for Goethe's (and Schubert's) noble *Meine Ruh' ist hin*. The close of the work, 'the ride to the abyss', was exceptionally well done, reminding us of another 'Faustian' work, the end of Mahler's enormous Eighth Symphony dedicated (like Berg's *Wozzeck*) to his wife, Alma Maria, a multiple setting of the really un-settable and un-stageable Part II of Goethe's poem, in which Fischer-Dieskau sang the baritone rôle of *Pater ecstaticus* in Rafael Kubelik's DG recording with the Bavarian Radio Symphony Orchestra, made in Munich in June 1970.

Just as interesting as these rôles is the enchanting RCA/Eurod-isc version of Humperdinck's *Hänsel und Gretel* recorded in July 1971 for the Humperdinck 50th anniversary celebrations with the Bavarian Radio Orchestra conducted by Kurt Eichhorn, but not issued in Britain until 1974. Fischer-Dieskau sang the rôle of the father Peter, perhaps too subtly for a simple peasant, but with some beautiful moments, as in Act One when the parents fear that the two children are lost, and all of Fischer-Dieskau's great art goes into the passage 'Wenn sie sich verirrten im Walde dort, in der Nacht ohne Stern' und Mond' (If they are lost in the woods in the night without star or moon) (Ex. 19) and again at the end of Act Three before the chorale when we hear Fischer-Dieskau scale his magisterial voice down in the simple prayer, 'Ja, wenn die Not aufs höchste steigt, Gott der Herr die Hand uns reicht', (When our need is greatest, God gives us his hand). (Ex. 20) The fine cast, Charlotte Berthold, Christa Ludwig, Anna Moffo and Helen Donath, with Arleen Auger and Lucia Popp, made this a truly moving recording, particularly, of course, for Germans who grow up with the legend and know the *Sandman's Prayer* from their

Ex. 19

Ex. 20

earliest childhood. (The recording did not deserve however the rather peculiar American 'praise' from *The Post* of Denver, Colorado: 'Fischer-Dieskau sings the father with a rollicking thumbs-under-the-suspenders tramping-in-lederhosen punch' (20 October 1974), which was both inaccurate and unfair!)

The baritone has made few forays into Russian music. He said in 1971 that Russian opera needed a 'particular depth and resonance in the voice which I fear I don't possess', and no doubt had one of his unhappiest stage experiences in his mind when he said it. I asked him on one occasion on which performances he looked back with *least* pleasure, and he answered: 'Liszt's *Heilige Elisabeth* (known to us as the oratorio The *Legend of St Elizabeth* KSW) doesn't bring back any blessed memories, and even although the costumes and the direction were perhaps unsuccessful, the much reviled *Eugen Onegin* in Vienna was really pretty well sung'. He was referring to his four appearances as Onegin with Sena Jurinac, Biserta Cvejic, Anton Dermota and Oskar Czerwenka at the Vienna State Opera in January and February 1961 in a performance of Tchaikovsky's 1879 opera, conducted by Lovro von Matačič and directed by Paul Hager. He was actually suffering from a heavy cold at the time, but would not suggest that that was the reason for the 'failure'. He just feels that, as he said once to a questioner in 1965, one probably has to sing Russian opera in the original language. (He can be heard in the rôle, in fact, in DG excerpts in German, made in July 1966, under Otto Gerdes).

His interpretation of the Landgraf Ludwig in Liszt's oratorio-cum-drama goes back to the 1949 performance under Leo Blech in Berlin shortly before he made his very first operatic record, the Act Three quartet *Lebt wohl, ihr süssen Stunden* (Addio, dolce svegliare), from Puccini's *La Bohème*, with Elfriede Trötschel, Rita Streich and Lorenz Fehenberger, and conducted by Paul Schmitz. Happy the artist who can rue only two blots on his escutcheon after thirty years!

Thus, with a look over our shoulders, so to speak, for completion's sake, at the scenes from Gustav Albert Lortzing's 1837 opera *Zar und Zimmermann* (now enjoying a revival), in which Fischer-

Dieskau sang the rôle of Czar Peter I to Fritz Wunderlich's Peter Ivanov in the latter's last recording for DG before his tragic death in the same month, September 1966, we can close this section with something of a surprise. By 1973, Fischer-Dieskau's versatility had been pretty well taken for granted, but even those who had followed his astounding career closely since his début were not prepared for what that year brought in "Fischer-Dieskaviana': his singing of the 'batman' Dr Falke in the Johann Strauss operetta *Die Fledermaus*. Strauss and Franz Lehár are often taken to be the Austrian equivalents of Britain's slightly less ebullient Gilbert and Sullivan's D'Oyly Carte operas – but the latter are rarely produced in Britain or America with the stellar casts found in the former in Germany and Austria.

Of course, to those who knew Fischer-Dieskau the actor-singer, his success in the rôle hardly came as a surprise. But to those who resolutely continued to pigeon-hole him solely as a *Lieder*-singer, his suave handling of that *ur*-Austrian passage at Orlofsky's party, 'Brüderlein, Brüderlein und Schwesterlein' (Brothers and sisters), leading into the erotic 'Erst ein Kuss, dann ein Du' (First a kiss, then a 'thou'), must have been a revelation! (Ex. 21) Nowhere

Ex. 21

better can we judge his marvellous sense of rhythm, his feeling for that *rubato* that Gerald Moore speaks about so often, than here, as he waltzes to Willi Boskovsky's *Dreivierteltakt*. The work was recorded by Electrola in Vienna in December 1971, with Anneliese Rothenberger, Renata Holm, Brigitte Fassbaender, Walter Berry, Nicolai Gedda and the Vienna Symphony Orchestra. The best summing-up that I have found of the singer in this rôle came from the British provincial paper, the *Derby Evening Telegraph*, whose

Elizabeth Thompson wrote: 'Fischer-Dieskau as Dr Falke . . . a ritzy piece of casting if ever there was one . . .'!

*   *   *   *   *

Hugo Wolf's rarely-performed opera *Der Corregidor* (1896) occupies a lonely position in the world of music. Frank Walker wrote in his 1951 book on the composer that the work had been revived from time to time and 'has achieved a *succès d'estime*, has delighted the connoisseur and lover of Wolf's music and has then been quietly dropped'. Hugo Wolf has found in Fischer-Dieskau one of the most loyal and sympathetic interpreters of his songs, but, in December 1974, the Deutsche Oper in Berlin produced a concert form of *Der Corregidor*, (realised by Gerd Albrecht), which was widely regarded as 'Fischer-Dieskau breaking a lance' for the work. His performance as the neurotic, betrayed miller, Tio Lukas, in music sounding like, as one reviewer put it, 'Richard Wagner on holiday in Spain', was greatly praised. The brilliant new Greek contralto, Agnes Baltsa, Horst Laubenthal and Gerti Zeumer sang the main rôles. But common critical consent was that the work which, after all, contains many quotations from Wolf's own *Spanisches Liederbuch*, belonged to the piano and not to the stage.*

Wolf, then, is the bridge to the last of the three great operatic names of the nineteenth century – even if this third name was with us until 1949. 'Wenn Richard, dann Wagner; wenn Strauss, dann Johann', one can still hear many Germans say, and Richard Strauss, the iconoclastic, 'vulgar' Bavarian with the 'Austrian' name, caused as much stir in the musical world of the turn of the century as does his ebullient Bavarian namesake, Franz Josef Strauss of the Conservative Christian Socialist Union in the world of Federal German politics in our day.

Although Strauss' last opera *Capriccio* had its première on 28 October 1942 in the middle of the Second World War where Strauss had earned opprobrium by his tacit acceptance of the Hitler régime – his music is still banned in Israel – his great operas can be regarded as 'Romanticism's long coda', to use Harold C. Schonberg's striking phrase. Fischer-Dieskau himself was

---

*The singer took part in a concert performance of the work (again under Gerd Albrecht) in Munich on 28 and 31 July 1980.

only too ready to agree with Strauss' own definition of the 'essential feature of opera' viz. 'that it was inseparable from *Kitsch*', and that the success of *Arabella* (1933) showed 'his real gifts' – 'and he said this with something approaching resignation', added the singer.

An Electrola recording of that last opera (*Capriccio*), to Clemens Krauss' libretto, was, strangely enough, Fischer-Dieskau's first appearance in a complete recording of a Strauss opera; Wolfgang Sawallisch conducted the Philharmonia Orchestra with a starry cast, including Elisabeth Schwarzkopf, Christa Ludwig, Anna Moffo, Nicolai Gedda, Hans Hotter (Strauss' first Olivier), and the Austrian baritone, Eberhard Wächter, as the Count. The work was recorded in London in September 1957. As has already been mentioned, other countries did not yet associate Fischer-Dieskau with 'modern' opera, so his performance as the poet Olivier locked in that well-worn argument 'prima la musica' or 'prima le parole' with the musician Flamand (Nicolai Gedda), did not receive much comment, although the recording was to become a much-praised and much-prized treasure later. This 'Conversation Piece', as Strauss called it, demands a fluent understanding of German to follow the at times complicated eighteenth-century discussion which is summed up in the celebrated lines 'Ton *und* Wort sind Bruder und Schwester', (Music *and* text are brother and sister).

More interesting Straussian rôles than that of Olivier offered themselves in the 1960's, and it was not until April 1971 that *Capriccio* reappeared in Fischer-Dieskau's diary – in another complete recording for Deutsche Grammophon (actually a studio broadcast) under the bâton of Karl Böhm, with the Bavarian Radio Symphony Orchestra. Directed by August Everding, Fischer-Dieskau's singing of the minor rôle of the Count brought life to a part that can have its *longeurs*.

The elderly Herr von Faninal in Strauss' 1911 opera *Der Rosenkavalier* is another fairly minor part which Fischer-Dieskau graced with his presence in the DG recording made in Dresden in December 1958, with Karl Böhm and the Saxon State Orchestra. Marianne Schech as the Marschallin and Irmgard Seefried as Octavian had many strong competitors in the rôles, and I should have thought that the Fischer-Dieskau name on the record-sleeve would not have hindered sales. It was a rôle often sung by much less distinguished artists. Certainly Deutsche Grammophon's representative Hans Rutz had no hesitation in declaring on one occasion in 1964 that Fischer-Dieskau's name on the 1960 recording of *Elektra* had helped to sell eight thousand copies in six months of an opera in which, according to one contemporary critic in America, 'Strauss lets loose an orchestral riot that suggests a murder in a Chinese theatre'! (H. T. Finck in *The New York Post* in 1910). Here the rôle of Orest, Elektra's brother, is a small but very important one. The DG recording, also made in Dresden with the Saxon State Orchestra under Karl Böhm in October 1960, gave his part a good deal of prominence, especially in the emotional *anagnorisis*, the 'Recognition Scene' of Greek tragedy, where Elektra's question 'Was willst du, fremder Mensch?' (What do you want, strange man?) is answered by the disguised stranger 'Orest lebt' (Orestes is alive), and he reveals himself as her brother. Fischer-Dieskau lends the simple words enormous conviction and makes something credible out of a rather cardboard character. (The *Musiklehrer* (Music Teacher) in *Ariadne auf Naxos* (1912) appears only in the Prelude to the opera, mainly in the opening disputation with the *Haushofmeister* (the Major-Domo), and is another small character-part. Fischer-Dieskau's treatment of his lines (and his superb top-notes!) were much admired. Karl Böhm conducted the Bavarian Radio Symphony Orchestra in this recording, made in September 1969).

But none of these rôles give any conception of Fischer-Dieskau as a Straussian singer; they are all fill-in parts, important in themselves, but undemanding for a great actor-singer. Challenges for the baritone first appear in performances of the great leading rôles: Jokanaan in *Salome* (1905), Barak in *Die Frau ohne Schatten* (1919), and, above all, Mandryka in *Arabella* (1933), the first two written for *Heldenbariton*, Mandryka for a 'lyric baritone'.

The libretti of *Elektra* (1909), *Der Rosenkavalier* (1911), *Ariadne auf Naxos* (1912), *Die Frau ohne Schatten* and *Arabella*, were all written by Strauss' major collaborator, the Austrian poet, Hugo von Hofmannsthal.

Much has been said and written about the contrast between the bluff, down-to-earth Bavarian from Garmisch and the hypersensitive, refined Austrian aristocrat examining what he called 'the bacteriology of the soul', and Norman del Mar has tried desperately hard (in his book *Richard Strauss*), to show how Hofmannsthal's 'conviction that Strauss was a being of inferior calibre, both as artist and as man', lay behind all the tempestuous disagreements of their relationship, and it is plain to see that the way to their eventual collaboration was prepared by Strauss' basing his 'Musikdrama' *Salome* on the Oscar Wilde play which he had seen in 1902. *Salome* was Strauss' first international *succès de scandale* in opera – it can still be strong meat for weak stomachs today! Not many works give such an insight into the *fin-de-siècle décadence* symbolised by Baudelaire in France, Schnitzler in Austria and, of course, Wilde himself in Great Britain. Salome's grisly request for the head of Jokanaan (John the Baptist) (Jochanaan in the German version), Herod's savage outbursts and Jokanaan's frightening declamation from the cistern were all wonderfully captured in the DG recording made from a live performance of August Everding's new production for the Hamburg State Opera in November 1970. This was Gwyneth Jones' first Salome – and Karl Böhm's first visit to Hamburg for thirty-seven years! The other major rôles were taken by Richard Cassilly as Herod and Mignon Dunn as Herodias. Here we can talk of Fischer-Dieskau's first major Straussian rôle. He had, in fact, sung Jokanaan for the first time in 1952 in Berlin, in a performance conducted by Artur Rother, and again in Munich in 1962, for example, at the beginning of his 'decade of opera', when he had begun to take over the greatest leading rôles and to maintain these alongside his pre-eminent position as Germany's principal male *Lieder*-singer. These were the sort of rôles which gave him the courage to 'sing out' in the concert hall. Most of them require vigorous declamation to rise above the huge Straussian orchestra, and it might be recalled that Sir Thomas Beecham was reputed to have shouted to the orchestra at a rehearsal of *Salome*: 'Louder! Louder! I can still hear the singers'!

Jokanaan is an unlovely rôle for any singer; for his Salome, Strauss wanted 'a sixteen-year old Princess with the voice of an Isolde' – and knew that he would never get *that*. His Jokanaan needs all the resources of a Wagnerian *Heldenbariton* to match the clamour of the orchestral part, but there are some beautiful lyrical passages, too, as where, with great pathos and beauty of tone, Jokanaan tells Salome to go and seek out Christ: 'Er ist auf einem Nachen auf dem See von Galiläa' (He is in a boat on the Sea of Galilee) – and again when he curses the 'Tochter der Unzucht':

'Ich will dich nicht ansehen, Salome. Du bist verflucht, Salome, du bist verflucht' ('I will not look on you, Salome. You are accursed), where Fischer-Dieskau takes a beautiful high E on the word 'verflucht'.

(On the lighter side of this tragic work: Fischer-Dieskau tells with gusto, and in broad Berlin dialect, an anecdote of an earlier Jokanaan who had never sung the rôle before and had to be initiated by a worldly-wise director: 'Now then', he said, 'you're a clever lad, so you'll soon get the hang of it. That's a hole', – he pointed to the famous cistern – 'In you go. Then you come out and act holy for a bit. Then you go back in again. That's all there is to it!')

The contrast between Strauss' practical nature and Hofmannsthal's spirituality (for want of a better word), is seen to best advantage in the libretto to *Die Frau ohne Schatten*. Even those well versed in Austro-German mysticism, like the poet's biographer, Hans Andreas Hammelmann, in his 1957 book on the writer, have found Hofmannsthal's 'ultimate intention, though undoubtedly high-minded, somewhat disappointing in proportion to the immense effort required to understand it' – readers who wish to try will find Norman del Mar's exposition, (on pages 151–218 of Volume II of his book on Strauss), as helpful as any. Not the least of the peculiarities is the contrast between the honest humanity of Barak der Färber (The Dyer) and the uncouthness of his wife, (who, after all, was supposed to have been at least partially modelled on Strauss' wife, Pauline de Ahna!) It is this contrast which makes the part such a powerful male rôle. 'You mustn't do anything on stage to *show* Barak's goodness', insists Fischer-Dieskau. 'You must *be* goodness'. Strauss' preference for the female voice is well documented – one recalls his great admiration for Elisabeth Schumann whom he met in 1917 – but he wrote some of his most touching music for the baritone here in what he himself often felt to be his 'greatest opera' – although few agree with him. 'As you know', said Fischer-Dieskau, 'Strauss thought that tenor voices led to abstract feelings – which is why he didn't like Italian opera where tenors rule the roost'.

Die *Fr*au *o*hne *Sch*atten (or 'FROSCH', as German musicians affectionately call it – from the underlined letters!) was chosen to open Munich's sumptuous National Theatre – over 2000 seats, cost: sixty-two million Marks – on 21 November 1963, a splendid event in a splendid city. Joseph Keilberth conducted the Bavarian State Orchestra; the cast included Ingrid Bjoner, Inge Borkh, Martha Mödl, Hertha Töpper, Jess Thomas and Hans Hotter. I had had the Ariola recording for some time (with Inge Borkh and Walter Berry (as Barak)), but must confess that it was Fischer-Dieskau's Barak which gave me an interest in this strange work. When we eventually reach the beginning of the third act, (on Side Six of the heavily-cut, four-record 'live' DG set), our puzzlement, perhaps even boredom, is relieved by the thrilling and beautiful scene between Barak and his wife, as they lie entombed, divided by a thick wall, ignorant of each other's presence, and surrounded by the voices of 'the unborn children'. The typically broad Straussian melody of 'Mir anvertraut, dass ich sie hege, dass ich sie trage auf diesen Händen' (She is mine to comfort, to carry on these hands), with its memories of *Rosenkavalier*, is wonderfully sung (and acted) by Fischer-Dieskau and Inge Borkh. The mixture of humanity, pity and servitude in the rôle of Barak allows him to use a broad palette of vocal colorations.

Fischer-Dieskau sang all these Straussian rôles with total commitment, interpreting the composer's intentions, not only as they manifest themselves in the printed score, but also from his conversations and correspondence on the work, for, here too, the singer had prepared himself for the rôle by immersing himself in the documented material. Would that more of our artists realise that this is necessary to get the most from, and give the most to a part! To me and to others, however, he has admitted that his favourite Strauss rôle is Mandryka in *Arabella*. He also told me that, although he held no high opinion of Hofmannsthal's libretti *qua* libretti, that for *Arabella* had always interested and moved him deeply. Significantly too perhaps, it is the only one of the great Strauss rôles written for a *lyric* baritone, as we saw earlier – yet it not only lies perfectly for the singer's voice but, like Almaviva, Rigoletto and Amfortas, it also suits his temperament. He said once that the shortest time that he had taken to learn a new part was five weeks – but that Mandryka had been one of the most difficult assignments. 'It is not a clear-cut rôle; there is nothing self-explanatory, and one can always find contradictory elements in the character', he said to Michael Marcus of *Records and Recordings* in November 1959.

Having scored a great success with his first Mandryka at Salzburg in 1958, (with Lisa della Casa as Arabella, directed by Rudolf Hartmann and conducted by Joseph Keilberth), Fischer-Dieskau was delighted to be asked to make his long-awaited Covent Garden début in the rôle on 29 January 1965. With Lisa della Casa as Arabella, Joan Carlyle as Zdenka and Michael Langdon as Waldner, in a Rudolf Hartmann production conducted by Georg Solti, (with wonderful sets by Peter Rice), he gave a performance whose power was described as 'hypnotising': 'What I mean is that when he's on stage, whether singing or not, whether moving or staying put, you can't keep your opera glasses off him', wrote Charles Read in *The Spectator* of 5 February 1965. That is what *I* meant when I wrote about his performance in *Le nozze di Figaro* in Edinburgh, that he 'is always in the action'. It is a feature of all great actors – whether on the stage, in Parliament – or at a dinner party. It is called *charisma*. It means total immersion in the rôle being played, and it is what also gives Fischer-Dieskau's singing of *Lieder* its immense sense of conviction. The 'mere' words and music are interpreted with vocal and intellectual 'truth'. His performance was certainly a revelation to those British journalists who had not managed to get to Germany to hear him in opera (since his début in 1948); a good deal of surprise was evident in the reviews, and one had to smile in the intervals at Covent Garden on hearing remarks such as: 'You wouldn't think it was the same man, would you?' from those who knew him only as a *Lieder* singer.

The triumph was repeated almost exactly two years later when he returned to Covent Garden to sing in *Arabella*, (again under Solti), followed by the *Falstaff* to which I have already referred.

This 'tenderest and happiest of love-dramas', as Norman del Mar eloquently describes it, had already been recorded by Fischer-Dieskau before his London début; it was made by DG in Munich's Prinzregententheater in August 1963, with the Bavarian State Orchestra conducted by Joseph Keilberth. By the time that it was issued, what the singer had called 'an abyss that seemed unbridgeable' had opened up before him – the death of his talented wife, Irmgard, on 15 December 1963, giving birth to their third son, Manuel. Waves of sympathy from his colleagues went out to Fischer-Dieskau. Of all those that I have read the most touching came from a distinguished artist, who should remain anonymous, but who wrote that, after trying to compose a letter, he had played, for Fischer-Dieskau alone, the second movement of the Mozart E flat Piano Concerto (K. 482), and that, in it, was everything that he had felt on hearing the terrible news.

Such knowledge lent an almost unbearable poignancy to his tender singing of 'Ich habe eine Frau gehabt' (I had a wife once) in the duet with Arabella in Act Two (Ex. 22) and to his general

Ex. 22

Molto tranquillo

Ich ha - be ei - ne Frau ge - habt,

interpretation of this 'Mr Right' (*Der Richtige*) who battles through the tangled, perhaps even incredible plot to the triumph of the 'Glass of Water' scene and ultimate possession of Arabella. Since his first appearance as Mandryka at Salzburg in 1958 under Keilberth, Fischer-Dieskau had taken this rôle to his heart, and it is indeed curious that it should have entered his life again at that particular tragic time.

His Mandryka is a very human figure who runs the gamut of emotions from initial shyness through boisterous joviality ('Teschek, bedien' dich') (Help yourself, old chap!), to the final searing melodies of the close. It has all that the singer would demand from an operatic rôle: deep humanity, 'singability', 'flesh-and-blood' credibility. His friend, the French critic of *Le figaro littéraire*, Claude Rostand, wrote to Fischer-Dieskau about his Paris Mandryka (on 12 August 1964): 'On ne sait plus ce qui chez vous est le plus grand et le plus génial: l'acteur ou le chanteur? Probablement tous les deux! Vous êtes vraiment l'artiste total'. (One doesn't know with you which is the greater, the actor or the singer? Probably both! You are truly the total artist).

* * * * *

Our study of Fischer-Dieskau's involvement in the operas of Richard Strauss has taken us well into the twentieth century, but it was firmly stated at the beginning of the section that these operas were to be seen as 'Romanticism's long coda', and before we proceed to discuss the singer's work in twentieth-century opera proper, we should look at two further composers whose works hover on the bridge between the two centuries: Giacomo Puccini and Claude Debussy.

The Act Three quartet from *La Bohème* was Fischer-Dieskau's first operatic record, made on 19 September 1949. Puccini's operas are the staple fare of all the world's opera houses, and Germany's are no exception. Throughout his thirty years' membership of the Berlin opera companies, Fischer-Dieskau has regularly sung the standard Puccinian *verismo* character-baritone rôles: Marcello in *La Bohème*, Sharpless in *Madame Butterfly*, Scarpia in *Tosca* and in the two one-acters, Michele in *Il Tabarro* and the name-part in *Gianni Schicchi*, Parts I and III of *Il Trittico*. He sang Marcel (Marcello) in a German version of the complete *La Bohème* for DG in June 1961 in a performance by Alberto Erede to follow his successful Electrola version of excerpts with Wilhelm Schüchter back in 1954. But the performance which aroused most public interest was his Scarpia in *Tosca* and the comparison it evoked with the singer whose name was synonymous with the rôle at the time: Tito Gobbi. The famous Callas/Gobbi recording of 1953, followed by the 1964 Zeffirelli production at Covent Garden, is believed to have set standards for all time – although one can ascertain that *it* was not all that enthusiastically received in general!

Fischer-Dieskau's Scarpia was recorded for Decca in the Accademia di Santa Cecilia in Rome in June 1966, with Birgit Nilsson as Tosca and Franco Corelli as Cavaradossi, conducted by Lorin Maazel. It was the German baritone's keenly intelligent feeling for the meaning of the words, contrasting so well with Birgit Nilsson's thrilling Tosca, which drew critical praise. I find that Fischer-Dieskau makes a superbly sinister police-chief; there is about him too that 'slimy piety' which Gobbi knows to bring out, and both baritones have the vocal technique to ride the top notes in the so-called *Cantabile di Scarpia* – the final 'Mia!' is a test for all but the greatest voices. Here, Fischer-Dieskau's *italianità* was put to a severe test – a comparison with arguably the greatest Italian singer of his day on his own ground. I cannot but think that honours are even here; listen to their 'Orsù, Tosca, parlate' as Scarpia menaces Tosca with the torturing of her lover – both men in their different ways bring enormous acting skills to the tiny phrase which lays bare the evil of the character.

Comparison with the Italian baritone would again be invited were Fischer-Dieskau to record *Il Trittico*. In December 1973, he had had an enormous success in the Munich Nationaltheater when he had sung the two one-acters *Gianni Schicchi* and *Il Tabarro* opposite his future wife, Julia Varady. There were golden reviews for his mastery of, on the one hand, the comic touch in the first, and, on the other, of the *verismo*, to me almost *Flying Dutchman*-like tragedy of the second. Günther Rennert's direction and Wolfgang Sawallisch's conducting, allied to the art of the singers, brought quite unprecedented applause at the end of the evening. Puccini's strange, almost haunted night-world of the barges of the Seine has certainly something impressionistic about it which has led to the opera being linked with the name and the style of Claude Debussy. (Fischer-Dieskau has, in fact, recorded the opera – but for West German Radio, in 1975).

We shall see that Fischer-Dieskau has a personal affinity with the world of French Impressionism, but first thoughts would not associate this vibrant, active artist with the cool, languid, muted world of Debussy's 1902 opera *Pelléas et Mélisande*. Rafael Kubelik had persuaded the singer, however, to sing the part of Golaud in a concert version in Munich's Herkulessaal on 17–19 November 1971, and, with Helen Donath as Mélisande and Nicolai Gedda as Pelléas, they gave a superlative performance of a work which could well claim to have destroyed the 'arch-poisoner's' *culte wagnérien* in Europe and paved the way for the operas of Berg and the twentieth century. Pierre Boulez' London performance and subsequent recording (1970) had reinstated the work for modern audiences – Boulez' long article in the set's booklet (almost a book!) had justified Kubelik's choice of a tenor Pelléas, while his description of Golaud as one who 'passe de la faiblesse à l'obsession névrosée' seemed to have been heeded by the Munich performers. Karl-Heinz Ruppel counted the Kubelik *Pelléas et Mélisande* as 'one of the greatest evenings in the history of the symphony concerts of Bavarian Radio', (in the *Süddeutsche Zeitung*).

* * * * *

A glimpse into Fischer-Dieskau's 'workshop' as he prepares a new rôle was given in an interview with Professor Karla Höcker printed in *Die Welt* on 29 November 1962, and which has appeared in many places since. The singer had just appeared in the Berlin première of Hans Werner Henze's *Elegy for young lovers* (q.v.). Professor Höcker asked him if it were true that, for modern singers, a page of Alban Berg gave no more difficulties than a page of Mozart or Debussy. Fischer-Dieskau felt that a singer's receptivity to serial music was part of a group of very varied complexes, including an awareness of the technicalities of the structure of the music. It was really a question of 'training'. There was more than musicality in this, he felt; it was really something intellectual – which is why one should not compare contemporary composers, (like Henze), with Berg, whose music, despite all its novel structures, could still be understood from a *musical* point of view. But *all* new music, he added, takes one to the limits, sometimes vocal, sometimes interpretative; that was the attraction of this pioneering work – one had to fight to open up the way for the works before they are accepted.

Just such a challenge had been *Wozzeck* (1925), by the Austrian composer, Alban Berg, dedicated to Alma Maria, Gustav Mahler's wife. The opera is based on an even more remarkable play by Georg Büchner (1813–1837) from Darmstadt near Frankfurt. *Woyzeck*, (as the play was called), was not published until 1879 and had an extraordinary influence on German writers, from Gerhart Hauptmann at the turn of the century, through Bertolt Brecht and the German Expressionist writers of the 1920's, to Friedrich Dürrenmatt, the controversial Swiss dramatist of the 1960's. Büchner, a brilliant young scientist and philosophical thinker, was fifty, perhaps a hundred years ahead of his times, even although he died at only twenty-four; his pitiful soldier Woyzeck, hunted, hounded and tormented, became one of the symbols of modern *Entfremdung*, man's alienation from his fellow-man and, ultimately, from himself. Writing about the opera before his début, (with Helga Pilarczyk as Marie, in Wolf Völker's production, under Richard Kraus in the Städtische Oper in Berlin on 2 February 1960), Fischer-Dieskau pondered on the reasons for the work still being thought of as 'difficult': 'There was, of course', he said, 'the sheer difficulty of the text itself, but also . . . there were four different vocal levels to comprehend: pure song, *Sprechgesang*, elevated speech and colloquial speech. What listener can comprehend all four – and what singer can sing or act them?' So, he asked, was Schoenberg right after all, when he said that there were not enough 'trained listeners'? The singer tended to agree that a work like *Wozzeck* could only be sung by hard-working singers – and understood by hard-working listeners!

After the première, Fischer-Dieskau sang several performances during that Berg 75th anniversary year, and later recorded the work for DG with Evelyn Lear, Karl Christian Kohn, Helmut Melchert, Gerhard Stolze and Fritz Wunderlich, with the Deutsche Oper Orchestra, Berlin, conducted by Karl Böhm, in March and April 1965. It was the first recording in the original German and gave Fischer-Dieskau the opportunity to set the standard of performance – which he has done for so many new works since. There seemed to me to be just a slight excuse for thinking his performance a little too 'artistocratic' for Büchner's 'arme Leut' (poor people), but who can forget his acting in the murder scene (Act III Scene 2), or when he drowns while looking for the murder knife in the woodland pool: 'Aber der Mond verrät mich – der Mond ist blutig' (But the moon betrays me – the moon is full of blood) – or his forced joviality in the inn? (Compare, too, the gaunt, close-cropped figure on the record sleeve with the suave, bewigged, aristocratic Almaviva and you will see something of the man's genius as an actor). At the same time, he did not fail to convey Wozzeck's almost maniacal humour, a forerunner of the *comédie noire* of our own times.

Much of the credit for his understanding of the problems of interpreting Wozzeck must go, he told me, to his great friend, the distinguished interpreter of Büchner's *Woyzeck*, Walter Franck, whose death in 1961 robbed the singer of one of his greatest advisers *and* admirers.

Fischer-Dieskau's next Berg rôle was Dr Schön, the *Heldenbariton* part in the incomplete 1937 'Zürich version' of *Lulu*. This text also comes from an established literary classic, or, to be precise, from two: *Die Büchse der Pandora* (Pandora's Box) (1904) and *Erdgeist* (Earth Spirit) (1895) by Bertolt Brecht's 'predecessor' in unconventional drama, Frank Wedekind. As the reader might know, after Helene Berg's death in 1977, a complete *Lulu* was given in Paris on 24 February 1979 with Friedrich Cerha's version of the unfinished Act Three, but the DG recording, made in February and March 1968, and based on a Deutsche Oper performance again, has retained its place in the catalogues. In this work, Fischer-Dieskau once again essayed a difficult *Heldenbariton* rôle – he ranks it indeed as the most difficult rôle of all that he has played – where he had to sing *forte* for long stretches. The plays themselves are read by Germanisten as preparatory studies to 'modern drama' and do not have a great deal of literary value, I feel. The opera abounds in passages which skirt the area of 'ham' – but, as always, Fischer-Dieskau manages to convey a credible character in a youngish, at times humorous, Dr Schön, who dies an 'actor's death' at the hands of Lulu: 'Da ... ist noch ... einer ...'! The 'complete' DG recording, conducted by Pierre Boulez and issued at the end of 1979, did not seem to me to match the Fischer-Dieskau/Evelyn Lear performance – *and* the German of the cast left something to be desired.

Perhaps, as a linguist, I am hypersensitive to poor pronunciation of the common European languages, yet surely it is his beautiful enunciation and pronunciation, allied to his obvious awareness of the *literary* significance of texts (both operatic and song), which place Fischer-Dieskau so far above so many of his contemporaries? The latter trait, (awareness of literary significance), is clearly present in his famous interpretation of Dr Faust in Ferruccio Busoni's opera, captured on a DG recording made under Ferdinand Leitner in May 1969, with William Cochran as Mephistopheles and Hildegard Hillebrecht as the Duchess of Parma; for this is not Goethe's *Faust*, but is derived rather from the Lutheran chapbooks and puppet plays, from that world which Goethe reviled as arising from 'the accursed, devil-ridden imagination of our Reformer, which was always seeing devils, peopled the entire visible world with devils and personified it *as* the devil', when he was talking to his friend Voss on 24 February 1805.

This 'Germano-Italic' opera (completed by Busoni's pupil, Philipp Jarnach and conducted by Fritz Busch at the Dresden première in 1925) had been reintroduced to contemporary audiences by Fischer-Dieskau in the Städtische Oper in Berlin in 1955, in a Wolf Völker-Richard Kraus production, one of Fischer-

Dieskau's first 'pioneering' acts, indeed; he did the same for it in the Royal Festival Hall in London in November 1959, when Sir Adrian Boult conducted a shortened version with Richard Lewis, Heather Harper, Ian Wallace and the London Philharmonic Orchestra and Chorus. Sir Adrian wrote to the singer afterwards, saying 'what a privilege it was to cooperate with you in your magnificent performance' – and apologising for the cold air to which English concert halls are subjected!

Once again, he found himself singing a *Heldenbariton* rôle; the 1955 performance was, indeed one of his first experiences of the problem. The rôle's mixture of abstract lyricism and practical black-magicry allows the singer an astonishingly wide range of vocal moods – from the hectoring to the seductive, and Fischer-Dieskau admits that he took some time to enjoy a rôle that he now truly loves and has made his own. Indeed, François Florent in a special number of the French periodical *Opéra* (June 1967) said of his *Dr Faust*: 'Il y nage comme poisson dans l'eau' (He swims in it like a fish in water)!

The singer has often been asked why he makes life so difficult for himself by continually offering his services in the promotion of new works, where so many great artists are content to underpin their reputations by repeated appearances in the classics. His answers always betray a certain desire to teach, to educate: 'To besprinkle our young people with lukewarm musico-historical treasures from the nation's reservoir is no substitute for living culture', he says; and again: 'It is the interpreter's task to build a bridge of comprehension, not to scorn a living exchange of thoughts with the composer – above all, to gain that 'certainty of taste', so as not to be crushed between that which is purely epigonal and that which is not yet understood'.

To record the one-act opera *Duke Bluebeard's Castle* (1911/1918) by Béla Bartók, in the original Hungarian (as *A Kékszakállú herceg vára*) at the age of fifty-four, might be thought to be proof that the singer has the courage of his convictions. His connections with the work go back over twenty years to a truncated DG recording (in German) with Ferenc Fricsay, the Hungarian conductor, (who had introduced him to the opera), on 7 October 1958 after a performance in the Berlin Academy of Music with Hertha

Töpper and the Radio Symphony Orchestra of Berlin, and he has sung it fairly regularly since. Listening to the latest DG recording in Hungarian, made with his Hungarian-speaking wife, Julia Varady (as Judith), with the Bavarian State Opera Orchestra under Wolfgang Sawallisch in March 1979, one had the impression that the baritone's voice had become more, rather than less flexible as he reached down for those low bass notes. Miss Varady's beautiful performance brings out the passion in the score, the *parlando rubato* rhythms being emphasised by the interesting accentuation of the Hungarian language. Fischer-Dieskau is most moving at the passage over throbbing strings 'Váram sötét töve reszket . . .' (The stones of my castle are trembling . . .), and I am assured by a Hungarian colleague that his Hungarian accent is remarkably good – which is more than can be said for the terrible translations; all three, English, German and French disagree with one another and are equally bad. With so many well-trained linguists available for employment, such shoddiness is nothing short of disgraceful. (Fischer-Dieskau had already sung in Hungarian of course – in the moving tribute to Zoltan Kodály at the Royal Festival Hall in London on 3 June 1960).

The reader might remember the work done by Fischer-Dieskau for yet another great contemporary composer, the German, Paul Hindemith, the inventor of that badly-translated term *Gebrauchsmusik*. I wonder if a look at Hindemith's own 'manifesto' might not have produced a better translation than 'useful music' (or *Groves'* 'workaday')? Hindemith wrote: '. . . the demand for music is so great that the composer *and the consumer* (my italics) ought most emphatically to come to at least an understanding'. So, is this not 'consumer music'? It seems to me to be a better translation for our day and age than even 'functional music'.

The composer's two great stage works, *Cardillac* (op. 39) (1926, revised 1952) and *Mathis der Maler* (1934–1938), the latter memorably linked with Wilhelm Furtwängler's defiance of Goebbels' ban on the work in 1934 – although he did have to eat humble pie a year later! – have always been favourite Fischer-Dieskau rôles. Like Hans Sachs, both characters are essentially concerned with the theme of the artist's relationship to his craft or art. I quoted

Fischer-Dieskau earlier on the theme: 'Creative artists can never worry about 'politics' or 'living conditions'. They can only be concerned with themselves and the work that they are called upon to do'.

Cardillac, one might think, takes this doctrine to its unfortunate extreme when, becoming obsessed with his jewellery and quite disinterested in 'people', he murders to recover his 'possessions'. Mathis the painter's thesis is that the artist is just not *competent* to dabble in politics; both viewpoints could be seen as justifying the so-called 'innere Emigration' (internal emigration) of so many leading German *Künstler* ('artists' in the widest sense) in the Nazi times.

After his stage début in the rôle in 1965 in Munich, Fischer-Dieskau recorded the part of Cardillac (in the 1926 version) for the Westdeutsche Rundfunk in June 1968, with Leonore Kirchstein, Elisabeth Söderström, Donald Grobe and Karl Christian Kohn, with the Cologne Radio Symphony Orchestra under Joseph Keilberth. This performance was then issued as a set by DG in April 1970. It was certainly a very 'functional' version of a very puzzling opera. On balance, however, I prefer E.T.A. Hoffmann's original *Novelle Das Fräulein von Scudéri*, which is much more concise and (*therefore*, perhaps) more chilling.

Excerpts only of Hindemith's second opera, *Mathis der Maler*, made with Pilar Lorengar in November 1961 had been issued by DG, so it was after years of neglect that the complete recording appeared in December 1979 in an Electrola recording made in June and December 1977. The superb cast, including James King, William Cochran, Donald Grobe and Gerd Feldhoff, (and a very fine Bavarian Radio Chorus), supported Fischer-Dieskau and Rafael Kubelik's Bavarian Radio Symphony Orchestra in a much more enjoyable operatic experience. Fischer-Dieskau as Mat(t)hias Nithardt (*dit* Grünewald) (Mathias was the name the singer gave to his first son, incidentally!), the painter of the wonderful Isenheim altarpiece and the unwilling leader of the sixteenth-century peasants' revolt, sings his philosophy as he packs his things away and makes preparations for his death, bidding farewell to each object as he does so. It is a most touching scene. The adaptations of well-known German folk-songs makes this one of the finest German operas of the century and a peculiarly suitable vehicle for the great master of the German *Lied*. (He had made his stage début in the rôle in Berlin in September 1959 under Richard Kraus).

The 'artist in society' is a well-worked vein in this century of anti-authoritarianism, particularly in modern German literature, and it evokes the names of Thomas Mann and Hermann Hesse, among others. As is probably well known, Thomas Mann wrote his *Doktor Faustus* (1949) on the theme of the 'musician in society'. *His* Faust, Adrian Leverkühn, loosely based on the character of Arnold Schoenberg and his dodecaphonic or twelve-note music, on the one hand, and the life of the philosopher, Friedrich Nietzsche, on the other, meets his Mephistopheles in Palestrina; Hans Pfitzner (1869–1949) died in the year of the publication of Mann's enormously long novel; his huge opera *Palestrina* had its première under Bruno Walter in Munich in 1917. Although its subject is the sixteenth-century composer rather than the town, the opera also treats the theme of the artist in an uncomprehending society. The work, Wagnerian in its scope – and in some of its themes –, and with a libretto by the composer, occupies a special place in Germanic hearts, although it receives scant mention in reference books. (Record collectors are always on the look-out, however, for Julius Patzak's Cologne radio broadcast!) Pfitzner earned opprobrium for his naive inter-war 'patriotism'; he left Germany in 1946 to die in embittered emigration in Salzburg in 1949.

Fischer-Dieskau first studied the work in 1952 when he sang the small part of Giovanni Morone, the Legate, in a Cologne broadcast under Richard Kraus in the October. In the DG recording, however, he took the demanding rôle of Cardinal Carlo Borromeo, who, having at first failed to persuade the tired, idealistic Palestrina (sung by Nicolai Gedda) to write the *Missa Papae Marcelli*, throws himself at the composer's feet when he hears the wonderful work, which proves that polyphonic music *is* compatible with that austerity represented by plainsong. This recording, (made in Munich in February 1973 under Rafael Kubelik), would probably be the only opportunity that a British or American audience would have of hearing the work – apart from everything else, it has thirty-four solo parts! – but the baritone sang Borromeo in a production at the Bavarian State Opera in Munich in December 1979. For me, it has, like so much of Pfitzner's music, (his songs, for example) a curious, dated charm.

It certainly could not be said that the final group of Fischer-Dieskau rôles are in any way 'dated'! All three composers of these works are still alive and have expressed their deep gratitude to Fischer-Dieskau for his cultivation of modern music in general – and theirs in particular. When I asked Gottfried von Einem, (born in Switzerland in 1918), if he could find any faults in Fischer-Dieskau's singing, he jovially replied: 'Just that he doesn't sing my songs often enough!' Von Einem's *Dantons Tod*, to a libretto by Boris Blacher, had had such an enormous success at the Salzburg première in 1947 with Paul Schöffler as Danton, Julius Patzak as Camille and conducted by Ferenc Fricsay, that one can well imagine Fischer-Dieskau's pleasure in singing the rôle for the first time in Berlin on 9 February 1963 under Heinrich Hollreiser. For Gottfried von Einem himself, that night was Fischer-Dieskau's, since he told me that the singer carried the whole production by his performance. (Von Einem has since written another opera, based on a play by the Swiss author, Friedrich Dürrenmatt: *Der Besuch der alten Dame* (The Visit) (premièred in Vienna in 1971 and staged at Glyndebourne in 1973). His latest work *Jesu Hochzeit* opened to attacks from irate Catholics in Vienna on 18 May 1980).

Hans Werner Henze felt the same about Fischer-Dieskau's performance as Gregor Mittenhofer in his *Elegy for young lovers* as von Einem had about *Dantons Tod*. The opera had its German language première (as *Elegie für junge Liebende*) in the lovely little rococo theatre in Schwetzingen, not far from Heidelberg, on 20 May 1961 to Henze's own direction. The Bavarian State Opera company was conducted by Heinrich Bender, with Karl Christian Kohn, Friedrich Lenz and Ingeborg Bremert in the important rôles. The original English libretto by W. H. Auden and his friend Chester Kallman which tried to see 'how much psychological drama and character' could be made 'compatible with the convention of the operatic medium' (Auden), paints a picture of human brutality; the artist-poet, having lost feelings and respect for other human beings, virtually murders for the sake of gaining an 'experience' for a poem, his 'elegy'. Fischer-Dieskau, white-haired, elegant in his monogrammed smoking-jacket, could once again run the gamut of artistic and vocal emotions – from artistic naivety to pathological brutality, from intellectual urbanity to uncivilised hatred, in music which is dodecaphonic, but tuneful. It seems strange that there is (as yet) no complete recording of the work, although Deutsche Grammophon did issue (although not until January 1968) a disc of excerpts in German, made in Berlin in April and May 1963, with the Radio Symphony Orchestra under Henze himself. Fischer-Dieskau sings most of his important solo work on this record, including the great 'worldly business', where he fills his voice with all the hate and malice that he feels. Although Fischer-Dieskau has always regarded the opera as an important modern work, it was a resounding flop at its Glyndebourne 'English' première on 13 July 1961 and the seven subsequent performances. Auden soon fell out of love with it, too, and always called it thereafter 'Allergy for young lovers', the title as typed on the score by his typist! (See Charles Osborne's book *W. H. Auden* 1980). The hymn-singing Auden had clearly very little sympathy for the modernist Henze. To be fair, Henze himself said sarcastically of his work: 'It's just old arias with new notes'!

Has there ever been a greater artistic triumph for Dietrich Fischer-Dieskau, I wonder, than the last work of our chapter – for many as great a night in the theatre as they had ever witnessed? On 9 July 1978, in Munich's Nationaltheater, Fischer-Dieskau created his greatest modern rôle to date – King Lear in Aribert Reimann's opera *Lear* written to the individual timbre and talents of the cast: Julia Varady as Cornelia, Helga Denesch as Goneril and Colette Lorand as Regan, with the Bavarian State Opera Orchestra under Gerd Albrecht.

Fischer-Dieskau had long had an opera on Lear in mind and had indeed broached the matter more than once with Benjamin Britten, he told me, but Britten had found the task too daunting – as, of course, had Verdi and Debussy *inter alia* before him! Reimann had become one of the singer's favoured accompanists and knew the Fischer-Dieskau voice well, having already composed several vocal pieces for him, and, incidentally, having acted as vocal coach for the Mittenhofer rôle above. In summer 1975, August Everding, the new *Intendant* of the Bavarian State Opera, commissioned Reimann to compose the opera; the composer turned to Claus Henneberg to provide a libretto which was eventually based on the 1777 translation of Johann Joachim Eschenburg which, they felt, was nearer the original than the better-known Schlegel-Tieck version. With constant advice from, and consultation with, Fischer-Dieskau, Reimann said that he lived and slept with the opera for the next two years. Rehearsals with Jean-Pierre Ponnelle began in May 1978. Describing the opera as a 'single metamorphosis', Reimann pointed out that as each person's character altered, so too did the music. 'The individual characters were surrounded by differing but always characteristic musical fields which changed as they changed, continually and mutually influencing each other'.

This huge opera – it lasted three hours with one interval – was dominated by Fischer-Dieskau's literally awe-inspiring presence, even, peculiarly, when he was not on stage; one knew that the opera revolved round the character Lear, round the actor-singer Fischer-Dieskau. His shaggy head (a likeness caught memorably in one of his own paintings shown at his Bamberg exhibition (q.v.)) was the cynosure of all eyes. His 'Ja, jeder Zoll ein König' (Ay, every inch a king), delivered lying on his back, had 'every word savoured, every tone judged·for a particular occasion', wrote William Mann in his *Times* review of 26 July, and in the wonderful final monologue 'Nein, nein, kein Leben mehr' (No, no, no life), delivered as, dying, Lear looks down on his dead Cordelia, Fischer-Dieskau let his voice trail away up into unearthly silence on 'Seht hier, seht' (Look there, look there!), accompanied by mysterious percussion. He had done nothing finer in his long and distinguished stage career.

There was a general chorus of acclaim when the DG recording made from four live performances of the first Munich revival in October 1978 with the same forces was released in September 1979. It was a magnificent testament to a work which Fischer-Dieskau is certain will remain one of the great operas of this or any other age and which he was happy to appear in again, in Munich in 1980.

Thus we come to the end of this chapter on Dietrich Fischer-Dieskau, operatic baritone. His place among contemporary singers is unchallenged; in an age rich in great voices, he, by dint of the sheer beauty of tone and command of vocal technique, added to his undoubted ability as an interpreter of the leading operatic rôles, would command the place as of right. There is also no doubt that, had he appeared in all the world's leading opera houses as often as he has appeared in the theatres of Germany and Austria, many more operagoers would have been able to confirm the impression of his great artistry gained from his recordings.

Over the last thirty years, I have heard all his recordings and seen many of his stage performances; when I play through my many records and compare his performances in Mozart, Verdi and Wagner, and his pioneering work for twentieth-century operas, with the great voices of the past and present, I am hard put to find his peer overall. Many singers have had as beautiful voices perhaps; many as strong, many as flexible instruments – but none, I am certain, have been able to put the voice to the service of the composer and his librettist as faithfully and as beautifully as this Mastersinger.

Dietrich Fischer-Dieskau as...

15 Don Giovanni, with Ferenc
   Fricsay, Berlin, 1958
16 Gregor Mittenhofer in *Elegy for
   young lovers*, with the composer,
   Hans Werner Henze,
   Schwetzingen, 1961

17 Mandryka in Richard Strauss'
   Arabella, with his wife Julia Varady,
   Munich, 1977
18 Wozzeck (Alban Berg), Berlin, 1965
19 Falstaff, in Verdi's opera
20 Macbeth, Salzburg, 1964
21 Count Almaviva in Mozart's
   Le nozze di Figaro, Berlin
22 Hans Sachs, in Wagner's
   Die Meistersinger von Nürnberg,
   Berlin, 1976

23 Lear in Aribert Reimann's *Lear*, with Julia Varady
as Cordelia, Munich, 1978

CHAPTER FOUR

Cameo: Fischer-Dieskau at Rehearsal

Place: The Philharmonie in Berlin.
Date: 10 September, 1979.
Time: 11 am.
Work: Rehearsal of Ferruccio Busoni's *Four Goethe Lieder* (1919–1924).
Players: Israel Philharmonic Orchestra.
Conductor: Zubin Mehta.

The orchestra sit in shirt-sleeves, a mixture of men and women chattering happily: Mehta, saturnine, in slacks and pullover. There is a general noise of disparate tuning – silence – then a note from the leader and more deliberate tuning. Mehta taps on the desk and says in English: 'Ladies and gentlemen, may I introduce Dietrich Fischer-Dieskau?" The singer, in a gray suit, shirt without a tie, grins broadly and stretches out his arms in greeting. (He knows many of them, of course, since this is the orchestra that he conducted in Israel in 1976).

After some general remarks about the evening's concert (the *Lieder*, Penderecki's *De Natura Sonoris* No. 2 and Mahler's 5th symphony), Mehta announces the order of the songs; the orchestra have them in separate parts and they have to be re-arranged. Mehta wants to start with the witty *Flohlied des Mephisto* (from *Faust*). As the orchestra begins the staccato figures, Fischer-Dieskau sits in his chair and sings half-voice to the music. Mehta turns now and then to take the tempo from him. Mehta is very strict with the orchestra; when the second violins have difficulty with one of his suggestions, he calls: 'Are we here to make it easy?' From time to time, Fischer-Dieskau stands up and points to places in the score in front of Mehta, who is worried that the orchestra is too loud. Fischer-Dieskau then tries the whole song through with full voice, first of all into the empty hall, then he turns and sings to the orchestra. After the final section (three p's), the orchestra clap him – although they are still not happy about 'the four bars before figure six'!

So to the second song *Lied des Unmuts* (from Goethe's *West-östlicher Divan*). Fischer-Dieskau enters with *Keinen Reimer wird man finden* straightaway (We shall not find a rhymer), seated first of all; then he stands and faces the orchestra. He half-conducts them where he wants the last three notes shortened. (His wife, Julia Varady, has come into the hall at 1140, and, after we have greeted each other, she goes to a seat directly in front of him and sits making notes and gesturing to him now and then). Then Mehta takes the song through with Fischer-Dieskau singing *piano* and indicating where he requires a *forte* or a *pianissimo*. Mehta watches the singer continuously for his reactions.

The third song *Schlechter Trost*, (which was actually Busoni's last composition), brings in the singer from the downbeat, (although Mehta has to ask two of the players to stop talking first!) The orchestra seem fascinated by Fischer-Dieskau's *mezza voce* and murmur approval. Fischer-Dieskau takes off his jacket when he stands up to sing and puts it on again as soon as he sits down, remembering no doubt that he has just recovered from the influenza which had made him cancel the European Broadcasting Union's broadcast concert of Schoenberg's *Ein Überlebender aus Warschau* (A survivor from Warsaw). Then he accompanies Mehta through the tempo, looking as if he would love to take over the conducting himself. There is a little contretemps with the violas; Mehta has them to his right. He speaks English to the orchestra, sometimes a little broken German, but the leaders of the various sections speak to their colleagues in Hebrew. Then Fischer-Dieskau stands up again and sings full voice to the three of us in the Philharmonie soon to be filled to sold-out capacity. The song ends with 'a vision of ghosts gliding past the sleepless man', as Fischer-Dieskau's friend, Professor H. H. Stuckenschmidt, put it in his Busoni biography. Three pp's are called for – and the cello has trouble in maintaining the note.

It is now 1210 and Mehta wants to take the songs right through, warning the orchestra first that they must have the music in sequence and not to make a noise turning over between songs – and begs them not to ask him to be allowed to re-tune. Fischer-Dieskau starts the *Flohlied* – he crosses his arms right over left, and the drooping left hand twitches in time to the music. Now and then the whole body reacts to the words; he looks up at the ceiling – smiles at 'wenn einer sticht' (when we are stung), tapping his foot to the fast tempo.

He makes a mistake at the start of the second song and leaps to the score to check what he has done. A smile, and all is in order once again. Similarly the third song, *Schlechter Trost* is begun too loudly and he asks for a more *piano* start. At the first word 'Mitternachts' (At midnight), he looks actor-like up at the ceiling and clasps his hands. The fourth song *Zigeunerlieder*, with its persistent semi-quavers, is marked *allegro* and rattles along like a tongue-twister ('Im Nebelgeriesel, im tiefen Schnee' (In misty drizzle, in deep snow)). He conducts the orchestra again behind Mehta, his whole body in the song. Here, the orchestra is the true accompanist, following Fischer-Dieskau's remarkable sense of rhythm. When the rhythm slackens, he turns and sings to the orchestra to re-establish it. The last bars go well, as the cello has conquered the problem of keeping his bow on the instrument with plenty of tone.

At 1230 precisely, the last notes, *ppp*, die away and Mehta says: 'Fine. Thank you all'. The orchestra clap and tap their bows on their desks to Fischer-Dieskau. He leaps forward and embraces Mehta in a bear-hug, picks up his jacket and stretches out his hand to help his wife over the bar up on to the stage. The rehearsal is over.*

*Fischer-Dieskau had recorded these *Goethe-Lieder* with Jörg Demus for Deutsche Grammophon in May 1964.

CHAPTER FIVE

The *Lied*

A statistically-minded reader might have been able to confirm that Dietrich Fischer-Dieskau has sung well over seventy operatic rôles on stage, T.V., radio and on record – an impressive enough figure for anyone engaged on operatic work alone but phenomenal for an artist who is regarded by the majority of music lovers first and foremost as a specialist in works for solo voice, and especially when the singer himself has no doubt where his love lies – with the solo song. He reminds us too in his Schubert book that singers originally undertook concert work when they could no longer either appear credible in operatic rôles, or satisfactorily sing and act the more difficult parts. Such was the case, as we shall shortly see, with Johann Michael Vogl (1768–1840), the baritone singer who, above all, made Schubert's *Lieder* popular.

Peter Glossop, the Yorkshire baritone, revealed in a BBC interview in 1979 that, as he grew older, he felt that it would suit him to begin to undertake more concert work, since his voice – and his physical attributes – were no longer suited to the more virile Italian rôles, although he added that he thought he would be able to sing the German repertoire, which lies a good deal lower than the Italian. Fischer-Dieskau would certainly not disagree with Glossop, but he continually stresses both the pleasure – and the pain – of solo concert work. These are two sides of the one coin: the pleasure lies in 'being one's own programme director, producer and conductor – and soloist'; the pain lies in the enormous toll such an evening takes of one's physical and mental resources. As he summed it up to me once: there is more perspiration expended in opera – more personal involvement in a *Lieder* recital. He told me too that many opera-singers shrink from the awesome responsibility of facing an audience *solo* for two or three hours. When asked what a great solo singer needed, he answered: 'Outstanding musicality, personality and presence, stylistic certainty in the changeover from one composer to another during the evening, and – above all – the ability to concentrate; it is this which welds an audience, however huge, into an entity'. For Fischer-Dieskau, this is the goal for every singer of *Lieder*.

Although he had raised an interesting issue in his book on Schubert, viz. 'Should one perform *Winterreise* in public at all? Should one offer such an intimate diary of the human soul to an audience whose interests are so varied?', he himself has no qualms about singing *Lieder* to audiences of nearly three thousand people, (as in the Salzburg Festspielhaus, for example). Indeed he has often said that not only do such halls have better acoustics some-times, but the singer actually has closer contact with his audiences in large halls, because 'there is less chance of his being disturbed by noises and so on' – and there is also always more 'electricity' generated in a large audience! All who have heard this singer in a huge auditorium will agree that he never needs to force his tone because of his superlative voice-production and diction. The more I listen to his records, the more I am convinced that the charge made now and then that some of his louder notes 'blast' should be laid at the door of the recording engineers, for I cannot recall an instant of aural discomfort in a Fischer-Dieskau recital in a concert hall over all the years that I have been listening to him.

These sentiments are shared of course by all his accompanists – in particular, by the two 'senior' men, Gerald Moore and Jörg Demus. Gerald Moore has written frequently on his work with the singer in his many books, and in conversation and correspondence with him and Jörg Demus, one is able to sense the admiration and loyalty that these fine musicians have for Fischer-Dieskau. Gerald Moore is clearly most impressed with the singer's eternally fresh approach to the music that he sings. Although everything was carefully thought-out and well-rehearsed, it was *never* taken for granted. 'He is a marvellous combination of intellectual power and wonderful vocal technique, and, above all, he has a tremendous imagination. He is much more imaginative than any other singer I've ever played for', he added.

Jörg Demus would agree: 'Fischer-Dieskau is very precise. In rehearsals he makes known his most detailed wishes, but before the microphone he concentrates on the *total* effect'. If he had to single out Fischer-Dieskau's one greatest contribution to the development of the *Lied*-form – what would it be? 'That, probably for the first time, he has shown that it is possible to transmit the verbal contents of a song in their full breadth and depth and thereby fully serve the poet, while showing at the same time that, as Schumann said, the voice is the most wonderful musical instrument for realising all the inspirations and intuitions of the composer'.

As in his operatic work, Fischer-Dieskau has covered an astounding range of periods, styles and composers of solo vocal music. He is however rather pessimistic about the future of the *Lied*-form which, he feels, died with Hugo Wolf, and he is perhaps all the more pessimistic, since, despite all his own efforts, so few modern composers have written *Lieder*. One must write 'so few', for, as we shall see, a not inconsiderable number of leading musicians have in fact been inspired by the singer's great gifts to write songs for him. But why is the *Lied*-form dead or dying, I asked him? 'Largely because suitable poetical texts are no longer being written,' he replied. Goethe himself felt that his own enormous lyrical output might well have exhausted the German language's ability to create lyrical poetry. But music, too, has exhausted itself – and, despite the efforts of these few composers, there are not many twentieth-century *Lieder* to be found in concert programmes. Opera, on the other hand, is still alive, he feels, because it is a 'mixture' of the arts – it has life and strength and vitality and these will always appeal to audiences. Strangely enough, he felt that that 'life, strength and vitality' might still be found in so-called 'pop-music'. Many of these musicians are serious and talented artists who may yet 'win back the lost ground', the 'lost paradise of non-decadence', as he called it. But the regeneration of the *Lied*-form would depend above all on the production of music that is 'singable'. 'When music doesn't give me what is singable, then I go on strike', he added!

Fischer-Dieskau's contribution to a comprehensive understanding of the history of solo vocal music begins in an unlikely quarter:

with François Couperin. (There would have been a case for including this music in Chapter Two, of course). Wilfrid Mellers calls Couperin's three *Leçons de ténèbres* (1713–1715) 'one of the most impressive examples of linear organisation and harmonic resource in late baroque music', in his *François Couperin and the French Classical Tradition*. The composer specifically permitted the music to be transposed down a minor third for baritone which encouraged Fischer-Dieskau to make the first recording on L.P. of the *Première Leçon* ('Pour le mercredy') i.e. for Ash Wednesday. This extraordinary music, composed for the Latin text which is then punctuated by elaborately beautiful vocalisation on the Hebrew latters of the alphabet (Aleph, Beth, Chimel et al), speaks, of course, the same spiritual language as the music of J. S. Bach, yet is light-years away from the great Protestant's faith. Fischer-Dieskau was accompanied by Edith Picht-Axenfeld on harpsichord, and his wife Irmgard Poppen on cello, in the last recording made together before her death. The recording was made in fact in their own Berlin Academy of Music in February 1963.

It is therefore an all the more moving experience to listen to those grave, deeply-felt 'Lamentations of Jeremiah' with their beautiful melodies e.g. 'Plorans ploravit in nocte' (She (i.e. Judah) weepeth sore in the night) (I,2), and the baritone's remarkably fluent baroque ornamentations (particularly his full trills) and exemplary breath-control. This record, (backed by Scarlatti's *Infirmata vulnerata* and Telemann's *Die Hoffnung ist mein Leben*), was a distinguished contribution to eighteenth-century musical studies.

The baritone performed a similar pioneering service to a second composer better known in other fields, when, in November 1969, he and Jörg Demus recorded seventeen of Carl Philipp Emanuel Bach's odes, psalms and *Lieder* for DG's Archiv series. Emanuel Bach was a superb harpsichordist, (having been excused learning a stringed instrument because he was left-handed!), who occupies an important position in the history of the *Lied*, since he was one of the first to supply singers with music beyond the trifles for voice available hitherto. Although these works, simple in vocal line and accompaniment, were meant to be played and sung by one person 'at home', J. H. Füssli claimed that, after C. P. E. Bach, the *Lied* now had the quality 'eines wichtigen Gegenstandes', (of an important subject). Bach bequeathed nearly three hundred settings;

Fischer-Dieskau made a quite excellent selection which, when accompanied by Jörg Demus on his own 1793 *Tangentenflügel* (an instrument somewhere between the clavichord and the *Hammer-klavier*), proved to be of such extreme musicological, as well as of general musical interest, as to win one of the many *Grands Prix du Disque* that have been awarded over the years to the singer. (One suspects that only a Fischer-Dieskau would have been able to make such a record in 1969!)

A scholarly review in *Musica*, the German specialist periodical, granting Fischer-Dieskau's 'most detailed interpretation in which every nuance of the performance is persuasively presented and vocally perfectly shaped', felt that it was difficult to make a great work of art out of many of the mediocre songs. Nevertheless, I believe that the three strophes of *Morgengesang* would teach the student of the German *Lied* a great deal about the historical state of the genre *circa* 1750–1780 before the Schubertian revolution. Whether these songs 'penetrate to the heart', as C. P. E. Bach intended them to, is perhaps more doubtful.*

Our student of the German *Lied* would already have been directed to more famous predecessors of Schubert, of course; here too, Fischer-Dieskau has been of enormous service to the world of musical scholarship. How many singers had included the *Lieder* of Haydn, Mozart and Beethoven in their repertoires before the German baritone put them on record? Harry Plunket Greene's *Interpretation in Song* (1913) has no mention of Haydn or Mozart in the index and only one reference to Beethoven, while his suggested programmes cover that range of compositions which Fischer-Dieskau called 'Feld-, Wald- und Wiesenprogramme' (i.e. 'pot-pourri' programmes). He told me that he had had to fight to establish his type of programme. So, what did he want to intro-duce? It would be too pedantic to have an orchestral concert devoted to the works of one composer, he said, yet that might be ideal for a *Liederabend*. 'The arrangement of the poems', he added, 'should create a unity – the key-sequences must be so arranged that there is a natural connection between the songs. There must

*cf. 'This collection (and others by Bach) is a staging post on the high road of the German *Lied*': Percy M. Young: *The Bachs 1500–1850* (1970). Maurice Brown, the eminent Schubert scholar, disliked this 'evolutionary' theory as an explanation of the Schubertian 'revolution'. One wonders, however, if all composers are not children of their age in some respects.

be variety; a sequence of *adagio* songs would be both ridiculous and boring. It is difficult for the listener to a miniature art-form like the *Lied* to penetrate to the heart of the composer until he has heard quite a few of the *Lieder*. It is not as easy as, say, with the first movement of a symphony. Unfortunately, a *Lieder* audience generally needs to be given some time before it is really listening'. He felt, too, that Schubert's idea of filling an evening with a unified song-cycle *did* make the point about striving for unity in a programme, and Fischer-Dieskau's itineraries seem to have been planned with this concept in mind. When one looks at them carefully, one notes that, to take a few examples at random, 1968 was a 'Mahler year' – he sang eight Mahler concerts; 1970 saw him touring with Schubert's Goethe settings and in 1978 there were many *Winterreise* performances – all these, of course, in addition to many other musical commitments.

Apart from *The Sailor's Song*, sung at innumerable school concerts in Great Britain, the person not particularly interested in Haydn's *Lieder* would be hard put to it, I suspect, to name five songs by Haydn. Fischer-Dieskau recorded eighteen Haydn *Lieder* with Gerald Moore, eleven to German and seven to English texts, for Electrola in April 1959. Their critical reception was unfortunately affected in Britain by their being only one of half-a-dozen Fischer-Dieskau records that appeared in 1961; some reviewers wondered at the singer's 'Niagara-like productivity', but Philip Hope-Wallace felt 'immediate joy' when he heard the Haydn record. My own joy is rather muffled, I must admit, since I find the *Lieder*, like many of the eighteenth-century examples of the genre, rather static and unimaginative. Genius will always out however; Haydn's setting of Viola's *She never told her love* (from Act Two, Scene 4 of *Twelfth Night*), with Fischer-Dieskau's magical enunciation of 'smiling at grief' in the well-known phrase, 'she sat like patience on a monument *smiling at grief*', has long been one of my model passages to demonstrate his feeling for the nuances of our language. (Ex. 23). (The song also shows one interesting connection (although probably just a musical coincidence) between Haydn and Schubert – the uncanny resemblance between the postlude to Haydn's *She never told her love* and the introduction to Schubert's *Nacht und Träume*). Professor Jack Stein in his *Poem and Music in the German Lied* says that Haydn here 'tried to make

Ex. 23

like   pa - tience   on   a   mon - u - ment,   smil - ing,

smil   -   ing   at   grief,

something dramatic out of what is the essence of pure lyricism'. I
do not hear that in Haydn's song.

The beautiful *The Spirit's Song* also finds the singer at his incomparable best, negotiating that difficult 'a' sound in 'where my cold
*a*shes sleep'; he certainly makes the song what Rosemary Hughes
claimed it should be: 'the first Haydn song to achieve a true
integration of words and music' (*Haydn* 1950). These two songs are
clearly further 'staging posts' on the high road of *Lieder*.

On 14 February 1961, Fischer-Dieskau and his wife Irmgard
had joined forces with Aurèle Nicolet (flute), Helmut Heller
(violin) and Karl Engel (piano), to record a group of arrangements
of Scottish folk-songs, five by Haydn, six by Beethoven and five by
Weber. Haydn published a hundred of these in 1791, and a further
fifty in 1794 for William Napier the Scottish publisher, and
although, to a Scot, they smack more of Vienna than Edinburgh,
they are further proofs of Fischer-Dieskau's interest in Scotland
and things Scottish which goes back to his first appearance at the
Edinburgh Festival in 1952. Here the songs were all sung in German translation; only later, in March 1970, did Fischer-Dieskau
gladden our ears with the native Scots, when he recorded the
Beethoven settings (q.v.).

Like Haydn, Mozart found song-writing a pleasant *divertissement*,
in his case, he would compose them for his Masonic friends and
for publication in the ever-popular annual almanacs. In 1971, out
of Fischer-Dieskau's new collaboration with Daniel Barenboim,
(after Gerald Moore's retirement in 1967), came a fascinating
record of Mozart *Lieder* for Electrola. A genius in other musical
fields, Mozart failed to see the way ahead as Schubert was to do,
largely, perhaps, because of his lack of literary taste. As is evi-

denced in his letters, Mozart had a very ordinary, indeed, at times, a downright vulgar mind, 'with various defects and blind spots surprising in a genius', as Eric Blom put it in his introduction to *Mozart's Letters*, and it would seem that great poetry scarcely moved him, if indeed he ever read it at all. This is evidenced in some way by the choice of poets on this particular record. One looks in vain for the great names of the German literary revival of the 1770's; Mozart composed these songs between 1768 and 1791, but seemed to find his inspiration in anthologies of second-class poets rather than in the works of, say, Goethe. In addition, most of his songs are strophic, (that is, the same melody is employed for each verse, even where the mood has changed), and the pianist is often left, as he was too at times in Haydn's *Lieder*, to decorate where he desired. As Fischer-Dieskau said once: 'The Viennese wanted songs that any cab-driver could sing'!

For Fischer-Dieskau the musicologist, however, these *Lieder*, crumbs from Mozart's operatic feasts though they may be, have their fascinating place in the overall mosaic of the *Lied*. The recording was made in July 1971 in London, two days before Daniel Barenboim conducted the performance of Mozart's *Requiem* mentioned earlier.

Three *Lieder* merit special attention: *Das Veilchen* (K476, written on 8 June 1785) – and this *is* a setting of a Goethe poem – *Abendempfindung* (K523) by Campe and *An Chloe* (K524) by Jacobi, both written in June 1787. The rococo *Das Veilchen* is often regarded as the first 'through-composed' (*durchkomponiert*) *Lied*, since Mozart does follow the sense of the poem and paint a little *scena*, as it were. I lived for years with Elisabeth Schumann's haunting version of the song and never guessed that the heavier baritone voice could make so much of the tripping 'mit leichtem Schritt und munterm Sinn' as the shepherdess approaches. Although Fischer-Dieskau has definite views about 'male' and 'female' songs, it is certainly not inappropriate for him to sing this song, since the poem is a narration about a flower being picked by a young shepherdess and could therefore be told by a voice of either sex. Normally, however, this is a song which I prefer to hear in the soprano register.

In the other songs, Fischer-Dieskau's wonderful word-painting and in particular his *mezza voce* singing in *Abendempfindung* (at 'Schenk auch du ein Tränchen mir' (Shed a tear for me)), and

the long melisma on 'dann die schönste Perle sein' (it will be the
fairest pearl), turn these workaday songs into treasures. (Ex. 24).

Ex. 24

die   schön-ste,   die   schön   -   ste   Per - le__ sein

His vocal acting in *An Chloe*, where he has to imitate the over-
worked lover on the thrice-repeated word 'ermattet' (exhausted),
betrays the opera singer's knowledge of Mozart's profound
sensuality.

We have already discussed Beethoven's attitude to word-setting
in Chapter Two; he, like Haÿdn and Mozart, saw song-writing as
a pleasant pastime for a society dominated by instrumental music
– or the social opera. Only with the revolution of the Romantic
movement – the 'studying of the soul' – and then the growth of
Biedermeier home-comforts, did 'songs around the piano' become an
established custom. In addition, Goethe's well-known view that
simple direct verses were to have simple direct melodies greatly
influenced the age. As Goethe wrote in a review of Arnim and
Brentano's *Des Knaben Wunderhorn* (1806):

'. . . may this volume rest upon the piano of the musical amateur
or professional, so that the songs in it may either be done justice
to by familiar traditional melodies or matched to their own
individual tunes – or if God wills it – they may elicit notable
new melodies'.

In his *Marginal Notes to a Beethoven evening* (written in August 1965
to accompany his recordings with Jörg Demus), the singer deplores the lack of attention given to Beethoven's songs (apart from
An die ferne Geliebte); Beethoven's own words, 'Ich schreibe ungern
Lieder' (I do not like writing songs), are often held against him as
proof of a lack of interest in vocal music. But, unlike Haydn or
Mozart, Beethoven *could* be moved by great lyrical poetry.
Fischer-Dieskau cites Beethoven on Goethe: 'This language moves
and excites me to composition – it raises itself to a higher order as
if through spiritual awareness and already bears the secret of

harmony within itself', and, as we know, Beethoven had always planned to set Goethe's *Faust* to music. Indeed from 1800 to 1807, says Fischer-Dieskau, he was continually engaged on compositions or sketches for settings of Goethe's poems.

Interestingly enough, it was with Beethoven's *Lieder* that the singer made one of his first British tours, being accompanied by (now Sir) William Glock on 26 August 1953 in Dartington Hall in Totnes, and then on 3 September by Gerald Moore in the Free-masons' Hall at the Edinburgh Festival (He had recorded *An die ferne Geliebte*, Beethoven's self-styled *Liederkreis* (the first true 'Song Cycle') of 1816 in his very first recording session with Gerald Moore on 2–7 October 1951). He sang *An die ferne Geliebte* for the first time in Berlin-Dahlem accompanied by Hertha Klust on 11 December 1949, and it was this pianist who also accompanied him in his first substantial two-record set of Beethoven *Lieder* made for DG in November 1954. Then for the 200th anniversary of Bee-thoven's birth (1970), Deutsche Grammophon undertook the stu-pendous task of recording all the composer's works on seventy-six L. P. records, (the vocal works can be found on the last seven records), and these works were conveniently re-issued in 1977 for the 150th anniversary of his death. Fischer-Dieskau recorded forty-two *Lieder* plus *An die ferne Geliebte* with Jörg Demus in April 1966 which, first issued in February 1967 in Britain, then became part of the 1970 and 1977 celebrations.*

There is doubtless something of the missionary spirit in Fischer-Dieskau's work with Beethoven. He has restored many of the songs to the concert repertoire, and many contemporary artists now feel able to include a Beethoven set in their programmes. I marginally preferred the older recording of the *Lieder* (with Hertha Klust), particularly the beautiful performance of the six *Gellert-Lieder* on religious texts (op. 48), to the Demus set – but, on the other hand, I found Fischer-Dieskau's *An die ferne Geliebte*, with Demus, incomparably more moving and meaningfully sung than in the earlier (ex-78 r.p.m.) recording with Gerald Moore. Listen to that magical passage from 'Wenn das Dämmrungsrot dann

*The Beethoven settings 'in the native Scots' mentioned on p. 185 were recorded by Fischer-Dieskau, Edith Mathis, Julia Hamari and Alexander Young in March 1970. The foreign singers make a noble effort at the accents, but the music remains nearer the Prater than Princes Street!

ziehet . . .' (When sunset moves away . . .) with the *ritardando pianissimo* up to 'hinter jener Bergeshöh' ' (behind those hills) (Ex.
25) and one might agree with me that fifteen years' experience has
helped the singer to fine down his voice for the succeeding extraordinarily compressed phrase, the broad *adagio* 'und du singst' (and
you will sing . . .), than which there is nothing finer in Schubert,
I am certain. (Ex. 26) As Joseph Kerman points out in *Beethoven*

Ex. 25
Ex. 26

Studies (1974), the cycle should have a firm place, not only in the
history of the *Lied*, but in what J. W. N. Sullivan called Beethoven's
'spiritual development' – and not the least of Fischer-Dieskau's
services to this composer has been his making his contemporaries
aware of the central position of Beethoven's *Lieder* in his total
oeuvre. Lieder like *Adelaide* (1795), *Andenken* (1809), the wonderfully
sonorous *In questa tomba oscura* (1807) and the Goethe settings,
Mailied (1785–7), *Neue Liebe, neues Leben* (1809), *Mit einem gemalten
Band* (1810), and the Schubertian *Wonne der Wehmut* (1810), would
still grace any *Lieder* recital.

A word finally on another important Fischer-Dieskau contribution to musicology: In September 1972 he recorded for the DG
Archiv series a fascinating programme of settings of Goethe by
those contemporary composers (i.e. circa 1776–1832) of whom the
Master himself approved, above all his 'court musicians', Carl
Friedrich Zelter (1758–1832) and Johann Friedrich Reichardt
(1752–1814), who were, in a sense, the arbiters of Goethe's musical
tastes.
It goes without saying that Fischer-Dieskau shares the disappointment of all Schubertians that Goethe spurned the Viennese
composer's settings of his poems; this fine recording, on which the
singer is most sensitively accompanied by Jörg Demus on his own
Gröber *Hammerflügel* (an early piano of circa 1815–1825), proves,
alas, that Goethe was unwisely advised. For me, only Zelter's *Um*

Mitternacht, with its remarkably effective plunge at the close of each of the three stanzas, bears any sign of true invention. Although Goethe believed that 'poetry only became complete with the addition of music' (1809), and we know that he actually called his poems *Lieder* and that they were written to be sung, he nevertheless meant the poems only to be 'clothed' in music – a setting like Schubert's *Erlkönig* filled him with dismay. 'To paint tones by tones: to thunder, to crash, to splash, to smack is detestable', he said to Zelter (2 May 1820)! The music, Goethe was quite certain, was to play a 'servant's role' to the mistress, Poesy. But every true lover of the *Lied* was grateful to Fischer-Dieskau for allowing him to hear these forgotten songs and to make his own comparisons.

The August 1968 Munich Festival witnessed a remarkable tribute to Goethe, incidentally, when Fischer-Dieskau, accompanied by Jörg Demus, gave a concert of settings of Goethe's poems by various hands – the Duchess Anna Amalie of Sachsen-Weimar, Reichardt, Zelter, Schoeck, Reger, Busoni and Hugo Wolf; the two artists recorded a similar programme on 26–27 September 1972. In his scholarly programme-note, the singer paid tribute to the wide range of Goethe's own musical interests, from a four-part setting of Psalm XXX to a projected Part II of *Die Zauberflöte*.

*   *   *   *   *

On no other composer has Fischer-Dieskau lavished so much of his artistry than on Franz Schubert; no other composer occurs so frequently in his itineraries, to no other composer has he given so much thought, time and love. Gerald Moore's simple statement on the cover of my translation of Fischer-Dieskau's book on Schubert sums it all up: 'This book comes', he wrote, 'from the hand of the supreme Schubert interpreter of our time'. Fischer-Dieskau had paid Gerald Moore a similar handsome compliment in his foreword to the German edition of Gerald Moore's popular book *Am I too loud?* (1968): 'Gerald Moore is always an equal with his partner', he wrote, 'and I believe that many of them have had no little difficulty in rivalling him'. Together, over their fifteen years of partnership in concerts (and nearly twenty years in recordings), they set new standards for *Lieder* performances. Just as Gerald Moore wrote: 'This man Fischer-Dieskau has taken me deeper into the hearts of Schubert, Schumann, Wolf, Brahms than I have ever been before', so Fischer-Dieskau felt that this 'master of the art of *legato*-playing' made him 'an almost ideal partner in solving even the most complicated technical problems posed by Schubert' – 'and', he added, 'he is probably the only pianist to have played every Schubert *Lied*'!

Strangely enough, both artists believe that the secret of the other's art lies in his feeling for *rhythm*, 'the lifeblood of music', as Gerald Moore calls it. Perhaps because neither artist seems to have had any worries about technical difficulties is this so marked; to hear Gerald Moore play the fiendishly difficult introductory bars to *Der Lindenbaum* (No. 5 of *Winterreise*), or master those extraordinary right-hand octaves of *Erlkönig*, or Fischer-Dieskau sing the fine-spun *legato* lines of *Am Meer* (No. 12 of *Schwanengesang*), or *Im Abendrot* (D 799), or that frightening climb up to his high G at the end of *Du bist die Ruh* (D776), is to realise that these are not ordinary artists; they have superlative gifts which set them apart.

At the conclusion of his article on Schubert in Volume VII of the German encyclopaedia *Die Grossen der Weltgeschichte* (Great men of world history) (Kindler Verlag, Zürich, 1976), Fischer-Dieskau wrote that the composer 'had to be reckoned as one of the miracles of art, as a composer who wrote in a natural style'. It was perhaps this very idea of Schubert's 'naturalness' which caused some people to feel that Fischer-Dieskau put too much 'art' into some of his interpretations. They believed what their prophet, Richard Capell, had claimed, that Schubert was a 'child', and 'simple' to boot. 'His simplicity, which we shall have to call a German simplicity, could not have been tolerated in a sophisticated society', Capell wrote on page 3 of his *Schubert's Songs*. Modern research has refuted this too-naive view of a young man who, as we are now well aware, knew the pangs of poverty, of lost love, of disabling disease (syphilis) and family grief: 'Eine lustige Musik gibt es nicht' (There is no cheerful music), he wrote once, and a perfunctory acquaintance with the social and political problems of early nineteenth-century Vienna would have corrected Mr Capell's view. I yield to none in my admiration for his matchless romantic prose; I regret, however, his false picture of Schubert – of a childlike, instinctive composer wandering by the babbling brooks of the Vienna Woods, piping his lays like *Der Musensohn* (the Son of the Muses). This is an English classical scholar's Virgilian or Sidney-esque Arcadia,

'where shepherd boys pipe as tho' they would never grow old' –
but which never was – and never could be. Schubert's life was,
alas, more as Harry Goldschmidt saw it in his 1971 book on the
composer, 'a life bordered by reactionary provincialism which poisoned even a capital city; a life for friendship which appeared to
him to be the surest protection against society's oppressions; a life
marred by poverty, pain and sickness'. Although Goldschmidt's is
an East German, anti-bourgeois view, I believe it to be much
nearer the truth than the normal, sentimentalised picture of Vienna
prevalent in this country – and substantiated for many by Richard
Tauber's inter-war Viennese *Schmalz*. The saccharine picture of
Schubert given in Heinrich Berté's *Dreimäderlhaus* (1916) (which
Sigmund Romberg turned into *Blossom Time* (1921) for America,
and G. H. Clutsam into *Lilac Time* (1923) for Britain), would have
been greeted sardonically by Schubert's melancholic, liberal-
thinking friend, Johann Mayrhofer, smarting under Austrian cen-
sorship, and by the Schubert who wrote to Leopold Kupelwieser
on 31 March 1824:

> 'In a word, I feel that I am the unhappiest, most miserable
> person in the entire world. Imagine someone whose health will
> never improve and who in despair (over this) makes things
> worse instead of better, whose brightest hopes have come to
> nought, to whom the joy of love and friendship can offer nothing
> but pain at the most, who is in danger of losing his enthusiasm
> (at least the sort which inspires) for beauty, and ask yourself if
> that is not a miserable unhappy wretch? . . .'

Not for nothing, I believe, have some writers claimed that
Fischer-Dieskau has done for Schubert what Rubinstein did for
Chopin: freed him from *Schmalz*.

Whose debt is the greater? Fischer-Dieskau's to Schubert for the
wealth of beautiful music given him to sing? Or Schubert's to
Fischer-Dieskau for the services rendered to the composer over so
many years, not only by his singing of the well-known *Lieder* and
cycles, but also by the resurrection of so many beautiful *Lieder*,
forgotten, in some cases, since they were written over 150 years
ago? Until Fischer-Dieskau began his artistic career, I suppose
that Schubert's six hundred or so *Lieder* would have been represented in the vocal repertory by – how many – thirty? – forty? –

of the best-known songs. When I heard Elisabeth Schumann in Edinburgh in 1948 her 'Schubert group' was: *Geheimes, Ave Maria, Das Mädchen, Die Forelle*, a fairly typical selection for the female singer. By the mid-1970's, one could hear out-of-the-way Schubert *Lieder* such as the settings of Hölty's *An den Mond* (D 193, 1815), Kosegarten's *An die untergehende Sonne* (D 457, 1816), Mayrhofer's *Der entsühnte Orest* (D 699, 1820) and Scott's *Lied des gefangenen Jägers* (D 843, 1825) on successive BBC 3 radio programmes.

It seems to me that Fischer-Dieskau is in some little way a reincarnation, if that is not putting it too fancifully, of Johann Michael Vogl, who, after some hesitation, embraced Schubert's cause, and, by his advocacy, persuaded their contemporaries that the tiny Viennese assistant schoolmaster was a musical genius. Michael Vogl was a high baritone who was old (he was forty-nine when he met Schubert in 1817) and famous enough to allow himself the luxury of decorating many of the Schubert *Lieder*; those 'embellishments' caused headaches for Schubert's later editors, Eusebius Mandyczewski and Max Friedländer. But when Schubert accompanied him '. . . we appear at that time to be one, . . . something quite new and unheard-of for these people', Schubert wrote in 1825.

From 1952 to 1967, the *Grand Trio*, Schubert, Fischer-Dieskau and Moore delighted audiences in all the major musical capitals of the world. For Gerald Moore, the memories of his partnership with Fischer-Dieskau are among the sweetest of a long life dedicated to music. He remembers particularly well the pleasures of rehearsing with a singer who knew exactly what he wanted and who would never demand the impossible from his accompanist. Fischer-Dieskau disliked the 'patchwork-quilt' type of recording where the final version was made from eight or nine 'takes'; he preferred to go through the *Lied* two or three times and when he felt that the performance was right, he would say: 'I cannot do it better than that' – and leave it. He was able to do this because his preparation of the song had assured him of its possibilities. Each song, Gerald Moore recalled, would have a 'high point' to which the interpretation would be directed. He still marvels at the singer's ability to maintain the exact tempo, the exact nuances of diction agreed on in rehearsal. But, and this Gerald Moore insisted on firmly, this was no mere pedantry. As he wrote, 'I cannot think of one single song that Fischer-Dieskau sings where he would keep strict time throughout'. Fischer-Dieskau's search for 'perfection' is no ice-cold intellectual's disinterested 'search for truth'. His passions are involved all the time; at rehearsal, (although rarely on the concert platform), his hands and feet will beat time to the music and his expressive features tense and relax with the emotions conjured up and released. One can well imagine why Gerald Moore found some rehearsals more enjoyable than the concerts!

Watch, too, as Fischer-Dieskau prepares for his first song in a *Lieder* recital; he bows to the tumultuous reception, calms the audience, then almost springs round to his accompanist to indicate that he is ready. By the second song, a lift of the head suffices; the nervous tension has subsided. Fischer-Dieskau has spoken of the 'heilige Angst' (literally, the 'holy fear') that he experiences before a concert. 'Shall I come up to expectations?' he asks himself each time, as he prepares to renew what Wilhelm Furtwängler in his essay *The Artist and his Public*, called the 'love relationship' between musician and audience.

For Fischer-Dieskau has what every artist seeks: *charisma*. When I watch the audience, young and old, flock to the front of the hall to be near him after a recital and fight my way through the crowds to the artists' room, I wonder just where those people have been who think of him, as some still do, as 'Olympian', 'remote', 'reserved'. They have certainly not been with him in the artists' room as he sits and signs, courteously and with a smile, the many requests for his autograph.

Fischer-Dieskau would say, I know, that his 'professional' début as a *Lieder* singer took place in those American POW camps in Italy where he spent the years 1945–1947 and sang impromptu concerts standing on a packing case in the open air. From those days on, Fischer-Dieskau's dedication to Schubert is awe-inspiring. First came the series issued on six 78 r.p.m. records made in that famous spell (from 2 to 7 October 1951), in London with Gerald Moore: *Ständchen/Du bist die Ruh* (DB 21349); *Erlkönig*/Schumann's *Die beiden Grenadiere* (DB 21350); *Nacht und Träume*/Schumann's *Mondnacht* (DB 21517); *Am Meer/Der Doppelgänger* (DB 21586) (all 12-inch); then the two 10-inch records: *Das Fischermädchen/Die Stadt* (DA 2045); *Der Atlas/Ihr Bild* (DA 2049) and finally *Die schöne Müllerin* (DB 21388–95), and Beethoven's *An die ferne Geliebte* (DB 21347–48). Of the *Erlkönig* record, the EMI *Monthly Letter* for January 1952 wrote: '. . . we were impressed by a singer who clearly has a fine sense of style coupled with a keen regard for the significance of the words he is singing', while, in the November 1952 issue (on *Nacht und Träume/Mondnacht*), we read: 'This is a wonderful record. Fischer-Dieskau's phrasing is impeccable, his intonation beyond reproach. Time and time again we were struck by the astonishing, almost mathematical fidelity [with] which singer and pianist adhered to what Schubert and Schumann wrote'. That keen critique recognised at such an early date what was to make Fischer-Dieskau the greatest *Lieder* singer of his or any other day – fidelity to what the composer wrote, accomplished by a matchless technique. Many singers change what a composer wrote because they cannot sing it – or play it, as in the case of Schubert's right-hand triplets accompaniment to *Erlkönig*, which Schubert himself played as eight quavers to the bar, since it was too difficult!

The Schubert singer has little need of vocal histrionics. Fischer-Dieskau believes that Schubert demands a variety of types of 'voices': an Italian *bel canto* representing Rossini's influence on Schubert; the 'Singspiel' voice for those *Volkslied*-like songs, and, finally, the 'declamatory' voice, (as Vogl's really was), for the narrative ballads. The singer also suggests that there are four typical Schubertian rhythms: what he called the 'death-rhythm' for those peaceful extended songs (long-short-short) such as *Der Tod und das Mädchen*; the dancing 6/8 barcarolle (*Das Fischermädchen*); the 'wanderer's' rhythm, usually 4/8, written 2/4, and finally, the 'riding' rhythm as in the *scherzo* or finale of a quartet – perhaps as in *Die Post* or *Abschied*.

I have often wondered which Fischer-Dieskau Schubert records I would take with me to that mythical 'desert island'. I eventually chose five which I regard as among the most difficult and beautiful Schubert *Lieder* and of which Fischer-Dieskau has given, in my opinion, the most satisfying performances: *Du bist die Ruh* (D 776) (Rückert); *Über allen Gipfeln* (D 768) (Goethe); *Im Abendrot* (D 799) (Lappe); *Nacht und Träume* (D827) (Collin) and *Am Meer*

(D 957 No. 12) (Heine), and, with some good fortune, I might be able to conceal the cassettes of *Winterreise* and *Die schöne Müllerin* somewhere on my person!

My choices are all 'late' Schubert, (as the Deutsch numbers show),* and all in the *Todesrhythmus* ('death rhythm') mentioned above. I believe that it is here that Fischer-Dieskau's voice and interpretations are *hors concours*. In *Du bist die Ruh* the singer has to keep a perfect *legato* from the very first long phrase, 'Du bist die Ruh, der Friede mild'. (Ex. 27.) Then, as the singer writes in his

Ex. 27

book, 'the concluding refrain takes up the melody of the opening stanzas and reaches its ecstatic climax by climbing up a veritable ladder of chords'. Nor does he forget to mention that the composer specified a *diminuendo* on the difficult *erhellt* (illuminated), 'something often overlooked', the singer adds pointedly, 'because of the general difficulties of execution'. That climb in Rückert's oriental imagery on 'Dies Augenzelt/Von deinem Glanz/allein erhellt' (The tent of my eyes is illuminated only by your radiance), is, as the singer writes, 'a far more difficult and far more valuable vocal exercise than all those found in the text-books'. (Ex. 28.)

Ex. 28

I should choose that first 78 r.p.m. recording of the song from all the others that he has made; it seemed to me to have a youthful passion and a creaminess of tone not quite equalled anywhere else.

---

*These 'Deutsch numbers' are taken from *Schubert: Thematic Catalogue of all his works in chronological order* by Otto Erich Deutsch, the Austrian musicologist, who emigrated to Britain to work at the University of Cambridge. The catalogue was published in 1951; the German translation was published by Bärenreiter in 1978. Otto Erich Deutsch, who died in 1967, was Honorary President of the International Schubert Society, an office now occupied with distinction and pleasure by Fischer-Dieskau himself.

The fourteen bars of Goethe's *Wanderers Nachtlied* II (*Über allen Gipfeln*), like *Du bist die Ruh*, written in 1823, are also a frightening test of a singer's *legato* singing. Goethe had written the poem (on 6 September 1780) on the wall of a hut on the Kickelhahn, a mountain near Ilmenau in Thuringia; the poem describes a balmy summer evening where all is quiet, no birds sing and soon all will be at rest – but when the old poet returned to the Kickelhahn thirty-three years later, the rest was to be the peace of God. Schubert captured this atmosphere in his setting ten years later – and Fischer-Dieskau magically brings it to life in the twentieth century. In his book he regrets that he had been unable to make more use of the new Bärenreiter *Gesamtausgabe* (edited by Walther Dürr, Christa Landon and Arnold Feil) which incorporates some new readings. One interesting alternative, which Friedländer omitted, but which Mandyczewski gives in his *Gesamtausgabe*, is the turn on the reprise of 'balde' in 'balde ruhst du auch' (Soon you too will be at rest).

Fischer-Dieskau has normally followed Friedländer, but he sang the turn in his wonderful 1979 Salzburg recital with Jörg Demus. Perhaps I have become accustomed to hearing it omitted, but I now prefer it that way. Not many singers manage that long last phrase including the *dimuendo* on 'balde' and the *portamento* to the *Abgesang* (the afterstrain), 'ruhest du auch' in one breath. (Ex. 29.) Fischer-Dieskau brings this off to perfection, a test without parallel in singing, as famous in its own way as the six bars of *fioriture* on the second syllable of *tornar* in 'nunzio vogl'io tornar' in the tenor aria *Il mio tesoro* in *Don Giovanni* – so memorably sung, in a single breath, by John McCormack on DB 324 (GEMM 158).

Ex. 29

war - te nur,   war - te nur,   bal - de   ru - hest du auch

Lappe's *Im Abendrot* (1825); this must surely be one of the most deceptively simple-looking songs on paper; to sing it however with the unbroken *legato* and the interpretative depth that it demands, needs a truly great singer. This is one of Schubert's religious songs; the singer must both paint a picture of the setting sun and celebrate this purely naturalistic description in religious symbolism. Fischer-Dieskau leads us from his perfectly-pitched 'O wie schön ist deine Welt' (Oh how beautiful is Thy world), to the central passage of doubt, 'Könnt' ich klagen, könnt' ich zagen' (Could I complain, could I despair?), where the music temporarily and correctly becomes disturbed, before the doubts are resolved and the voice sinks back to the peace of 'Trinkt noch Glut und schlürft noch Licht' (Drinks in the glow and the light). This last phrase always poses a problem – the potentially ugly word 'schlürft'. The singer's enunciation of it, the softening of the opening 'sch-', is an object lesson.

I was surprised to note that John Steane did not include any of Fischer-Dieskau's versions of Collin's *Nacht und Träume* (1825) in his selections for comparison in *The Grand Tradition*. He states, in fact, that none of his six singers: Julia Culp, Emma Bettendorf, Karl Erb, Elisabeth Schumann, Irmgard Seefried and Gérard Souzay, do it justice – and I must say that I agree with him. Of all the great and difficult Schubert songs, this, above all, is mastered best by Fischer-Dieskau – in all his recordings, starting with that 1951 78 r.p.m. It is the song most famous for what Maurice Brown, the Schubert scholar, used to call 'the sudden swerve into new keys'. As Richard Capell wrote so memorably: 'A perfectly calm and steady flow of beautiful tone' is needed here; 'not a moment's agitation or constriction, nor a misshapen syllable, can be forgiven'. No Schubert song moves me more in performance than this one and I have seen tears flow when Fischer-Dieskau makes that effortlessly simple, but heartbreaking 'drop' or 'swerve' in the reprise of the phrase 'Die belauschen sie mit Lust' (They listen to them with joy). (The modulation from B major to G major became a Schubertian fingerprint). This modulation has to be sung without an increase in volume, I believe – and few singers achieve this. The effect, as Ernest Porter rightly says, is 'to express a tender ecstasy of feeling as the last note in one key becomes the mediant in the next', (in his interesting book *Schubert's Song Technique*). In a Fischer-Dieskau recital, as the singer looks upward while the piano murmurs the closing bars, I feel that most audiences would have an answer to John Steane's question: Has it (the song) ever been perfectly sung?

Lastly, Heine's *Am Meer* (1828) from the *Schwanengesang*, the 'cycle' which isn't one. The monotony of the C major melody must be compensated for by interpretative skill. For the interpreter, the song moves so slowly that any fault in a singer's technical equipment will be mercilessly exposed; first of all, in the long *mezza voce* introductory bars – then, with a key change, the singer has to recall the swelling seas and the rising mists before he sinks back to the heartache of the falling tears, 'Ich sah sie fallen auf deine Hand' (I saw them fall on your hand); Fischer-Dieskau memorably makes the open 'a' on 'fallen' express the lover's despair. Another outburst of passion as he describes his wasted hours since the girl left him, and then to the close, the vindictive 'Mich hat das unglücksel'ge Weib/Vergiftet mit ihren Tränen' (This unfortunate woman has poisoned me with her tears). (Ex. 30.) The turn within

Ex. 30

mich hat das un glücksel 'ge Weib.   ver - gif - tet mit ih - ren— Trä   - nen

'Tränen', which Fischer-Dieskau sings with heartbreaking agony, might *just* be construed as a touch of Heinesque irony on Schubert's part – that things are not really as desperate as they appear – but, in performance, as Richard Capell says: 'Nothing else, nothing, is like it'. Fischer-Dieskau's remarkable control of his great voice in this song, his complete comprehension of the dynamics needed to interpret these contrasting emotions – bliss in nature, unhappiness, sorrow, then despair – in this, one of the last of Schubert's songs, make him indeed 'the supreme Schubert interpreter of our time'.

Since he could naturally never have imagined that, one day, he would be able to record most of Schubert's *Lieder* for the male voice in one collection, Fischer-Dieskau started his first Schubert collection on an L.P record made in May 1955, and issued in Great Britain as ALP 1295. Over the next fifteen years, he was to record a series of selections of Schubert *Lieder*, (the song cycles excluded), accompanied variously by Gerald Moore, Jörg Demus or Karl Engel. As will now be well known, however, Fischer-Dieskau and Gerald Moore were invited by Deutsche Grammophon to undertake the mammoth task of recording some five hundred of Schubert's more than six hundred *Lieder* in three volumes of twenty-nine L.P. records, between December 1966 and March 1972.* Gerald Moore, who had 'technically' retired in 1967, remembers that these recording sessions in Berlin were occasions of great joy, although they must have been extraordinarily strenuous for a man of nearly seventy. Fischer-Dieskau recalls that he studied the *Gesamtausgaben* for a whole year – mainly Friedländer's, and, as far as he could, the new Bärenreiter. He felt that he had to leave out a few *Lieder* (Goethe's *Gott und die Bajadere*, for instance, which he felt was too 'bieder' (commonplace)), and those which he believed were more suited to the female voice. (Interestingly enough, his colleague, Gundula Janowitz, picked up his gauntlet and, in 1978, issued an excellent selection of the female songs on five records).

By recording sometimes for three months at a stretch, the first two volumes were completed in three and a half years. It would be too tedious to quote even a few of the extraordinary reviews of these recordings: suffice to say perhaps that, by February 1971, Volumes I and II had been honoured by the following awards: The Edison Prize – the Grand Prix National du Disque Belge – the Grand Prix International du Disque (Académie Charles Cros) – the Grand Prix des Discophiles – the Prix mondial du Disque Montreux – the Record Academy Prize, Tokyo – the Grand Prix du Disque (Académie française) and the Deutscher Schallplattenpreis, and others were to follow.

But it was in the United States, above all, that these records received their most enthusiastic welcome, for it must be remembered that there – even more than in Britain – Fischer-Dieskau is seen mainly as a *Lieder* singer, since he has never appeared in opera on an American operatic stage. The Americans have a rather different way of expressing critical approval from the more sober British, and, at times, make no distinction between their critical approval of a Fischer-Dieskau and of a Frank Sinatra. Why should they indeed? It was Mr Winthrop Sargent in the *New Yorker* of 30 January 1971 who summed it all up with my favourite American

---

*To accompany the enterprise, Fischer-Dieskau had written his book *Auf den Spuren der Schubert-Lieder* (1971); during 1974 and 1975 I had the pleasure of translating and editing this book which was published in Great Britain by Cassell as *Schubert: A biographical study of his songs* (1976) and in the U.S.A. by Alfred A. Knopf of New York as *Schubert's Songs: A biographical study* (1977). It is discussed in Chapter Six below. Deutsche Grammophon have since re-issued the set of records.

eulogy of Fischer-Dieskau: 'If you haven't heard Mr Fischer-
Dieskau, you haven't lived life to the full'! Bernard Jacobson in
the *Chicago Daily News* of 9/10 January 1971 and Martin Bernheimer in the *Los Angeles Times* subjected the Schubert volumes to
long criticisms; small cavillings apart, (mainly about the dreadful
English translations), Bernheimer found the singer 'at the peak of
his intellectual and musical powers' with Gerald Moore 'a Schubertian of equal authority', while Jacobson, (entitling his article
'Can he sing Schubert?'), found Fischer-Dieskau, at his best,
'which is to say in the large majority of the songs', the equal of
any of the great voices of the past, and Gerald Moore 'on the same
pinnacle of artistry and technique'. During his American tour that
year (1971), many critics felt able to comment on the freshness
with which he sang the Schubert songs. '. . . it is indeed a pleasure
just to watch him sing', wrote Robert C. Marsh in the *Chicago
Sun-Times* of 17 January 1971, 'since it is so plainly a free and
spontaneous act of recreative art . . .'

The singer and his accompanist received the highest accolade of
the record world when he was awarded the 1970 'Grammy' as the
'best vocal artist of 1970', at the 15th Annual Academy of Recording Arts and Sciences in Nashville, Tennessee in March 1971, for
the Schubert recordings. (He was to win a second 'Grammy' in
1972 for his recording of Brahms' *Die schöne Magelone* with Sviatoslav Richter).

Volume Three of the great enterprise, issued in 1973, contained
Die schöne Müllerin, (recorded in December 1971), *Winterreise*,
(recorded in August 1971), and *Schwanengesang*, (recorded in March
1972). Gerald Moore, among many others, has discussed these
masterpieces in full-length books.* Here, I should like to discuss
and document Fischer-Dieskau's various recordings. There are
three *Schöne Müllerin* performances on record: with Gerald Moore,
(made for Electrola on 2–7 October 1951), and again in December
1961 (the only one with the poet Wilhelm Müller's ironical prologue and epilogue, which reveal that the poetical cycle was, in
essence, part of an ironical intellectual charade); and thirdly, the
version mentioned above, in 1971.

The singer is naturally well aware of the ambivalent nature of

---

*cf. Gerald Moore: *The Schubert Song Cycles* (Hamish Hamilton, 1975).

the cycle, but is of the opinion that, since Schubert himself elected to take the verses at their face-value, (as seriously-intended sentiments), the singer should do so too. Alan P. Cottrell's scholarly analysis of the two great cycles, (*Wilhelm Müller's Lyrical Song Cycles*, 1970), reveals the true meaning of the first one, and Fischer-Dieskau would not now recommend the inclusion of the spoken verses. He also feels that this cycle (*Die schöne Müllerin*) is best sung in the original tenor keys, which is why he has not sung it in public for some time, not indeed since June 1973, with Karl Engel in Tel Aviv. As he writes, 'the brook murmurs all too frequently in the bass clef', and he believes that, if the songs are to be transposed at all, they should never go down by more than a minor third. It is important too to realise the interdependence of the twenty songs, both in textual and in key relationships. None were meant to be sung out of context, but were meant to form part of an evening's domestic music-making, such as we can see depicted in Moritz von Schwind's charming sepia drawing, 'Schubert-Abend bei Josef von Spaun' (1868), now to be seen in Vienna's Schubert Museum in Schubert's birthplace in Nussdorferstrasse 54, in the Ninth *Bezirk*.

Fischer-Dieskau has sung the cycle on countless occasions with various accompanists throughout the world since that first famous sold-out performance with Hertha Klust in Berlin's Titania Palast on 29 June 1949. Who could forget his magical enunciation of 'Es singen wohl die Nixen' (The water-nymphs are singing down below) in *Wohin?* (No. 2); his *mezza voce* in *Der Neugierige* (No. 6), particularly at the end of the reprise of 'Sag', Bächlein, liebt sie mich?' (Tell me, little brook, does she love me?); (Ex. 31.) the

Ex. 31

sag', Bäch - lein,_ liebt ___ sie mich?

ironical 'side-glance' in the voice, as it were, in *Tränenregen* (No. 10), when the girl gets up to go home as the rain threatens; the beautiful melismatic phrase in *Pause* (No. 12) on 'dass kein Klang auf Erden es in sich fasst' (that no sound on earth can contain it); the painstricken cry on 'grün, alles grün, so rings und

rund' (green, everything green all around), when the lover curses
the colour of the hunter's green coat in *Die liebe Farbe* (No. 16); the
suppressed passion in *Trockne Blumen* (No. 18), the melody of which
Schubert turned into a set of not very distinguished variations for
flute and piano (D 802), and then the final rocking lullaby to the
drowned lover, *Des Baches Wiegenlied* (No. 20), with its unearthly
conclusion 'Und der Himmel da oben, wie ist er so weit!' (And
how broad are the heavens above!). Here, more than anywhere
else in Schubert, can be found what the singer believes to be the
Austrian composer's outstanding characteristic: his *Weltfrömmig-
keit*, a sort of 'secular piety', quite unconfessional, and shot through
with scepticism.

I would not pretend that words alone could do justice to, or
explain the genius of this work or of its two great interpreters.
Gerald Moore rightly quotes Georges Braque: 'In art only one
thing counts: that which cannot be explained' – and there we
might leave this cycle.

Yet we leave it only to encounter another 'inexplicable' phenomenon – *Winterreise*. Among Schubert's last works – he was correcting the proofs of the final twelve songs on his deathbed in
November 1828 – this cycle of twenty-four searing songs can be
regarded as the summit of the *Lieder* composer's art. Benjamin
Britten ranked it, and the B Minor Mass of J. S. Bach, as the 'twin
peaks of Western culture'. Britten's own performances with Peter
Pears are unforgettable and much admired by Fischer-Dieskau,
who makes particular mention of them on page 267 of his book on
Schubert. Yet I feel that this cycle *does* demand the lower voice,
even although the first song *Gute Nacht* was first sung by a tenor,
Ludwig Tietze (or Titze), on 10 January 1828, and the original
version was written for the higher voice. One hundred years later,
Richard Tauber showed – in his Parlophone-Odeon recordings of
twelve of the *Winterreise* songs (RO 20037/42) – the great *Lieder*
singer that he might have remained.

These 'frightening' songs, which, Schubert told his friends, 'have
taken more out of me than was ever the case with other songs',
represent the greatest challenge to any solo singer. Fischer-Dieskau
can appear physically drained after a *Winterreise* performance where
the singer sings the twenty-four songs without a break in something
approaching eighty minutes.

'I first played *Winterreise* on the piano when I was fifteen'', the singer said to me, 'first of all thinking through and feeling the music. The journey is, of course, a series of sufferings and despairs, and therefore we can take it to be a gradual freezing of the emotions – that is certainly how Schubert understood it''. Fischer-Dieskau would not wish these songs to be transposed in such a way as to misinterpret the composer's intentions – these can be read from the key signatures of the successive songs.

Apart from the 1947 RIAS radio recordings and that first Zehlendorf appearance in 1943 (see p. 23), Fischer-Dieskau gave his first public performance of the cycle with Hans-Peter Olshausen in Siemensstadt outside Berlin on 7 December 1948. He has recorded the work five times: with Gerald Moore for Electrola/HMV in January 1955, in November 1962, and for the DG Collected Edition in August 1971; once with Jörg Demus for Deutsche Grammophon in May 1965, and his latest DG recording with Daniel Barenboim, made in January 1979.

In *Winterreise* more than in any other work, I think that I see that 'honesty' of Fischer-Dieskau's artistic intention in which he takes so much pride. Here, above all, he can be faithful to the composer, the poet and himself. This artistic honesty actually frightened Heinz Tietjen when he first heard the young Fischer-Dieskau sing *Lieder* back in 1948; this young 'beginner' seemed to be uncovering undreamt-of depths in these familiar songs.

Many critics would say that, in *Winterreise*, Fischer-Dieskau is in his natural element; sixteen of the songs are in minor keys, the atmosphere is predominantly sombre, the mood is of death. I have tried to show that much of the music that Fischer-Dieskau has had to sing is, of its nature, sombre. Few *Lieder* are humorous, at the most, some are 'merry'. Here there is neither, but instead an intensity which borders at times on the pathological, and which shows us the same Fischer-Dieskau in essence as we met in Berg's Wozzeck or in the mad King Lear. No mere 'singer' can perform the cycle – he, (and despite Elena Gerhardt's exciting 1907 records with Arthur Nikisch, I just cannot accept a woman in the rôle) – he must be able to portray this anguished man, the alienated, lonely, shadowy figure set against the unceasing lament of the inhospitable winter landscape. Thrasybulos Georgiades makes the vital distinction between these two cycles, it seems to me: the songs of *Die schöne Müllerin* can be taken as 'schöne Lieder' (lovely songs), he writes, directed to an audience; the *Winterreise Lieder*, both vocal and piano parts, are inextricably woven together and directed inwards, to the listener's heart. (cf. Georgiades in *Schubert: Musik und Lyrik*, 1967). Fischer-Dieskau put his finger on the genius of *Winterreise*, too, when he said once that 'the *Lied* is a situation, a snapshot of a state of mind, though with dramatic colorations; opera shows stages of a development' – and in *Winterreise*, the actor-singer must combine the two, I believe.

If in his first recording of 1955 Fischer-Dieskau seemed to make the man snap his fingers at cruel fate (in No. 23 *Mut*, for example), his later recordings show that *Winterreise* is not written for the young at heart. Although Schubert was only thirty when he wrote the songs in the year before his death, he seemed to me to be fulfilling that grim remark made by Hugo Wolf years later, that 'man lives only until his work is done'. The singer's later recordings, and particularly his singing of the last five songs, from *Der Wegweiser* to *Der Leiermann* spread a numbness, a chilling despair, impossible to describe. Gerald Moore, too, by common consent of his peers the incomparable accompanist, seems to find a more wintry tone than in his other recordings. As he plays these final bars, our mind's eye travels over snowy wastes, accompanying the crazed youth and his strange companion.

As Fischer-Dieskau himself writes: '*Der Leiermann* is not only the emotional nadir of the cycle – this song is the culmination of everything that Schubert ever wrote, for there is no escape from this agony . . . Life has little more to offer in these lines. The effect on the listener is paralysing'. There is an almost unbearable silence at the end of a Fischer-Dieskau/Gerald Moore *Winterreise* as the audience tears itself back to reality. Nowhere is there better proof that the *Lied* is a *Drama im kleinen* (a miniature drama) – and no contemporary singer has been able to transport us more easily than this great baritone.

In January 1979, Fischer-Dieskau allowed the TV cameras of *Sender Freies Berlin* to film his *Winterreise*, with Alfred Brendel at the piano, in the Siemens-Villa in Lankwitz near Berlin. The event was not a complete success, I felt, largely because, as so often with televised music, the camera would not 'stay put', but would insist on wandering, now to the singer, now to the pianist, missing the beginning of a song or the climax of an important passage. What *was* extremely interesting, however, was to note how much Fischer-Dieskau now acts each song with expressive facial gestures; closed eyes, a look upwards at *Die Krähe* (No. 15), a glassy stare at the numbing monotone on 'Einen Weiser seh' ich stehen' (I see a signpost) in *Der Wegweiser* (No. 20) (Ex. 32.), complete immobility as the piano whispers the closing notes. One realised once

Ex. 32

Ei- nen Wei- ser   seh' ich   ste - hen   un-ver - rückt vor mei-nem Blick,

again what an eternal challenge this masterpiece must be for a performer, and wondered if Richard Capell, (who died in 1954), would have rewritten his famous remarks on *Winterreise* had he heard Fischer-Dieskau first?

'The *Winterreise* as a whole awaits one (an interpreter). A fine voice is wanted to hold the attention for so long, but the most musical tone will pall here if it is not the servant of the imagination. The singer must have sympathy with the passionate temper. For the dry of heart, the 'Winterreise' might as well not exist'.

*(Schubert's Songs, 1928).**

It was in the late 1950's that Fischer-Dieskau's reputation as a *Lieder*-singer was made in North America and elsewhere outside Germany. Those of Central European descent, in particular, flocked to his concerts, and the reviews in German-language newspapers, such as *Aufbau* in New York, were in much the same tone

---

*It would be a pity to leave Fischer-Dieskau and Schubert without a mention of three DG recordings which have given a great deal of pleasure, I know; the domestic duets with Janet Baker, including that remarkable *Singübung* (D619), wordless, like Rachmaninov's beautiful *Vocalise* (op. 34/14), trios with Elly Ameling, Horst Laubenthal and Peter Schreier, and, finally, quartets with Elly Ameling, Janet Baker, Peter Schreier and Gerald Moore. If, as John Warrack suggested, the quartet was really too distinguished for such humble music, the recordings might have stimulated some less distinguished singers to try these charming trifles for themselves.

as those which appeared after his first concerts later in Israel. On 29 January 1971, *Aufbau* reported: 'The Carnegie Hall was like a church; one could have heard a pin drop, so devoutly did the congregation receive the High Priest of the Lied'. On 26 April 1972, the *San Francisco Chronicle* reported that he 'received one of the longest standing ovations in memory', (for his *Winterreise* with Norman Shetler). In Israel, in July 1971, the *Al-Hamischar* critic, Awner Bahat, suggested that Fischer-Dieskau was 'a unique miracle, a miracle that is repeated whenever the artist performs, for this perfection is in the highest degree an artistic one, and therefore, to a certain degree, a perpetual miracle', while, in a report about the not-too-successful 'Kulturwoche' (Cultural Week) of the Federal Republic of Germany in Israel later that same year, Fischer-Dieskau's ecstatic reception in the July was recalled in *Die Zeit* of 17 December as a contrast: 'The singer was drowned in flowers; one encore after another was demanded from an audience which hummed the *Lieder* with tear-filled eyes and openly expressed its sorrow and its disappointment that its patriotic love had been despoiled'. Nowhere had Fischer-Dieskau's rôle as a bridge between the 'good' Germany of nineteenth-century Romanticism, of Emil Staiger's 'heile Welt' (sane world), over the fearful chasm of Nazism to the *Lieder*-less post-war Federal Republic been more clearly demonstrated.

An Israeli writer, Peter Gradenwitz, summed up in the *Frankfurter Allgemeine Zeitung* on 21 July 1971 what a Fischer-Dieskau visit to countries with large, formerly German-speaking populations meant:

'For the older people who came from Central Europe, this was the building of a bridge; for the younger ones, the opening of a hardly-known world – for all, an unforgettable experience'.

After his Herculean endeavours on behalf of Franz Schubert up to, say, 1973, Fischer-Dieskau, now bereft of Gerald Moore, turned his attention more to the *Lieder* of Robert Schumann and to other accompanists, and now promises to do for the German composer what he has already done for the Austrian, that is, record most of his *circa* two hundred and fifty *Lieder*. He is at work at the moment on a book on the composer and has already lectured to the Berlin

Akademie der Künste on Schumann and his works. His short introduction, written in August 1969, to Jörg Demus' collection of
Schumann's Piano Works, (issued in Japan), gives us a clue to the
singer's own approach to this composer.

'To know Schumann requires, above all, a deep study of his
works for piano. Some of his most profound compositions were
begun at this instrument and the essential character of the remainder of his work can only be understood from it as well'. Again,
in his introductory essay on the *Lied* in his *Texte deutscher Lieder*,
Fischer-Dieskau writes of Schumann: 'Schumann's main characteristic is his receptivity to what is psychological and atmospheric
and the mirroring of these emotions by an alteration of the balance
towards the harmonics. Rhythm is relegated to a minor rôle . . .
The poem's internal logic yields pride of place to a more general
impression. This is particularly important in the case of Goethe'.

Schumann's enthusiastic embracing of Goethe, as well as of
Heinrich Heine and Joseph Freiherr von Eichendorff (1788–1857),
would seem to posit a literary taste superior to Schubert's. Yet the
doom-laden *Sprechgesang* in Schubert's unforgettable setting of *Der
Doppelgänger* (D 957, No. 13) of 1828, of which Fischer-Dieskau
gave such a heartrending performance in Volume Three of the
complete Schubert recordings, does give some inkling of the path
this genius would have followed, had he been spared. Fischer-
Dieskau is convinced that this song binds Schubert to the future,
and to Wagner for example, more closely than has yet been realised. Heine's peculiar irony, evinced in the 'sting in the tail' of
his poems, was, some claim, ignored by the 'naive' Schubert in his
late six Heine *Lieder* in *Schwanengesang* (i.e. Nos. 8–13). It is a
debatable point. I will always believe that the turn on the word
'Tiefe' in 'in seiner Tiefe ruht' (rests in its depths) of Schubert's
Das Fischermädchen (No. 10) *does* indicate Schubert's awareness of
Heine's intention, since it colours the otherwise 'naive' 6/8 setting.
Those who know of Heine's last terrible years in Paris, spent in
creeping paralysis on his 'mattress grave', watched over by his
faithful 'Mouche', the former prostitute Elise von Krienitz (Camille
Selden), might tend to see more genuine tragedy in Heine's seemingly off-hand writings. I for one believe that it was *always* present,
even in his early poems. There has been much scholarly debate on
the point: Eric Sams, in *The Songs of Robert Schumann*, is certain

that, for Schumann, the poetry always took second place to the piano; Stephen Walsh, in *The Lieder of Robert Schumann*, agreeing that, for many, Schumann is the most discriminating of the great *Lieder* composers, is of the opinion that he was really only the most orthodox. Fischer-Dieskau suggests too in his essay that Schumann's alteration of the second line of Julius Mosen's poem *Der Nussbaum* from 'blättrig die *Blätter* aus' to 'blättrig die *Äste* aus' (in op. 25, No. 3) is a sign of Schumann's 'literary sensitivity', since it avoids an unpleasant alliteration. On the other hand, the fact that Schumann made such a beautiful song out of a not very inspiring poem could be yet another sign of a genius. (It was, of course, Schumann who wrote to his friend Hermann Hirschbach in June 1839: 'All my life, I have thought vocal music inferior to instrumental and have never considered it to be a great art'!)

Such general considerations make it hardly surprising that a literary-orientated singer like Fischer-Dieskau should take a deep interest in Schumann from his earliest years as an artist. *Dichterliebe* (op. 48) (1840), to Heine's poems, appears on his programmes as early as 20 May 1948, and he has continued to sing what I noted above as one of his favourite programmes: Schubert's six Heine-*Lieder* paired with Schumann's *Dichterliebe*, one of my first experiences of his art, back in 1950 in Bonn.

Dichterliebe, one of the cycles of Schumann's 'year of song', 1840, written after his temporary estrangement from his beloved Clara Wieck, whom he eventually married in May 1840, has become his most celebrated vocal work. Although it may sound best in the brighter tenor register, the psychological depths do bear a Fischer-Dieskau-type interpretation. The cycle starts with the innocence of the strophic *Im wunderschönen Monat Mai* and the merry abandon of *Die Rose, die Lilie, die Taube, die Sonne*, then moves to the first traces of sorrow at the 'deceitful' close of No. 4, 'doch wenn du sprichst: ich liebe dich!' (Yet when you say: I love you) (which the girl doesn't!), 'so muss ich weinen bitterlich' (Then I must shed bitter tears), Fischer-Dieskau's wonderful *mezza voce* on 'ich liebe dich' in his latest DG recording with a new accompanist, Christoph Eschenbach, (born 1940), is a miracle, quite the most impressive of any of his recordings. (Ex. 33) But it is with the remarkable song *Ich grolle nicht* that a singer must come to terms with the 'psychology' of a Schumann setting. The poet tries to

Ex. 33

convince himself that the girl who left him, (and Heine himself was twice 'jilted'), is, in fact, miserable without him – but he bears her no grudge for abandoning him. The singer therefore has to present a gallimaufry of emotions: insouciance, hurt pride, jealousy, sorrow and, not least, grim satisfaction! The song rises to a splendid top A for tenor on 'die dir am *Herzen* frisst' (the serpent gnawing at your *heart-strings*), which Fischer-Dieskau, even in the latest version recorded in April and May 1976, soars up to *like* a young tenor! (Ex. 34) Eric Sams points out indeed that, in the

Ex. 34

sixteen songs of this cycle, the voice must cover two full octaves from that A on 'Herzen' to a bottom A in No. 14 *Allnächtlich im Traume* on 'Perlentränentröpfchen', while, in contrast to Schubert's modest range, the piano covers six octaves.* (It was interesting to hear Gerald Moore say, incidentally, that he had found Fischer-Dieskau able to range through nearly three octaves in rehearsal).

In many ways, Schumann's sensitivity to words makes Fischer-Dieskau his most natural interpreter. True, Schumann did write: 'The poem must wear the music as a garland or yield to it like a bride', but, in *Dichterliebe*, can the singer ever be *unaware* of the importance of the poem? In No. 11 *Ein Jüngling liebt ein*

*See Eric Sams: *The Songs* in *Robert Schumann: The Man and his Music* (1972).

Mädchen, the jaunty 2/4 tempo and the brightness of the *allegretto* tune has to be set against the realisation that the theme is Heine's own experience of being rejected, firstly by Amalie Heine (his cousin) in 1823, and then by her sister Therese. (The *Buch der Lieder*, from which most of the *Dichterliebe* songs were taken, appeared in 1827). As Fischer-Dieskau's voice hardens on 'Es ist eine alte Geschichte' (it's an old, old story), and he sings the last two lines depicting the broken heart, there is no doubt of *his* awareness of the text. (I have heard the song sung, however, with a 'vocal laugh'). His singing of these songs led the American critic, Bernard Jacobson, to remark, (anent a Fischer-Dieskau/Daniel Barenboim Heine recital in Chicago in 1973), that Schumann, not Schubert, was 'Fischer-Dieskau's composer', and that his 'gift for irony, for polished elegance' allied the singer clearly closely with Heine. (*Daily News*, 18 January 1973).

The mature Fischer-Dieskau has altered his approach to the cycle in two ways, I feel: the gentler, less bitter songs (e.g. Nos. 1–6) are 'sung through' more – the line is firmer, the tone lighter, whereas the later heart-rending songs are sung with the maturity of years of personal and vocal experience. One might expect no more, except that some have felt that Fischer-Dieskau has never changed his interpretations of some *Lieder* over the years. This is clearly just not true, and such people should compare, for example, Fischer-Dieskau's 1951 performance of Schumann's *Die beiden Grenadiere* with his later version with Eschenbach and note the tempi from the beginning of the *Marseillaise* motif. This would only be one example of many that could be cited.

I must confess that I treasure Fischer-Dieskau's early Schumann recordings. As we have seen, among his first were *Mondnacht* (from op. 39), which displayed his matchless *legato* singing from the very first words, 'Es war, als hätt' der Himmel die Erde still geküsst', (Ex. 35.) *Die Lotosblume* and *Du bist wie eine Blume* (from *Myrten*, op. 25), and Heine's exciting ballad *Die beiden Grenadiere* (op. 49 No. 1.) with that great voice trumpeting out the *Marseillaise* theme in the closing bars: 'So will ich liegen und horchen still' (So I'll lie there and listen in silence); all these were recorded with Gerald Moore on 2–7 October 1951. Then, on 16 September 1956, he recorded that first beautiful collection with Hertha Klust for Electrola (and the BBC). The record included the *Liederkreis* (opus 24)

Ex. 35

(Nos. 1–9) and a chilling *Belsatzar* (Heine's own spelling) (op. 57), where the vocal acting of the closing lines depicting Belshazzar's death ('Belsatzar ward aber in selbiger Nacht/von seinen Knechten umgebracht') (Belshazzar was murdered that same night by his servants), presaged Fischer-Dieskau's 'decade of opera'. That Stephen Walsh (op. cit.) can write that the voice-part 'leaves little impression on the memory', suggests that he has never heard a Fischer-Dieskau version!

That recording seemed to be almost a rehearsal for the German Schumann-tour which the baritone undertook in the next month, October, and for the Schumann cycles which he sang with that fine accompanist, Leo Taubman, in the subsequent tour, (21 October–7 November 1956), of Canada and the United States. (The first DG *Dichterliebe* with Jörg Demus was recorded in Vienna in February 1957 where the duo also included it in a memorable concert for the Schumann 150th anniversary in the Grosser Konzertsaal on 8 June 1960. I did not think too highly of that *Dichterliebe* recording – nor does Jörg Demus, as he told me – but the next DG version, of May 1965, is very fine indeed).

Those of us present at Fischer-Dieskau's Schumann concert, (with Wolfgang Sawallisch), at Covent Garden on 10 February 1980 marvelled with William Mann of *The Times* that, thanks to his pioneering, we can hear these 'unfamiliar but marvellous songs', even though 'the cause, admirable, of a larger Schumann repertory may bring lesser interpreters to despair, spurred as they will be by such champions'. Earlier in his career, the singer shed new light on *old* favourites, too. All lovers of *Lieder* would know Schumann's masterpieces, the opus 24 Heine *Liederkreis* (Nos. 1–9)

(1840), the twenty-six songs of opus 25, *Myrten*, (Schumann's wedding-gift to Clara), the moving settings of Justinus Kerner (*Liederreihe* opus 35, Nos. 1–12), and, before *Dichterliebe*, the Eichendorff *Liederkreis* (opus 39, Nos. 1–12).

The Kerner songs are, I believe, much undervalued. Fischer-Dieskau has indeed a particular love of this cycle, particularly of No. 6 *Auf das Trinkglas eines verstorbenen Freundes*, which he associated with his old friend, Walter Franck, who died in 1961. It was Franck who had persuaded Fischer-Dieskau in a holiday postcard, (signed 'Justinus Kerner'), to revive this long-neglected group of songs. In his moving *Abschiedsbrief* to his departed friend, Fischer-Dieskau quoted the last lines which he sings with such moving pathos: 'Leer steht das Glas! Der heil'ge Klang tönt nach/ in dem kristallnen Grunde' (The glass stands empty. The solemn notes ring round its crystal depths). (Ex. 36) The last two poems

Ex. 36

of this group, *Wer machte dich so krank?* and *Alte Laute* set to the same melody, gave us surely the quietest *pianissimos* ever recorded – on Fischer-Dieskau's first DG recording, made with Günther Weissenborn in January 1957? Eric Sams, unbelievably, finds the two songs 'maudlin' – although Clara Haskill, in a charming letter to the singer, remarked how pleased she was to find that he, too, found these *Lieder* closely related to Schumann's fine *Bunte Blätter*. For myself, Fischer-Dieskau's final 'Und aus dem Traum, dem bangen/weckt mich ein Engel nur' (And only an angel can wake me from this tortured dream) is one of his most unforgettable performances. I am almost moved to tears by that tiniest of breaths taken between 'mich' and 'ein Engel', so significant for the meaning of the poem. (Ex. 37)

Ex. 37

und aus dem Traum, dem ban - gen,___ weckt mich ein En - gel nur

Fischer-Dieskau's next 'enterprise', his complete Schumann recordings for Deutsche Grammophon, was undertaken with the brilliant young pianist Christoph Eschenbach, who first played for the singer in a concert on 24 September 1973 in Berlin. The baritone has often been asked why he has more than one accompanist: his answer is typical of his attitude to music generally. A fresh accompanist means a fresh approach, he will say; the new accompanist and the singer have to re-think familiar music, work together to form a new 'unity'. Each strikes sparks from the other. To date, the new duo has recorded three volumes of Schumann *Lieder*, the first group in January 1974, the second in April 1975 and a final group in April/May 1976. The records issued were an amalgam of these recordings.

Eric Sams remarked wittily in a review that Fischer-Dieskau's accompanists are like Fred Astaire's dancing-partners: 'Some were ideally matched, like Ginger Rogers; those of unusual stature obligingly modified it, like Cyd Charisse'. He no doubt meant that a concert pianist like Christoph Eschenbach has to adapt more than a 'professional' accompanist like Gerald Moore. Although there is no question but that these former are great artists, I find less 'inwardness' in these concert pianists' *pianissimo* passages and less awareness of the textual significance: take the songs mentioned above, for example, the last two songs of the Kerner cycle. I feel that Mr Eschenbach leans too heavily on the bridge-passage between the two songs and disturbs the almost spiritual atmosphere. Overall, however, the Fischer-Dieskau/Eschenbach collection is a most distinguished addition to the Schumann recorded repertory. As John Warrack said of Volume III: 'To listen through these three records is to marvel anew at the richness of Fischer-Dieskau's gifts'. (*The Gramophone*, September 1979).

Finally, a mention of these very domestic Schumann duets which the singer recorded, firstly, with Elisabeth Schwarzkopf at Gerald Moore's Farewell Concert on 20 February 1967, then with Janet

Baker and Daniel Barenboim as part of an issue titled simply *Duets*, and then with his wife, Julia Varady, and Christoph Eschenbach for DG in December 1977. The couple sang the duets with Wolfgang Sawallisch in Tokyo, during their 1979 tour of Japan, and again in New York in May 1980.

There is a rather strange appendix to Fischer-Dieskau and Schumann. He was persuaded to take part in a 'Concert of the Century' in aid of the Carnegie Hall Endowment Fund on 18 May 1976, when, just before a riotous appearance at the close with Yehudi Menuhin, Mstislav Rostropovich, Isaac Stern and Vladimir Horowitz in the *Hallelujah Chorus* from *Messiah* (and conducted by Leonard Bernstein!), Fischer-Dieskau and Horowitz gave a very strange account of *Dichterliebe*. On the subsequent recording (CBS 79200/2XS), neither artist seems to be in communion with his partner, the rhythms are pulled about and interpretation is at a minimum. Fischer-Dieskau told me that he had had to wait for four hours in a small room, with Rostropovich practising on his right and Horowitz on his left, and that he was nearly exhausted when he was finally called upon to sing! My faith in critics was sorely tried when one of them suggested afterwards that this was such an outstanding performance that it should be issued separately.

*   *   *   *   *

Like his contemporary Karl Marx, Johannes Brahms always appears to be one of the most forbidding, unyielding, and didactic figures of the nineteenth-century's intellectual hierarchy. In how many of our music colleges and schools do his heavily-bearded features scowl down on the students? I must admit that I often find myself reminding audiences that this daunting character actually started his career, a slim, fair-haired, blue-eyed youth, playing the piano in dubious cafés and bordellos on the Reeperbahn in Hamburg! That news seems to put them in a more receptive mood to listen to his music!

Schumann's last article *Neue Bahnen* (New Paths) in the publication which he had founded in 1834, *Neue Zeitschrift für Musik*, was on Brahms, predicting that the 'true apostle' would do great things in music, and, as is well known, Brahms befriended Clara Schumann, (how closely is still not certain), until her death in

1896. In his book *Abenteuer der Interpretation*, Jörg Demus relates that Pablo Casals was a close friend of Brahms' intimate colleague, Edward Speyer. When Casals asked Speyer if 'il y avait quelque chose' between Brahms and Clara, the old man answered, 'No, never', for Brahms' enormous respect for Robert Schumann excluded such thoughts! Fischer-Dieskau is sure that Clara influenced the music of neither composer.

As was made clear in Chapter Two, Fischer-Dieskau was early attracted to the music of Brahms, and we saw how closely he identified himself with the *German Requiem* (op. 45). It was however the *Vier ernste Gesänge* (op. 121) (1896), one of the composer's last works, which Fischer-Dieskau had first sung, aged twenty-two, at the University of Freiburg in 1947, and which has, as he puts it, 'a place of honour' in his repertoire.

He gave four performances of these 'serious songs' in that first 'public' year 1948, thrice accompanied by Ludwig Hoffmann and once, in Leipzig, by Karl Maria Zwister, and he was asked to sing them at his first Salzburg concert in the Mozarteum in August 1949, accompanied by Dr Ernst Reichert. The reader might recall that it was the Brahms' work which brought Fischer-Dieskau and Furtwängler together, too. Interestingly enough, Fischer-Dieskau chose the original version of these songs for his contribution to the Furtwängler 'Gedenkkonzert' (Memorial Concert) in the Titania Palast in Berlin on 9 December 1954, shortly after the conductor's death. Hertha Klust accompanied him, as she had done in his first commercial recording of the songs for DG in September 1949. Fine though that version is, I do not believe that it compares with his second version with Jörg Demus made in October 1958, (but not released until October 1961 in Britain when it was coupled with Dvořák's *Biblische Lieder* (q.v.)). The pianist told me that he believed this to be one of their best recordings in their twenty-eight years of partnership. I certainly agree. It was made at a time when reviewers were critical of concert pianists accompanying singers, but I prefer Demus' quiet assurance to any of the other versions available – even to Barenboim's more assertive performance in the 1972 recording mentioned below.

The songs, written towards the close of Brahms' life and obviously influenced by Clara Schumann's death, too, are not really religious, despite the religiosity of the texts. Brahms and Clara

hardly ever discussed religion nor the solace which their age believed it could bring. Yet the Lutheran-Jewish texts of the *Four
Songs* do breathe a compassion and a concern for humanity which
Fischer-Dieskau clearly found relevant in those grim post-war
years. Hans Gàl in his *Johannes Brahms* writes: 'What the preacher
says are inexorable facts; the music transfigures them into expres-
sions of abounding humanity; everything has become pure expression, flowing melody'. In 1979, Fischer-Dieskau said that he had
interpreted the songs in a more religious way in 1949, but that,
since they are really four symphonic movements, he interprets
them now in 'the Brahms' way', since Brahms was not a particularly religious man.

Brahms' music to the songs lies perfectly for Fischer-Dieskau's
great, grave voice; he whispers those frightening words 'und der
noch nicht ist, ist besser als alle beide' (but he who not yet is, is
better than both), (Ex. 38.) and yet is able to find the ringing tones
needed for those seven bars (such a gift to a powerful baritone
voice) at the end of the fourth song, 'Nun aber bleibet Glaube,
Hoffnung, Liebe, diese drei . . .' (But now remain faith, hope, love,
these three . . .) with the climaxes on the three nouns. (Ex. 39.)

Ex. 38

Although the singer has no difficulty with the three notes, I did feel that they were less opulent on the Barenboim DG record, (made in September 1972), than in the earlier performance, which I prefer on all counts.

1972–1973 were 'Brahms' years' for Fischer-Dieskau. After recording the *Requiem* with Daniel Barenboim in August 1972, he and Günther Weissenborn toured America in 1973 with a programme of Brahms' *Lieder* and included them in an unforgettable recital in Carnegie Hall on 23 January 1973, when the overflow audience had to be accommodated on the stage. Harold Schonberg (in the *New York Times*) found 'the highest level of artistry' from 'this complete interpreter' and his excellent accompanist. Their programme included many lesser known songs, but also the lovely *Ständchen* (op. 106 No. 1), and, of course, *Wie bist du, meine Königin*, (op. 32 No. 9), the first song that Fischer-Dieskau ever consciously 'studied'. *Ständchen* was included on a fine Electrola record, (accompanied by Karl Engel), of twenty Brahms' songs made in March 1957, and there followed a DG recital with Jörg Demus, (recorded in February 1958), which proved enormously popular in Great Britain. The *Feldeinsamkeit* (op. 86 No. 2) on this record is one of the singer's finest versions of one of Brahms' finest strophic songs. The baritone's tranquil evocation of a hot summer's day as the music spirals up to the sky on the lines 'und ziehe selig mit durch ew'ge Räume' (and drift with you through eternal spheres), with that magical turn within *Räume*, reminds us that the author of the poem, Hermann Allmers, took exception to Brahms' composition. One wonders how many people would have heard of him but for Brahms! (Ex. 40)

Ex. 40

und zie - he se - lig mit durch ew' - ge Räu - - me.

To the 'Grammy' that he had won in 1970, Fischer-Dieskau now added the 1972 award for his Electrola recording of *Die schöne Magelone* (opus 33, Nos. 1–15), set to poems by Ludwig Tieck

(1773–1853), in retrospect, a rather unusual winner of this illustrious recording 'Oscar'. (The singer's first recording of the cycle had been with Jörg Demus for DG at the end of April 1957 during one of his extended Brahms' periods when he used to narrate the Tieck poems as well as sing them). Prophetically, Eric Sams, (in the *Musical Times* in January 1972), had suggested that whoever had had the idea of bringing Fischer-Dieskau and Richter together to record this 'rather quaint old cycle' deserved a special award. Presumably the writer did not know that it was Benjamin Britten who had brought them together to perform the cycle in the Parish Church in Aldeburgh on 20 June 1965; they also performed it at the Menton Festival on 28 August 1969, while Brahms' enthusiasts in Britain are sure to remember the memorable performance with Gerald Moore in the Festival Hall in February 1965.

The love and care lavished on this recording could not make me believe that Tieck's mushy pseudo-medieval verses had been improved upon by Brahms. No. 9 *Ruhe, Süssliebchen*, will, of course, always remain one of my favourite Brahms' songs, (I remember Elisabeth Schumann just brushing the ascending notes on 'Schlafe, schlaf' ein' (Fall asleep)), but I do remain puzzled about the reasons for the award to this particular record. Not that it is not very fine. Far from it – but there were so many other outstanding examples of Fischer-Dieskau's art to choose from!

The work was recorded in Munich in July 1970 and performed again at the Mozarteum in Salzburg on 30 July; only two days later Fischer-Dieskau sang it yet again, this time with Jörg Demus, in the Residenztheater in Munich, a proof, surely, of his affection for the 'quaint old' cycle.

Fischer-Dieskau's view that Brahms' *Lieder* are characterised by, firstly, a strongly conservative belief that the strophic is the superior *Lied* form, and, secondly, the 'robust' nature of his accompaniments which forces the singer to think 'instrumentally', is reflected in his recording of forty-two of the many beautiful *Volkslieder* (1894) with Elisabeth Schwarzkopf and Gerald Moore for Electrola in August 1965. Not all of these are, of course, genuine folk-songs, but when one listens to the infectious duet *Jungfräulein, soll ich mit euch gehen* (Young girl, shall I walk along with you), with Gerald Moore's bubbling accompaniment to the female part, one scarcely worries about scholarly accuracy. Fischer-Dieskau was at his melodious best, I thought, in the exquisite *Nur ein Gesicht auf Erden lebt* (No. 19), but I prefer a female voice for the miraculous *Mein Mädel hat einen Rosenmund* (My girl has a rose-red mouth) (No. 25). It has always seemed to me that Brahms made a mistake in setting so obviously a 'female' melody to so obviously a 'male' poem. Listening to this selection, one is reminded that Brahms sent them to Clara Schumann as dedications of devotion, and they should always be sung as such – and never as scholarly antiquities.

It will surprise no one that Electrola decided to issue in February 1975 a fairly complete Fischer-Dieskau 'Brahms' collection' on seven records, the first of which, (accompanied by Gerald Moore), had been recorded as early as March 1964, four with Wolfgang Sawallisch, recorded in September 1970, in March 1971 and then again in August 1973, and two with Daniel Barenboim, recorded in March 1972. This collection, (minus *Die schöne Magelone*) comprises about one hundred and fifty Lieder, just about three-fifths of Brahms' total output. The reviews were enthusiastic, although a reading between the lines suggested that not many of the reviewers could imagine themselves spending many evenings by the central heating listening through the entire collection. Published as they were just before the celebrations for the singer's fiftieth birthday on 28 May 1975, they perhaps put a darker mantle round his fame than a Schubert collection, say, would have done. Brahms' poets were not among the nineteenth century's greatest, and I believe that his *Lieder* are not among Fischer-Dieskau's greatest personal favourites. It certainly takes Fischer-Dieskau's persuasive advocacy to make me enjoy some of the darker songs. The singer is interesting in his vigorous defence of Schubert's setting of Ludwig Hölty's *Die Mainacht* (D 194) in a seemingly unadventurous strophic form, compared to Brahms' more famous *da capo* setting (op. 43 No. 2) (here with Gerald Moore). Schubert's, he claims, is stylistically much nearer the form of the original poem. Brahms, who worshipped Schubert, (my 'love-affair', he called it), might not have disagreed. His friendship with the great baritone Julius Stockhausen (who was the first singer to present song-cycles on the concert platform, including the first complete performance of *Die schöne Müllerin* in Vienna in 1854, and *Die schöne Magelone*, which is dedicated to him), probably did more for the *Lied* than the majority of Brahms' own largely forgotten songs. These and the similarly largely forgotten *Lieder* of our next composer, Felix Mendelssohn-Bartholdy, will have been preserved for posterity by Fischer-Dieskau's albums.*

Mendelssohn's *Lieder* had rarely been heard in public before the singer recorded his two-record set with Wolfgang Sawallisch in September 1970 for Electrola in Berlin. Mendelssohn, who, of course, knew the great Goethe and was only nineteen when Schubert died, wrote seventy-five *Lieder* in all – and is probably remembered in Great Britain for one – *Auf Flügeln des Gesanges* (opus 34, No. 2), known to, and in, countless tea-shops as *On Wings of Song*! It was Fischer-Dieskau's sensitive rendering of this song which made me want to examine the Berlin composer's *Lieder* more closely. His singing of the last lines, 'und träumen seligen Traum' (and dream a blissful dream), without exaggerated *portamenti*, without sentimentalisation, restored greatness to a wonderful melody.

Amateur singers, (and professionals too, for that matter), looking for new material, could do worse than try out some of these resurrected treasures. Lenau's *Schilflied* (op. 71 No. 4), the very beautiful *Frühlingslied* (op. 19a, No. 1) by Ulrich von Lichtenstein, the *Erntelied* (op. 8 No. 4), where Fischer-Dieskau gives an almost Brahmsian interpretation to 'Es ist ein Schnitter, der heisst Tod' (There is a reaper, his name is Death), and the gentle refrain 'Hüte dich, schön's Blümlein' (Beware, sweet flower), are among the loveliest. The setting of Eichendorff's *Pagenlied* (op. posth.), with Sawallisch's ingratiating mandoline-like accompaniment, reminds us that Schumann admired Mendelssohn's music greatly – and the strophic simplicity of Klingemann's *Es lauschte das Laub* (op. 86. No. 1), that Mendelssohn was a pupil of Goethe's friend, Zelter!

Wolfgang Sawallisch was at this time busy preparing a new edition of Mendelssohn's symphonic works; he no doubt had Fischer-Dieskau's amazing pioneering efforts for the composer's *Lieder* in mind when he wrote me that it was due to Fischer-Dieskau alone that the art-form, the *Lied*, had found such a wide and enthusiastic circle of admirers since the war; that the singer was

*Four Brahms' duets were recorded for DG with the contralto Kerstin Meyer and Jörg Demus in May 1967; the same duets were included in the two recitals with Janet Baker and Daniel Barenboim given in the Festival Hall in London in August 1969.

still, after thirty years, its undisputed principal interpreter, (thanks
to his *disciplined* approach to his art), was one of the most fascinating aspects about singers in general. (It might not be known
that Sawallisch began his own musical career as a concert pianist).

Mendelssohn would be the first of a group of nineteenth-century
composers whose *Lieder* Fischer-Dieskau has made known to wider
circles; the names of Carl Loewe, Franz Liszt, Giacomo Meyerbeer
and Antonin Dvořák rarely figured on recital programmes until
the baritone recorded his choice of their *Lieder*. I became aware of
Loewe's talents as a song composer when I heard Fischer-
Dieskau's recording of *Tom der Reimer* (op. 135a), so beautiful that
my palms moistened as the young baritone sang 'Er küsste sie, sie
küsste ihn, ein Vogel sang im Eschenbaum' (He kissed her, she
kissed him, a bird sang in the ash tree), with such a wonderful
mezza voce. When that first volume of *Loewe Ballads* was issued by
Electrola in 1968, (recorded in September 1967, with Gerald
Moore), the reviewers waxed lyrical at the discovery of such unknown gems. Philip Hope-Wallace's review in *The Gramophone*
(August 1968) was typical; he, like me, seriously wondered if
Loewe's *Erlkönig* (op. 1 No. 3) (dated 1818; Schubert's was written in 1815), is not, in fact, superior to the Austrian composer's.
(Wagner, we know, certainly thought so!) Fischer-Dieskau's per-
formance is given 'the characterisation of a miniature opera', and
the piano part is actually more of a horse's gallop than Schubert's!
Fischer-Dieskau's record spurred other artists, I believe, (Theo
Adam and Elly Ameling, *inter alia*) to try Loewe out on their
respective publics – and the baritone himself followed the first
album with a *Lieder und Balladen Vol. I*, (but for DG), made in July
1968, accompanied by Jörg Demus, as was Volume II, made in
November 1969. Volume III followed in November 1979.

The fifteen Goethe settings, (in Volume II), included, again, at
least one masterpiece: the setting of Goethe's lines from *Faust*, Part
II, *Lynkeus der Türmer auf Fausts Sternwarte singend* (Lynceus, the
watchman, singing on Faust's observatory tower) (op. 9); the slow
bass progressions in the piano support an extraordinary upsurging
melody line – the singer needs a perfect *legato*, supported by
unimaginable resources of breath, to enable him to reach these low
and high notes, finally, from 'gesehen' to the succeeding miraculous
ornamentations of 'es sei, wie es wolle, es war doch so schön'

(whatever may come, it was *so* beautiful). Would that my inadequate prose could make the reader dash to listen to Fischer-Dieskau's remarkable performance of this remarkable song – and one other: The baritone's great voice has to be pared down to a nothing to sing the butterfly-like *Canzonette* (op. 79), a love song full of tenor-like *coloratura*. I play this song to recital-groups to demonstrate the flexibility of Fischer-Dieskau's voice – it compares well with that strange little Schubert *Lied Blondel zu Marien* (D 626), also full of quasi-Italian *fioriture*.

Writing in November 1970 about Carl Loewe, Fischer-Dieskau reminded us that the German composer at least managed to *speak* to Goethe – which is more than Schubert ever did – but as Goethe had no piano available at the time, Loewe was not able to play the Master his compositions. Later however, Goethe entrusted Loewe with the musical education of his grandson, Walter.

The Berlin composer, Giacomo Meyerbeer, was also brought to the *Lieder*-loving public's awareness, when Deutsche Grammophon issued in 1975 a Fischer-Dieskau record of his *Lieder* and *mélodies* in their Archiv Produktion. The singer had just returned, (at the end of October 1974), from an exhausting Japanese tour and was in the middle of preparations for the production of Hugo Wolf's *Der Corregidor* in Berlin.

The Meyerbeer *Lieder*, (made with Karl Engel in December 1974), a selection of the composer's sixty or so songs dating mainly from the 1830's, are clearly meant for amateur voice and accompaniment, and I cannot but think that the enterprise was, once again, a piece of pioneering, even missionary (although I know that he dislikes the word!), work on Fischer-Dieskau's part. He admitted as much in a note in 1975, when he said that hardly anyone knew of their existence, but that the charm of Meyerbeer's works, the moulding-together of three heterogeneous elements, Italian *bel canto*, Parisian salon-music and Schumann-inspired German *Lieder* was one worth succumbing to!

I believe that his voice is simply too good for most of these settings; one feels this most forcibly when he sings Meyerbeer's versions of well-known poems: Heine's *Hör' ich das Liedchen klingen*, with its simple strumming accompaniment, for example, or worse, his *Die Rose, die Lilie, die Taube, die Sonne* – comparisons with

Schumann's *Dichterliebe* settings are extremely odious. Fischer-Dieskau treats this poor song rather like an operatic aria with a *forte* top note on the beautifully gentle word *Wonne* in the first verse. I can find no trace of his having sung Meyerbeer songs in public.

The songs of Franz Liszt are, however, something completely different. Although Fischer-Dieskau has not yet recorded Liszt's rather quaint orchestral settings of Schubert's *Lieder* (e.g. *Erlkönig*), which Hermann Prey included in a recording in 1977, I am certain that a programme of Liszt's songs performed by artists of the class of a Fischer-Dieskau and a Jörg Demus would astound and delight those who know Liszt only as a heaven-storming symphonic or keyboard composer. For those who know and love these *Gesänge*, *Oh, quand je dors*, *Es muss ein Wunderbares sein*, *Ihr Glocken von Marling* and the three Petrarch sonnets could be included without hesitation in a mythical Top Fifty *Lieder*. Andrew Porter, reviewing the DG record made by Fischer-Dieskau and Demus in November 1961, sent it to the top of his Christmas present list, and, for years now, it has been one of my favourite Fischer-Dieskau records. I play to friends two passages to show Liszt's genius as a song-composer – and Fischer-Dieskau's as a *Lieder* singer! The first comes at the very end of the setting of Victor Hugo's poem *Oh, quand je dors* (1842), when the beloved is compared to Petrarch's Laura: 'Oh viens, comme à Pétrarque apparaissait Laura' – the baritone sings this soaring phrase in a way only approached in my opinion by Heddle Nash's wonderful old 78. (Ex. 41) It encompasses all that is unique to Fischer-Dieskau – beauty of tone, amazing breath control, astounding vocal technique. Then again, in the setting of Petrarch's sonnets (Liszt's

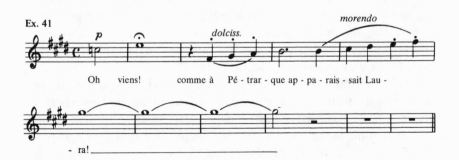

Ex. 41

first versions date from 1838–1839, and the melodies appear, of
course, also in the piano versions in *Années de pèlerinage* (in Nos. 4–
6, 1839)). My second example, my 'model' passage, is, curiously
enough, also about Laura – at the end of the second sonnet, where
the poet declares that he is in a state of unrest because of the
beloved – 'in questo stato son Donna, per Voi': Once again the
voice soars up on a thread of tone to the repetition on 'O Laura
per Voi'. (Ex. 42) Even in the transposition the effect is magical.

Ex. 42

O   Lau   ra   per   Voi

Andrew Porter wrote: 'Fischer-Dieskau breathes the phrase in a
blissful transfigured ecstasy that seems the very apotheosis of devoted love'. Liszt's songs had a great influence on many composers
– the celebrated 'Tristan chords' are always traced back to his *Ich
möchte hingehen* – and Fischer-Dieskau is keen to show other Wagner borrowings in his book on Wagner and Nietzsche. (This recording of Liszt's songs was made in November 1961, and the
sonnets reappeared in a later record (1974) of *Sonette von Francesco
Petrarca* along with settings by Reichardt, Pfitzner and Schubert.
The baritone made another selection of Liszt's *Lieder*, accompanied
by Daniel Barenboim, in November-December 1979).

In his book *Abenteuer der Interpretation* (1976), Jörg Demus wrote
of an experience that he had had with Fischer-Dieskau and a
performance of Dvořák's *Biblische Lieder* (opus 99) (1894).
Fischer-Dieskau had found the German translations that he was
to sing so clumsy, Demus said, that he sat down the evening before
the recording-session and rewrote the translation to suit the music:
'On the next day', wrote Demus, 'he sang the new texts without
error into the microphone – and he certainly had not rehearsed
them'. This selection (Nos. I, III, IV, VIII and X) was recorded
on 1 April 1960, and it was issued on the reverse of the Brahms'
Vier ernste Gesänge in October 1961.

Antonin Dvořák, the least literate of composers, set these texts
from the 1613 Czech Protestant Bible while in America in the
1890's under the influence, as Fischer-Dieskau wrote, of the deaths

of his mentor, Hans von Bülow (on 12 February 1894), and of his father. Fischer-Dieskau finds in these songs 'a surprisingly plastic form of declamation' and a 'fire and inspiration' which he found irresistible even although they lack Dvořák's friend Brahms' 'melancholic individuality'. The unaccompanied opening of No. 4. (Psalm 23) *Gott ist mein Hirte* (The Lord is my shepherd) is most impressive in Fischer-Dieskau's beautifully controlled *mezza voce*, while Dvořák's natural gaiety breaks through in No. 10 (Psalm 98) *Singet ein neues Lied* (O, sing unto the Lord a new song) which has an infectious dancing melody. Fischer-Dieskau makes impressive propaganda indeed for these simple songs, which bear comparison with Dvořák's equally melodious and, in my opinion, vastly underrated *Zigeunerlieder* (op. 55) (1880). One wondered indeed with an American critic, after one of the Brahms' recitals in New York, whether these Dvořák *Lieder* might not make an interesting contrast to Brahms in a recital?

*   *   *   *   *

The 'Golden Age of *Lieder*' which began with Franz Schubert and the first 'true' *Lied*, *Gretchen am Spinnrade* (D118), written on 19 October 1814, came to an end with Hugo Wolf and Richard Strauss. The argument as to whether Schubert or Wolf is the 'greater' *Lied* composer, could be answered, I suppose, in Goethe's words when he was asked whether he or Schiller had contributed more to the development of German literature: 'They should be glad that there were two like us for them to argue about!' Fischer-Dieskau, writing in 1977, thought that, where Wolf set the same poems as Schubert (for example, the Goethe poems *Prometheus, Ganymed, Grenzen der Menschheit*), he had felt sure that he could emulate the earlier composer because he possessed musical means, (largely obtained from his idol, Wagner), not available to Schubert. This would enable him to present the *true* Goethe, 'warts and all'. The singer compares Schubert composing 'as if in his sleep', based on a long secure tradition, with Wolf struggling to the point of suicide with the uncertainties of his own era – but successfully, so that the *music* is an immeasurably greater inheritance than the *poetry* of his contemporaries. The baritone is clearly attracted by, and to, both composers, and attempts to evaluate the 'other side' of their personalities: thus he will not accept that Schubert was just the naive peasant-boy, so takes pains to present the darker side of his genius, and he will not accept, on the other hand, that Wolf was just the neurotic manic-depressive. He enjoys singing Wolf's lighter songs, (as in the Mörike *Lieder*). Nevertheless, a careful reading of Fischer-Dieskau's book on Schubert will reveal hardly a complimentary word about Wolf, but a good deal of implied criticism of his (over)-psychological settings. For Wolf, Gluck, Mozart and Wagner were the holy trinity, 'a holy trinity', he wrote, 'that only in Beethoven becomes one'. By Wolf's day, the Romantic Movement had lost its innocence – and it was as an innocent that he saw Schubert, which may be why he tried so hard to write songs so complicated in harmony, rhythm and changing tonalities. 'Was he perhaps impelled towards the 'characteristic' song by the riches of the Schubertian heritage?' asks Frank Walker in *Hugo Wolf* (op. cit.) I am sure that he was, and this is why he was a composer who *knew* that he was not writing for 'die breite Masse', for mass consumption.

Wolf has been in Fischer-Dieskau's repertoire since his earliest years; indeed, the very first entry in his 'musical diary', for 18 and 25 April and 2 May 1948, is of a selection from the *Italienisches Liederbuch*, a *RIAS* broadcast with Marie-Louise Mansfeld and Walter Welsch, and he sang Wolf's *Lieder* in six separate recitals that year. Deutsche Grammophon recorded seven songs from the *Italienisches Liederbuch* (with Hertha Klust) in April 1950 and January 1951, and when he came on his first visit to Great Britain in June 1951 to sing in *A Mass of Life* under Sir Thomas Beecham, the BBC invited him to record the *Goethe-Lieder* with Ernest Lush, on 8 June. His first concert in the Mozartsaal in Vienna with Jörg Demus featured *Die schöne Müllerin* (on 25 February 1952), but that was followed on the 28th by selections from the *Spanisches* and the *Italienisches Liederbuch*. He and Gerald Moore recorded some Goethe, Eichendorff and Mörike *Lieder* for Electrola in London on 14 October 1952, and I heard Fischer-Dieskau and Irmgard Seefried, with Gerald Moore, sing the *Italienisches Liederbuch* in the Freemasons' Hall during the Edinburgh Festival on 9 September 1953.

Great Britain's introduction to Fischer-Dieskau on record in Wolf was the Electrola record accompanied by Gerald Moore, issued here in 1953. British reviewers, still largely unaware of the new phenomenon, carefully compared the voice with their pre-war favourites, Friedrich Schorr and Heinrich Schlusnus. There was a feeling, too, that a way had not yet been found to do complete justice to his recorded voice. Few however failed to remark on the singer's extraordinary ability to make a familiar old song new.

In a later chapter, I shall discuss Fischer-Dieskau's general development as a vocal artist in more detail; it might be of interest here to look at three of his recordings of one collection, principally, I must admit, because it is my own favourite Wolf group: the *Lieder* set to texts by the south German clergyman Eduard Mörike (1804–1875), who, apart from his poems, published in 1855 a most fascinating account of his hero Mozart's 'journey to Prague' with his 'difficult' wife Konstanze to attend the première of what Mörike called *Don Juan (Don Giovanni)* in 1787. Mörike, who, himself highly musical, disliked Beethoven, found Schubert's *Erlkönig* wanting, and was revolted by Wagner's vulgarity, wrote of the 'pure gold of the art of a Gluck, Handel and Mozart'. His poems are among the most widely-studied of the nineteenth-century German authors in British universities.

The fifty-three settings of *Mörike-Lieder* were Wolf's first great musical outpouring; they were written in two remarkable creative bursts, forty-three between 16 February (*Der Tambour*) and 18 May 1888 (twenty in March alone!), the final ten between 4 October (*An den Schlaf*) and 26 November (*Auf eine Christblume II*). Fischer-Dieskau recorded forty of these (the 'male' songs) for Electrola with Gerald Moore in September 1957 in Berlin. These were the first extensive recordings of Wolf-*Lieder* since those of Walter Legge's pre-war Hugo Wolf Society-recordings by Elena Gerhardt, Elisabeth Schumann, Friedrich Schorr, Helge Roswaenge, Gerhard Hüsch, Herbert Janssen and Alexander Kipnis – treasures indeed! The Fischer-Dieskau/Moore box was an instant success. His singing of the extremes, from the quiet religious devotion of *Auf ein altes Bild* or *Schlafendes Jesuskind* to the outrageous comic vocal acting of *Warnung* (with his famous alcoholic's croak!) or *Abschied* where the obnoxious critic is unceremoniously booted downstairs to an intoxicating Viennese waltz, was captivating. Gerald Moore's *echt* Viennese *Kunstpause* in the piano postlude to *Abschied* has never been emulated in my opinion, and indeed

distinguishes these performances from the baritone's other recordings of the *Lieder*. After Moore's retirement in 1967 and the swim-
ming of the *Wunderkind* Daniel Barenboim into the Fischer-Dieskau
ken, Deutsche Grammophon engaged them for a complete Wolf
set which they began in Berlin in December 1972 with the Lenau,
Heine and Mörike *Lieder* I and II, continued in Paris in June 1973
with more Mörike, the Eichendorff, Goethe and Michaelangelo
Lieder, concluding these in January and February 1974. There were
further recordings in Berlin (*Goethe Lieder*) in October and November 1974, and, finally, some more Eichendorff and Michelangelo
settings in Berlin in November 1976 – another mammoth under-
taking, and further proof of Fischer-Dieskau's unique devotion to
the art of the *Lied* in our century! (DG issued Volume I (Mörike
Lieder) in Britain in December 1974, Volume II in November 1976
and Volume III in August 1977. Fischer-Dieskau's third Mörike
recording was from a 'live' performance in the Stadtsaal,
Innsbruck, accompanied by Sviatoslav Richter in October 1973.
The singer did not seem to me to be well recorded).

All these recordings bear witness to the singer's deep love of,
and commitment to these songs which I too believe are Wolf's
greatest. I believe too that Wolf's genius and inspiration, (unlike
Schubert's), flagged somewhat and that the post-Mörike *Lieder*
lost a little of that early freshness.

Walter Legge had mooted the possibility of issuing a 'complete
Wolf' for the anniversary year 1960, but, since nothing came of it,
it is not surprising that Fischer-Dieskau has gone his own way and
supplied us with his own 'complete' Wolf. Although he has to
transpose some of the *Lieder* and concedes that Wolf had been in
principle against transpositions, he reminded me that Hugo Faisst,
Wolf's close friend and an amateur bass-baritone, had begged the
composer to allow at least a few to be sung by the lower voice.

Fischer-Dieskau's unwillingness to sing any of the 'female' songs
gave rise (in April 1971) to an interesting discussion in the columns
of *The Gramophone* when a Swiss reader suggested that the art of
Lieder singing lay in *interpretation* and not in *impersonation*, and went
on to cite Elena Gerhardt's singing of *Winterreise* and Michael
Vogl's reported singing of Schubert's *Ellens Gesänge*. I must say
that if, as with Fischer-Dieskau, the *Lied* becomes a miniature
drama where the words are as important as the music, it is difficult

to accept a woman singing what is quite clearly a male rôle – and vice-versa. Where the singer either does not know the language of the song well and is only concerned with making a 'beautiful sound', it is clearly not as important. There are certain words and phrases in all languages which are not 'unisex' however, and these are sung at the singer's peril!

The overwhelming impression gained from a comparison of these three *Mörike-Lieder* performances is how little the voice has changed over twenty years. Obviously, a little bloom has disappeared from the tone; one or two top notes (cf. at the end of *Storchenbotschaft* on the Richter record) are less opulent, but listen to the smooth *legato* of *Verborgenheit* which follows! Eric Sams was one of those who expressed slight surprise that the *interpretations* had not changed in that time – but would he listen to the three versions of *Abschied*, for example, again? He will find innumerable differences in detail: with Gerald Moore, Fischer-Dieskau sings 'ich tat ihm leuchten' (I lit his way) through clenched teeth; with Richter, only 'leuchten' is sung like this, and with Barenboim he achieves the effect wanted by colouring his tone only. With both Richter and Barenboim, he begins the song at a much faster tempo, and all three versions have a different emphasis on the final 'Gerumpel' – and I have heard other differences on many occasions in concert. There is, of course, a basic interpretation which a singer of Fischer-Dieskau's vast experience and learning has come to adopt over these many years. His answer to that other charge – that he sings 'too perfectly' – covers the first one as well: 'I've never felt this' (that he sings too perfectly), he said, 'You can never do the same thing exactly the same twice running. That is why interpreters who can improvise and who have imagination have the best careers on the concert platform. Those with fixed model interpretations are doomed – you can only succeed when you experience the music at that instant, out of the mutual relationship with your audience' – and he could have added, 'with your partner', since Gerald Moore has said just this about Fischer-Dieskau on many occasions. Fischer-Dieskau went on to pour scorn on the idea that the gramophone record sets 'golden immutable standards'. 'A record is a snapshot, the confession of a moment which can not be taken as an eternally valid interpretation'. Which is why a great interpretative artist, like a great playwright, (such as

Bertolt Brecht), is continually renewing his acquaintance with the masterpieces of his art. Brecht, for example, called his early plays *Versuche* (Experiments) and they exist in several versions, like Fischer-Dieskau's Wolf, Schubert and Schumann performances. An interpretation, particularly a musical one, must perforce change with the years – the artist, a human being, has changed.

Fischer-Dieskau's involvement with Hugo Wolf has been second only to that with Schubert. He recorded sixteen of Wolf's last song book, the forty-six *Lieder* of the *Italienisches Liederbuch* (1890–1896) for the first time for DG with Hertha Klust as early as 1950–1951, the first seven recorded in April 1950, the others in January 1951. His most popular performance, with Irmgard Seefried and Erik Werba, was heard at the Brussels Expo. and at Salzburg in 1958, and it was then recorded for DG for the Wolf Centenary Year in 1960 (Fischer-Dieskau's contribution was actually made with Jörg Demus in October 1958). He then joined with the most distinguished female Wolf singer of the day, Elisabeth Schwarzkopf, to record the songs for Electrola in January and February 1966, accompanied by Gerald Moore. Although I am always bowled over by the sheer beauty both of her person and her voice in the concert hall, Miss Schwarzkopf's vocal mannerisms have always rather detracted from my complete enjoyment of her art on record. So here too. Fischer-Dieskau did not seem to me to be quite at his best here either. His pianissimo on 'von purem Golde' in *Und willst du deinen Liebsten sterben sehen* was indeed 'pure gold', but he seemed to be forcing some of the bigger climaxes, as on 'Willst du nicht Liebe, nimm Verachtung hin' in *Hoffärtig seid Ihr, schönes Kind*. His latest recording of the *Italienisches Liederbuch* (with Christa Ludwig and Daniel Barenboim), made for DG in 1979, has a masterly *Geselle, woll'n wir uns in Kutten hüllen*. Frank Walker's description of this song as a 'scene out of Boccaccio's *Decameron*' seemed to match perfectly Fischer-Dieskau's interpretation and to give Mr Walker the 'artist of the calibre of a Chaliapin' that he demanded. Nor would one wish to overlook the magic of the Fischer-Dieskau *mezza voce* at the *pianissimo* passage 'Er schuf die Schönheit und dein Angesicht' (He created beauty and your face) in *Gesegnet sei, durch den die Welt entstund*. (Ex. 43)

The forty-four songs of the *Spanisches Liederbuch* (1889–1890), translations by Emanuel Geibel and Paul Heyse of sixteenth- and

Ex. 43

er schuf die Schön-heit und dein An - ge - sicht.

seventeenth-century Spanish poems, seem to have attracted Fischer-Dieskau's attention rather less. *Herr, was trägt der Boden hier* and *Nun wandre, Maria* were both beautifully sung on a single record of twenty-three songs which he recorded for Electrola with Gerald Moore in May 1958, before recording the complete Book with Elisabeth Schwarzkopf and Gerald Moore for DG in December 1966, a recording which Alec Robertson in *The Gramophone* needed a 'cornucopia of adjectives' to praise worthily enough. For myself, I find these songs rather less appealing than those of the *Italian Book*, even although I appreciate that they represent an important phase in Wolf's development, his attempt, as Frank Walker put it, 'to attain that Nietzschean Mediterranean spirit' as a counter to Wagner's oppressive influence.

The Electrola recording of the *Goethe Lieder* (1888–1889) with Gerald Moore, (nine recorded in October 1952 and the others in April 1960), remains a touchstone of quality for these *Lieder*.* Gerald Moore was in particularly fine form for these recordings of songs which, as Fischer-Dieskau always points out, seem to lie stylistically miles away from the *Mörike Lieder*, yet are separated by one year only. Wolf tried hard to avoid those poems which had already been set by other composers, and by Schubert in particular, unless, as was the case with *Prometheus, Ganymed* and *Grenzen der Menschheit*, he felt that Schubert had simply not understood the poem. As Frank Walker put it, Wolf's setting of those poems was a criticism *and* a challenge. Even Fischer-Dieskau finds that overwhelming climax of *Prometheus* a strain, for it is *the* song above all which demands (and indeed found) an orchestral accompaniment and, in so doing, it heralded the end of the nineteenth-century

---

*The reader will find John Steane's *Essays in Comparison* at the end of his book *The Grand Tradition* fascinating material. *Anakreons Grab*, in versions by McCormack, Janssen, Lehmann, Schumann, Schwarzkopf and Fischer-Dieskau, is discussed. Fischer-Dieskau carries off the palm: 'Out of the song itself, he and his accompanist have made something Wordsworthian', Steane writes (page 608).

tradition of 'Solostimme mit Klavierbegleitung', (solo voice with piano accompaniment). As Fischer-Dieskau rightly says, Eduard Mörike was possibly the last lyric poet whose verses deserved a musical setting, and it was fitting that he should have found a genius like Hugo Wolf to gild them – and, we might add, an interpretative genius like Dietrich Fischer-Dieskau to recreate them for our times.

I do not think that it would be unfair to say that Fischer-Dieskau finds the *Lieder* of Richard Strauss an anti-climax to what has gone before, and that he might even agree with Ernest Newman's rather severe judgement passed in his book on Strauss that 'one very small volume might well contain all the *Lieder* of Strauss that are worth living with day-by-day'. Fischer-Dieskau is severe, too, on the composer's choice of poets, and critical of the sentimentality of many of Strauss' two hundred or so songs. Strauss was not particularly enamoured of the male voice and composed most of his songs with a female voice in mind (particularly – from 1888 on – that of his fiancée, then his wife, Pauline de Ahna) – and certainly sopranos have cause to be grateful to Strauss for some beautiful *Lieder*.

The composer's love-affair with *Lieder* served as 'an outlet for his urge to compose for the voice', Norman del Mar reminds us, since the failure of his first opera *Guntram* (1891) had made Strauss *persona non grata* in opera houses. In six years, he composed fifty-nine songs, many of which e.g. *Freundliche Vision* (op. 48 No. 1), *Traum durch die Dämmerung* (op. 29 No. 1) *Ständchen* (op. 17 No. 2), *Morgen* (op. 27 No. 4) and *Ruhe, meine Seele* (op. 27 No. 1) now rank as classics of the genre. Writing on Strauss in 1964, Fischer-Dieskau said of the *Lieder*: 'However often I sing them, and however much pleasure I have from interpreting them – *ratio* and *sensus* should be held in balance in the *Lied* or else one begins to have doubts. There *are* some successful songs, but they are in the minority. Strauss was not really looking for success in this field – although they would have proved him to be a total musician'.

Fischer-Dieskau performs Strauss *Lieder* on the concert platform mainly in programmes of 'turn-of-the-century' music, as he calls his programmes; he had a favourite programme of *Lieder* by

Strauss, Pfitzner and Mahler which he gave regularly in the late 1950's and early sixties. His first Strauss record for Electrola with Gerald Moore, recorded in January 1956, and re-issued for the Strauss Centenary celebrations in 1964, evoked great praise. It contained sixteen 'favourite' Strauss songs, those of 'motionless ecstasy' like *Traum durch die Dämmerung* (composed in twenty minutes, we are told!) and *Morgen*, as well as wonderful examples of Fischer-Dieskau's matchless *legato* singing, such as *Die Nacht* (op. 10 No. 3), with its wonderfully spun *pianissimo* on 'sie stehle/ dich mir auch' (It (the night) will steal you from me too), and, above all, *Ruhe, meine Seele*. His *Ständchen* was inevitably compared with Elisabeth Schumann's radiant version of 1927 (found, *inter alia*, on HMV/COLH 154), where the soprano conjures magic out of the top A on '*hoch* glühen von den Wonneschauern der Nacht'. The lower voice has not got this radiance, of course, but I for one believe that Fischer-Dieskau made much more of phrases like the whispered 'dass nichts sich regt' (that nothing stirs) or 'nur die Liebe ist wach' (only love is awake) – and *he* has Gerald Moore, of course! I felt incidentally that the recording engineers of this Strauss record, and the next selection made in September 1967, had brought the microphones too close to the singer for comfort – misjudging, not for the first time, the extraordinary sonority of Fischer-Dieskau's voice.

Fischer-Dieskau's love of 'something fresh', something new, has led him to espouse the cause of a Strauss work which might never have found a popular following. The work is a treasure for the literary person with an allusive mind, since its enjoyment depends largely on a knowledge of German literary history – and of puns. It was typical of Fischer-Dieskau that he should make two full recordings of this 'cycle' – *Krämerspiegel* (op. 66) (1918) (literally 'Shopkeeper's mirror') – one with Jörg Demus for DG in March 1964, and one for Electrola in November 1969 and May 1970 with Gerald Moore, which was included in the six-record set of 135 Strauss *Lieder* issued in Britain in January 1972.

This cycle, the result of a feud between the composer and the Berlin publishing house, Bote und Bock, can only be sung, I believe, by an artist of 'literary leanings'. He has to understand fully the allusions, puns and witty satire of Alfred Kerr's indifferent verses to interpret the work satisfactorily. Indeed, I have often claimed that this work could serve as a touchstone of interpretative gifts, and it was interesting that Gerald Moore should choose the cycle for a lecture in the Festival Hall in London on 13 April 1976, illustrated by this recording. (Fischer-Dieskau has said that he believes the cycle to be Strauss' most effective work for the piano).

The work abounds in musical references to Strauss' earlier compositions (*Der Rosenkavalier* and *Don Quixote*, for instance), and to works by other famous composers (e.g. Beethoven's Fifth Symphony), and is a severe test for any singer, with its plethora of frightening high notes. In No. 4 for example *Drei Masken sah ich am Himmel stehen* (I saw Three Masks in the sky), a pun on the name of the music firm Drei-Masken-Verlag as well as a parody on the Schubert *Lied, Drei Sonnen sah ich am Himmel stehn* (No. 23, *Die Nebensonnen* from *Winterreise*), Fischer-Dieskau takes the remarkable top B flat on 'O Schreck . . . dahinter sieht man Herrn Friedemann' (O horror, there is Mr Friedemann behind them), full voice *fortissimo* with no suspicion of a *falsetto*, and, as Gerald Moore rightly said in the lecture mentioned above, 'in a way that would make many a tenor jealous'!

The Berlin firm continues to find the work offensive and finds support among those musicians who dislike Strauss' failure to rebuff Nazi approaches in the 1930's – but it is to Fischer-Dieskau's credit that he has rescued what Norman del Mar, in Volume III of his great work on the composer, called 'one of the most extraordinary works in the whole field of song', for modern listeners. Fischer-Dieskau sings the cycle only rarely in public, the last occasion being during the Strauss Festival in Munich in October 1978.

His fine DG recording sessions of the cycle with Jörg Demus included also a performance of *Enoch Arden* (op. 38); although the singer acknowledges that Strauss did make a few technical advances – in the songs dedicated to his mother, for instance (*Blindenklage* and *Im Spätboot*, op. 56 Nos. 2 and 3), with their difficult plunges down to low notes – he has said that the Bavarian's major contribution to the *Lied* form was to rescue it from the 'Spasslosigkeit' (lack of 'fun') which had perhaps militated against the international acceptance of the genre!

The baritone found himself excellently qualified to profit from the growing interest in the 1960's in the music of Anton Bruckner, and especially of Gustav Mahler. In an essay on Mahler, written in October 1967, Fischer-Dieskau recalls how it was only after the Second World War that Mahler's music became truly accepted, how up till then 'the neo-classicists, anti-Semites, those against "expression" of any kind' would have been able to relate Mahler's major theme, 'Man's loneliness', to the composer's own position in the world of music. Fischer-Dieskau accepted that the ignorance of Mahler's own music probably arose from his fame as a conductor and as Director of the Vienna State Opera from 1897 to 1907, and he believed that many of the difficulties for singers in Mahler's music can be traced back to Mahler's operatic experiences. It was Mahler's music, of course, that had brought the young singer into close contact with Wilhelm Furtwängler, who told him after their performance of the four *Lieder eines fahrenden Gesellen* (recorded for CETRA) in August 1951 in Salzburg, that the singer had 'converted' him from the 'reserve' that he had hitherto felt towards Mahler's music. Perhaps it was Mahler's unashamed expression of sorrow, of almost neurotic grief, that had initially repelled the older man? (Furtwängler was born in 1886). At any rate, I am certain myself that it was precisely that quality which attracted post-1945 audiences to the symphonies, and, after concerts by artists like Kathleen Ferrier, Elisabeth Schwarzkopf and Dietrich Fischer-Dieskau, to the *Lieder*.

Kathleen Ferrier's now legendary performance of *Das Lied von der Erde* with Bruno Walter at that first sun-lit Edinburgh Festival in 1947 had certainly fostered interest in the Austrian composer; it was in 1952, the year in which Fischer-Dieskau had recorded the Mahler *Lieder eines fahrenden Gesellen* with Furtwängler for Electrola (in the June), that the composer begins to feature in the baritone's programme-diary. Since then, he has recorded *Das Lied von der Erde* twice, once for Electrola with Murray Dickie under Paul Kletzki and the Philharmonia Orchestra in October 1959, and for Decca, with James King and the Vienna Philharmonic Orchestra, conducted by Leonard Bernstein, in April 1966. He also much enjoys singing the five Rückert *Lieder* (1901–1904), particularly that great trio *Um Mitternacht, Ich atmet' einen linden Duft* and *Ich bin der Welt abhanden gekommen* (I am lost to the world), that last title being suggested by Fischer-Dieskau to be an echo of

Mahler's own despairing cry: 'There's nothing left to compose'. Fischer-Dieskau's singing of those aching lines 'Ich leb' allein in meinem Himmel, in meinem Lieben, in meinem Lied' in the version with piano accompaniment by Daniel Barenboim, made in February 1978, seems particularly to underline that thought. (Ex. 44)

Ex. 44

One cannot deny that Fischer-Dieskau seems to have doubts about the modern 'popularisation' of Mahler's work; in October 1967, he wrote that it was no coincidence that Leonard Bernstein was a distinguished Mahler-interpreter, finding the American's outgoing genial personality a blend of those contrasting qualities which mark Mahler for him too. The singer remembers receiving on a flight to the United States a prospectus which bore a symbolical design incorporating the Empire State Building, the Statue of Liberty, the United Nations' Building – and Bernstein conducting! 'That gives the musical blue-stocking and the esoteric experimentalist something to think about', he joked. Bernstein and he did, in fact, give a Mahler evening in the Philharmonic Hall in New York on 8 November 1968. The Rückert *Lieder* (with the piano accompaniments) were excerpted from this concert and issued by CBS as *Lieder und Gesänge aus der Jugendzeit* (with others) in April 1972. Eric Salzmann in *Stereo Review* thought that the songs 'took some getting into'. I feel that they are much more impressive in the orchestral versions – as in the singer's first recording for DG with the Berlin Philharmonic Orchestra under Karl Böhm made in June 1963. As Roger Fiske wrote in August 1964, this was 'a record to treasure'. (Nevertheless, the record with Bernstein gained the 1972 *Académie du Disque Lyrique* award). For many people, the thrilling trumpet finale in *Um Mitternacht* goes for nothing in the piano version, and the *frisson* from Fischer-Dieskau's great climax on 'Herr über Tod und Leben/Du hältst die Wacht/um Mitternacht' (Lord over death and life, you keep watch at midnight) is not quite as strong. (Ex. 45.)

However, no one could deny the magnificence of the versions made with Daniel Barenboim. Here, the Fischer-Dieskau voice is as supple as ever with an extraordinary use of that wonderful *mezza voce* in No. 7 of the *Lieder und Gesänge aus der Jugendzeit, Ich ging mit Lust durch einen grünen Wald* (I walked joyfully through a green forest), for example, while the Rückert *Lieder* receive a heartfelt performance.

The recording with Karl Böhm mentioned above also contained a superlative rendering of the *Kindertotenlieder* (1905), settings of those strangely depressing poems, by Rückert again. Rückert (1788–1866) was a Romantic poet much affected by the fatalism and the quietism of oriental poetry. When Mahler lost his elder daughter (as Philip Barford in his *Mahler: Symphony and Song Cycles* reminds us), the composer admitted that he had set these poems 'in an agony of fear lest this should happen'. Friedrich Weidemann, the baritone from the Vienna State Opera, gave the first performance of the songs on 29 January 1905, so, fine though the performances of Janet Baker and Christa Ludwig are, I just cannot believe that they make textual sense – particularly in the third song *Wenn dein Mütterlein tritt zur Tür herein* (When your mother comes in at the door), where the *husband* is clearly watching the grief-stricken mother as she seeks the missing daughter. The wonderful *pianissimo* end to the last song 'Von keinem Sturme erschrecket/von Gottes Hand bedecket' (Protected by God's hand, they need fear no storm) is sung by Fischer-Dieskau with Schubertian tones, re-

minding us that Mahler's fated characters inhabit the same alienated world as did Schubert's grief-stricken journeyman in
Winterreise. (Ex. 46.) (I thought that Rudolf Kempe's accompanying of Fischer-Dieskau in the singer's very first recording for Electrola, also with the Berlin Philharmonic Orchestra in June 1955,
was even more poignant).

Ex. 46

von   kei - nem Sturme er - schrek - ket, von Got - tes Hand be - dek - ket,

Mahler's 'Winterreise' would certainly be his *Lieder eines fahrenden
Gesellen* (1883–1885); the baritone's famous first recording with
Furtwängler, made just after their recording of Wagner's *Tristan
und Isolde* with Flagstad in June 1952, proved, I think, that this
cycle really did have to be sung by a man – it was first performed,
Donald Mitchell writes in his *Gustav Mahler: The Wunderhorn Years*,
by the Dutch bass Anton Sistermans, on 16 March 1896; it also
proved that the English title 'Songs of a Wayfarer', a title handed
down over the years, was not, as I have already suggested elsewhere, an accurate one. The *Geselle* is really a 'journeyman', setting
out on his seven years' travel to master his trade, and, as he plods
away 'übers Feld', broken-hearted, he too, like Schubert's lad, will
find a *Lindenbaum* as the symbol of lost hope. As Fischer-Dieskau
wrote in his Schubert book, 'only the most wilful critic' would deny
the inner relationship of this cycle to *Winterreise.* (pp 298–299)

Fischer-Dieskau sang Mahler's own folk-song-like verses with
the same artistic conviction that he had lavished on Wilhelm
Müller's equally simple and equally moving poems; one catches
one's breath at that wonderful musical moment where the harp
arpeggios lead into the Schubert-like melody of 'Auf der Strasse
steht ein Lindenbaum' (A linden-tree stands by the wayside),
(Ex. 47) and again at the conclusion, where the singer hardly sings,
rather breathes, the quasi-comforting words 'Welt und Traum'
(world and dream), promising 'eternal rest'. I recall Fischer-
Dieskau's 1974 Edinburgh Festival performance with Daniel Barenboim and the London Philharmonic Orchestra, where his voice
almost vanished in tears at these last words as did Kathleen Fer-

Ex. 47

Auf der Stra - sse steht ein— Lin - den - baum, da—

hab ich zum er - sten Mal im Schlaf ge - ruht!

rier's at 'ewig, ewig', the closing words of *Das Lied von der Erde*, in 1947.

Since that first Salzburg performance in 1951, Fischer-Dieskau has sung the *Gesellen-Lieder* with, seemingly, every famous conductor in the world: with Solti (in Frankfurt), with Walter (at the Festival Hall in May 1955), at the 1955 Edinburgh Festival with Keilberth, in 1957 with Schüricht in Besançon, Kletzki at the Paris UNESCO Concert in 1960, with Jochum in Tokyo, Ansermet in Lausanne, with many conductors during his USA tours, with Haitink in Amsterdam, and frequently with Wolfgang Sawallisch in Germany. His second recording, (for DG), with Rafael Kubelik and the Bavarian Radio Symphony Orchestra in December 1968 seemed to me to be marginally less satisfying. But wherever and whenever he sings it, the reaction is usually that of the *Los Angeles Herald-Examiner*'s music critic Bernard Soll after a Fischer-Dieskau performance in April 1974: 'This was the kind of vocal expression that drives strong men (and critics) to unashamed tears'.

The debate about whether a contralto or a baritone should sing the lower voice part in the 'song *and* symphony', *Das Lied von der Erde*, has continued for years. Fischer-Dieskau told me that he believed that he had been the only baritone to sing it since Friedrich Weidemann in Mahler's day, but admitted that 'it goes very high' for him. Deryck Cooke, the British Mahler expert, reviewing the Fischer-Dieskau/King/Kletzki Electrola recording of October 1959, wrote: 'I personally find the male voice less satisfactory from the point of view of colour and contrast, but Fischer-Dieskau is at his incomparable best, penetrating right to the heart of this tormented music . . .' (*The Gramophone*, July 1960) which reminded me of Gerald Moore's remark about *Die schöne Müllerin*: 'It should always be sung by a tenor – except for Fischer-Dieskau!'

Mahler himself allowed the alternative, as we know, and the problem of textual 'accuracy' is not so important here, since Hans Bethge's translations show that, although the 'story' clearly concerns two *men*, the narrator could be either a man or a woman. 'Er stieg vom Pferd und reichte ihm den Trunk des Abschieds dar', says the narrator. (He dismounted and handed him (i.e. his male friend) the farewell cup).

The contrast between tenor and baritone did seem to me to be more marked in Fischer-Dieskau's second superlative reading (with Leonard Bernstein), recorded in April 1966 shortly after their great *Falstaff* triumph in Vienna. James King's ringing operatic tenor tones seem to set off Fischer-Dieskau's graver baritone voice more effectively than those of the Scot, Murray Dickie. There are indeed some cruel notes for the baritone (on 'Wo bleibst du?' in *Der Abschied* and in some of these *fortissimo* passages in *Von der Schönheit*), but no one, not even Kathleen Ferrier, has ever sung that cruelly high tessitura at the beginning of *Der Abschied* 'O sieh wie eine Silberbarke schwebt der Mond am blauen Himmelssee herauf', (Look how the moon glides like a silver barque o'er the heavenly blue) with such perfectly-placed notes and clarity of diction, while the whole wonderful song is full of magical singing, and equally magical playing by the Vienna Philharmonic. (Ex. 48)

Ex. 48

If Fischer-Dieskau would dismiss some of Mahler's music as 'pseudo folk-music', he seems to enjoy singing the composer's settings from the Arnim-von Brentano *Des Knaben Wunderhorn* (1888), and has given many concerts of them, as well as recording them for Electrola with Elisabeth Schwarzkopf, the London Symphony Orchestra and George Szell, in March 1968 at the Festival Hall in London. The very beautiful duet *Wo die schönen Trompeten blasen* was held to be 'the most touching account of any Mahler song that I have ever heard' by one critic; Fischer-Dieskau's enunciation of the words 'Die grüne Heide, die ist so weit', would remind almost every Schubert lover of the great tragic Schubert-*Lieder*.

Thus, Fischer-Dieskau is clearly fascinated by this Freudian case-study of a 'modern' composer who, as he writes, 'has grappled with those elements which are irreconcilable, and in whose works all the artistic problems of our century are mirrored'.

Fischer-Dieskau dislikes clichés and generalisations about 'the greatest *Lieder* singer in the world', 'the singer with the largest repertoire', 'the most-recorded classical vocalist' and so on, and often reminds his questioners that Julius Stockhausen or Heinrich Schlusnus might well have sung more than he – Schlusnus said once indeed that he had six hundred *Lieder* in his repertoire. Fischer-Dieskau really does not know how many songs he has 'in his head', although he must have sung 'thousands' in recordings and elsewhere. When I asked him 'what was left to be recorded?' he mentioned Loewe, (there are twenty-odd volumes of his songs!), Robert Franz, Grieg – and the French repertoire. When he received the honorary degree of Doctor of Music at the Sorbonne in 1980, it was ostensibly for his books on Schubert and the Wagner-Nietzsche relationship, but also, I am sure, for his services to French music. He has always found French audiences among his most knowledgeable and most enthusiastic – he was the first singer to dare to give a programme devoted entirely to Wolf in Paris – and one French critic was heard to say that Fischer-Dieskau would be the only person to keep him in Paris over summer – for the 'Festival estival'! Fischer-Dieskau's friendship with the Soviet pianist, Sviatoslav Richter, (dating from their Aldeburgh partnership in 1965), led to visits to the Tours Festival and to Richter's famous 'La Grange', for Wolf-Mörike evenings (in 1967, for example). Nevertheless, Fischer-Dieskau has rarely included French *chansons* or *mélodies* in his programmes for the concert platform.

Gabriel Fauré, who, with Debussy and Ravel and the last three composers mentioned, set twentieth-century music on its way, produced one of the few French song-cycles to compete with the great German tradition: *La bonne chanson* (op. 61) (1893). Fischer-Dieskau recorded the work for Electrola, with Gerald Moore after a six-day recording session which included, interestingly enough, Wolf's *Spanisches Liederbuch* and twelve Schubert songs, in May 1958, and immediately invited comparison with the illustrious Pierre Bernac and his own contemporary, Gérard Souzay, who sings so fluently and idiomatically in German. I have shown that I disagree with the view that only a national can sing his or her nation's music; there are many witnesses to the ability of truly great interpreters to cross linguistic or stylistic boundaries. Dietrich Fischer-Dieskau is surely one? The warmth and restraint of his singing of the Fauré cycle seemed to match perfectly the *pudeur* of this chaste music and Verlaine's wonderfully calm verses. Just now and then however, (as in 'une *Sainte* en son auréole'), his accent slipped – but in his second version, recorded in Fauré's alternative form for piano (Wolfgang Sawallisch), two violins, viola, cello and bass (all from the Berlin Philharmonic Orchestra), and made in November 1975, I really could find no fault. His ability to adopt this 'classical' style, so different from the *Innigkeit* required to interpret German *Lieder*, is nowhere better illustrated than in his singing of that magical line, 'la lune blanche luit dans les bois' (The white moon gleams in the woods) (Ex. 49.) with the poem's wonderful last sigh, 'c'est l'heure exquise'. It is a superb musical moment.

Ex. 49

Andantino

dolce

La lu - ne blan - che luit dans les bois,____

That recording also contained his second version of the three haunting *Chansons madécasses* (1926) of Maurice Ravel, which Fischer-Dieskau had first recorded with Aurèle Nicolet (flute), his wife Irmgard Poppen (cello) and Karl Engel (piano) for DG in October 1959. This is, as Ravel said, 'a sort of quartet in which

244   DIETRICH FISCHER-DIESKAU

the voice plays the part of the main instrument'; Fischer-Dieskau's
'Femmes, approchez', (Women, approach) has the right air of
'l'abandon de la volupté'! (The earlier record also included an
infectious account of Ravel's *Cinq mélodies populaires grecques* of
1907).

In such music, and in that of Claude Debussy, who was Fauré's
pupil, colour and rhythm are as important as harmony or melody.
Fischer-Dieskau's sense of rhythm, his feeling for the correct
tempo, for the 'style' of this music, enables him to enter a world
which, at first sight, would not seem to be his natural element.
Yet, again and again, one finds his interpretations of this music as
'natural' as his recordings of his 'native' *Lieder*. There are some
who, like Andrew Porter in his *Gramophone* review (July 1961) of
the Debussy songs, thought indeed that he was *over*-interpreting
these songs – but a comparison of Fischer-Dieskau's style with,
say, that of Maggie Teyte would show that the incomparable Miss
Teyte made much of the words too. In particular, the baritone's
singing of Debussy's setting of Verlaine's *Mandoline* seems to me to
be unsurpassed; the huge voice scurries over the words in an
irresistible fashion.

After a Fischer-Dieskau recital in the Théâtre des Champs-
Elysées on 27 October 1979, Claude Lully wrote in *Le Parisien
libéré* that 'he sang these songs with a sensitivity whose exquisite
finesse stemmed from the extraordinary economy of the means
employed'. 'These songs' were Debussy's *Trois Ballades de François
Villon* (1910) which he had already recorded with Karl Engel in
October 1959, and which he has sung on many occasions with
great success in France. (He has since – October 1979 – recorded
them again with Daniel Barenboim for Deutsche Grammophon).

Finally, Francis Poulenc: Poulenc was to Pierre Bernac what
Benjamin Britten was to Peter Pears. ('Has Benjamin Britten
over-written? Not to the ears of Peter Pears', ran a waggish couplet
in the 1960's!) Together, they made one of the great partnerships
in the history of song; their recital in Edinburgh in February 1949
introduced me to Debussy's Villon ballades as well as to Poulenc's
own music for the voice, in this case, his *Chansons villageoises* with
the intoxicating *Chant du clair tamis*. On the 1975 recording already
mentioned, Fischer-Dieskau sang Poulenc's setting of Max Jacob's
nonsense verses *Le bal masqué* (1932); surrealistic parody at its best

(or worst), the music and the verses have a sad faded air which the (en)forced gaiety does nothing to dispel. One could say that it gives Fischer-Dieskau an excellent opportunity to show his command of French idiom – but, above all, of his innate sense of humour (in '. . . son nid, son nid . . .') at the very end of the cycle, in No. 6 *Caprice*, where the 'réparateur perclus de vieux automobiles' (the paralysed repairer of old cars) returns to 'his nest' and the word 'nid' is repeated – to end on three comical falsettos. In addition, his singing of the dance/jazz rhythms recalls Gerald Moore's story of Fischer-Dieskau rushing away from an engagement so as not to miss hearing Ella Fitzgerald and Duke Ellington!

* * * * *

Fischer-Dieskau's work with these composers takes us into our own times. As has been mentioned more than once, the singer has never ceased to relish the challenge of contemporary music; no singer surely has put the contemporary composer more in his debt by his readiness to lend his enormous prestige to their new works. Fischer-Dieskau has always said that 'he does not plan ahead'. 'It's part of my attitude to life to let things happen to me', he said – but then to put all his energy into the work on hand, be it singing, writing, conducting, painting, collecting or whatever. So it has been with modern music too; where impresarios or record companies have suggested works, he has been ready to oblige. Clearly, he is aided by the phenomenal speed with which he learns new works. He has them put on to tape and spends every available moment learning them. His huge Mercedes car is fitted with stereo/quadraphonic equipment which enables him to follow the music with the score, as his secretary, Diether Warneck, drives him the few miles from his home to the recording studios in Munich.

Although others besides Fischer-Dieskau are of the opinion that the romantic *Lied* died with Hugo Wolf, the genre nevertheless took 'a most unconscionable time dying'. It seems appropriate that one of his first recitals with the then thirty-four year old Aribert Reimann at the piano should have been of the *Lieder* of Schoenberg, Webern and Alban Berg in October 1970, for Reimann, a pupil of Boris Blacher, has become, with Hans Werner Henze, Fischer-Dieskau's musical companion in the world of new music. The songs of the misleadingly-called *Second Viennese School* were issued by DG in December 1971 and introduced a public often antipathetic to these three outriders of the twelve-note revolution to some surprisingly melodic and beautiful music: Webern's tiny 1899 song *Vorfrühling*, written when Hugo Wolf was still alive, with its magical conclusion on 'leise tret auf', and Berg's *Warm die Lüfte* (opus 2, no. 4) with the poignant closing lines to Alfred Mombert's poem 'Der Eine stirbt, daneben der Andre lebt' (One dies while the other lives), seemed to me to prove that music like other forms of art is evolutionary and that, as Arnold Schoenberg wrote in 1948, 'no new technique in the arts is created that has not had its roots in the past'. (Needless to say, Fischer-Dieskau was not tackling Schoenberg for the first time with these songs; on 16 February 1955 in the Stadthalle in Heidelberg, he sang the small part of the *Bauer* (the peasant) in a performance of Schoenberg's mammoth *Gurrelieder* conducted by his wife's uncle, Professor Hermann Meinhard Poppen).

The baritone's choice of these very songs for his first-ever recital (with Aribert Reimann) at the Komische Oper in East Berlin on 16 April 1978 was an astute one, since he must have known that there is nothing more conservative than a communist culture! Yet the audience would have the sensation of listening to rather daring 'modern' music. The singer was delighted with the ecstatic reception that he was given. 'The greatest singer of modern times', as the G.D.R. Press called him in uncharacteristic hyperbole, had built another bridge between countries. Whether they would have enjoyed Fischer-Dieskau's performance in another Schoenberg work with an Eastern European theme, *Ein Überlebender aus Warschau* (A survivor from Warsaw) (op. 46 of 1947), written for a narrator, male chorus and orchestra, is perhaps more doubtful. Fischer-Dieskau performed this seven-minute long piece in Munich on 31 January 1979 under Gary Bertini, but was prevented by influenza from repeating it at what would have been a moving occasion with the European Community Youth Orchestra under Claudio Abbado in Berlin that August. The work showed how Schoenberg (with Berg) had moved away from the *Lied* in order, as Fischer-Dieskau wrote once, to be able to express themselves, musically, in a more discriminating fashion.

No two composers owe more to Fischer-Dieskau than Max Reger

and his former pupil, the Swiss musician Othmar Schoeck. Through his persuasive advocacy, their songs have been brought to the attention of a public largely ignorant of their worth. The reader might recall that Fischer-Dieskau's affection for Reger stemmed largely from his admiration for the art of Emmi Leisner; throughout his long career, the singer has continued to perform Reger's otherwise seldom-performed works. As early as July 1949 indeed, he sang Reger's solo cantata *Der Einsiedler* (op. 144) in Heidelberg and there again, in February 1953, his *Hymnus der Liebe* (op. 136), as well as *Der Einsiedler*.

Reger's chamber and organ works are quite well represented in Anglo-Saxon record catalogues, but Fischer-Dieskau's recording of a selection of his *Lieder* does not seem – so far at any rate – to have had its usual effect and called forth emulants, although Hermann Prey has recorded four of Reger's orchestral settings of Schubert *Lieder*. Fischer-Dieskau's Reger selection, (made for DG in November 1965 with Günther Weissenborn), places these songs firmly in the Romantic tradition – indeed the conclusion of Reger's setting of Otto Julius Bierbaum's *Traum durch die Dämmerung* (op. 35, No. 3) has more than echoes of Strauss' better-known setting.

Fischer-Dieskau was one of the celebrants at the centenary *Reger-Fest* in Bonn in 1973 where he sang the *Hymnus der Liebe* and *Der Einsiedler*. The 'profound meditative calm' which Ronald Crichton experienced while listening to these works in the Beethovenhalle was shared by many (including myself); Fischer-Dieskau could not have given more support to a composer who continues to present a problem to critics and musicians alike. (That Reger had a wicked sense of humour is borne out by the story of his witty riposte to a critic of one of his works: 'Dear Sir, I am sitting in the smallest room of my house. Your review is in front of me. Soon it will be behind me'!)

Schoeck, who died in 1957, had studied under Reger in Leipzig in 1907–8 and has had no more faithful interpreter than Fischer-Dieskau. There are four separate records devoted in part or in whole to this composer's works – persuasive advocacy indeed. Schoeck, like Reger, looks backwards to the great *Lieder* tradition, and particularly to his idol, Hugo Wolf – his two song-cycles *Lebendig begraben* (op. 40) (1927), to poems of his fellow-Swiss,

Gottfried Keller, and *Notturno* (op. 47), are full of Austro-German melodies and memories as well as 'new' techniques. The first was recorded for DG in March 1962, when the singer was accompanied by the Radio Symphony Orchestra of Berlin under Fritz Rieger; the second on 8 April 1967 by CBS in New York, accompanied by the Juilliard Quartet, after a performance in Hunter College a few days earlier.

Lebendig begraben is, like *Winterreise*, 'a cycle of frightening songs', about a man buried alive, but lacks the Schubertian cycle's lyricism, while *Notturno* (1931–1933), to nine poems by Nikolaus Lenau and a final prose hymn by Keller, is, I suspect, a modern masterpiece. Fischer-Dieskau's blend here of lyricism and dramatic intensity sets off to perfection the spare sound of the Juilliard strings. The third and fourth songs, (from 'Die dunklen Wolken hingen . . .'), coming after the quartet's long introspective 'solo', catch Lenau's Austrian melancholy with uncanny accuracy. The work requires a singer of Fischer-Dieskau's distinction and not many singers have attempted it; Fischer-Dieskau himself sang it most recently in February 1979, with the Schoeck Quartet in Munich. His pioneering work for Schoeck was recognised in a moving letter from the Othmar-Schoeck-Gesellschaft in Berne who wrote in February 1963 that Fischer-Dieskau's recording of *Lebendig begraben* would have allowed the composer to die with a lighter heart and a more hopeful view of the future. Schoeck himself had written the singer some years earlier when he had learned that Fischer-Dieskau would sing his *Notturno*: 'After the enormous experience of your *Lebendig begraben* – to hear *Notturno* sung by you – these are 'Göttergaben' (gifts from the gods) for me; I feel new-born when I think of it!'

Schoeck had also been among the first composers to set the poems of the naturalised Swiss poet Hermann Hesse (1877–1962) who was to become – rather surprisingly – the *guru* of Jack Kerouac's hippy generation in the America of the 1960's. Hesse had calculated in 1950 that there were – even then – over two thousand settings of his poems; the Centenary Celebrations of 1977 invited Fischer-Dieskau to make a contribution to making some of these known. In March 1977, he and Karl Engel recorded a fine selection (for DG) of settings by Schoeck and the Swiss-born composer Gottfried von Einem. It was particularly instructive to compare the settings of one of Hesse's most famous, and loveliest poems *Seltsam, im Nebel zu wandern*; Schoeck gives it a jaunty 'walking rhythm', slightly reminiscent of the Schubertian, and sets the final aching lines 'Kein Mensch kennt den andern/Jeder ist allein' (No man knows his neighbour, each is alone) in 'Romantic' *Weltschmerz*. The younger von Einem set the poem as the first of the seven songs of his song-cycle *Leb wohl, Frau Welt* (opus 43) written in 1974; his setting clearly reflects the thirty-year difference in the ages of the two composers – spiky discords stress rather the contrast made in the poem between loneliness as sadness and the loneliness that brings wisdom. Fischer-Dieskau gave a masterful interpretation of both composers' very different styles of setting Hesse – as he had already done for another twentieth-century composer, Mark Lothar, when he recorded *his* Hesse settings (*Musik des Einsamen*, op. 67) in August 1967.

Von Einem's first work for Fischer-Dieskau, the eight 'Rosa mystica' songs, to poems by H. C. Artmann, was performed at the Vienna Festival on 4 June 1973 with the Vienna Philharmonic Orchestra conducted by Karl Böhm. One writer thought that they were 'weltschmerzlich, nostalgisch' (pessimistic and nostalgic) and the huge ovation at the end of the concert showed that they were much to the taste of the distinguished audience. (Von Einem has also written a cantata *An die Nachgeborenen* (1975) for Fischer-Dieskau who, he wrote to me, possesses 'inborn musicality . . . and great self-discipline').

Before considering, finally, some other twentieth-century composers whose songs have attracted Fischer-Dieskau's attention, I might direct the reader to the Discography; there he will find a quite remarkable number of 20th century composers whose *Lieder* Fischer-Dieskau has somehow or other found time to perform and record. Among these are Bartók, Busch, Dallapiccola, Fortner, Kempff, Křenek, Martin, Pfitzner, Schwarz-Schilling, to name only a few.* Special mention might be made of his collaboration with Ernst Křenek who was born in Vienna in 1900 and whose

---

*The reader will be interested to know that many of these *Lieder* are issued by Electrola on a series of records under the generic title of *Stilwandlungen des Klavierliedes, 1850–1950* (lit. "Changes in the style of the art-song, 1850–1950").

first wife was Gustav Mahler's daughter, Anna. Křenek, who had attained fame with his opera *Jonny spielt auf* in 1927, wrote his cycle *Spätlese* (opus 218) to his own poems for Fischer-Dieskau. The première on 22 July 1974 during the Munich Festival puzzled some of the audience; the plucking of the piano strings and the knocking on the piano wood alienated those who had perhaps expected something more 'Romantic'. When it was performed at the Edinburgh Festival on 3 September of that year, however, the applause was tumultuous, (as it had been in Lucerne and Berlin). The six poems of the cycle are hardly great poetry, with their fleeting reminiscences of Hölderlin and Stefan George, but, once again, the baritone brought all his great art to the service of a new work. It has not been heard much since however.

Fischer-Dieskau first became friendly with Benjamin Britten when the composer wrote the baritone part in his *War Requiem* (1962) for him; the singer soon became a frequent visitor to the Red House in Aldeburgh and to Britten's festival. His admiration for the Pears-Britten performances of the Schubert song-cycles has already been mentioned; it was therefore not surprising that Britten should suggest writing a cycle for Fischer-Dieskau. The tenor Peter Pears chose six of William Blake's *Songs of Experience* (1794) punctuated, as it were, by, as musical *ritornelli*, six *Proverbs of Hell*. The dodecaphonic music underpins Britten's favourite theme of lost innocence; Fischer-Dieskau's magisterially sombre tones (in *The Chimney Sweep*, for example: 'A little black thing among the snow') present a winter scene of utter desolation. The greatest song of the cycle is, I think, *The Tyger*, a superb example of Fischer-Dieskau's declamatory powers in a foreign language. What artistry at the words 'Did he who made the lamb make thee?' and what chill there is in the frightening monotones of the proverbs! When Britten sent the singer the finished score of the songs in April 1965, he paid the singer a charming compliment: 'I hope the tessitura is good for you', he wrote. 'Once or twice it is rather high, but you can sing anything!' (He actually found his own piano accompaniment just as difficult). The actual score bears the dedication 'To Dieter: the past and the present'.

They first performed the cycle together on 24 June 1965 in the Jubilee Hall in Aldeburgh, and recorded it for Decca on 4 December, repeating the work at London's Croydon Hall on 6 December. Strangely, the recording only appeared in May 1969, when it met with uniform acclaim and was praised as one of the great works of the twentieth century. Nevertheless, Fischer-Dieskau has performed it only rarely since the première – with Britten at the Edinburgh Festival in 1968, for example.

The baritone remains a devoted admirer of Benjamin Britten. 'Ben was a man of imagination', he told me in Berlin in 1980. 'He heard things in a particularly individual way. A man with 'melos', not *the* most important ingredient of music, but *a* most important ingredient, because it is melody that brings people together, because 'cantabile' presents human emotions'. He was impatient with present critics of Britten: 'We do not have so many good composers that we can afford to attack him', he said.

He had said the same to me once about Ferruccio Busoni whose *Goethe-Lieder* he had done so much to popularise, and I suppose that he might stand up and be counted for the American composer, Charles Ives, in the same way. Ives, who died in 1954, is something of a cult figure at the moment; he grew up under the strong influence of his father, a Union Army bandmaster with Puritanical leanings. While at Yale (from 1894–1898), he was introduced to German *Lieder* by his professor, Horatio William Parker. It was at Yale, too, that he began to write the first of his one hundred and fourteen songs which he published – at his own expense – in 1922, and which, as he wrote, were not 'composed in the spirit of competition; neither Schumann, Brahms or Franz will be the one to suffer by a comparison . . .', as David Wooldridge tells us in *From the steeples and the mountains*.

Fischer-Dieskau encountered Ives' songs on one of his American tours and was encouraged to record them – rightly or wrongly? Wooldridge's rather hectic book suggests that the songs are very 'American', and that they cry out for a black singer. Fischer-Dieskau's vocal timbre certainly suits the songs – one just has to decide whether Ives ever envisaged an 'English' accent singing them. But this argument is no different from that which raged about 'foreigners' singing German *Lieder* or French *mélodies* – while non-Americans have been singing first 'dance' tunes, and then 'pop music', for decades. Fischer-Dieskau's record – *Songs, Lieder and Chansons* – was made with Michael Ponti in December 1975 in

Berlin and is always interesting, in places very beautiful. The 1917 song *Tom sails away* is haunting, but the overtones for a Britisher of Henry Francis Lyte's *Abide with me* (1890) are too strong for us to appreciate Ives' very idiosyncratic setting. The baritone soars up to the (to me) unnatural high note on 'Help of the *help*less' and 'In life, in *death*' with amazing ease, but the song remains earthbound. Yet I doubt whether there was one reviewer who did not admire his enterprise, so typical of the artist. Personally, I prefer the songs of another American composer, Samuel Barber (1910–1981), whose 1931 setting of Matthew Arnold's *Dover Beach* (op. 3) is among the most beautiful of twentieth-century vocal works. The baritone sang it for the first time as early as July 1950 with the Rudolf Schutz Quartet in the Titania Palast in Berlin, and then recorded it with the Juilliard Quartet, along with Schoeck's *Notturno*, on 8 April 1967. I regard this performance as one of Fischer-Dieskau's major contributions to the cause of twentieth-century music, and it is tragic that more singers have not emulated him. To paraphrase Fischer-Dieskau: 'There are not so many good twentieth-century vocal works around that we can afford to ignore it'. (i.e. the Barber work).

Looking back over his long musical life in 1979, Barber the composer, (whose aunt was the great contralto, Louise Homer), jokingly recalled that he had once recorded *Dover Beach* himself. 'Fischer-Dieskau studied very carefully what the composer had done', he said. 'I don't mean to pat myself on the back vocally, but he sounds just like me'! (Barber's recording displays, in all truth, a fine tenorial voice).

Yet it is in his own country and in his own language that Fischer-Dieskau has found two major modern composers of vocal music to support: Hans Werner Henze and Aribert Reimann. The former's *Fünf Neapolitanische Lieder* (1956), written for Fischer-Dieskau, and which he once described as one of the 'hopes for the rediscovery of that lost *melos*', were recorded with members of the Berlin Philharmonic Orchestra under Richard Kraus on 15 December 1956 and were issued in Great Britain in June 1959 as part of Deutsche Grammophon's 'musica nova' series. Fischer-Dieskau seems never to have lost his affection for these very original love-songs in Neapolitan dialect which received their première in the *musica nova* series in Hesse Radio on 26 May 1956, in a performance conducted by Otto Matzerath. They have much in common – both in mood and in construction – with Hugo Wolf's Italian and Spanish creations, but Henze is very much his own man and one could not say of him, as one could of so many twentieth-century composers of *Lieder*, that he is 'derivative' or an 'epigone'. Since, like Britten's, his works are also both interesting and original in harmonic structure and, at the same time, 'melodious', they should remain in the repertoire when other *Lieder* of the period have become 'case-studies' for the musicologist. For Fischer-Dieskau the actor-singer, they represent a worthy challenge of interpretation, ranging from bitter raging to seductive charm.

Lastly, Aribert Reimann: As accompanist, conductor and operatic composer, Reimann has been very close to Fischer-Dieskau for the last twenty years. He was a pupil of Boris Blacher who was Professor of Composition at Fischer-Dieskau's Berlin *Hochschule für Musik* from 1953. Fischer-Dieskau gave the première of Blacher's *Drei Psalmen* on 4 October 1962 in a performance conducted by the twenty-six year old Reimann, and he had previously taken the rôle of *Der Fischer* in Blacher's earlier radio opera *Die Flut* (1947) in 1956 under Otto Matzerath. He had also sung in *Der Grossinquisitor*, under Christoph von Dohnanyi, in Berlin in 1963. Thus, the singer had an almost paternal relationship to his young fellow-Berliner.

Reimann's great opera *Lear* was the culmination of these years of cooperation, of mutual musical interests. In a BBC 3 interview broadcast on 18 March 1979, Reimann, whose mother was a singing teacher, mentioned that he had already written over a hundred songs and vocal works; a major work for Fischer-Dieskau, settings of five poems by Paul Celan (whose *Todesfuge* (Death Fugue) of 1948 is generally regarded as one of the greatest post-war German poems on the theme of the destruction of the Jews), was premièred in 1961. Fischer-Dieskau told Karla Höcker in 1971 how deeply impressed he had been with this cycle which 'seems to be improvised, even though all the notes are written out. The declamation and the musical symbolism are extremely subtle'. The very first song, *Blume*, with its murderously high *tessitura* presented the baritone with the sort of challenge that he clearly relishes, since he has encouraged the young composer to continue to write for him. He had asked Reimann to compose a Lear opera as long ago as 1968, but the composer felt that the task was beyond him then. However, having now composed three major works for the Fischer-Dieskau voice viz. *Ein Totentanz*, première on 29 September 1961 with the Berlin Philharmonic Orchestra under Werner Egk, the six *Celan Lieder, Zyklus für Bariton und Orchester)* on 15/16 April 1971 at the Dürer 500th anniversary concert in Nuremberg under Hans Gierster, and the requiem *Wolkenloses Christfest* (première on 2 June 1974), Reimann felt ready to tackle *Lear*.

However inadequate the attempt, I have tried in this chapter to document and comment on what I believe to have been Fischer-Dieskau's major artistic achievements in the field of solo vocal music. No one can seriously challenge this artist's pre-eminence in this field of music. There are many reasons to advance for his position – the sheer beauty of his voice as an instrument, the astounding vocal technique, the keen intelligence at work on the overall meaning of, and the fine linguistic sense for, the less obvious nuances in the poem – all these are trenchant, genuine and valid, but they would not in themselves account for his pre-eminence. To all of these, he added the operatic singer's histrionic gift for characterisation, for leading an audience beneath the superficial level of the text, so that, partly by his intimate knowledge of the poet's and composer's intentions, partly by his extraordinary and fine sensitivity to language, partly by his ability to employ that matchless vocal technique in the coloration of vowels and the enunciation of consonants, he presented his listeners with a *fuller* experience of the song than had ever been vouchsafed them before. His industry too, both intellectual and physical, has enabled him to bring to the public *Lieder* treasures unknown until he sang and recorded them. I have tried in the preceding pages to document at least some of these pioneering efforts which have not only enriched the experience of his audiences but also – I am sure that they would agree – the repertoires of his colleagues in the field.

If, in the last analysis, I were to single out his amazing contribution to our knowledge of Schubert's *Lieder* and his devotion to the works of the Viennese composer, it is only because I know that his recitals and recordings of these songs have entranced and influenced a wider public than any others and made his name proudly synonymous with that of Schubert. To maintain these standards over thirty years of ceaseless journeying and artistic activity is richly to deserve the epithet once bestowed on him in France: 'le miracle Fischer-Dieskau'.

Dietrich Fischer-Dieskau and...

24 Karl Engel, 1957
25 Jörg Demus
26 Gerald Moore, rehearsing the
   Schubert *Lieder*, December, 1966
27 Victoria de Los Angeles, Elisabeth
   Schwarzkopf and Gerald Moore at
   a rehearsal for Gerald Moore's
   Farewell Concert, London,
   20 February 1967

34 Tamas Vasary
35 Sviatoslav Richter
36 Daniel Barenboim
37 Wolfgang Sawallisch
38 Christoph Eschenbach

CHAPTER SIX

Aspects of Dietrich Fischer-Dieskau

It will have become clear to the reader that the subject of this study is no ordinary musician, no ordinary singer who makes his annual rounds of the cities of the globe to sing a well-rehearsed, familiar repertoire. He is rather an artist *hors concours* who, in his thirty or so years of professional life to date, has sung the songs of all the best-known, and many of the not-so-well known composers, and has performed in opera and oratorios, dramatic and sacred music, ranging from the eighteenth to the twentieth century on stage and on record. The Discography attached carries titles of over five hundred recordings, a figure unmatched by any other recording artist.

When, on 21 June 1978, the University of Oxford bestowed the honorary degree of Doctor of Music on Dietrich Fischer-Dieskau, the Public Orator's *laudatio* presenting this 'idol of the citizens of Berlin and the non-pareil of baritone singers throughout the world' for the degree, made specific mention of yet another aspect of this 'Proteus personified, no mere mortal' – his literary work. Mr Griffiths, the Public Orator, spoke of Franz Schubert, 'cuius vestigia insecutus librum doctissimum hic conscripsit', ('about whose songs our guest has written a learned book *Auf den Spuren der Schubertlieder*, 1971', as Mr Griffiths translated his own Latin); these, and his other writings, form the first of the many other 'aspects of Dietrich Fischer-Dieskau'.

No doubt, someone someday will have to collect Fischer-Dieskau's many articles on composers, singers and on musical themes for publication. My own archive and that of the *Dietrich Fischer-Dieskau Gesellschaft e.V.* in Munich (directed by F. Axel Mehrle), contain writings going back to his earliest years as a musician. Many of these have already been quoted in the preceding pages, since they often appeared as contributions to boxes of records. Among the most important and interesting are: *Randnotizen zu einem Beethoven-Liederabend* (Marginal notices to a Beethoven *Liederabend*) (August 1965); *Der Podiumslöwe* (The lion of the rostrum) (on Gustav Mahler) (October 1967); on *Richard Strauss* (October 1969); on Goethe settings (August 1968); on *Carl Loewe* (November 1970); on the 'New German School' (March 1971) and on settings of Eichendorff's poems, written in December 1974, to name but a few. Clearly, this singer enjoys writing about music as much as performing it. The articles bear witness, too, to his intense involvement in the job at hand. With the *Lieder* composers, he is fascinated by their methods of working, with their attitudes to the poets and the poems they set, with the contemporary world around them; with operatic composers, he wants to know about the theatres, orchestras and singers for whom they wrote, of their early intentions and final thoughts. This is why, I am sure, his own favourite reading is the correspondence of poets and composers. From these, he says, he can learn so much more about the *Lied* or opera on which he is engaged: 'You get back to the origins', he said to me – not just the music, not just the poem or the libretto – a thorough knowledge of both is essential.

Some of these articles seem to me to have had an influence, too, on Fischer-Dieskau's fellow-musicians and their work; the Beethoven article was a powerful plea for the revaluation of the songs; the numerous *Lieder* should not be regarded as peripheral work, Fischer-Dieskau wrote, but rather as being 'among the most important, forward-looking works in the whole *oeuvre*', reminding us not only that to Beethoven must be credited the very first 'song-cycle' (*An die ferne Geliebte*, op. 98, 1816), but also that it was he who anticipated Schubert's extraordinary gift for blending words with music. Fischer-Dieskau quoted Beethoven's words to Bettina von Arnim: 'Melody is the sensual life of poetry. Does not the intellectual content of a poem become sensual feeling *through* the melody?' Fischer-Dieskau's Beethoven recordings, (which appeared as early as 1954), have encouraged younger singers to include such fine *Lieder* as *Adelaide, Ich liebe dich* and the almost Mozartian *Neue Liebe, neues Leben* in their programmes, since they knew that the public would have heard these songs in a Fischer-Dieskau recording.

Similarly with Richard Strauss's lesser-known songs; Fischer-Dieskau's collection of Strauss *Lieder* recorded with Gerald Moore in 1969–1970 contained an essay which gave powerful support to that strange, rarely-performed cycle *Krämerspiegel*, which encouraged Gerald Moore to devote a whole lecture to it in the Festival Hall in 1976, and other artists, such as the Norwegian baritone, Knut Skram, to include it in their repertoire and, in his case, to record it (CRD Bis LP49). It is in this essay too that we find a remark that Fischer-Dieskau seems to have adopted as a motto for his own philosophy of life, his 'Weltanschauung' perhaps: 'Dass nichts besser's sei, denn dass der Mensch fröhlich sei in seiner Arbeit' (There is nothing better than that a man should rejoice in his own works) – and he repeated this to me in Berlin in 1980. (The source is Ecclesiastes, Chapter 3, verse 22).

Fischer-Dieskau is also generous in writing prefaces and forewords to books by friends and colleagues; books by or on David Ffrangcon-Davies, Charles Panzéra, Fritz Busch, Jörg Demus, Gerald Moore, Aksel Schiøtz and Rudolf Kempe for example, all carry warm and interesting introductions by the singer, while a selection of Fischer-Dieskau's extensive correspondence with the great figures of the musical world since the war will no doubt also see the light of day at some future date; I have been privileged to read, and to use in this study, some of this material already.

Our main concern at the moment must be with Fischer-Dieskau's three publications to date: They are *Texte deutscher Lieder: Ein Handbuch* (Deutscher Taschenbuch Verlag, München 1968) first published as a paperback of 475 pages and then translated in large, imposing, hardback format as *The Fischer-Dieskau Book of Lieder* by George Bird and Richard Stokes (Victor Gollancz/Pan Books, London 1976, pp. 433); secondly, *Auf den Spuren der Schubert-Lieder: Werden-Wesen-Wirkung* (F. A. Brockhaus, Wiesbaden, 1971 pp. 371, and a second edition in paperback, 1976). The translation by Kenneth S. Whitton appeared in Great Britain as *Schubert: A Biographical Study of his Songs* (Cassell, London, 1976, pp. 331) and in the United States as *Schubert's Songs: A Biographical Study* (Alfred A. Knopf, New York 1977), and, thirdly, *Wagner und Nietzsche: Der Mystagoge und sein Abtrünniger* (Deutsche Verlags-Anstalt, Stuttgart 1974, pp. 312), translated by Joachim Neugroschel as *Wagner and Nietzsche* (Seabury Press, Inc., USA 1976), and in Great Britain under the same title with Sidgwick and Jackson, London 1978, pp. 232.*

A word, firstly, on Fischer-Dieskau's literary style. He writes in a reflective, at times quasi-philosophical vein with a wide and varied vocabulary culled from all ages of German prose writing. It is undeniably difficult to translate, but it is also the style of a well-read, scholarly man *au fait* with his subject(s), eager to share his enthusiasms and not afraid to engage in professional *querelles*. He is not usually submitting the results of musicological or academic researches, but presenting an intelligent and experienced musician's views of composers with whose vocal works he must surely be as familiar as any living musician. Accepted as such by the public, they have given enjoyment, and not a little instruction, to many.

Texte deutscher Lieder, (dedicated to Heinz Friedrich of the dtv-Verlag), has proved to be of enormous value to concertgoers; in the English translation's official 'blurb', Sir Peter Pears wrote that it was a 'very valuable, indeed essential book of reference for students of the *Lied*'.

The work contains the texts of circa 750 *Lieder* that one might encounter in the concert hall or on record, and although Professor Siegbert Prawer, sometime Taylorian Professor of German in the University of Oxford, warned that the translations are often of the composer's *setting* and not of the original poem, and can therefore not serve as texts for the study of German literature, he wrote in his review of the translation in the *Times Literary Supplement* (5 November 1976) that Fischer-Dieskau had presented a 'well-conceived volume'.

Fischer-Dieskau prefaces the work with 'Ein Versuch über das Klavierlied deutscher Sprache' translated, rather inadequately, I thought, as 'German Song – An Essay', seventeen pages long in the English version. The singer here attempts an 'Überblick' ('overview'!) of the whole field of German *Lieder* from 1736 (Sperontes' *Singende Muse an der Pleisse*) to Hans Werner Henze's *Neapolitanische Gesänge* (sic). Taken as this, as a general survey of an enormous field and an introduction to the detailed texts which

---

*The Schubert book has also been translated into Hungarian and Japanese; French and Czech translations are in preparation. The Wagner-Nietzsche book is available in French and Japanese translations.

follow, then the essay must be of great interest to the tyro and general reader. He will certainly be fascinated to learn Fischer-Dieskau's views on some of the composers with whom his name has been so closely identified: his defence of Schubert's choice of texts, for example: 'A poem had above all to inspire him musically', Fischer-Dieskau writes, 'and his extraordinary fecundity in *Lieder* composition should not mislead anyone into regarding him as one who would set anything' (p. 14); or his firm opinion that he does not share the common belief that Schumann 'achieves a *more* integral fusion of voice and piano' than Schubert. (I have set *more* in italics, since the translators have overlooked the force of the comparative in the original 'nahtlos*ere*').

The essay seems to be leading to a rather pessimistic conclusion; the singer believes that today's poets and composers have lost their sense of responsibility towards their public and have exhausted the possibilities of the German language, although, he grants that Goethe himself had this impression! He feels, too, that since 'perfection is (now) stereophonically preserved', the amateur at home must regard himself as reduced to the status of a 'mere imitator'. Nevertheless, he concludes that it is the singer's 'glorious task', his duty indeed, to be a 'kind of builder of bridges', to preserve by his performance the great creations of the past. Thus, his conclusion asks us not to be led into a state of 'mere resignation'. He writes, (I quote from the translation):

Music and poetry have a common domain, from which they draw inspiration and in which they operate: the landscape of the soul. Together, they have the power to lend intellectual form to what is sensed and felt, to transmute both into a language that no other art can express. The magic power that dwells in music and poetry has the ability ceaselessly to transform us.

In its limited compass, this essay does confirm Fischer-Dieskau's thoughtful and informed attitude towards his art and his profession. He is proud not to be one of those singers of whom the French critic Gérard Mannoni once wrote: 'La voix résonne là où devrait se trouver la cervelle' (The voice is where their brains should be'!) As Fischer-Dieskau said in 1980: 'After all, we are dealing with the products of highly-intelligent people (i.e. the composers), and we can only get along with them if we try to match our own meagre intelligence to their efforts'.

It would indeed have been strange had an artist like Fischer-Dieskau not been interested in the whole phenomenon 'Franz Schubert', and not just in his musical compositions. Fischer-Dieskau's own predilection for *Lieder*, his early involvement with the composer's works, the enthusiastic critical acclaim leading to his almost unrivalled position as 'the supreme Schubert interpreter of our time', as Gerald Moore has called him, had led Fischer-Dieskau to amass an imposing archive of material on the composer, and when that mammoth Deutsche Grammophon project – to record nearly all of Schubert's *Lieder* for male voice – was initiated in the 1960's, Fischer-Dieskau believed that it should be accompanied by more than an essay.

On top of his unremitting schedule of concert recitals, operatic engagements and recording commitments, he somehow found time to produce, after three years' work, his *Auf den Spuren der Schubert-Lieder*, published in 1971. It is a more or less chronological survey of Schubert's *Lieder*, relating them to their poets, their time and place of composition and, of course, to Schubert's own life. The original version contained some eighty well-chosen illustrations, either of contemporary musical figures or of musical scores, most of them drawn from the singer's own collection. Some four hundred and fifty *Lieder* appear in the index as having been mentioned in the text, which was intended, of course, to accompany the three boxes of twenty-nine L.P. records issued between 1970 and 1973, and to give a background to the booklets of texts and translations included with the boxes.

Leading post-war writers on Schubert such as Maurice Brown, Alfred Einstein, Arnold Feil, Thrasybulos Georgiades and Harry Goldschmidt had already corrected Richard Capell's rather romanticised 1928 view of the composer. The self-indulgent memoirs of Schubert's erstwhile friends, Anselm Hüttenbrenner, Benedikt Randhartinger, Franz Lachner, Eduard von Bauernfeld and Joseph von Spaun and the others, had all been critically evaluated and incorporated into many twentieth-century biographies after their appearance in the three volumes of Otto Erich Deutsch's *Franz Schubert: Die Dokumente seines Lebens und Schaffens* (1913/1914, translated in 1946). Fischer-Dieskau's publishers claimed however that his book was the first to have both a 'biblio-graphical and lexical' character, which was probably true. For anyone coming to Schubert for the first time, for anyone wanting a short, lucid description of all the important songs, I am certain that Fischer-Dieskau's book has performed a valuable service. In it, the reader will find a detailed description of Schubert's personal development, of his early promise as a chorister in the church at Liechtenthal, and of his astoundingly mature musical intelligence. Fischer-Dieskau manages too to place all this firmly against the background of contemporary political events; we are made aware of the unrest and unhappiness of the patriotic Austrians among Schubert's fellow-students in the Imperial *Konvikt*, (the seminary for Chapel Royal choristers), as Napoleon's French troops attacked and finally defeated the Austrian Army in 1809. Schubert's own unhappy family life and the misery caused by his inability to find the woman of his desires after he had been rejected by Therese Grob, are skilfully contrasted with the sunny, uninhibited nature of so much of his music, a paradox which continued to that last year 1828, when he wrote not only those tortured songs *Die Stadt*, *Der Atlas* and *Der Doppelgänger* (in the *Schwanengesang*, D957), but also that wonderfully heart-easing and peaceful adagio of the C major Quintet (D956).

Fischer-Dieskau is continually at pains to stress the *naturalness* of Schubert's art – but he will not have it that this means that he was a purely 'intuitive' composer and cites the proof of Schubert's continual wrestling with the structural and contextual problems of composition. 'He didn't live', Fischer-Dieskau often says, 'he only composed'! There are so many examples of different versions of songs that Fischer-Dieskau's point must be accepted – think only of the six settings of Goethe's Mignon's song *Nur wer die Sehnsucht kennt* – without having to add the usual information that Schubert is said to have approached Simon Sechter for counterpoint lessons shortly before his death.

Throughout the work, the singer stresses the jewels that one discovers when one takes the time and trouble to dig deep into the Schubertian treasure-chest. He is justified in deploring the shame-fully small number of Schubert songs which are sung in recital programmes, and, although he is elsewhere critical of the effect of recorded music on the musical life of our times, he has a warm word of praise for the record companies who have had the courage to allow artists to record less familiar *Lieder*. Certainly, I firmly believe that the appearance of Fischer-Dieskau's 'Complete Schubert', and of this book too, has led to more performances of out-of-the-way songs.

Much of the detailed information on German writers and the German/Austrian scene was deemed to be of less interest to the Anglo-Saxon reader and the reader will find it omitted from my edited translation, *Schubert: A Biographical Study of his Songs* (1976), but I did regret that room could not be found for at least some of the charming illustrations which gave some indication of Schubert among his friends.

The German version was well received on the whole; critical notices fell into three groups: firstly, those who were not particularly well informed either about Schubert's *Lieder* or the Austro-German literary scene of the time and who welcomed such a work from a man whose name had become synonymous with that of Schubert. This group welcomed the book enthusiastically and they are, I surmise, among its most frequent buyers and users. The second group, the musicians and musicologists, took the view that, although Fischer-Dieskau had presented no particularly novel view of Franz Schubert, his work was valuable as the studied opinion of a man with as much *practical* experience of performing Schubert's songs as anyone in the world. The third group, the 'Germanisten', those who read the book more from the standpoint of literature specialists and who were interested in, and at times critical of, the author's account of the literary background to the music compositions, conceded that he had managed to weave the various strands skilfully together. Some forgot however, and continued to forget when the second edition was published in 1976, that the book was meant to accompany the recordings, and that this had conditioned both its style and its format. The publication of that second edition (in paperback) was, of course, an eloquent testimony to the success of the book, and the author could bear with equanimity the cavillings of those few newspapers whose general tenor was that a 'cobbler' should stick to his 'last'.

In Great Britain and America, the book was welcomed very positively; Paul Hamburger (in *Music and Musicians*, July 1977) wrote that 'if he were not the best-known lieder (*sic*) singer of our age, one could, on the strength of this book, take Fischer-Dieskau for one of our foremost musicologists', since 'in the discussion of the music itself, Fischer-Dieskau never puts a foot wrong'. William Bender in *Time* magazine in the United States gave a more 'man-in-the-street' welcome: 'The industry and productivity of Schubert's new and brilliant critic should drive music-lovers to the bookstore' (18 April 1977), while Martin Bernheimer, reviewing the book in the *Times* of Los Angeles in May 1977, put the 'cobbler-stick-to-your last' remark in another perspective:

'Fischer-Dieskau of course has never been an orthodox anything. No one could be too surprised if his next tome turned out to be a definitive evaluation of contradictory developments in nuclear physics or a revolutionary treatment of the mating habits of the prehistoric amoeba . . .'!

After an interesting and useful discussion of some of the great Schubert interpreters – from Johann Michael Vogl to his own contemporaries, Fischer-Dieskau shows his profound knowledge, gleaned of course largely from his own enormous record collection, of developments in the art of interpretation. He tells, or reminds, us that it was Brahms' friend Julius Stockhausen (1826–1906) who first performed Schubert's (and other) song-cycles in their entirety and who was probably the first singer to give a *Liederabend* in its modern form. (Raimund von Zur Mühlen (1854–1931) was the first singer to give a *Liederabend* in London, in 1882 it seems).

Fischer-Dieskau's preference for male singers of 'male' songs is demonstrated by his remark anent Jenny Lind, the 'Swedish Nightingale', that she sang 'the male Schubert songs with as little compunction as many lady singers after her', and his (vain) hope that such 'breeches-rôles' would no longer be a feature of our concert platforms. Indeed, he goes on to remind female singers of Schubert that they have quite an extensive repertoire of 'female' songs to choose from if they would only be a little bolder. He cites *Gretchen am Spinnrade, Suleika I and II*, the Mignon songs, the much too rarely performed songs from Walter Scott's *Lady of the Lake*, as well as some of the admittedly rather tiresome 'flower songs' e.g. *Die Rose* (D745), *Viola* (D786), and the lovely *Nachtviolen* (D752).

On more modern interpreters, Fischer-Dieskau writes with un-bounded admiration of Elena Gerhardt, whom he knew, of course, of Karl Erb, 'whose richness of expression is something to marvel at', of Hans Hotter, who is given credit for reviving many long-neglected Schubert songs, Lotte Lehmann, Gerhard Hüsch and many others. Fischer-Dieskau's more immediate German forebears were Herbert Janssen, of whom he does not however say very much, Heinrich Rehkemper, whose recordings 'reveal a vitality which counterbalances the rather heavy voice', and Heinrich Schlusnus, who had a 'seductively beautiful voice', although Fischer-Dieskau felt that his 'uncertainties in intonation and musical inaccuracies' might not satisfy present-day standards. When I discussed his relationship to these two great singers, Fischer-Dieskau was of the opinion that Rehkemper was the more word-conscious, Schlusnus more concerned with *cantabile*, and that it might be fair to say that he (Fischer-Dieskau) had consciously attempted to make a compromise between these two types. (A special word is reserved for Gerald Moore, the 'King of Accompanists' whose 'feeling for rhythm' and mastery of the art of *legato* playing made him such an outstanding partner).

That chapter and the closing 'Ausblick' (*Final Thoughts*) are a unique feature of the work. The pessimism which we have noted elsewhere in Fischer-Dieskau's remarks about the *Lied* in particular, and the music of our age in general, is present here too. He longs for a transitional period in which we might find our way back to the peace and quiet of past ages out of the cacophony of the present. Above all, he longs to re-discover the lost art of melody, the 'non-decadence' that Friedrich Nietzsche was seeking too, and he puts the central question: 'Will musical theorists ever pluck up enough courage to admit the impossibility of making music *without* melody?' Fischer-Dieskau suggests finally that perhaps the *Lied* might come to our aid as we struggle to gather up the shattered remains of past art forms.

Such thoughts are revealing and suggest that Fischer-Dieskau, despite his amazing pioneering work on behalf of 'new music' and support for modern composers, has his heart in the music of the nineteenth century. Indeed I asked him once which age he would have chosen to have been born in, had he had the chance to choose. He answered: 'Last century certainly, where beginnings and endings were all determined. I am disturbed by the emptiness and chaos that followed. Exceptions only prove the rule'.

When I spoke to Fischer-Dieskau about his next book on Wagner and Nietzsche, he told me that he had read one of Elisabeth Förster-Nietzsche's books on the philosopher when he was about sixteen which had revealed, not only Nietzsche's friendship with Wagner, but also the break which led to their estrangement. From that point on, he had begun to collect material on this peculiar relationship, long before, that is, he knew that he himself was going to be so intimately involved with Richard Wagner and the whole Bayreuth industry.

Friedrich Nietzsche (1844–1900) is now recognised as one of the most important of modern philosophers. For many years, Anglo-Saxon scholars and laymen under-estimated or indeed neglected his work, the main themes of which were then distorted when, with the rise of Hitlerian National Socialism in the 1920's and 1930's, certain of Nietzsche's leading concepts, the 'Übermensch' (superman), the 'Herrenvolk' (the master race), Zarathustra's remark that 'God is dead', were bandied about out of context in close connection with Nazi ideology. It was perhaps Professor Walter Kaufmann's book *Nietzsche – Philosopher, Psychologist, Anti-Christ* (1950) which corrected these false impressions and allowed Nietzsche's name to be linked with such representatives of 'existentialist thought as Søren Kierkegaard in Denmark, Martin Heidegger and Karl Jaspers in Germany and Jean-Paul Sartre in France', to quote Janko Lavrin in his useful little 'biographical introduction' to Nietzsche (1971).

The very fact of his break with Wagner, indeed, should have proved that Nietzsche's thought was inimical to the Nazi hierarchy, since it is well known that Wagner's music, above all, represented for them everything that was pan-Germanic, noble, heroic, and, of course, 'Aryan'. Nietzsche's doctrine that the values bequeathed to us by Christianity and humanism were out-dated and that these and others should be adapted in the 'transvaluation of all values' only *seemed* to echo the Nazi philosophy peddled by men like Houston Stewart Chamberlain and Alfred Rosenberg. Professor Peter Stern's excellent book *A Study of Nietzsche* (1977) deals in some detail with the perversion of Nietzschean philosophy, particularly the notions of his 'God-less theology' and the 'heroism of strenuousness', by the Nazi party hacks. This, Stern shows, was unfortunately common ground to the greatest philosophers and the worst demagogues of the Germany between the wars.

Fischer-Dieskau's early experience of Nazi ideology, his early days in the Hitler-Jugend and his four years' service in the *Wehrmacht*, must have left their mark on an intelligent, sensitive youth; it is certain that he must have heard Nietzsche's name bandied about – and more certain that he pondered over Nietzsche and his relationship to Wagner after he had started to appear at Bayreuth from 1954 onwards and become part of that great quasi-religious cult.

In his foreword to the book, the singer explains his approach: 'The author believes that Wagner's attraction for and influence on Nietzsche were tightly interwoven with the philosopher's ambitions as a composer – a side of Nietzsche's work which readers have scarcely noted', and he attempts to disarm any criticism of a musician's having written a book on this unusual relationship by claiming an intimate awareness of the musical products of both men – a claim that it would surely be foolhardy to deny. It is perhaps still not widely known outside musical circles in Germany that Nietzsche has a fair number of musical compositions – both instrumental and vocal – to his name. It was Thomas Mann indeed who wrote of Nietzsche: 'Er war Musiker. Keine andere Kunst stand seinem Herzen so nahe', (He was a musician. No other art form lay so close to his heart.) *Grove* (Volume VI) lists the following: Seventeen songs (1864), *Manfred-Meditation* (after Byron) and *Une monodie à deux* for pianoforte (1872), *Sylvesternacht* for pianoforte (1874), *Hymne an die Freundschaft* for chorus and pianoforte (1874), *Hymne an das Leben* for chorus and orchestra (1887), and pianoforte pieces and songs (MS). It is certainly not well known that Fischer-Dieskau has played the Nietzsche *Manfred-Meditation* (a four-handed piano work) in public – with Aribert Reimann at a concert in the Berlin *Akademie der Künste* on 13 May 1975! He also sang some of Nietzsche's *Lieder* then, along with those of Nietzsche's friend, Peter Gast (the pseudonym of Heinrich Köselitz), Liszt and Wagner, and repeated that programme in Bamberg in August 1980 during the exhibition of his paintings (q.v.)

It is obvious that the majority of books on Nietzsche would lay greatest stress on his philosophical writings; Fischer-Dieskau's aim was to show the profound psychological effect that Wagner, his music, and his entourage had on the ailing younger man. The singer demonstrates in his early pages that Nietzsche was not only profoundly affected and emotionally disturbed by music, but that he had gained a good grasp of the technical fundamentals during his student days in Bonn during 1864–1865, having written a three-part essay *Über das Wesen der Musik* (On the Essence of Music) during 1862–1863 – and that he was always of the opinion that the 'musical' *Romantik* in Germany had been immeasurably superior to the 'literary' *Romantik* which had 'remained a promise'. We know too from his early discussions with friends in Bonn, (with Wilhelm Pinder, for example), that he was fully aware of the 'word-music' dichotomy, and that, at one time, he believed that Wagner's *Gesamtkunstwerk* (total work of art) might be the solution. (Later, he was to despise Wagner for having given 'the word' supremacy over 'the music').

The friendship with Wagner and his visits to the family home in Tribschen on Lake Lucerne opened up new intellectual horizons for the young professor of Classics at the University of Basel; he was able to discover and discuss music in philosophical terms with a man who shared his early admiration for Schopenhauer, the early nineteenth-century German philosopher who, they both believed, was the only philosopher really to comprehend the essence of music. Nietzsche wrote enthusiastically to his friend Erwin Rohde: 'What I am learning, seeing, hearing and understanding there (i.e. in Tribschen) is indescribable', (16 June 1869).

Fischer-Dieskau advances two major reasons for the eventual break with Wagner: Wagner's arrogance and Nietzsche's own feelings of inferiority as a dilettante musician. Wagner wrote to Nietzsche in 1870: 'Had you become a musician, you would be roughly what I should have been had I tried to become a philosopher', and Wagner's wife Cosima told Felix Mottl in 1886 that she had tried to play Nietzsche's *Sylvesterglocken* (sic) but: 'I confess that I . . . couldn't play on for laughing'. Such attitudes eventually alienated the sick philosopher.

But Nietzsche's own growing distaste for the Wagner cult, (soon to be publicly manifested at the opening of the Bayreuth Festival on 13 August 1876), is described by Fischer-Dieskau in words which reveal more than a little sympathy with the philosopher. Fischer-Dieskau writes of the 'self-indulgent, bored, unmusical male and female patrons, mixing with the *jeunesse dorée* of Europe, as if it were a sports festival that was taking place at Bayreuth'. He shows how Nietzsche had become gradually disillusioned with certain facets of Wagner's character: his arrogance, his play-acting, his narcissism, his anti-Semitism, his rudeness and vulgarity, all these now hung over Nietzsche like a ghastly spectre. The 'apostate' had rejected the 'mystagogue', the 'pious seducer'.

Fischer-Dieskau writes that, as a result of these musical and personal experiences with Wagner, Nietzsche was weaned away from the Romantic, the Dionysiac and the Idealistic, and that his literary works show that he grew to regard these as 'negative' qualities, not only in music, but in life itself. The great anti-Wagner essay, *Der Fall Wagner* (The Case of Wagner, 1888), lists those qualities that Nietzsche now missed in Wagner's music – and which he found, for example, in Bizet's *Carmen*:

> . . . la gaya scienza; light feet; wit, fire, grace; great logic; the dance of the stars; overjoyous intellectuality; the southern shower of lights; the *smooth* sea, perfection . . .

and earlier in the same work Nietzsche summed up his feelings about Wagner more succinctly: 'He made music sick'.

In Chapter Three, I tried to indicate what I took to be Fischer-Dieskau's scepticism about the Wagner cult; he has not appeared at Bayreuth since 1961 when he sang the role of Wolfram von Eschenbach in *Tannhäuser* and has clearly missed the opportunity of rising to the challenge that Wagner's music sets each and every singer. Yet, in this book, while never questioning the worth of the *music*, he clearly discerns that side of Wagner's character which eventually disturbed Nietzsche too. The singer writes: 'Wagner's German-ness, which, in truth, supplied the national dictatorship of the thirties and forties with a musically convincing background, his chauvinism, just could not be accepted by Nietzsche', and he very revealingly refers to Wagner's sub-title for *Parsifal* (a 'Bühnenweihfestspiel', a Sacred Dedication Festival Play) as 'schwülstig', bombastic.

In conversation with Fischer-Dieskau on the subject of the book, however, Fischer-Dieskau stresses again and again how important it is to keep the 'man' and the 'music' separate. 'Whether Wagner was a 'pleasant' person or not should only interest the biographers really', he said to me. Wagner's ability to 'present characters' was unmatched, he added, and this alone made Wagner the 'musical phenomenon' that he undoubtedly was.

As in the Schubert work, Fischer-Dieskau concludes here too on a pessimistic note. He deplores the victory of the anti-classical forces and believes that this led directly to the age of 'consumer music', where the average citizen can 'get hold' of all music too easily. He writes: '(Nietzsche) saw as early as the first *Thoughts out of Season* that the over-cultivation of the classical composers would be a possible alibi for the philistine; he declared it a danger to 'edify' oneself regularly on their works, to yield to those tired egoistical emotions which our concert halls and theatres promise to every ticket-purchaser', and the singer concluded: 'Nietzsche complained that music had lost its affirmative character with Wagner. Yet he experienced only the beginnings of that loss'. (Nietzsche had prophesied, of course, that art would lose its dominant rôle in society and that the artist would soon be regarded as a 'herrliches Überbleibsel', a 'magnificent relic').

The original version was widely reviewed when it appeared in Germany in 1974, and I can claim to have read every important review; the majority were highly appreciative. Joachim Kaiser, rather less appreciative in the *Süddeutsche Zeitung* of 14 November 1974, did however suggest an answer to his own question: Why did Fischer-Dieskau write the book? He thought that the impulse had come from the singer's innate desire to 'inform', to be a teacher of 'Kulturgeschichte', cultural history. There may well be something in the remark.

Some colleagues took the opportunity to write to Fischer-Dieskau when the book was serialised in the *Frankfurter Allgemeine Zeitung* in September and October 1974; one old friend, for example, was moved by the *nobility* and *rightness* of his judgements of the two main characters, a remark repeated, interestingly enough, in quite a few of the *critiques* who clearly credited the author with a unique insight into the lives of Wagner and Nietzsche.

Every writer has to bear at least one cross – that critics are prone to assert that he has not written the book that *they* would have written – had they had the opportunity and the time. Both Fischer-Dieskau books set out to achieve an objective: the Schubert book was intended to make known those many unknown and undeservedly neglected *Lieder* and to relate them to their genesis – *and* to their performance on record; the Wagner book was intended to depict anew 'the memorable relationship between two giants in our cultural history'. It can surely be claimed that both books achieved these objectives? To regret that Fischer-Dieskau has not written an 'Interpretation in Song', like Plunket Green, or a book of memoirs like Elena Gerhardt's *Recital*, or a study of *Eighteen Song Cycles* like Lotte Lehmann, is surely to miss the point and is unfair to the artist? In his Schubert book indeed, the singer is at pains to make quite clear why he did not want to write such an 'Interpretation in Song'. Writing of Hans Joachim Moser's fine book *Das deutsche Lied seit Mozart*, he says:

> '. . . the advice which he offers to the student in his *Singakademie* ('Singer's studio') could lead to misunderstandings, which is the reason why, in this book, such advice or suggestions as to interpretations have largely been avoided. Neither recordings nor the printed word can be a substitute for a course of study tailored to the individual needs of a student under the supervision of a teacher or an accompanist',

and to date Fischer-Dieskau has been as good as his word. In August 1980, he held his first masterclass for young students of *Lieder* in Berlin, but there is no sign that he wishes to produce a 'manual of instruction' for singers.

The English translation of the Wagner-Nietzsche book, by Joachim Neugroschel, appeared in 1976 in America, in 1978 in Great Britain. It posed a slight problem for British readers, since Herr Neugroschel had translated the work into a very colloquial 'Americanese'. One grants at once, of course, that British and American English have drifted far apart and that we are indeed often 'divided by the same language' – words and phrases like 'in high feather', 'concertized', 'happen-stance', 'rambunctiousness' and 'oldies' are, of course, part and parcel of the modern American language – but when we read that Nietzsche was 'delighted that his tailor had promised to finish a *tuxedo* for him', or that 'Nietzsche never failed to *drop by when in town* . . .', there seems to me to be a clash of what linguists call 'registers'.

This version was accepted in British and American circles as a remarkable testimony to the many-sidedness of a remarkable artist. George Martin in the *Yale Review* saw it indeed as 'a good antidote to Ernest Newman's account', where he felt the British author, in his eagerness to correct Nietzsche's notoriously biased sister Elisabeth, had 'put down Nietzsche too hard'. This does seem to me to be one of Fischer-Dieskau's most interesting contributions to the literature on the subject.

At the very end of his book, Fischer-Dieskau implores the reader not to feel that he is taking sides in the debate, but most readers – and the critics certainly – felt that the work was a polemic. *The New York Times* wrote: 'It may not be too much to say that no question in contemporary art is more important or more fascinating right now than the one implicit in this provocative book: where is the new Wagnerism headed, and do we go along?'

Fischer-Dieskau has not, of course, 'abjured' Wagner, but, like Nietzsche, he seems to have grown weary of Wagner's theatricality and found in his study of the two men that, although Nietzsche was an amateur as a musician, a dilettante even, he had seen as clearly as any writer before or since that music should have a cultural and revivifying, a *positive*, power. Fischer-Dieskau, like Nietzsche, is dismayed at the influence of the *extra*-musical forces in the world of opera, at the often almost neurotic attempts to mount productions which 'symbolise' the music. He would hope that we would soon return to the intentions of the composer, to the music as it was written.

Thus, strangely, it was in the 'non'-musician Nietzsche's devotion to the *music*, in contradistinction to the musician Wagner's love of the *drama*, that the singer-author Fischer-Dieskau found his soul-mate. In the two books that he has written to date, his emphasis on the importance of 'what the composer wrote' seems to tally with his own insistence on recording what is 'on the page', in the score. That it was Nietzsche too who declared that the loss of melody (*melos*) in modern music was the surest sign of oncoming *décadence* and barbarism, was yet another reason for Fischer-Dieskau's interest in the philosopher, since, as we have seen, this has been one of his own most enduring laments. New technical *forms* will not save music – rescue will have to come from within, from the *substance* of music itself.

Critics are happy for distinguished musicians to write their memoirs or to appear out of rôle in guest performances, (as at the Met.'s famous New Year *Fledermaus*), but they look askance at any attempt to run two or even three careers in harness. Leonard Bernstein, Daniel Barenboim, Peter Ustinov, Placido Domingo, Sherill Milnes, and lately Peter Schreier, have had to shrug off 'critical' disapproval in recent years – not that that has disturbed the artists in any way! The announcement in 1969 that Dietrich Fischer-Dieskau was proposing to appear on the conductor's rostrum, albeit as a professional 'hobby', inspired a few critics to adverse comment. To be fair to some of them, their concern was that the public might be losing a great singer and gaining a mediocre conductor, a loss that the world of music could ill afford. Ulrich Schreiber's article, 'The myth of total vocal art' in the journal *Hi-Fi* in August 1969, was mainly inspired by his just having received the 'almost perfect' Fischer-Dieskau recording of Benjamin Britten's settings of William Blake's poems.

The Press had mentioned that Fischer-Dieskau would be conducting a performance of *Così fan tutte* (in a production by Elisabeth Schwarzkopf) at Glyndebourne – which of course did not take place – although it was well known to his friends that the singer had always had a desire to conduct. In Chapter One we saw that this desire belongs to his earliest childhood memories, and he has talked about it continually since he attained international fame as a singer. I am sure that there are many reasons for this: his wonderfully-developed sense of rhythm for one. At an orchestral rehearsal, he is never still, as now his hands, now his feet, move to accompany the music. Again, he enjoys the feeling of 'controlling' the musical performance, a feeling that he has at a *Liederabend* when the singer has to be his own conductor, director and producer – and I quoted him earlier as saying that he found few conductors nowadays who conducted Bach as he wished to have it conducted. There was also his unbounded admiration for the art of Wilhelm Furtwängler. With Sir Georg Solti, Fischer-Dieskau would agree that Furtwängler was 'the greatest influence on modern conducting'. The singer treasures Furtwängler's Schumann recordings, in particular – the *Manfred* overture and the wonderful fourth symphony – and of course the memories of their *Lieder eines fahrenden Gesellen* in Salzburg in 1951 when the sixty-five year old conductor became something of a father-figure to the twenty-six year old fledgling singer and remained so up to his death from pneumonia in Baden-Baden in November 1954. Of course, by that time, as Fischer-Dieskau told me, Furtwängler's hearing was impaired and the conductor would really have preferred to have been composing, but the memory of his quiet authority on the rostrum, the lack of histrionic gestures, his demand for 'naturalness', all contributed to Fischer-Dieskau's own style of conducting. He was very touched to learn that Furtwängler's wife Elisabeth was reported to have said in America that she had always seen Fischer-Dieskau as a successor to her husband. He heard this, he said, 'with a tear in his eye'.

For Fischer-Dieskau, conducting, like authorship is another way of making music, a way of 'doing something fresh', of experimenting with the medium, and I do not believe that he had ever seriously contemplated giving up singing to conduct full-time. His experience as a singer, he was certain, could be of value when he began to conduct. He told me once that he had always been impressed by Furtwängler's way of allowing the music to 'breathe', and that he was sure that singing, where correct breathing was so important, would be a valuable training for any conductor. Indeed, when Josef Krips, the distinguished Austrian conductor, read that Fischer-Dieskau had said as much once, he wrote to him: 'A conductor who knows that breathing is the most important thing for a conductor, is a born conductor'!

The 'experiment' began in public in the Stadtsaal in Innsbruck on 16 October 1973 when Fischer-Dieskau conducted the Camerata Academica of Salzburg, whose conductor, Bernhard Paumgartner, had recently died, in what was described as a 'bold programme' of Haydn works: Symphonies Nos. 22, 94 and 104, and the C major cello concerto with the Berlin Philharmonic Orchestra cellist, Wolfgang Böttcher. The Camerata Academica was a group of young people, Fischer-Dieskau said, very keen on their work, but not yet set in a routine like the more famous orchestras, so that a conductor could enjoy a mutual learning relationship, as it were.

Dr Johnson's celebrated remark about a woman's preaching: 'It is not done well, but you are surprised to find it done at all', was certainly not the reason for the critical surprise at Fischer-

Dieskau's performance as a conductor. He was adjudged indeed to have been very professional, both in approach and method. The critic in *Die Welt*, for example, found that, after the initial nervousness, he was eventually conducting 'almost casually, elegantly, as if it was the easiest and most natural thing in the world'. (The concert was televised by the Austrian Television Service).

Michael Höltzel, the first horn-player of the Camerata, had invited Fischer-Dieskau to conduct a further two concerts, in the Mozarteum in Salzburg (on 17 October), and in the Stadtsaal in Linz on 18 October, which led one critic to remark that Fischer-Dieskau had begun his conducting career in the best Broadway manner – 'out of town'! But it is true to say, I think, that the singer's next venue surprised everybody – strange new pastures indeed! He made his British début in the Usher Hall in Edinburgh, the scene of so many of his singing triumphs. On 26 October 1973, he conducted the Scottish National Orchestra in an all-Schumann programme: the *Manfred* overture, Symphony No. 3 (The Rhenish) and the A minor piano concerto with the young French pianist, Jean-Bernard Pommier, as soloist. I attended the second performance in Glasgow's Town Hall on the next night and came away with mixed feelings, I must confess. Having watched Fischer-Dieskau full-face as it were for twenty-five years, it was a shock to see his back only and not to hear his voice. He seemed to me to start very fussily, leaping from side to side of the rostrum, pointing here and there, but, as in Innsbruck, he settled down as the nervousness left him and gave an easy and professional-looking performance. Most of the critics were impressed that it *sounded* professionally conducted as well. *The Guardian* and *The Scotsman* wrote what was rapidly to become a cliché about 'Fischer-Dieskau, the conductor': that he conducted with the 'sensitivity of nuance and interpretation which we know so well from his lieder singing'. (*The Glasgow Herald* was slightly less impressed, feeling that the conductor had lavished too much attention on detail!)

We were not surprised when these favourable comments were made about his first recording as a conductor with Electrola. This had been made somewhat earlier in fact, in February 1973: Schubert's Symphonies Nos. 5 and 8, with the New Philharmonia Orchestra. His joy at the event is mirrored in the three underlinings of the words '1. Dirigieren' (First conducting) in his diary! The Electrola record was exceptionally well received and has maintained its place as one of the most appealing versions of these most appealing works. The cliché mentioned above, which, like most clichés, has an element of truth in it, can be substantiated in the Fifth Symphony where Fischer-Dieskau makes magic of the second movement *andante con moto* which, as Ralph Hill once wrote, 'is a lyric, not a theme for treatment'. Edward Greenfield, writing in *The Gramophone* for December 1973, found the interpretations of both symphonies 'riveting' and was certain that they would 'stand up convincingly in a hotly competitive field', while Joseph McLellan in *The Washington Post*, after comparing Fischer-Dieskau's interpretations with five 'distinguished performances', (Toscanini, Bernstein, Cantelli, Walter and Szell), declared that his performance had set off his new career 'at the top'.

It was to Schumann that Fischer-Dieskau the conductor turned next, in collaboration with an artist who shared his Protean proclivities, Daniel Barenboim, and with whom he had shared many memorable musical moments – and jokes. I was talking once to Fischer-Dieskau in the artists' room after a recital in which he had been accompanied by Barenboim. As the pianist entered the room, the singer patted him on the head – Barenboim is quite a few inches shorter than the massive singer – and said: 'You played very well. You should take it up professionally'! By 1973, Barenboim had international reputations as a conductor and a solo pianist and he himself had said once: 'When I am playing the piano, I am trying to get an orchestral sound, and when I am conducting, I am playing piano on the orchestra' – Fischer-Dieskau's problem in another medium.

On 30 October 1973, Fischer-Dieskau conducted a fine performance in Wembley Town Hall in London of the Schumann Piano Concerto, with Barenboim as soloist, and accompanied by Barenboim's orchestra, the English Chamber Orchestra.* The concert was repeated on 31 October in Chichester and on 1 November at the Queen Elizabeth Hall in London. Schubert's Symphony No. 5 and Haydn's No. 104 completed the programme. The reviews were

*They recorded the work (along with the *Introduction* and *Allegro appassionato*, op. 92) with the London Philharmonic Orchestra for Electrola in June 1974.

good and the general opinion decisive: This was no fly-by-night amateur, but a leading musician taking a new professional challenge seriously. So might it be what Fischer-Dieskau jokingly, I believe, once prophesied: A hobby that might degenerate into a profession?! He had certainly had a happy relationship with all the orchestras that he had worked with, and was proud to have been invited back to conduct them again.

But it was not to be: By 1980, Fischer-Dieskau had decided that too much physical and nervous energy was required to keep two strenuous professions going side by side; he was fifty-five, after all, and as he said once: 'It took me almost a week to get over the pains in my back after conducting'. There had never been what he calls an 'iron necessity' behind his decision to take up conducting, he said, and it cost him no tears to lay it down, although he naturally regretted the absence of such an absorbing interest. He looks back now with great pleasure on the achievements of these six years; in 1974, he had gone to Israel to conduct the Israel Philharmonic Orchestra, firstly, in February, with Alfred Brendel in a Mozart piano concerto, along with Schubert's fifth and Schumann's third symphonies – this was in Tel-Aviv – and then a few days later with Uri Shoham (flute) in a Mozart Flute Concerto and the same two symphonies in Haifa. He had always found the Schumann symphony a particular challenge, he said, with its three slow middle movements – even the scherzo is a slow movement!

Then, in March, during his American tour, he conducted Zubin Mehta's Los Angeles Symphony Orchestra in his all-Schumann programme (with Horacio Gutierrez as pianist); some American critics missed his singing more than they would say – they, of course, heard and saw Fischer-Dieskau so much less frequently than Europeans did. After three concerts with the Radio Symphony Orchestra in Berlin in September 1974, he made a German tour with the fine Bamberg Symphony Orchestra with Mendelssohn's *Hebrides* Overture, Schumann's second symphony and Chopin's Piano Concerto No. 1, with Jorge Bolet as soloist. His last appearances as a conductor, (to date anyway), were in Israel in 1976, when he conducted the Israel Philharmonic Orchestra in six concerts in Tel-Aviv and Jerusalem, and then the Czech Philharmonic Orchestra in Prague, where he recorded a performance of Brahms'

Symphony No. 4 and Berlioz' *Harold in Italy*, for Supraphon. The Brahms was enthusiastically reviewed on release as a 'performance in a thousand' by Robert Dearling in June 1979. Beside this performance, he wrote, Lorin Maazel's interpretation (issued in the same month) had a 'studied artificiality'.

If one adds to the recordings already mentioned, his fine versions of Schumann's second and third symphonies, recorded for BASF in August and September 1975 with the Bamberg Symphony Orchestra, we can see that Fischer-Dieskau has made a distinguished contribution to the conductor's catalogue – one in which he can take legitimate pride, as I know that he does. The reviews make plain that the critics took him seriously as a conductor and were prepared to measure and praise him by the highest standards – but I think that it would also be true to say that they breathed a sigh of relief, when he turned his face to them again – and began to sing!

Singing, authorship, conducting – does one cry: Enough? Throughout this study, I have had cause to mention the singer's intense interest in the world of art – as a collector of paintings and drawings, and, since his earliest childhood, as an enthusiastic artist himself. The reader might recall that his interest in art was aroused by his piano-teacher at the age of nine. It has proved to be an abiding interest; over the many, many years of journeying all over the world making music, his painting has been an oasis to which he could return to refresh his senses. I have admired these colourful, individual paintings in both his houses, in Berlin and Munich, but, until recently, they have been 'for friends' eyes' only. In 1980 however, the Kunstverein in Bamberg invited him to participate in an exhibition entitled 'Künstlerische Doppelbegabungen von E. T. A. Hoffmann bis Dietrich Fischer-Dieskau' (Artistic dual talents from . . .) which was held in the Neue Residenz in Bamberg, not far from Munich, from 6 July to 29 September. The exhibition's aim was to present examples of the participants' 'Nebenbegabung' ('Secondary talent'), which, of course, did not mean that they were just to be regarded as 'talented dilettantes'. In the exhibition was work by Paul Hindemith, Hermann Hesse, Günter Grass, Federico Fellini, Friedrich Dürrenmatt and Ernst Křenek, among others. Fischer-Dieskau was represented by no less than forty-three works: portraits of his secretary Diether Warneck among others, landscapes, for example, the painting mentioned in Chapter One, the view in Edinburgh, 'Douglas Gardens', and some abstract paintings.

John Russell wrote in the introduction to the catalogue of Fischer-Dieskau's work: 'In music he can do and become everything; is it surprising that he still has to decide on *one* idiom as a painter?' Certainly the Fischer-Dieskau 'art-style' is extremely heterogeneous, and can range from an oil painting like 'Selbstgespräch' of two females facing each other, both blonde-haired, both intense, via a chalk study, simple but effective, of his Austrian accompanist, Jörg Demus, (1979), to an almost surrealistic 'self-portrait' in oils of his make-up and costume as King Lear in Aribert Reimann's 1979 opera *Lear*.

As with his music, Fischer-Dieskau sets himself ambitious goals in his chosen hobby as well, goals as varied and as exciting as could be imagined. His hobby, like his profession, bears witness to his imaginative use of the medium, his awareness of what has been done before him and his desire to keep up with what is being done now. But, above all, it is surely an expression of that joy which he clearly feels art should express. And joy is grace, which, as he wrote twenty years ago, we find when we give pleasure to others.

Aspects of
Dietrich Fischer-Dieskau...

39 From Clive Barda's exhibition 'An eye for an
    ear', 1979
40 Dietrich Fischer-Dieskau conducting

41 Fischer-Dieskau in the recording studio
42 Listening to a playback of Verdi's *Otello*,
   London, 1968

43 At the Edinburgh Festival; cartoon by Emilio
   Coia in *The Scotsman*, 6 September 1962
44 During a recording session

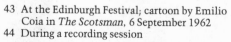

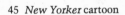

"*Just a minute! You don't get three years of my life and the Dietrich Fischer-Dieskau!*"

CHAPTER SEVEN

Conclusion

This study set out to document the career of a musician who, at fifty-six, is, I believe, the greatest singer of his time. In my early pages I dubbed him a 'musical Colossus' and I trust that the documentation of his career has justified the choice of epithet. The French critic, Jean Cotte, writing in the *Journal du dimanche* on 13 January 1974, ended a touching description of the artist by declaring: 'He is more than a baritone, he is a monopoly'!

But Fischer-Dieskau is a modest man who dislikes such sweeping generalisations and gushing eulogies as much as he mistrusts unfair criticism from unqualified sources. Like all great artists, he has had to put up with his fair share of such critics and would probably not disagree with Max Reger's trenchant riposte to them (see p. 247 above)! Fischer-Dieskau said once that positive and negative press reviews could only be taken as information about what opinions were 'in fashion' at that particular moment; *genuine* criticism could only come from those who knew the artist, his circumstances and his work intimately, since a press review only represented the critic's opinion on that particular occasion and was in any case conditioned by the acoustics of his seat in the hall! 'Nothing must deter an intelligent musician from following the path which he sees before him', he added.

It will be understood that I share his distaste for the modern custom of prying into the private lives of famous performers; rarely do these sensational reports correspond to the truth and, if sometimes they do, then often only as the description of a certain state of affairs at a certain time in the creative artist's career which, if taken as the norm, would give a distorted view of the subject's true feelings and circumstances. Fischer-Dieskau has not been spared these either; he has always treated sensation-seeking journalists with civility and courtesy, often giving them more information than they deserved – information which then appeared in a warped form in the eventual journalistic article. Indeed, for an artist who does have the reputation of being difficult to meet, Fischer-Dieskau has given a surprising number of interviews over the thirty years of his career. I am sure that his natural politeness makes it difficult for him to refuse what appears, at first sight anyway, to be a genuine request for information about his art. Although nothing can be more tedious for a musician after a tiring concert than to be asked 'searching' questions about the work(s) just performed, I am sure that there are few who can recall Fischer-Dieskau's failing to answer such questions fully and with interest.

'Unbuttoned' and at home, Fischer-Dieskau is an easy and fluent conversationalist who has a ready wit and a bubbling laugh and whose reminiscences and opinions are often illustrated by remarkably vivid and comical impersonations – in voice and gesture – of the character under discussion. After his housekeeper has brought in the sandwiches, biscuits or whatever, Fischer-Dieskau will pour the coffee or tea himself before settling down to talk.

We once discussed the 'music of the future'; readers will recall the views expressed in his books on Schubert and the Wagner-Nietzsche relationship. Fischer-Dieskau said that he believed that music had come to an 'interval', it was 'down in a valley', so to speak, and we now had to wait for someone new, someone who could re-organize the musical material available – yet, before that occurred, the present musical 'technology' would have to be adapted. Although the orchestral instruments themselves would probably not change, he foresaw some alterations in our concert-going habits and maybe even a reduction in the number of orchestras, if only because so few new works were being written for them. Indeed, he thought that it would not be impossible to imagine the creation of a few 'Weihestätten', (literally, 'holy places'), where the works of the great masters of the past would be cultivated, almost as 'rites'. When I asked him if he thought that the record industry had contributed to this apparent decline by its flooding of the market with recordings of the 'classics', his answer was one which he has given so often on so many occasions that one could fairly take it as a basic element in his *Weltanschauung*:

'Jeder Fortschritt bringt seinen Rückschritt mit sich', perhaps, 'Every step forward is a step back' – you lose as you win.

Although we were talking about the future, and the singer was at pains to stress that the present position was not all that unsatisfactory, in that music could be heard all over the world in small and large towns, and that the record industry had made an enormous contribution to the public's comprehension of music, he felt nevertheless that the situation had markedly deteriorated over the thirty or so years of his own professional career. He recalled how thrilled he and his fellow German musicians had been after the last war to hear all the music that had been forbidden during the Nazi era – Schoenberg, Stravinsky and so on. To hear and to perform this music had been an enormous artistic impetus for audience and musician alike. But that had all been done – it all lay in the past. One of the reasons for the decline in music, Fischer-Dieskau believed, was what he called, in German, 'das Sich-Auflösen des Nationalen in Schulen', the dissolving of the national element into schools of music, that is, that one can no longer distinguish German music from English, American from Italian. It all sounded the same. Diversity, that special something, a *je ne sais quoi*, characteristic of each nation, was essential for the healthy growth and development of music, he believed.

From these more general remarks about the state of music, it was a small step to a discussion of that area of music with which his name will be indelibly associated: the 'solo song with piano accompaniment' and, in particular, the German *Lied*. I reminded the singer of George Steiner's provocative book *The Death of Tragedy*, and asked him if he believed that the *Lied* was, similarly, 'dead'. He answered that, although there might still be a few 'late blossoms' here and there, the *Lied*, as a musical genre, had had its day, principally because, firstly, the texts which would be suitable for musical setting were no longer being written, and secondly, because that particular genre had exhausted itself as all other genres had done. He thought that opera alone had remained vital and alive, perhaps because it was now an admixture of film, musical and other forms, and, in a sense, was on the way to becoming the genuine *Gesamtkunstwerk*, the total work of art. Nor could he imagine that the great operas of Verdi or Puccini, for example, would ever 'die', since they continued to offer audiences so much vitality, strength and excitement.

Yet Fischer-Dieskau does not deal with these matters as a pessimistic soothsayer, it seems to me, but rather as a very realistic, practising musician who knows full well of course that what a Fischer-Dieskau achieves – and *can* achieve – is not necessarily proof of what others can or could achieve. He knows full well too that other *Liederabende* do not necessarily fill great halls as his do. Indeed, he makes the point that, as with all art-forms, his too suffers from what he himself called 'ups-and-downs'! There was, for example, I recall, a heated discussion among *Intendanten* in Germany in 1968 as to whether it would be worthwhile to continue to hold *Lieder* concerts in. the future; one prominent promoter announced that he would no longer do so, since only two to three hundred people had been prepared to book their seats in advance ('abonnieren', in German) for concerts in halls which held fourteen hundred seats, and that only singers of the status of a Fischer-Dieskau or a Prey would fill them. But that was at a time when, as the promoter added, 'only introverted or older people wanted evenings of *Lieder*, the younger generation preferring symphony concerts'. Much has changed however since 1968, and I have found *Lieder* concerts in Britain, France and Germany quite well attended recently. Young groups, such as the Songmakers' Almanac in Britain, no doubt encouraged by the sales figures of *Lieder* records made by great artists like Fischer-Dieskau, have made an even larger public aware of the possibilities – and the beauties – of the *Lied*, or of solo songs with piano (or orchestral) accompaniment.

Since my own professional work is largely concerned with the training of young people, I am always interested to hear the views of colleagues in other professions about how to pass on one's knowledge and experience. As has been indicated, Fischer-Dieskau is no friend of the sweeping generalisation, above all, where the subject is the training of the voice. 'Such general statements almost always lead to misunderstandings and misinterpretations', he will say. Singers, like people in general, have such individual physiological characteristics, (vocal chords, physique etc), that one could only teach individual to individual, 'eye-ball to eye-ball', as he puts it graphically – if he were to write a book on 'interpretation' and to state that 'one' should do this or that 'one' should sing like this, then these misunderstandings and misinterpretations would be bound to arise. He fears, I believe, that some of such books on 'Interpretation' tend to become projections of the writer's own artistic personality rather than genuine aids to learning – which is why Fischer-Dieskau wanted to keep the masterclasses which he held in Berlin in 1980 as small and as intimate as possible. He wanted to avoid any suspicion of giving a 'performance'.

The singer has always been very conscious of the pitfalls that lie in the way of those who want to teach. He sees teaching as a very 'altruistic' activity, one which he, up to the present at any rate, had felt unable to consider, since his attentions have had to be concentrated on himself and his own artistic development over the last thirty years and more. Yet he would clearly enjoy passing on some at least of his enormous experience, if he could be sure that he could teach the technique of singing *along with* the art of interpretation. The two are indissolubly connected, he feels. As soon as the teacher is satisfied that the technique is 'there', however, then the teaching of interpretation should begin – the pupil should not need to continue vocal or breathing exercises for years on end. But he would qualify that statement, too, by saying that it would all depend on the individual student!

Many of his professional colleagues have expressed the wish that he would somehow pass on this wealth of experience to younger singers and, in so doing, they have stressed those aspects of his art which make Fischer-Dieskau – for them – 'unique'. It is fascinating to observe that these distinguished fellow-artists do not always underline the *same* aspect. For Gerald Moore, for instance, his 'unique-ness' lay in his unparalleled mastery of rhythm: 'Dieter has this dynamic potential', wrote the accompanist, 'and it imbues his singing with authority . . . fluctuation of tempo is performed with such subtlety that the listener, while captivated by the life-enhancing buoyancy of it all, is unaware that the musical phrase has lost its fixed mould and now is pliable'. Gerald Moore was writing principally of Fischer-Dieskau, the *Lieder* singer of course. Wolfgang Sawallisch, on the other hand, wrote to me of Fischer-Dieskau, the operatic baritone, although, as we know, Sawallisch has regularly accompanied Fischer-Dieskau on the concert-platform, too. As an operatic baritone, Fischer-Dieskau impresses

Sawallisch by his faultless and problem-free musicianship. That, allied to his profound knowledge of the particular musical 'style' of the performance, gave a stage personality *hors concours*. Sawallisch would certainly agree with Fischer-Dieskau's distinguished elder colleague, Hans Hotter, that Fischer-Dieskau's greatest contribution to music over the last thirty years has been, as Professor Hotter wrote to me, to bring about a 'far-reaching revival and renewal' of the classical German *Lied* by means of a 'musicality', 'sensitivity' and an 'intelligence' rarely found in one singer.*

Fischer-Dieskau's Austrian accompanist, Jörg Demus, believes that Fischer-Dieskau's 'unique-ness' lies in his possession of the most phenomenal – and yet the simplest – musical technique. 'Even after thirty years', Herr Demus wrote me, 'Fischer-Dieskau's voice shows no tendency to disintegrate into the notorious three registers – the voice is controlled like a cello from the lowest to the highest note of its range. Every sound, every note is possible in every dynamic crescendo or diminuendo and all this is carried by almost inexhaustible reserves of breath which permit a truly sovereign breadth of phrasing'. Jörg Demus acknowledged that Fischer-Dieskau had received this technique from his teacher, Professor Weissenborn, and that he had had to learn how to control, polish and refine this technique over the years – but since it was, in essence, founded on the simplest of basic principles, Herr Demus believed that it must be able to be passed on to others – which is what he hoped that Fischer-Dieskau would do in the years to come.

With Gerald Moore, Jörg Demus could only marvel at the singer's ability to learn new music quickly and without seeming effort. 'Two, at the most three rehearsals were sufficient, even for the most difficult music', he recalled, while for normal *Lieder* concerts, a longer rehearsal together, followed by a shorter one in the concert hall, sufficed. Similarly with recordings: Gerald Moore recalled how they only needed to record a song once, listen to the playback, discuss it together and with the Artistic Supervisor and the recording engineers, and then record it again. Only rarely would they need to record, say, a section of a longer *Lied* again,

---

*Elisabeth Schwarzkopf said to Edward Greenfield: 'A very few [artists] are really born gods, like Fischer-Dieskau, who has it all anyway. All we others have is the imagination which has to be kindled'. (in *Recorded Sound*, Jan. 1981).

but, after that, the singer would say that they should leave it there: 'It's the best that I can do'.

It is not easy to put one's finger on the most innovatory aspect of Fischer-Dieskau's art, but I suspect that Jörg Demus who, with Gerald Moore, was probably as close to the singer as a professional colleague could be, came very near to the truth when he wrote to me:

> 'What was absolutely new in his singing – and, of course, it is no longer new now because we have heard Fischer-Dieskau so often in the meantime – was his significant and absolutely clear-sighted awareness that the composer had been inspired by the *poem*. There are few great *Lieder* where the composer woke up with a melody in his head and then looked for a poem to set to it (as Beethoven did with the *Choral Fantasia*). With the great, the genuine *Lieder*, it was always the other way round and that is the way that Fischer-Dieskau leads us. Beside and before him, there was hardly another singer with whom one could enjoy the *poem* so much, in all its purity . . .'

This is certainly what makes Fischer-Dieskau unique for me; his ability to bring out the meaning of a phrase – or a word even – in a poem by a subtle coloration of the vowel or the tiniest stressing of the consonant is, I believe, unmatched. It is, in essence, a histrionic quality, and it is what has made him such a fine operatic singer as well. More than once I have wondered if Fischer-Dieskau would ever appear in a stage-play; he would not be the first singer to make the sidewards move, of course – that fine singer-actor Leo Slezak comes to mind, among others – and his fine, clear diction, married to his gift for comic and serious characterization, would fit him well for stage rôles.* It would also be interesting to hear him read poetry – ever since I heard his beautiful rendering of that strange Schubert 'Lied' *Abschied von der Erde* (D829), a poem spoken to a simple, but sensitive piano accompaniment, I have thought that a record of Fischer-Dieskau reciting some of the great German poetic masterpieces, by Goethe, Heine, Eichendorff or Mörike, would be an enthralling experience.

---

*In late 1980, the singer took his first speaking-role as an actor when he appeared as the Kaiser (Emperor) in Heinrich von Kleist's play *Käthchen von Heilbronn* (1810) on West German television.

Thus we take leave of Dietrich Fischer-Dieskau at the pinnacle of his career, heaped with honours and distinctions. How many honorary doctorates are to follow those bestowed upon him by the University of Oxford and the Sorbonne, we do not know. Undeniably moved by, and genuinely grateful for these tokens of recognition by such prestigious institutions, Fischer-Dieskau can still think back on the ceremonies in warm, human terms. Just as the Oxford ceremonial with the Latinization of his name ('Praesento vobis Dietrichum Fischer-Dieskau' – I present to you Dietrich Fischer-Dieskau) pleased and intrigued him enormously, so too did the Sorbonne event in 1980 have its moments. This was one of the first honorary degree ceremonies to be held at the famous Paris university since the *événements* of 1968. There were six other distinguished recipients, including a venerable scholar who, when introduced to Fischer-Dieskau, whispered: 'So, you are the lad who is the pin-up boy of my wife!' which both touched and amused the singer.

In 1971, Sweden had elected Fischer-Dieskau a member of the Royal Swedish Academy, the first time a German singer had been so honoured, and, in 1975, another Scandinavian country, Denmark, awarded him the Léonie-Sonning Prize for Music, worth about £7000. The singer is now an Honorary Member of many societies, among them the Schubert, the Schumann, the Hugo Wolf and the Richard Strauss, as well as being a distinguished Honorary Member of the Royal Academy of Music in London. Thus, official acclaim has certainly not lagged behind public.

For countless numbers in countless audiences throughout the world, the 'miracle Fischer-Dieskau' has been the means to an enrichment of human experience; he has led his audiences and his listeners into new musical paths, has introduced them to unimagined musical and musicological treasures, and, at the same time, presented them with a fresh and vital approach to old and well-loved favourites which, in his renderings, seem newly-minted. Dame Janet Baker, writing to me about the programme of duets which she and Fischer-Dieskau gave with Daniel Barenboim in London and New York in 1970 and 1971, recalled how moved she was when 'Dieter said how good it was to work with people whose minds are on the same path'. Dame Janet, whose own contributions to vocal music in our time are so distinguished, added: 'If my musical mind was in any way on the same path as his, I am indeed content. No greater compliment could ever be paid me', and Fischer-Dieskau's fellow-artists would, I am sure, share Dame Janet's closing thought: 'How lucky we are to work in his time'.

For many years now, I have closed my lectures on 'The Art of Dietrich Fischer-Dieskau' with an extract from a John Amis' review in *The Scotsman* of one of Fischer-Dieskau's early Edinburgh Festival concerts. Its unobtrusive prose sums up what I myself feel as we wend our way homewards after a Fischer-Dieskau recital, musing on yet another unforgettable musical experience. To have known such an artist, and to have been privileged to call him 'my dear friend', imposes a debt which I can only hope this study has in some small measure repaid.

'Providence gives to some singers a beautiful voice, to some, musical artistry, to some (let us face it) neither, but to Fischer-Dieskau, Providence has given both. The result is a miracle and that is just about all there is to be said about it. It is difficult therefore to write a long notice about Fischer-Dieskau. Having used a few superlatives and described the programme, there is nothing else to do but write 'finis', go home, and thank one's stars for having had the luck to be present.'

BIBLIOGRAPHY

Works Mentioned in the Text

ABRAHAMS, G. (ed.): *Schumann: A Symposium* (O.U.P., 1952).
ANDERSON, E. (ed.): *The Letters of Mozart and his Family* (3 vols. Macmillan, 1938). Second edition prepared by A. Hyatt King and Monica Carolan, (2 vols., Macmillan, 1966).
BACHARACH, A. L. (ed.): *The New Musical Companion* (Gollancz, 1957).
BARFORD, P.: *Mahler: Symphony and Song-Cycles* (BBC Music Guides, 1970).
BATLEY, E. M.: *A Preface to 'The Magic Flute'* (Dobson, 1969).
BLOM, E. (ed.): *Mozart's Letters* (Penguin, 1956).
BLYTH, A. (ed.): *Opera on Record* (Hutchinson, 1979).
BROPHY, B.: *Mozart the Dramatist* (Faber and Faber, 1964).
BROWN, M. J. E.: *Schubert: A Critical Biography* (Macmillan, 1958).
——: *Essays on Schubert* (Macmillan, 1966).
BUDDEN, J.: *The Operas of Verdi* (2 vols., Cassell, 1973).
CAPELL, R.: *Schubert's Songs* (Macmillan, Duckworth, 1928) (2nd edn., revised by Martin Cooper, 1957).
CHAILLEY, J.: *La flûte enchantée, opéra maçonnique* (Laffont, Paris, 1968) (Translated by Herbert Weinstock, Gollancz, 1972 as *The Magic Flute, Masonic Opera*).
COOPER, M.: *Gluck* (London, 1935).
COTTRELL, A. P.: *Wilhelm Müller's Lyrical Song Cycles (University of North Carolina Press, 1970).*
CULSHAW, J.: *Ring Resounding* (Secker and Warburg, 1967).
DAIBER, H.: *Deutsches Theater seit 1945* (Reclam, Stuttgart, 1976).
DEL MAR, N.: *Richard Strauss* (Barrie and Jenkins, Vol. I, 1962, Vol. II, 1969, Vol. III, 1972).
DEMUS, J., HÖCKER, K, LEWINSKI, W. E. von, OEHLMANN, W.: *Dietrich Fischer-Dieskau* (Rembrandt Verlag, Berlin, 1966).
DEMUS, J.: *Abenteuer der Interpretation* (Brockhaus, Wiesbaden, 1976).
DENT, E.: *Opera* (Book III of *The New Musical Companion*, see Bacharach, A.L.).
DEUTSCH, O. E.: *Schubert: A Documentary Biography* (Dent, 1946) (*A Schubert Reader*, New York, 1947)

———: *Schubert: Thematic Catalogue of His Works in chronological order* (Dent, 1951).

DICKINSON, A. E. F.: *The Art of J. S. Bach* (Hinrichsen Edition Ltd., London, 1936) (2nd revised edition, 1950)

———: *The Music of Berlioz* (Faber and Faber, 1972).

FEIL, A.: *Franz Schubert* (Reclam, Stuttgart, 1975).

FISCHER-DIESKAU, D.: *Auf den Spuren der Schubert-Lieder: Werden-Wesen-Wirkung* (Brockhaus, Wiesbaden, 1971). (Translated and edited by Kenneth S. Whitton as *Schubert: A Biographical Study of his Songs* (Cassell, 1976) and in the United States as *Schubert's Songs: A Biographical Study* (Knopf, 1977))

———: *Texte deutscher Lieder: Ein Handbuch* (Deutscher Taschenbuch Verlag, München, 1968) (Translated by George Bird and Richard Stokes as *The Fischer-Dieskau Book of Lieder* (Gollancz/Pan Books, 1976)).

———: *Wagner und Nietzsche: Der Mystagoge und sein Abtrünniger* (Deutsche Verlags-Anstalt, Stuttgart, 1974) (Translated by Joachim Neugroschel as *Wagner and Nietzsche* (Seabury Press, Inc. 1976) and in Great Britain by Sidgwick and Jackson, 1978)).

FISCHER-FABIAN, S.: *Die ersten Deutschen* (Droemer Knaur, 1975).

FLORENT, F.: *Dietrich Fischer-Dieskau* (in *Opéra*, No. 7, juin 1967).

GÀL, H.: *Johannes Brahms* (Fischer, 1961) (Translated by Joseph Stein, Weidenfeld and Nicholson, 1963).

GARTEN, H. F.: *Wagner, the Dramatist* (Calder, 1977).

GAY, P.: *Weimar Culture* (Secker and Warburg, 1969) (Penguin, 1974).

GEORGIADES, Th.: *Schubert: Musik und Lyrik* (Vandenhoeck und Ruprecht, Göttingen, 1967).

GERHARDT, E.: *Recital* (Methuen, 1953).

GOBBI, T.: *Adrian Boult Lecture* (5th March 1979) in *Recorded Sound*, January 1980, pp. 1–12, with Harold Rosenthal.

GODWIN, J.: *The Layers of Meaning in The Magic Flute* (in *The Musical Quarterly*, October 1979, Vol. LXV, No. 4, pp. 471–492).

GOLDSCHMIDT, H.: *Franz Schubert* (VEB Deutscher Verlag für Musik, Leipzig, 1976).

HALTRECHT, M.: *The Quiet Showman: Sir David Webster and the Royal Opera House* (Collins, 1975).

HAMMELMANN, H. A.: *Hofmannsthal* (Bowes and Bowes, 1957).

HERMAND, J. and TROMMLER, F.: *Die Kultur der Weimarer Republik* (Nymphenburger Verlagshandlung, München, 1978).

HERZFELD, F.: *Dietrich Fischer-Dieskau* (Rembrandt Verlag, Berlin, 1958) (3rd edn, 1962).

HUGHES, R.: *Haydn* (Dent 1950, revised 1974).

ILLING, R.: *A Dictionary of Music* (Penguin, 1950).

JACOBSON, B.: *The Music of Johannes Brahms* (Tantivy Press 1977)

KAUFMANN, W.: *Nietzsche – Philosopher, Psychologist, Anti-Christ* (Princeton, 1950).

KENDALL, A.: *Benjamin Britten* (Macmillan, 1973).

KERMAN, J.: *An die ferne Geliebte* (in *Beethoven Studies*, 1974, pp. 123–157, see Tyson, A (ed.)).

LARVIN, J.: *Nietzsche* (Studio Vista, London, 1971).

LEHMANN, L.: *Eighteen Song Cycles* (Cassell, 1971).

MANN, W.: *The Operas of Mozart* (Cassell, 1977).

MELLERS, W.: *François Couperin and the French Classical Tradition* (London 1950).

MITCHELL, D.: *Gustav Mahler: The Wunderhorn Years* (Faber and Faber, 1975).

MOORE, G.: *The Unashamed Accompanist* (Methuen 1943) (1959 edn.)

———: *Am I too loud?* (Hamish Hamilton, 1962)

———: *The Schubert Song Cycles* (Hamilton, 1975).

———: *Farewell Recital* (Hamilton, 1978).

MOSER, H. J.: *Das deutsche Lied seit Mozart* (2 vols., Berlin 1937).

NEWMAN, E.: *Richard Strauss* (London, 1908).

———: *Testament of Music* (Selected writings chosen by Herbert van Thal, Putnam, 1962).

———: *Wagner: Man and Artist* (1924) (Gollancz, 1963).

OSBORNE, C.: *The Complete Operas of Mozart* (Gollancz, 1978).

———: *W. H. Auden* (Methuen, 1980).

PAHLEN, K.: *Great Singers* (translated by Oliver Coburn, W. H. Allen, 1973).

PASLEY M. (ed.): *Germany: A Companion to German Studies* (Methuen, 1972).

PLEASANTS, H.: *The Great Singers* (Gollancz, 1967).

PLUNKET GREENE, H.: *Interpretation in Song* (Macmillan, 1913).

PORTER, A.: *Music of Three Seasons* (1974–1977) (Chatto and Windus, 1979).

PORTER, E.: *Schubert's Song Technique* (Dobson, 1961).

PRAWER, S. S.: *The Penguin Book of Lieder* (Penguin, 1964).

PRAWY, M.: *The Vienna Opera* (Weidenfeld and Nicholson, 1970).

ROBERTSON, A.: *Bach* (Clive Bingley, London, 1977).

ROBERTSON, J. G.: *A History of German Literature* (Blackwood, 1947).

ROBINSON, G.: *Karajan* (Macdonald and Janes, 1975).

ROSENFELD, P.: *Musical Impressions* (ed. by Herbert A. Leibowitz) (Allen and Unwin, 1969) (Great Britain, 1970).

ROSENTHAL, H.: *Great Singers of Today* (Calder and Boyard, 1966).

———: *Two Centuries of Opera at Covent Garden* (Putnam, 1958).

SAMS, E.: *The Songs of Robert Schumann* (Methuen, 1969, Eulenburg, 1975).

———: *The Songs* in *Robert Schumann: The Man and his Music* (see Walker, A. (ed.)).

SCHIØTZ, A.: *The Singer and His Art* (Hamilton, 1970).

SCHONBERG, H. C.: *Lives of the Great Composers* (Davis-Poynter, 1971).

SCHWEITZER, A.: *J. S. Bach* (translated by Ernest Newman, Black, 1923)

294 DIETRICH FISCHER-DIESKAU

SHAW, G. B.: *Music in London* (Constable 1932)
——: *GBS on Music* (Penguin, 1962).
SOLOMON, M.: *Beethoven* (Cassell, 1977).
STASSINOPOULOS. A: *Maria: Beyond the Callas legend* (Weidenfeld and Nicholson 1980).
STEANE, J. B.: *The Grand Tradition* (Duckworth, 1974) (1978).
STEIN, J.: *Poem and Music in the German Lied* (Harvard University Press, 1971).
STERN, J. P.: *A Study of Nietzsche* (Cambridge University Press, 1979).
SULLIVAN, J. W. N.: *Beethoven* (Cape 1927) (Pelican, 1949).
TAYLOR, R.: *German Music* (In *Germany: A Companion to German Studies,* see Pasley M. (ed.)).
TERRY, C. S.: *Bach. A Biography* (Oxford University Press, 1928) (2nd edn. 1933).
TOLAND, J.: *Adolf Hitler* (Doubleday, 1976).
TOVEY, Sir D. F.: *Essays in Musical Analysis* (6 vols. Oxford University Press, 1935–1939) (Vol. V: *Vocal Music*).
TOYE, F.: *Verdi: His Life and Works* (Gollancz 1931) (1962).
TURING, P.: *New Bayreuth* (Jersey Artists/Neville Spearman, 1969).
TYSON, A. (ed.): *Beethoven Studies* (Oxford University Press) (1974 et al.).
WALKER, A. (ed.): *Robert Schumann: The Man and his Music* (Barrie and Jenkins 1972).
——: *Franz Liszt* (Barrie and Jenkins 1970).
WALKER, F.: *Hugo Wolf* (Dent 1951) (2nd edn. 1968).
WALSH, S.: *The Lieder of Schumann* (Cassell, 1971).
WALTER, B.: *Themes and Variations* (London 1946).
WEAVER, W. and CHUSID, M.: *The Verdi Companion* (W. W. Norton, 1979).
WHITTAKER, W. G.: *The Cantatas of Johann Sebastian Bach, Sacred and Secular,* (2 vols., London 1959).
WOOLDRIDGE, D.: *From the Steeples and the Mountains* (Knopf, 1974).
YOUNG, P.: *The Bachs, 1500–1850* (Dent, 1970).

Index of Names

List of Illustrations
and Acknowledgements

Picture Credits

Erich Auerbach, London, 31
Clive Barda, London, 39
Ilse Buhs, Berlin 11, 16, 37
Photo Ellinger, Salzburg, 20, 25, 35, 41
EMI Electrola, 40
Isaac Freidin, Tel Aviv, 36
Douglas Glass, London, 28
Elfriede Hanak, Vienna, 29
Siegfried Lauterwasser, Überlingen, 33
Werner Neumeister, Munich, 17, 19, 23, 41, 42, 44 and jacket
Oxford Mail & Times, 47
Polydor International, 10, 18, 22, 38
Sabine Toepffer, Munich, 32
Diether Warneck, Berlin, 26, 27, 30
Cartoons:
The Scotsman (Emilio Coia), 43
The New Yorker (Wm. Hamilton), 45
Painting reproduced from Catalogue Kunstverein Bamberg (photo Anne Kirchbach, Starnberg), 2

Other illustrations from private collections and archives

Back flap photograph by kind permission of Colin Mellors, University of Bradford

Discography

Compiled by
Maurice R. Wright

Acknowledgements

We should like to offer sincere thanks to Dietrich Fischer-Dieskau for correcting the material for this discography and to his secretary, Diether Warneck, for help in providing the original lists on which it is based. Thanks for helpful information are also due to:

Jörg Demus, Karl Engel, Gerald Moore and Aribert Reimann.

Further information was obtained from the following sources to whom our thanks are likewise due:

Polydor International GmbH   Ilse Koefod
EMI Ltd   A. B. Locantro
Ariola-Eurodisc GmbH   Lydia Störle
EMI Electrola   Dr Herfrid Kier
BBC   Derek Lewis, Librarian

Decca Record Company Ltd.   Wergo Schallplatten GmbH
Vox Productions Inc.   BASF AG.
Schallplatten-Antiquariat
Alma Hoehn.

NB. 1. The date after each entry is the date of the recording.
    2. The recordings are those released before 1st August 1980.
    3. Where no numbers are given, the record is not yet issued or the number has proved to be untraceable.

Maurice R. Wright
Kenneth S. Whitton

1. Adolphe Adam
i. Vernimm, o Welt, gekommen ist die Stunde.
Jörg Demus (DG)
[2530 219]   Nov 1970

2. Anna Amalie von Sachsen-Weimar
1. *Goethe Lieder*
Auf dem Land und in der Stadt. Sie scheinen zu
spielen
Jörg Demus (DG)
[2533 149]   Sep 1972

3. Hans-Erich Apostel
1. Nacht op. 3 No. 4.
Aribert Reimann (Elec)
[C065–02 677]   Mar 1974

4. Bettina von Arnim
1. *Goethe Lieder*
O schaudre nicht.
Jörg Demus (DG)
[2533 149]   Sep 1972

5. Carl Philipp Emanuel Bach
1. *Oden, Psalmen, Lieder*
Abendlied. Bitten. Demut. Der Frühling. Die
Güte Gottes. Jesus in Gethsemane.
Morgengesang. Passionslied. Prüfung am
Abend. Psalmen 19, 130, 148. Der Tag des
Weltgerichts. Weihnachtslied. Wider den
Übermut.
Jörg Demus (DG)
[2533 058]   Nov 1969

6. Johann Christian Bach
1. *Duet*
Ah, lamenta, oh bella Irene.
Victoria de los Angeles
Gerald Moore (Elec)
[E91 098]   Dec 1960

7. Johann Sebastian Bach
1. *Matthäus-Passion* (BWV 244) (Christ)
Elfriede Trötschel
Diana Oistrati
Helmut Krebs
Friedrich Härtel
Choir and Orchestra of Berlin Radio
Fritz Lehmann (Vox)
[PL 6070]   Apr 1949

2. *Matthäus-Passion*
Elisabeth Grümmer
Marga Höffgen
Anton Dermota
Otto Edelmann
Vienna Philharmonic Orchestra
Wilhelm Furtwängler (CETRA)
(Recorded live in Vienna)
[L 0508/3]   1954

3. *Matthäus-Passion* (Bass arias)
Ernst Häfliger
Kieth Engen

Irmgard Seefried
Antonio Fehberg
Hertha Töpper
Max Proebst
Münchener Bach-Chor
Münchener Chorknaben
Münchener Bachorchester
Karl Richter (DG)
[ApM 14125/8   198009/12
2538126   2564044/7
2712001   EPA 37189
3336001 (Tape)
LPEM 19 233 (Choruses and arias)]
                                              Aug 1958

4. *Matthäus-Passion* (Christ)
Elisabeth Schwarzkopf
Christa Ludwig
Janet Baker
Helen Watts
Nicolai Gedda
Peter Pears
Wilfred Brown
John Carol Case
Otokar Kraus
Geraint Evans
Walter Berry
Instrumental soloists
Philharmonia Choir
Hampstead Parish Church choirboys
Philharmonia Orchestra
Otto Klemperer (Elec)
[SLS 827
C80693 (Highlights)]   Jan 1961

5. *Matthäus-Passion* (Christ)
Gundula Janowitz
Christa Ludwig
Peter Schreier
Walter Berry
Horst Laubenthal
Vienna Singverein
Berlin Philharmonic Orchestra
Herbert von Karajan (DG)
[2720 070   2711 012
Tape 3371 007   Jan 1972

6. *Matthäus-Passion* (Christ)
Edith Mathis
Peter Schreier
Janet Baker
Munich Bach Choir
and Orchestra
Karl Richter (DG)
[2723 067
3376 016 Cassette]   Aug 1979

7. *Johannes-Passion (BWV 245)*
Berliner Symphoniker
Karl Forster (Elec)
80 668/70
80 727 (Highlights)
ALP 1975/77
C 147 28589/91
ASD 526/8   Jun 1961

8. *Christ lag in Todesbanden* (BWV 4)
Helmut Krebs
Chor der Hochschule für Musik, Frankfurt
Orchester des Bach-Festes, Göttingen
Fritz Lehmann (DG)
[14079   2722 018
2420/21 AVM   Jul/Aug 1950

9. *Christ lag in Todesbanden*
Munich Bach Choir and Orchestra
Karl Richter (DG)
[198 465
2722 018
2564 18]   Aug 1968

10. *Ich will den Kreuzstab gerne tragen* (BWV 56)
Ich habe genug (BWV 82)
Hermann Töttcher (Oboe)
Berliner Motettenchor und Kammerorchester
Karl Ristenpart (DG)
APM 14 004   2548 128
                                   Jun 1951

11. *Ich will den Kreuzstab gerne tragen*
Ich habe genug
Munich Bach Choir and Orchestra
Karl Richter (DG)
SAPM 198 477
2538 231   2548 128
2564 127   2722 019
                                   Aug 1951

12. *Ich will den Kreuzstab gerne tragen*
Festival Strings, Lucerne
Rudolf Baumgartner (DG)   Aug 1963
[LPM 18969]

13. *Ich habe genug*
Hermann Töttcher, Oboe
Berlin Kammerorchester
Karl Ristenpart (DG)
[APM 14004 2548 128]
                                   June 1951

14. *Ich habe genug*
Münchener Bach Orchester
Karl Richter (DG)
[2538 231]   Aug 1968

15. *Cantata Arias*
Herr, so du willt, (BWV 73.)
Doch weichet ihr tollen, vergeblichen Sorgen
(BWV 8)
Der Friede sei mit dir, (BWV 158)
Ächzen und erbärmlich Weinen (BWV 13)
Ich halte meinen Jesum feste, (BWV 157)
Es ist vollbracht (BWV 159)
Chor der St. Hedwigskathedrale
Berliner Philharmoniker
Karl Forster (Elec)
[E90 022 WALP533]   Feb 1958

16. *Christmas Oratorio* (BWV 248)
Agnes Giebel
Marga Höffgen
Josef Traxel
Thomanerchor

Gewandhausorchester Leipzig
Kurt Thomas (in the Thomaskirche in Leipzig)
(Elec)
[ASD 5014   ALP 1950–3
SME 8063065   E80467
C147–28583/5
SME 80 662 (Highlights)]   Dec 1958

17. *Christmas Oratorio*
Elly Ameling
Janet Baker
Robert Tear
Choir of King's College, Cambridge
Academy of St. Martin-in-the-Fields
Philip Ledger (Elec)
[(SQ)SLS 5098   IC 153–02 890/92Q
Tapes 1C 285-02 890/892]   Dec 1976

18. (*Amore traditore*) (BWV 213)
Edith Picht-Axenfeld, Harpsichord
Irmgard Poppen, Cello (Elec)
[FALP PM 30544]   Feb 1960

19. *Peasant Cantata* (BWV 212)
Coffee Cantata (BWV 211)
Lisa Otto
Josef Traxel
Berliner Philharmoniker
Karl Forster (Elec)
[SME 80 618]   Oct 1960

20. *Magnificat in D Major* BWV 243
Münchener Bach-Chor
Münchener Bach-Orchester
Karl Richter (DG)
[ALP 13 078   APM 14 197
SAP 195 078   198 197]
2564 114]   Feb 1961

21. *Mass in B minor* (BWV 232)
Münchener Bach-Chor
Münchener Bach-Orchester
Karl Richter (DG)
[APM 14191   198 191
2564 104   2710 001
2722 017   Tape 3376 008
136 300   LPEM 19 300
(Choruses and Arias)]   Feb 1961

22. *Was mir behagt, ist nur die muntre Jagd* (BWV
208)
Members of the choir of the St. Hedwig-
Kathedrale Berlin
Karl Forster (Elec)
[ALP 1985   ASD 534
80 823   E 70475]   Nov 1961

23. *Easter Oratorio* (BWV 249)
Süddeutscher Madrigalchor
Südwestdeutsches Kammerorchester
Wolfgang Gönnenwein (Elec)
[SME 91 424   ST 95
ASD 624   ALP 2076]   Mar 1964

24. *Wie schön leuchtet der Morgenstern* (BWV 1)
Ernst Häfliger
Münchener Bach-Chor und Orchester
Karl Richter (DG)
[198 465   2722 018
2538 231   2564 117 and 144]
Aug 1968

25. *Ich hatte viel Bekümmernis* (BWV 21)
Edith Mathis
Ernst Häfliger
Münchener Bach-Chor und Orchester
Karl Richter (DG)
[2533 049   2538 231
2564 125   2722 019]
Jul 1969

26. *Cantatas*

4.	Christ lag in Todesbanden	Oct 1976
5.	Wo soll ich fliehen hin	May 1978
6.	Bleib bei uns	Jun 1973 & Oct 1976
9.	Es ist das Heil uns kommen her	Oct 1976
11.	Lobet Gott in seinen Reichen	Jan 1975
13.	Meine Seufzer, meine Tränen	Jul 1971
17.	Wer Dank opfert, der preiset mich	Oct 1976
26.	Ach, wie flüchtig, ach, wie nichtig	May 1978
27.	Wer weiss, wie nahe mir mein Ende	Oct 1976
33.	Allein zu dir, Herr Jesu Christ	Oct 1976
38.	Aus tiefer Not schrei' ich zu dir	May 1978
39.	Brich dem Hungrigen dein Brot	Jan 1975
44.	Sie werden euch in den Bann tun	Jan 1975
58.	Ach Gott, wie manches Herzeleid	Jun/Jul 1970
61.	Nun komm, der Heiden Heiland	Jun/Jul 1970
63.	Christen, ätzet diesen Tag	Jun/Jul 1970 Jul 1971
64.	Sehet, welch' eine Liebe hat uns der Vater erzeiget	Jun/Jul 1970
67.	Halt im Gedächtnis Jesum Christ	Jun 1973
70.	Wachet, betet, seid bereit allezeit	May 1978
80.	Ein' feste Burg ist unser Gott	May 1978
87.	Bisher habt ihr nichts gebeten in meinem Namen	Jun 1973
92.	Ich hab' in Gottes Herz und Sinn	Jun 1973
93.	Wer nur den lieben Gott lässt walten	Jan 1975
96.	Herr Christ, der ein'ge Gottessohn	May 1978
100.	Was Gott tut, das ist wohlgetan	Jan 1975
102.	Herr, deine Augen sehen nach	Jan 1975

	dem Glauben	
104.	Du Hirte Israel, höre	Jun 1973
105.	Herr, gehe nicht in's Gericht	Jan 1975
115.	Mache dich, mein Geist, bereit	May 1978
116	Du Friedefürst, Herr Jesu Christ	May 1978
129.	Gelobet sei der Herr, mein Gott	Jan 1975
130.	Herr Gott, dich loben alle wir	Oct 1976
137.	Lobe den Herren, den mächtigen König der Ehren	Oct 1976
139.	Wohl dem, der sich auf seinen Gott	May 1978
140.	Wachet auf, ruft uns die Stimme	May 1978
158.	Der Friede sei mit dir	Jul 1969
178.	Wo Gott der Herr nicht bei uns hält	Oct 1976
179.	Siehe zu, dass deine Gottesfurcht nicht Heuchelei sei	Oct 1976
180.	Schmücke dich, o liebe Seele	May 1978
187.	Es wartet alles auf dich	Oct 1976
212.	Mer hahn en neue Oberkeet	Jul 1971

[2722 018   2722 019
2564 119   2564 123
2533 355   2564 114
2564 146   2564 126
2564 120   2564 123
2564 146]

27. *Advent and Christmas Cantatas*
Nun komm der Heiden Heiland BWV 61
Christen, ätzet diesen Tag BWV 63
Sehet, welch eine Liebe hat uns der Vater erzeiget BWV 64
Gottlob! Nun geht das Jahr zu Ende BWV 28
Gott, wie dein Name, so ist auch dein Ruhm BWV 171
Ach Gott, wie manches Herzeleid BWV 58
Meine Seufzer, meine Tränen BWV 13
Edith Mathis
Sheila Armstrong
Peter Schreier
Münchener Bach-Chor und Orchester
Karl Richter (DG)
[2722 055   2722 018   1970–72

28. *Cantatas*
Liebster Immanuel BWV 123. *Aria*-Lass, o Welt.
Meine Seufzer, meine Tränen BWV 13. Aria –
Ächzen und erbärmlich Weinen.
J-P. Rampal, Flute
R. Veyron-Lacroix, Harpsichord
J. Neilz, Cello (Elec)
[ASD 2903]   Sep 1971

29. *Cantatas*
Ich hab' in Gottes Herz und Sinn BWV 92
Erhalt' uns, Herr, bei deinem Wort BWV 126
Münchener Bach-Chor
Münchener Bach-Orchester
Karl Richter (DG)
[2533 312]   1974

30. *Cantatas*
Du wahrer Gott und Davids Sohn BWV 23
Bisher habt ihr nichts gebeten in meinem Namen
BWV 87
Anna Reynolds
Peter Schreier
Münchener Bach-Chor and Orchester
Karl Richter (DG)
[2533 313]   1974

31. *Freue dich, erlöste Schar* BWV 30
Edith Mathis
Anna Reynolds
Peter Schreier
Münchener Bach-Chor and Orchester
Karl Richter (DG)
[2533 330]   Mar/May 1974
                                         Jan 1975

32. *Cantatas*
Meine Seel' erhebt den Herren BWV 10
Ach Herr, mich armen Sünder BWV 135
Ein ungefärbt Gemüte BWV 24
Edith Mathis
Anna Reynolds
Peter Schreier
Münchener Bach-Chor and Orchester
[2533 329]   1976

33. *Whitsun Cantatas*
O ewiges Feuer, O Ursprung der Liebe BWV 34
Also hat Gott die Welt geliebt BWV 68
Er rufet seinen Schafen mit Namen BWV 175
Edith Mathis
Anna Reynolds
Peter Schreier
Münchener Bach-Chor
Münchener Bach Orchester
Karl Richter (DG)
[2533 306   2564 122]

34. *Easter Cantatas*
Edith Mathis
Anna Reynolds
Peter Schreier
Münchener Bach-Chor und Orchester
Karl Richter (DG)
[2722 022]   1977

35. *Cantatas for Ascension Day, Whitsun & Trinity*
Edith Mathis
Anna Reynolds
Peter Schreier
Kurt Moll
Münchener Bach-Chor und Orchester
Karl Richter (DG)
[2722 025]   1977

36. *Cantatas for the Sundays after Trinity* – I
Edith Mathis
Julia Hamari
Peter Schreier
Münchener Bach-Chor und Orchester
Karl Richter (DG)
[2722 028]   1977

37. *Cantatas for the Sundays after Trinity* – II
Edith Mathis
Trudeliese Schmidt
Peter Schreier
Münchener Bach-Chor und Orchester
Karl Richter (DG)
[2722 030]   1977

8. Samuel Barber
1. Dover Beach op. 3
Juilliard Quartett (CBS)
[72687]   Apr 1967

9. Belá Bartók
1. *Duke Bluebeard's Castle*
(Herzog Blaubarts Burg) (in German)
Hertha Töpper
Radio Symphonie-Orchester, Berlin
Ferenc Fricsay (DG)
[138 030]   Oct 1958

2. *Duke Bluebeard's Castle* (in Hungarian)
Julia Varady
Orchester der Bayrischen Staatsoper
Wolfgang Sawallisch (DG)
[2531 172]   Mar 1979

3. *Im Tale op. 15*
Hermann Reutter (Elec)
[ASD 2714/5   C065 02 676
1E191 02180/1]   May 1970

10. Conrad Beck
1. Herbst
Aribert Reimann (Elec)
[C065 02 677]   Mar 1974

11. Ludwig van Beethoven
1. *An die ferne Geliebte* op. 98
Gerald Moore (Elec)
[DB 9681/2   DB 21347/8
ALP 10666]   Oct 1951

2. *Songs Vol. I*
Mailied. Marmotte. Neue Liebe, neues Leben.
Aus Goethes Faust. Wonne der Wehmut.
Sehnsucht. Mit einem gemalten Band. In questa
tomba oscura. Ich liebe dich. Andenken. An die
Hoffnung. Der Kuss. Adelaide.
Hertha Klust (Elec)
[ALP 509   ALP 1317
E90 005   ERW 5014 EP
*DA 5527   **DB 11595]   Nov 1954
* Separate recordings of
** one or more of the *Lieder*

3. *Songs Vol. II*
Der Wachtelschlag. Der Zufriedene. Ohne Liebe
lebe, wer da kann. Das Liedchen von der Ruhe.
Lied aus der Ferne. Abendlied. L'amante
impaziente (Stille Frage). L'amante impaziente
(Liebesungeduld). Resignation. Sehnsucht.
Gellert-Lieder.
Bitten. Die Liebe des Nächsten. Vom Tode. Die

Ehre Gottes aus der Natur. Gottes Macht und
Vorsehung. Busslied.
Hertha Klust (DG)
[ALP 510   ALP 1318
ERW 5333 EP   C053–01 138]
                                        Nov 1954
4. *Fidelio* op. 72 (Don Pizarro)
Leonie Rysanek
Irmgard Seefried
Keith Engen
Ernst Häfliger
Gottlob Frick
Friedrich Lenz
Chor und Orchester der Bayrischen Staatsoper
Ferenc Fricsay (DG)
[136 215   2705 037
2548 118]   Jun 1957
5. *Fidelio* (Don Fernando)
Hans Sotin
René Kollo
Gundula Janowitz
Manfred Jungwirth
Lucia Popp
Adolf Dallapozza
Karl Terkal
Alfred Sramek
Vienna State Opera Chorus
Vienna Philharmonic Orchestra
Leonard Bernstein (DG)
[2537 048   3306048
2709 082]   1977
6. *Symphony No. 9 in D minor* op. 125
Irmgard Seefried
Maureen Forrester
Ernst Häfliger
Chor der St. Hedwigs-Kathedrale
Berliner Philharmoniker
Ferenc Fricsay (DG)
[2700 108]   Jan 1958
7. Oh! Would I were but that sweet linnet. He
promised me at parting. They bid me slight my
Dermot dear. The dream.
Victoria de Los Angeles
Gerald Moore (piano)
Edward Drolc, (violin)
Irmgard Poppen, (cello) (Elec)
[E91098 YKM 5005]   Dec 1960
8. *Scottish Songs and Folksongs*
Horch auf, mein Liebchen. Canzonetta
veneziana. O köstliche Zeit. Trinklied. Der treue
Johnie. Kommt, schliesst mir einen frohen Kreis.
Helmut Heller, Violin
Irmgard Poppen, Cello
Karl Engel (piano) (DG)
[2720 017]   Feb 1961
9. *Lieder – An die ferne Gelbeite* op. 98
Schilderung eines Mädchens Wo O 107
Als die Geliebte sich trennen wollte Wo O 132
Sehnsucht WoO 146
Ruf vom Berge WoO 147
An die Geliebte WoO 140

Adelaide. Andenken. Zärtliche Liebe.
Italienische Liebeslieder:
Dimmi, ben mio, che m'ami. T'intendo, si mio
cor. L'amante impaziente op 82 no. 3 L'amante
impaziente op. 82 no. 4. Vita Felice. La
partenza. In questa tomba oscura.
Sechs Lieder von Gellert op. 48
An die Hoffnung op. 32. Das Liedchen von der
Ruhe. An die Hoffnung op. 94. Opferlied. Der
Wachtelschlag. Der Bardengeist. Das Geheimnis.
Resignation. Die laute Klage.
Lieder to poems by Goethe
Maigesang. Marmotte. Neue Liebe, neues
Leben. Flohlied. Wonne der Wehmut.
Sehnsucht. Mit einem gemalten Band. Uraniens
Reise um die Welt. Die Liebe. Das Blümchen
wunderhold. Der Zufriedene. Der Kuss. Lied aus
der Ferne. Der Jüngling in der Fremde. Der
liebende Seufzer eines Ungeliebten und
Gegenliebe. Abendlied unterm gestirnten
Himmel.
Jörg Demus (DG)
[139 216/8   2721 138]   Apr 1966

10. *Folksong arrangements.* (Scottish, Irish and
Welsh)
Music, love and wine. Once more I hail thee.
Behold, my love. The pulse of an Irishman. To
shepherds of this pleasant vale. Sunset. Put
round the bright wine. Robin Adair. Oh sweet
were the hours. Duncan Gray. Faithfu' Johnie.
Could this ill world. Farewell bliss and Farewell
Nancy. The Miller of Dee. Oh, had my fate been
join'd with thine. O Charlie is my darling. Come
fill, fill, my good fellow. Lochnagar. Sion, the
son of Evan. The return to Ulster.
Edith Mathis
Alexander Young
RIAS Chamber Choir
Andreas Röhn, Violin
Georg Donderer, Cello
Karl Engel (DG)
[2530 262   2721 138
2535   2720 017]   Mar 1970

11. *Goethe-Lieder*
Mit Mädeln sich vertragen (from *Claudine von
Villa Bella,*
Jörg Demus (DG)
[2533 149]   Sep 1972

12. Alban Berg
1. *Wozzeck* (Title Rôle)
Evelyn Lear
Karl-Christian Kohn
Helmut Melchert
Gerhard Stolze
Fritz Wunderlich
Chor und Orchester der Deutschen Oper Berlin
Karl Böhm (DG)
[2707 023]   Mar/
                                        Apr 1965

2. *Lulu* (Dr. Schön)
Evelyn Lear
Patricia Johnson
Loren Driscoll
Donald Grobe
Walther Dicks
Orchester der Deutschen Oper Berlin
Karl Böhm (DG)
[2709 029]   Feb/
                                      Mar 1968

3. *Vier Lieder op. 2*
Schlafen, schlafen. Schlafend trägt man mich.
Nun ich der Riesen Stärksten überwand. Warm
die Lüfte.
Aribert Reimann (DG)
[2530 107]   Sep 1970

13. Hector Berlioz
1. *Le trébuchet* op. 13 No. 3.
from *Fleurs des Landes*
Victoria de Los Angeles
Gerald Moore (Elec)
[E91098]   Dec 1960

2. Auf den Lagunen
Aribert Reimann (Elec)
[IC065 02674]   Mar 1974

3. Sur la lagune. Méditée
Orchestre de Paris
Daniel Barenboim (DG)
                                     Oct 1979

4. *Harold in Italy* op. 16
Joseph Suk, Viola
Czech Philharmonic Orchestra
Conductor – Dietrich Fischer-Dieskau (Eurodisc)
[110 2077]   Feb 1976

5. *Damnation of Faust* (Méphistophélès) (in
French)
Yvonne Minton
Placido Domingo
Jules Bastin
Orchestra de Paris and Chorus
Daniel Barenboim (DG)
[2740 199   2709 087]   Jan 1978

6. *Béatrice et Bénédict*
Orchestra de Paris
Daniel Barenboim (DG)
                                     Oct 1979

14. Georges Bizet
1. *Carmen*
Escamillo's aria (Votre toast!)
Radio Sinfonieorchester Berlin
Ferenc Fricsay (DG)
[17092   LPM 18700
135008]   Apr 1961

2. *Les pêcheurs de perles*
Zurga's Recitative and aria
Radio Sinfonieorchester, Berlin
Ferenc Fricsay (DG)
[LPM 18700   138700]   Apr 1961

15. Boris Blacher
1. *Three Psalms*
Psalm 142 – Ich schreie zum Herrn.
Psalm 141 – Herr, ich rufe zu dir.
Psalm 121 – Ich hebe meine Augen auf.
Aribert Reimann (Elec)
[E91 189]   Nov 1961

2. *Aprèslude* op. 57
Gedicht. Und was bedeuten diese Zwänge.
Worte.
Hermann Reutter (Elec)
[ASD 2714/5   C065-02 676
IE 19102180/1]   May 1970

16. Johannes Brahms
1. *Vier ernste Gesänge* op. 121
Hertha Klust (DG)
[17047   68 414/15]   Sep 1949

2. *Vier ernste Gesänge*
Jörg Demus (DG)
[18644   135 161]   Oct 1958

3. *Vier ernste Gesänge*
Daniel Barenboim (DG)
[2707 066]   Sep 1972

4. *Lieder from op. 32*
Wie rafft ich mich auf in der Nacht. Nicht mehr
zu dir zu gehen. Ich schleich umher betrübt und
stumm. Der Strom, der neben mir verrauschte.
Du sprichst, dass ich mich täuschte. Wehe, so
willst du mich wieder. Wie bist du, meine
Königin.
Hertha Klust (Elec)
[ALP1270   DB11595]   May 1955

5. *Ein deutsches Requiem* op. 45
Elisabeth Grümmer
Chor der St. Hedwigs-Kathedrale
(Director – Karl Forster)
Berliner Philharmoniker
Rudolf Kempe (Elec)
[ALP 1505   ALPS 1506
ALP 1351/2   FALP 394/5
XLP 30073/4   SMVP 8046/7]
                                     Jun 1955

6. *Ein deutsches Requiem*
Elisabeth Schwarzkopf
Philharmonia Choir and Orchestra
Otto Klemperer (Elec)
[SLS 821   STC 91 224/5
ASD 2789/90   33CX1781/2
SAXS 2430/1]   Jan 1961

7. *Ein deutsches Requiem*
Edith Mathis
Edinburgh Festival Chorus
London Philharmonic Orchestra
Daniel Barenboim (DG)
[2707 066]   Sep 1972

8. Sommerabend. Mondenschein. Es liebt sich so
lieblich. Meerfahrt. Es schauen die Blumen. Der
Tod, das ist die kühle Nacht.
Jörg Demus (DG)
[18370]   Feb 1957

9. *Von ewiger Liebe*
Meine Liebe ist grün. Heimkehr. Dein blaues
Auge. Wir wandelten. Serenade. Eine gute, gute
Nacht. Der Gang zum Liebchen. Ein Sonett.
Minnelied. Sonntag. Ständchen. Die Mainacht.
Botschaft. Geheimnis. Salamander. Komm bald.
In Waldeseinsamkeit. Mein wundes Herz
verlangt. Es träumte mir. Von ewiger Liebe.
Karl Engel (Elec)
[ALP 526   ALP 1584
ERW 5343 EP]   Mar 1957

10. *Wundersame Liebesgeschichte der schönen Magelone*
15 Romanzen op. 33
Jörg Demus (DG)
[18480   18 388/9
2700 102]   Apr 1957

11. *Wundersame Liebesgeschichte der schönen Magelone*
Sviatoslav Richter (Elec)
[SAN 291]   Jul 1970

12. Auf dem Kirchhofe. Feldeinsamkeit. O
wüsst ich doch den Weg zurück. Auf dem See.
Jörg Demus (DG)
[109 108B]   Jan 1958

13. *Ein Johannes-Brahms-Liederabend*
Mit vierzig Jahren. Steig auf, geliebter Schatten.
Mein Herz ist schwer. Kein Haus, keine Heimat.
Herbstgefühl. Alte Liebe. Abenddämmerung. O
wüsst ich doch den Weg zurück. Auf dem
Kirchhofe. Verzagen. Regenlied. Nachklang.
Frühlingslied. Auf dem See. Feldeinsamkeit.
Jörg Demus (DG)
[18 504   138 011]   Feb 1958

14. *Späte Lieder*
Auf dem Kirchhofe. Frühlingslied. Regenlied.
Kein Haus, keine Heimat. Steig auf, geliebter
Schatten. Alte Liebe. Mit vierzig Jahren.
Feldeinsamkeit. Verzagen.
Jörg Demus (DG)
[135 161]   1958

15. *Lieder des jungen Brahms*
In der Fremde. Lied. Liebe und Frühling.
Nachtigallen schwingen. Parola. Anklänge. Der
Kuss. In der Ferne. Wie rafft ich mich auf.
Nicht mehr zu dir zu gehen. Ich schleich umher.
Der Strom, der neben mir verrauschte. Wehe, so
willst du. Du sprichst, dass ich mich täuschte.
Bitteres zu sagen. So steh'n wir. Wie bist du,
meine Königin.
Gerald Moore (Elec)
[ASDF 859]   Mar 1964

16. *German Folksongs*
Elisabeth Schwarzkopf
Gerald Moore (Elec)
[SMA 91 487/8]   Aug 1965

17. *Lieder and Duets*
Kerstin Meyer
Jörg Demus (DG)
[139 328]   May 1967

18. *Four duets for Alto and Baritone* op. 28
Die Nonne und der Ritter. Vor der Tür. Es
rauschet das Wasser. Der Jäger und sein
Liebchen.
Janet Baker
Daniel Barenboim (Elec)
[ASD 2553]   Aug 1969

19. *Lieder*
Gerald Moore
Wolfgang Sawallisch
Daniel Barenboim (Elec)
[SLS 5002
OC191 50379-85]   Mar 1964, Sep 1970
                       Mar 1971, Mar 1972
                                    Aug 1973

20. *Symphony No. 4 in E minor* (op. 98)
Czech Philharmonic Orchestra
Conductor: Dietrich Fischer-Dieskau (Eurodisc)
(110 2077 ZA)   Feb 1976

17. Benjamin Britten
1. *War Requiem* op. 66
Galina Vischnevskaya
Peter Pears
The Bach Choir
Highgate School Boys' Choir
London Symphony Orchestra
Melos Ensemble
Benjamin Britten (Decca)
[SET 252/3   K27 K22
PA74   SPA 74]   Jan 1963

2. *Cantata Misericordium* op. 69
Peter Pears
London Symphony Orchestra
Benjamin Britten (Decca)
[LXT 6175   SXL 6175
SXL 6640]   Dec 1963

3. *Songs and Proverbs by William Blake*
Benjamin Britten (Decca)
[SXL 6391   5BB120]   Dec 1965

18. Adolf Busch
1. *Lieder* op. 3
Nun die Schatten dunkeln. Wonne der Wehmut.
Aus den Himmelsaugen.
Rudolf Nel, Viola
Jörg Demus (DG)
[138946]   May 1964

19. Ferruccio Busoni
1. *4 Lieder nach Gedichten von Goethe:*
Lied des Unmuts. Zigeunerlied. Schlechter Trost.
Lied des Mephistopheles.
Jörg Demus (DG)
[138 946]   May 1964

2. *Doktor Faust* (Title Rôle)
Hildegarde Hillebrecht
William Cochran
Karl Christian Kohn
Chorus and Symphony Orchestra of Bavarian
Radio
Ferdinand Leitner (DG)
[139 291-3   2709 032]   May 1969

20. Dietrich Buxtehude
1. *5 Geistliche Kantaten*
Members of the Bach Orchestra, Berlin
Carl Gorvin (DG)
[14088]   Mar 1957

21. Domenico Cimarosa
1. *Il Matrimonio Segreto*
Julia Varady
Arleen Auger
Julia Hamari
Alberto Rinaldi
Ryland Davies
English Chamber Orchestra
Daniel Barenboim (DG)
[2709 069]   Sep 1975/
                                              Aug 1976

22. Louis-Nicholas Clérambault
1. *Cantata: Orphée*
Aurèle Nicolet, Flute
Koji Toyoda, Violin
Edith Picht-Axenfeld, Harpsichord
Georg Donderer, Cello
Hans Nowak, Double Bass (Elec)
[IC063-02 258]   Aug 1969

23. Peter Cornelius
1. *6 Weihnachtslieder* op. 8
Gerald Moore (Elec)
[ASD 2630]   Feb 1966

2. *Duets*
Der beste Liebesbrief. Heimatgedanken. Ich und
du. Verratene Liebe.
Janet Baker
Daniel Barenboim (Elec)
[ASD 2553]   Aug 1969

3. *Lieder* op. 4 no 2
Trauer und Trost, Liederzyklus op. 3
Hermann Reutter.
[IC 065-01 251]   May 1970

4. *Vater unser* op. 2 No. 3
Zu uns komme dein Reich.
Jörg Demus (DG)
[2530 219]   Nov 1970

5. Liebe ohne Heimat. Sonnenuntergang.
Aribert Reimann (Elec)
[C065–02 674]   Mar 1974

24. François Couperin
1. *Leçons de Ténèbres*
'Pour le Mercredy', Cantata
Edith Picht-Axenfeld, Harpsichord
Irmgard Poppen, Cello (Elec)
[E 80822   ALP 2066]   Feb 1963

25. Claude Debussy
1. *Trois ballades de François Villon*
1. Faulse Beauté. 2. Dame du ciel. 3. Quoy qu'on
tient.
La Grotte. Mandoline.
Karl Engel (DG)
[138 115]   Oct 1959

2. *Trois ballades de François Villon*
Orchestre de Paris
Daniel Barenboim (DG)
[2531 263]   Oct 1979
3. Pour ce que Plaisance est morte. Le temps a
laissié son manteau.
Hermann Reutter (Elec)
[ASD 2714/4   C065-02 676
IE063 02241]   May 1975

26. Paul Dessau
1. Such nicht mehr, Frau. Noch bin ich eine
Stadt.
Aribert Reimann (Elec)
[C065-02 677]   Mar 1974

27. Antonin Dvořák
1. *From the 'Biblische Lieder'* op. 99
Rings um den Herrn sind Wolken und Dunkel.
Gott, erhöre mein inniges Flehen. Gott ist mein
Hirte. An den Wassern zu Babylon sassen wir.
Wende dich zu mir. Singet ein neues Lied.
Jörg Demus (DG)
[18644   138 644]   Apr 1960

2. *Duets*
Möglichkeit op. 38 No. 1
Der Apfel op. 38 No. 2
Victoria de Los Angeles
Gerald Moore (Elec)
[E91098]   Dec 1966

28. Gottfried von Einem
1. Ein junger Dichter denkt an die Geliebte op. 8
No. 4. In der Fremde op. 8 No. 2.
Aribert Reimann (Elec)
[C065 02 677]   Mar 1974

2. *Cantata: An die Nachgeborenen*
Julia Hamari
Wiener Symphoniker. Wiener Singverein.
Carlo Maria Giulini (DG)
[0666 543]   Nov 1975

3. *Liederzyklus*
Leb wohl, Frau Welt op. 43
Karl Engel (DG)
[2530 877]   Mar 1977

29. Hanns Eisler
1. An die Hoffnung. In der Frühe. Spruch 1939.
Aribert Reimann (Elec)
[C065 02 677]   Mar 1974

30. Philipp zu Eulenburg
1. Liebessehnsucht
Aribert Reimann (Elec)
[C065 02 674]   Mar 1974

31. Gabriel Fauré
1. *La bonne chanson* op. 61
Gerald Moore (Elec)
[SME 91660   WBLP 548]
                                              May 1958

2. *La bonne chanson*
Members of the Berlin Philharmonic Orchestra
Wolfgang Sawallisch (BASF)
[EA22 765–0]   Nov 1975

3. *Duet*
Pleurs d'or op. 72
Victoria de Los Angeles
Gerald Moore (Elec)
]E91 098]   Dec 1960

4. *Requiem* op. 48
Victoria de Los Angeles
Choeurs Elisabeth Brasseur
Conservatoire Orchestre de Paris
André Cluytens (Elec)
[CFP 40234   IC065 00 632]
                                                May 1962

5. *Requiem* op. 48
Sheila Armstrong
Orchestre de Paris
Daniel Barenboim (Elec)
[Q ASD 3065]   Feb 1974

32. Dietrich Fischer-Dieskau
1. *Erzähltes Leben*
Ein Selbstporträt (DG)
[LPM 18 727   SME 2025/26
2705 016]   1961

33. Wolfgang Fortner
1. *The Creation*
Sinfonieorchester des Norddeutschen Rundfunks
Hans Schmidt-Isserstedt (DG)
[18405]   Mar 1957

2. *4 Gesänge to words by Hölderlin*
An die Parzen. Hyperions Schicksalslied.
Abbitte. Geh unter, schöne Sonne.
Aribert Reimann (Elec)
[E91 189]   Nov 1961

3. *Lieder*
Abbitte. Hyperions Schicksalslied.Lied vom
Weidenbaum.
Hermann Reutter (Elec)
[C065-02 676]   May 1970

34. Robert Franz
1. Auf dem Meere op. 5 no. 3. Wie des Mondes
Abbild op. 6 no. 2. Gewitternacht op. 8 No. 6.
Bitte op. 9 No. 3. Für Musik op. 10 no. 1.
Abends op. 16 No. 4. Auf dem Meere op 26 No.
6. Auf dem Meere op. 36. No. 1. Wonne der
Wehmut op. 33. No. 1. Mailied op. 53. No. 3.
Aribert Reimann (Elec)
[C065 02 673]   Mar 1974

35. Umberto Giordano
1. *Andrea Chénier*
Gérard's monologue.
Radio Sinfonieorchester, Berlin
Ferenc Fricsay
[LPM18 700   138 700
30 425   30 269
2705 001]   Apr 1961

36. Christoph Willibald Gluck
1. *Orpheus und Eurydike* (in German)
Maria Stader
Rita Streich
RIAS Kammerchor. Berliner Motettenchor.
RIAS-Symphonie-Orchester
Ferenc Fricsay (DG)
[19311   18343/46
2700 103]   Sep 1956

2. *Orfeo ed Euridice* (in Italian)
Gundula Janowitz
Edda Moser
Bach-Chor und Orchester, München
Karl Richter (DG)
[2726043   136556]   Aug 1967

3. *Iphigenie in Aulis* (Agamemnon) (in German)
Anna Moffo
Manfred Schmidt
Thomas Stewart
Arleen Auger
Chor des Bayerischen Rundfunks
Münchener Rundfunkorchester
Kurt Eichhorn (Eurodisc)
[RCA ARL 2 1104]   Jun 1972

37. Charles Gounod
1. *Faust*
Valentin's Farewell (in German)
Radio Sinfonieorchester
Ferenc Fricsay (DG)
[LPM 18 700 138 700]   Apr 1961

2. *Faust* (Highlights in German)
Edda Moser
Nicolai Gedda
RIAS-Kammerchor
Berliner Rundfunkorchester
Guiseppe Patane
[C063-28 961]   Sep 1973

38. Edvard Grieg
1. Dereinst, Gedanke mein op. 48 No. 2. Lauf
der Welt op. 48 No. 2. Wo sind sie hin op. 4 No.
6. Hör ich das Liedchen klingen op. 39 no. 6.
Morgentau op. 4 No. 2. Abschied op. 4 No. 3.
Jägerslied op. 4 No. 4.
Aribert Reimann (Elec)
[C065 02 673]   Mar 1974

39. Joseph Haas
1. Die beweglichste Musika
Jörg Demus (DG)
[2530 219]   Nov 1970

40. George Frideric Handel
1. Cuopre tal volta il cielo'. (Solo Cantata.)
Dalla guerra amorosa. (Solo Cantata.)
Edith Picht-Axenfeld, Harpsichord
Aurèle Nicolet, Flute
Lothar Koch, Oboe
Irmgard Poppen, Cello (Elec)
[STE91063 FALP PM30544]
                                                Feb 1960

2. *Giulio Cesare* (in Italian)
Arias and scenes of Cleopatra and Caesar
Irmgard Seefried
Berliner Radio-Symphonie Orchester
Karl Böhm (DG)
[LPM 18 637   138 637]   Apr 1960

3. *Giulio Cesare* (Cesare) (in Italian)
Tatiana Troyanos
Julia Hamari
Peter Schreier
Franz Crass
Münchener Bach Chor und Orchester
Karl Richter (DG)
[2561 026–9   2720 023]   Apr 1969

4. *Apollo e Dafne* (in Italian)
Agnes Giebel
Berliner Philharmoniker
Günther Weissenborn (DG)
[139 153]   Jan 1966

5. *Duets*
Giu nei Tartarei regni. Quando in calma ride il mare.
Janet Baker
Kenneth Heath, Cello
George Malcolm, Harpischord (Elec)
[ASD 2710]   Live Feb 1970

6. *From 'Rinaldo'*
Cara sposa
Jean-Pierre Rampal, Flute
Robert Veyron-Lacroix, Harpsichord
Jacques Neilz, Cello (Elec)
[ASD 2903]   Sep/Oct 1971

7. *From 'Berenice'*
Si, tra i ceppi
Münchener Bach-Orchester
Karl Richter (DG)
[2563 555]   1975

8. *Bass arias*, from
Alexander's Feast.
Xerxes. Samson. Saul. Belshazzar. Ottone.
Berenice. Susanna. Agrippina. Solomon (in
English and Italian)
Munich Chamber Orchestra
Hans Stadlmair (DG)
[2530 979]   Aug 1977

41. Karl Amadeus Hartmann
1. *Gesangsszene*
Radio-Sinfonie Orchester
Dean Dixon (HR)
Live from première
[WER 60061]   13 Nov 1964

2. *Gesangsszene* for Baritone and Orchestra to
words from *Sodom and Gomorrha* by Giraudoux
(1963). Symphonie-Orchester des Bayerischen
Rundfunks.
Rafael Kubelik (WERGO)
     Dec 1968

42. Joseph Matthias Hauer
1. Der gefesselte Strom op. 23 No. 2. An die
Parzen op. 23 No. 4.
Aribert Reimann (Elec)
[C065-02 677]   Mar 1974

43. Joseph Haydn
1. *Songs and Cauzouettas*
Gebet zu Gott. Zufriedenheit. Das Leben ist ein
Traum. Gegenliebe. Eine sehr gewöhnliche Ge-
schichte. Die zu späte Ankunft der Mutter. Lob
der Faulheit. Auch die Sprödeste der Schönen.
Abschiedslied. Gott, erhalte Franz den Kaiser.
The Spirit's song. Fidelity. Recollection. Piercing
eyes. She never told her love. The Wanderer. Sai-
lor's song.
Gerald Moore (Elec)
[ALP 1829   IC053-01 436]   Apr 1959

2. Schlaf in deiner engen Kammer
Victoria de Los Angeles
Gerald Moore
Eduard Drolc, Violin
Irmgard Poppen, Cello (Elec)
[E91098   ALP 1891]   Dec 1960

3. Schläfst oder wachst du. Heimkehr. Maggy
Lauder. Dort, wo durchs Ried. Fliess leise, mein
Bächlein.
Aurèle Nicolet (Flute)
Helmut Heller, Violin
Irmgard Poppen, Cello
Karl Engel (DG)
[18706   138706]   Feb 1961

4. *Trios*
An den Vetter. Daphnes einziger Fehler.
Elisabeth Schwarzkopf
Victoria de Los Angeles
Gerald Moore (Elec)
[SB 3697]   Feb 1967

5. *Die Schöpfung (The Creation)*
Gundula Janowitz
Walter Ludwig
Fritz Wunderlich
Werner Krenn
Walter Berry
Wiener Singverein
Berliner Philharmoniker
Herbert von Karajan (DG)
[139282-3   643515-6
2704 044   136 439
2535 146   3370 005]
     Sep 1968

6. *Die Schöpfung* (The Creation)
Edith Mathis
Catherine Denley
Aldo Baldin
Academy & Chorus of St Martin-in-the-Fields
Neville Marriner (Philips)
[6769 047   (Tape 7699 154)]
     Jan 1980

7. *Arias*
Tergi i vezzosi rai. Un cor si tenero. Spann deine
langen Ohren. Dice benissimo.
Wiener Haydn-Orchester
Reinhard Peters (Decca)
[SXL 6490]   Oct 1969

44. Hans Werner Henze
1. *Fünf Neapolitanische Lieder*
Berliner Philharmoniker
Richard Kraus (DG)
[18406]   Dec 1956

2. *Elegie für junge Liebende)* (Elegy for young
lovers) (Mittenhofer's scenes)
Thomas Hemsley
Liane Dubbin
Martha Mödl
Catherine Gayer
Members of the Radio Symphony Orchestra and
the Orchestra of the Deutsche Oper, Berlin
Hans Werner Henze (DG)
[138 876]   Apr/May 1963

3. *Das Floss der Medusa*
Edda Moser
Charles Régnier, Norddeutscher Rundfunk
Chor und Orchester. RIAS Kammerchor
Hamburger Knabenchor
Hans Werner Henze (DG)
[139 428/9   2707 041Q]   Dec 1968

45. Ferdinand Hiller
1. *Gebet*
Aribert Reimann (Elec)
[C065-02 673]   Mar 1974

46. Paul Hindemith
1. *Mathis der Maler* (– Highlights) – (Title Rôle)
Pilar Lorengar
Donald Grobe
Radio-Symphonie Orchester Berlin
Leopold Ludwig (DG)
[18769   138769]   Nov 1961

2. *Mathis der Maler* (Title Rôle)
James King
Gerd Feldhoff
Manfred Schmidt
Peter Meven
William Cochran
Donald Grobe
Trudeliese Schmidt
Urszula Koszut
Rose Wagemann
Bavarian Radio Chorus & Radio Symphony
Orchestra
Rafael Kubelik (Elec)
[SLS 5182]   Jun/Dec 1977

3. *Cardillac* (original version) – (Title Rôle)
Leonore Kirchstein
Elisabeth Söderström
Donald Grobe
Eberhard Katz
Karl Christian Kohn

Chor des Westdeutschen Rundfunks
Kölner Rundfunk-Sinfonie-Orchester
Joseph Keilberth (DG)
[139435/6]   Jun 1968

4. *Lied*
Fragment: Das Angenehme dieser Welt
Hermann Reutter (Elec)
[ASD 2714/5   C065-02 676
IE 191 02180/1]   May 1970

47. Johann Nepomuk Hummel
1. *Goethe-Lieder*
Zur Logenfeier
Jörg Demus (DG)
[2533 149]   Sep 1972

48. Engelbert Humperdinck
1. An das Christkind
Jörg Demus (DG)
[2530 219]   Nov 1970

2. *Hänsel und Gretel* (Besenbinder)
Charlotte Berthold
Anna Moffo
Helen Donath
Christa Ludwig
Arleen Auger
Lucia Popp
Tölzer Knabenchor., (Director – Gerhard
Schmidt-Gaden). Bayerisches Rundfunk-
orchester, München.
Kurt Eichhorn (Eurodisc)
[27103-44 XDR   27105 XDR
ARL 20637]   Jul 1971

49. Charles Ives
1. *Songs, Lieder, chansons*
At the river. Elegie. Ann Street. Christmas Carol
from 'The Swimmers'. West London. Farewell to
Land. Abide with me. Where the Eagle.
Disclosure. White Gulls. Childrens Hour. Two
little flowers. Autumn. Tom sails away. Ich
grolle nicht. Feldeinsamkeit. Weil' auf mir. In
Flanders Fields..
Michael Ponti (DG)
[2530 696]   Dec 1975

50. Adolf Jensen
1. Lehn deine Wang' an meine Wang' op. 1 no.
1
Aribert Reimann (Elec)
[C065–02 673]   Mar 1974

51. Wilhelm Kempff
1. *4 Lieder from poems by C. F. Meyer*
Wilhelm Kempff (DG)
[138 946]   May 1964

52. Fürchtegott Theodor Kirchner
1. Sie weiss es nicht op. 1 no. 3. Frühlingslied
op. 1 no. 2. Frühlingslied op. 1 No. 4.
Frühlingslied op. 1 No. 9.
Aribert Reimann
[C065–02 673]   Mar 1974

53. Armin Knab
1. *Marienkind*
Jörg Demus (DG)
[2530 219]   Nov 1970

54. Ernst Křenek
1. Die frühen Gräber op. 19 No. 5.
Erinnerung op. 19. No. 1.
Aribert Reimann (Elec)
[C065–02 677]   Mar 1974

55. Conradin Kreutzer
1. *Goethe-Lieder:*
Ein Bettler vor dem Tor.
Jörg Demus (DG)
[2533 149]   Sep 1972

56. Henry Lawes
1. *Duet*
A Dialogue on a Kiss
Janet Baker
Kenneth Heath, (Cello)
George Malcolm, (Harpsichord) (Elec)
[ASD 2710]   Live Feb 1970

57. William Lawes
1. *Duets*
A Dialogue between Charon and Philomel
A Dialogue between Daphne and Strephon
Janet Baker
Kenneth Heath, (Cello)
George Malcolm, (Organ) (Elec)
[ASD 2710]   Live Feb 1970

58. Ruggiero Leoncavallo
1. *Pagliacci*
(Prologue)
Radio-Sinfonieorchester Berlin
Ferenc Fricsay (DG)
[LPM 18700   138700
135008]   Apr 1961

59. Frantiszek Lilius
1. *Duet*
Tua Jesu delictio
Janet Baker
Kenneth Heath, (Cello)
George Malcolm, (Organ) (Elec)
[ASD 2710]   Live Feb 1970

60. Franz Liszt
1. Die Vätergruft. Die drei Zigeuner. Tristesse.
Vergiftet sind meine Lieder. Der Alpenjäger. Es
muss ein Wunderbares sein. Blume und Duft.
Die Glocken von Marling. Oh quand je dors.
Three Petrarch-Sonnets
Benedetto sia'l giorno, e'l mese e'l anno. Pace
non trovo e non ho da far guerra. I vide in terra
angelici costumi.
Jörg Demus (DG)
[18793   138798
135026   2530352]   Nov 1961

2. Es rauschen die Winde. Wieder möcht ich dir
begegnen. Ständchen. Über allen Gipfeln ist
Ruh.
Aribert Reimann (Elec)
[IC065 02674]   Mar 1974

3. *Ausgewählte Lieder*
Daniel Barenboim (DG)
                                    Nov/Dec 1979

61. Carl Loewe
1. Tom der Reimer. Die Uhr.
Leo Stein (Elec)
                                     2 Jun 1948

2. Erlkönig
Gerald Moore (Elec)
[DB 21350   ASD2423
ERW 5044EP]   Jan 1955

3. *Ballades*
Der Schatzgräber. Tom der Reimer. Kleiner
Haushalt. Süsses Begräbnis. Herr Oluf.
Edward. Der Mohrenfürst auf der Messe.
Erlkönig. Archibald Douglas.
Gerald Moore (Elec)
[SME91 665   ASD2423
IC063 00388]   Sep 1967

4. *Lieder und Balladen* Vol. I
Prinz Eugen. Trommel-Ständchen. Die drei
Lieder. Die Uhr. Hochzeitslied. Elvershöh. Der
heilige Franziskus. Odins Meeresritt. Der Nöck.
Die Gruft der Liebenden. Heinrich der Vogler.
Jörg Demus (DG)
[139416   1643007]   Jul 1968

5. *Lieder und Balladen* Vol. II
Der getreue Eckhart. Wanderers Nachtlied. Im
Vorübergehen. Canzonette. Frühzeitiger
Frühling. Ich denke dein. Freibeuter. Der
Zauberlehrling. Der Totentanz. Gutmann und
Gutweib. Türmwächter Lynkeus zu den
Füssen der Helena. Lynkeus der Türmer auf
Fausts Sternwarte singend. Wenn der Blüten
Frühlingsregen. Die wandelnde Glocke. Gottes
ist der Orient.
Jörg Demus (DG)
[2530 052]   Nov 1969

6. *Lieder und Balladen* Vol. III
Jörg Demus (DG)
                                        Nov 1979

7. Der Hirten Lied am Krippelein op. 22, H. 1
No. 3
Jörg Demus (DG)
[2530 219]   1971

62. Albert Lortzing
1. *Undine*
Nun ist's vollbracht.
Rita Streich
Wilhelm Schüchter (Elec)
[DB11550   ERW 501]

2. *Undine*
Du kehrst zur Heimat wieder (Elec)
[DB11550]

3. *Der Wildschütz*
Wie freundlich strahlt die helle Morgensonne.
Heiterkeit und Fröhlichkeit.
Berliner Philharmoniker
Wilhelm Schüchter (Elec)
[EH 1465]   Dec 1955

4. *Zar und Zimmermann*
Einst spielt' ich mit Zepter
Berliner Philharmoniker
Wilhelm Schüchter (Elec)
[EH1465   ERW549
C04728 181]   Dec 1955

5. *Zar und Zimmermann* (Highlights – Peter I)
Ingeborg Hallstein
Friedrich Lenz
Fritz Wunderlich
Karl-Christian Kohn
Chor des Bayerischen Rundfunks
Bamberger Symphoniker Orchester
Hans Gierster (DG)
[136432   2537 004]   Sep 1966

63. Mark Lothar
1. *Musik des Einsamen* op. 67
Liederzyklus for voice und 7 instruments (Hesse)
Mark Lothar (Elec)
[SME 91660]   Aug 1967

64. Gustav Mahler
1. *Lieder eines fahrenden Gesellen*
Vienna Philharmonic Orchestra
Wilhelm Furtwängler
(Live at Salzburg Festival) (CETRA)
[L0510]   19 Aug. 1951

2. *Lieder eines fahrenden Gesellen*
Philharmonia Orchestra
Wilhelm Furtwängler (Elec)
[ALP1270   XLP30044
5C063 00898X   HTB409]   Jun 1952

3. *Lieder eines fahrenden Gesellen*
Symphonie-Orchester des Bayerischen
Rundfunks
Rafael Kubelik (DG)
[2806 002]   Dec 1968

4. *Kindertotenlieder*
Berliner Philharmoniker
Rudolf Kempe (Elec)
[BLP1081   BLP1511
SME91387   5C063 00898]
                                              Jun 1955

5. *Kindertotenlieder*
Berliner Philharmoniker
Karl Böhm (DG)
[18879   138879]   Jun 1963

6. Phantasie from 'Des Knaben Wunderhorn'
Ablösung im Sommer. Selbstgefühl. Des

Antonius von Padua Fischpredigt. Zu Strassburg
auf der Schanz.
Karl Engel (DG)
[18058   138058
135026]   Jun 1959

7. *Das Lied von der Erde*
Murray Dickie
Philharmonia Orchestra
Paul Kletzki (Elec)
[ALP 1773–4   ASD351–2
SXLP30165   Tape TC EXE72 and
8X-EXE72]   Oct 1959

8. *Das Lied von der Erde*
James King
Wiener Philharmoniker
Leonard Bernstein (Decca)
[SET331   Tape KCET331]   Apr 1966

9. *Rückert-Lieder*
Blicke mir nicht in die Lieder! Ich atmet' einen
linden Duft. Um Mitternacht. Ich bin der Welt
abhanden gekommen.
Berliner Philharmoniker
Karl Böhm (DG)
[18879   138879]   Jun 1963

10. *Lieder from 'Des Knaben Wunderhorn'*
Elisabeth Schwarzkopf
London Symphony Orchestra
George Szell (Elec)
[SAN218   IC065–00 098]
                                              Mar 1968

11. *Lieder und Gesänge aus der Jugendzeit*
Um schlimme Kinder artig zu machen.
Selbstgefühl. Scheiden und Meiden. Ablösung
im Sommer. Nicht Wiedersehen! Serenade aus
'Don Juan'. Zu Strassburg auf der Schanz. *Lieder
von Rückert*: Ich atmet' einen linden Duft. Blicke
mir nicht in die Lieder. Ich bin der Welt
abhanden gekommen. Um Mitternacht.
Leonard Bernstein (CBS)
[S72973]   Nov 1968

12. *Symphony No. 8 in E flat.*
Edith Mathis
Julia Hamari
Donald Grobe
Symphonie-Orch des Bayrischen Rundfunks
Rafael Kubelik (DG)
[2561 086]   Jun 1970

13. *Lieder*
Lieder und Gesänge aus der Jugendzeit
Lieder aus *Des Knaben Wunderhorn*
Fünf Rückert-Lieder
Lieder eines fahrenden Gesellen
Daniel Barenboim (DG)
[SLS 5173]   Feb 1978

65. Enrico Mainardi
1. Uomo del mio Tempo (Quasimodo). Con una
Fronda mi Mirto (Archilochos/Quasimodo)
Jörg Demus (DG)
[138 946]   May 1964

66. Frank Martin
1. *6 Monologues from 'Jedermann'*
Berliner Philharmoniker
Frank Martin (DG)
[138871 SLPM]   May 1963

2. *The Tempest* (3 Fragments)
Berliner Philharmoniker
Frank Martin (DG)
[138871 SLPM]   May 1963

67. Emil Mattiesen
1. Herbstgefühl
Heimgang in der Frühe
Aribert Reimann (Elec)
[C065–02 675]   Nov 1971

68. Felix Mendelssohn-Bartholdy
1. *Gerald Moore's Farewell Concert*
Duets
Abendlied. Gruss. Ich wollt' meine Lieb'. Lied
aus 'Ruy Blas'. Wasserfahrt.
Victora de Los Angeles
Gerald Moore (Elec)
[SB 3697]   Feb 1967

2. *Elijah* op. 70
Gwyneth Jones
Janet Baker
Nicolai Gedda
New Philharmonia Choir and Orchestra
Rafael Frühbeck de Burgos (Elec)
[SMA91 784/6   SLA935/3
ASD2609   YKM5008]   Jun/Jul 1968

3. *Duets*
Abschiedslied der Zugvögel. Herbstlied. Suleika
und Hatem. Wie kann ich froh und lustig sein.
Janet Baker
Daniel Barenboim (Elec)
[ASD 2553]   Aug 1969

4. *Lieder*
Wolfgang Sawallisch (Elec)
[SLS805]   Sep 1970

5. *St Paul* op. 36
Helen Donath
Hanna Schwarz
Werner Hollweg
Knabenchor
Chor des Städtischen
Musikvereins e.V. Düsseldorf
Düsseldorfer Symphoniker
Rafael Frühbeck de Burgos (Elec)
[IC157–30   701/03Q
SLS5092]   Oct 1976

6. *Die Heimkehr aus der Fremde*
Hanna Schwarz
Helen Donath
Peter Schreier
Benno Kusche
Munich Radio Orchestra
Conductor Heinz Wallberg (Elec)
[IC065 30741]   Jul/Aug 1978

7. *Die beiden Pädagogen*
Kristina Laki
Gabriele Fuchs
Adolf Dallapozza
Klaus Hirte
Günter Wewel
Ingrid Heitmann
Munich Radio Orchestra and Chorus
Heinz Wallberg
[IC068 45416]   July 1978

69. Friedrich Mergner
Weihnachtslied
Jörg Demus (DG)
[2530 219]   Nov 1970

70. Giacomo Meyerbeer
1. Menschenfeindlich. Hör ich das Liedchen
klingen. Die Rose, die Lilie, die Taube, die
Sonne. Komm, der Garten des Herzens. Sie und
ich. Sicilienne. Ständchen. Die Rosenblätter. Le
chant du dimanche. Le poète mourant.
Cantique du Trappiste. Scirocco. Mina.
Karl Engel (DG)
[2533 295]   Dec 1974

71. Darius Milhaud
1. Lied: Lamentation
Hermann Reutter (Elec)
[ASD 2714/5   C065–02676
IE191 02180/1]   May 1970

72. Wolfgang Amadeus Mozart
1. *Die Zauberflöte* (Papageno)
Rita Streich
Maria Stader
Lisa Otto
Josef Greindl
Ernst Häfliger
Kim Borg
Howard Vandenburg
Roger Vantin
RIAS-Chamber Choir. RIAS Symphony
Orchestra
Ferenc Fricsay (DG)
[18 26466   18 26769
135 008   138 981/83
2701 003   89 653]   Jun 1955

2. *Die Zauberflöte* (Papageno)
Evelyn Lear
Lisa Otto
Roberta Peters
Franz Crass
Hans Hotter
Fritz Wunderlich
Berliner Philharmoniker
Karl Böhm (DG)
[2563 318/20   2709 017
2720 058   2740 108
136 440   2537 003
3371 002]   Jun 1964

3. *Die Zauberflöte* (Speaker)
Pilar Lorengar
Cristina Deutekom
Renate Holm
Stuart Burrows
Hermann Prey
Martti Talvela
Chor der Wiener Staatsoper
Wiener Philharmoniker
Georg Solti (Decca)
[SET 497–81   K2A4 (Tape)]
                                          Oct 1969

4. *Don Giovanni* (Title Rôle) (in Italian)
Sena Jurinac
Maria Stader
Irmgard Seefried
Ernst Häfliger
Ivan Sardi
Karl Christian Kohn
Walther Kreppel
RIAS Chamber Choir
Radio-Symphony-Orchestra Berlin
Ferenc Fricsay (DG)
[138 050/52   2728 003
136 224]   Sep 1958

5. *Don Giovanni* (Highlights – Title Rôle – in German)
Claire Watson
Irene Salemka
Rita Streich
Ernst Häfliger
Walter Berry
Radio-Symphony-Orchestra, Berlin
Hans Löwlein (DG)
[Q135 127   Q136 415
2548 230]   Feb 1963

6. *Don Giovanni* (Title Rôle – in Italian)
Birgit Nilsson
Peter Schreier
Martti Talvela
Martina Arroyo
Ezio Flagello
Alfredo Mariotti
Reri Grist
Orchestra of the Prague National Theatre
Karl Böhm (DG)
[135008   2563 314/317
2711 006   2740 108
136 282   1643 007
2537 014   3371 014 (Tape)]
                                      Feb/Mar 1967

7. *Le nozze di Figaro* (Count Almaviva – in Italian)
Irmgard Seefried
Maria Stader
Rosl Schwaiger
Hertha Töpper
Renato Capecchi
Paul Kuen
Friedrich Lenz
Ivan Sardi

Georg Wieter
RIAS-Chamber Choir. Radio-Symphony-
Orchestra Berlin
Ferenc Fricsay (DG)
[138 697/99   2728 004
19406]   Sep 1960

8. *Figaros Hochzeit* (Highlights – Graf Almaviva – in German)
Maria Stader
Rita Streich
Hanny Steffek
Walter Berry
Berliner Philharmoniker
Ferdinand Leitner (DG)
[136 406]   Dec 1961

9. *Figaros Hochzeit* (Graf Almaviva)
Edith Mathis
Hermann Prey
Gundula Janowitz
Tatiana Troyanos
Chor und Orchester der Deutschen Oper Berlin
Karl Böhm (DG)
[104962–5   2563 310/313
2740 108   2537 023
(Tape) 3371 005]   Mar 1968

10. *Le nozze di Figaro* (in Italian)
Heather Harper
Judith Blegen
Geraint Evans
Teresa Berganza
Birgit Finnilä
English Chamber Orchestra
Daniel Barenboim (Elec)
[Angel (SQ)   SLS 995]   Aug 1976

11. *Così fan tutte* (Don Alfonso)
Irmgard Seefried
Nan Merriman
Erika Köth
Ernst Häfliger
Hermann Prey
RIAS-Kammerchor. Berliner Philharmoniker
Eugen Jochum (DG)
[2537019   136278]
                (Highlights)   Dec 1962

12. *Trios*
La partenza K.436
Più non si trovano K.549
Victoria de Los Angeles
Elisabeth Schwarzkopf
Gerald Moore (Elec)
[SB 3697]   20 Feb 1967

13. *Arias*
Così dunque tradisci K. 432. Hai già vinta la
causa (*Le nozze di Figaro*). Nach der Welschen
Art. Ich möchte wohl der Kaiser sein K. 539.
Männer suchen stets zu naschen K.433. Mentre
ti lascio, o figlia K. 513. Un bacio di mano
K.541.
Vienna Haydn-Orchestra
Reinhard Peters (Decca)
[SXL6490]   Oct 1969

14. *Lieder*
Kleine deutsche Kantate K.619
Gesellenreise K.468
Die Zufriedenheit K.473
Die betrogene Welt K.474
Das Veilchen K.476
Lied der Freiheit K.506
Lied der Trennung K.519
Abendempfindung K.523
Geheime Liebe K.125e
Die Zufriedenheit im niedrigen Stande K.125g
An die Freundschaft K.125h
Die grossmütige Gelassenheit K.125d
Das Traumbild K.530
An die Hoffnung K.340c.
An Chloe K.524
Daniel Barenboim (Elec)
[ASD2824   SEOM25*]
                                    Jul 1971

15. *Requiem* K.626
Sheila Armstrong
Janet Baker
Nicolai Gedda
John Alldis Choir. English Chamber Orchestra
Daniel Barenboim (Elec)
[ASD 2788 (Tape) TC ASD2788]
                                    Jul 1971

16. *Mass in C major* No. 16 K. 317 (Coronation Mass)
Vesperae solennes de confessore in C K.339
Edda Moser
Julia Hamari
Nicolai Gedda
Bayrisches Radioorchester und Chor
Eugen Jochum (Elec)
[(SQ)ASD 3373]
                                    Jul 1976

73. Christian Gottlob Neefe
1. *Goethe Lieder:*
Serenate
Jörg Demus (DG)
[2530 119]
                                    Sep 1972

74. Otto Nicolai
1. *Die lustigen Weiber von Windsor*
(Duet: Herr Fluth)
Gottlob Frick
Wilhelm Schüchter (Elec)
[DB11580   BLP 1098
WBLP 1510   SMVP8030
7EGW 11-8395]
                                    Apr 1955

75. Friedrich Nietzsche
1. Nachspiel, No. 6
Wie sich Rebenranken schwingen, No. 2
Verwelkt, No. 5 – from 7 Lieder
Aribert Reimann (Elec)
[C065-002 674]
                                    Mar 1974

76. Jacques Offenbach
1. *Hoffmanns Erzählungen*
Siegfried Jerusalem

Jeanette Scovotti
Norma Sharp
Kurt Moll
Julia Varady
Friedrich Lenz
Ilse Gramatzki
Hanna Schwarz
Münchner Rundfunkorchester
Heinz Wallberg
[IC157-45 351/53
IC289-45 351/53 (Tape)]   Jan 1979

77. Carl Orff
1. *Carmina Burana*
Gundula Janowitz
Gerhard Stolze
Schöneberger Sängerknaben Chor und
Orchester der Deutschen Oper, Berlin
Eugen Jochum (DG)
[139 362]   Oct 1967

2. *Carmina Burana* (3 scenes)
Anny Schlemm
RIAS Orch
Ferenc Fricsay (Rex/DG)
                                    1949

78. Hans Pfitzner
1. Sie haben heut' abend Gesellschaft. In
Danzig. Eingelegte Ruder. Säerspruch. Hussens
Kerker. Zorn. An die Mark. Tragische
Geschichte. Zum Abschied meiner Tochter.
Karl Engel (DG)
[138 058]   Jun 1959

2. *Lieder from poems by Joseph von Eichendorff*
Karl Engel (Elec)
[C065 29036]   Sep 1969

3. Hussens Kerker op. 32 No. 1 Es geht mit mir
zu Ende.
Hermann Reuter (Elec)
[ASD 2714/5   C065-02676
IE191 02180/1]   May 1970

4. An den Mond op. 18
Mailied op. 26 No. 5
Aribert Reimann (Elec)
[C065-02 675]   Nov 1971

5. *Sonett nach Petrarca*
Voll jener Süsse, die, nicht auszudrücken op. 24
No. 3
[2530 332]   Sep 1972

6. *Palestrina* (Borromeo)
Helen Donath
Brigitte Fassbaender
Nicolai Gedda
Karl Ridderbusch
Hermann Prey
Chor und Orchester des Bayrischen Rundfunks
Rafael Kubelik (DG)
[2530 364-7   2711 013]   Feb 1973

7. *Gesänge für Bariton und Orchester* (Songs for baritone and orchestra)
Herr Oluf op, 12. An den Mond op. 18. Sie haben heut' abend Gesellschaft op 4 No.2. Lethe op. 37. An die Mark op 15 No. 3. Dietrichs Erzählung. Zorn op 15 No. 2.
Bayrisches Radio-Symphonieorchester
Wolfgang Sawallisch (Elec)
[IC065–45 616]   Jan 1979

79. Francis Poulenc
1. *Le bal masqué*
Karl Steins, Oboe
Karl Leister, Clarinet
Manfred Braun, bassoon
Konradin Groth, trumpet
Thomas Brandis, violin
Wolfgang Boettcher, Cello
Fredi Muller, percussion
Wolfgang Sawallisch (BASF)
[EA22 765–0]   Nov 1975

80. Giacomo Puccini
1. *La Bohème* Quartet, 3rd Act (in German)
Lebt wohl, ihr süssen Stunden
Elfriede Trötschel
Rita Streich
Lorenz Fehenberger
Orchester der Deutschen Komischen Oper
Paul Schmitz (DG)
[68435 LM]   19 Sep 1949

2. *La Bohème* (Marcel) (Highlights in German)
Erna Berger
Lothar Koth
Rudolf Schock
Hermann Prey
Gottlob Frick
Chor der Deutschen Oper
Berliner Knabenchor
Berliner Symphoniker
Wilhelm Schüchter (Elec)
[(W)ALP 1502   SMVP8013]   Sep 1954

3. *La Bohème* (Marcel) (in German)
Pilar Lorengar
Rita Streich
Sandor Konya
Horst Günter
Hans Bertram
Chor der Staatsoper Berlin
Staatskapelle Berlin
Alberto Erede (DG)
[18720/21   Q136 404
2537 007]   Jun 1961

4. *Madame Butterfly* (Sharpless) (Highlights in German)
Erna Berger
Sieglinde Wagner
Rudolf Schock
Erich Zimmermann

Frauenchor der Deutschen Oper und Orchester
Wilhelm Schüchter (Elec)
[(W) BLP1507   SMVP8011]   Dec 1954

5. *Tosca* (Scarpia) (in Italian)
Birgit Nilsson
Franco Corelli
Silvio Maionica
Alfredo Mariotti
Piero de Palma
Choir and Orchestra of the Accademia di Santa Cecilia, Rome
Lorin Maazel (Decca)
[SET 341/2   SET 451
KCET 451]   Jun 1966

6. *Tosca* (Arias and Scenes, Scarpia)
Anja Silja
James King
Choir and Orchestra of the Accademia di Santa Cecilia, Rome
Lorin Maazel (Decca)
[SET 451]   Jun 1966

7. *Gianni Schicchi*
Gerti Zeumer
Hertha Töpper
Robert Ilosfalvy
Manfred Schmidt
Wilma Lipp
Cologne Radio Symphony Orchestra
Alberto Erede (WDR) (West German Radio)
[F666 205]   Dec 1975

81. Henry Purcell
1. *Duets*
Let us wander. Lost is my quiet.
Victoria de Los Angeles
Gerald Moore (Elec)
[E91098   STL 144/1]   Dec 1960

2. *Duets*
My dearest, my fairest. No, resistance is but vain. Shepherd, leave decoying. Sound the trumpet.
Janet Baker
Daniel Barenboim (Elec)
[ASD2553]   Aug 1969

3. *Cantata*
When night her purple veil.
Aurèle Nicolet, Flute
Koji Toyoda, Violin
Edith Picht-Axenfeld, Harpsichord
Georg Donderer, Cello
Hans Nowak, Bass (Elec)
[IC063 02 258]   Aug 1969

82. Joseph Joachim Raff
1. Unter den Palmen
Aribert Reimann (Elec)
[C065 02 674]   Mar 1974

83. Jean-Philippe Rameau
1. *Cantata: Thétis*
Jean-Pierre Rampal, Flute
Robert Veyron-Lacroix, Harpischord
Jacques Neilz, Cello (Elec)
[ASD 2903]   Sep/Oct 1971

84. Maurice Ravel
1. *Chansons Madécasses*
Cinq Mélodies populaires grecques
Don Quichotte à Dulcinée
Karl Engel, piano
Aurèle Nicolet, Flute
Irmgard Poppen, Cello (DG)
[18615   138115]   Oct 1959

2. *Chansons Madécasses*
Karlheinz Zöller, Flute
Wolfgang Boettcher, Cello
Wolfgang Sawallisch (BASF)
[EA22 765–0]   Nov 1975

85. Max Reger
1. *Selected Lieder*
Günther Weissenborn (DG)
[139 127]   Nov 1965

2. Warnung op. 104 no. 2. Sommernacht op. 98
no. 5.
Aribert Reimann (Elec)
[C065 02 675]   Nov 1971

3. *Geistliche Lieder* op. 137
3. Uns ist geboren ein Kindelein
10. Christkindleins Wiegenlied
Neue Kinderlieder op. 142
3. Maria am Rosenstrauch
Jörg Demus (DG)
[2530 219]   Nov 1970

86. Johann Friedrich Reichardt
1. *Petrarch Sonnets*
Jörg Demus (DG)
[2530 332]   Sep 1972

2. *Goethe-Lieder*
Jörg Demus (DG)
[2533 149]   Sep 1972

87. Aribert Reimann
1. *5 Gedichte von Paul Celan*
Aribert Reimann (Elec)
[E91 189]   Nov 1961

2. *Lear*
Helga Dernesch
Colette Lorand
Julia Varady
David Knutson
Hans Günther Nöcker
Richard Holm
Rolf Boysen
Chor und Orchester der Bayrischen Staatsoper
Gerd Albrecht (DG)
[2709 089]   Jul 1978

88. Carl Reinecke
1. Weihnachtslied
Jörg Demus (DG)
[2530 219]   Nov 1970

89. Hermann Reutter
1. Meine dunklen Hände (Fünf Negergedichte)
Bänkelsänger. Trommel. Schwarzes Mädchen.
Lied für ein dunkles Mädchen. Wenn Susanna
Jones trägt Rot.
Aribert Reimann (Elec)
[E91 189]   Nov 1961

2. *Johann Kepler* op 64, 5
Hermann Reutter (Elec)
[C06502 676]   May 1970

3. Weihnachtskantilene
Jörg Demus (DG)
[2530 319]   Nov 1970

90. Emil Nikolaus von Reznicek
1. Vier Bet– und Bussgesänge nach Worten der
Heiligen Schrift.
Günther Weissenborn (Elec)
                              Mar 1960

91. Joseph Rheinberger
1. *Der Stern von Bethlehem* op. 164
(Weihnachts-Kantate)
Rita Streich
Chor des Bayerischen Rundfunks
Symphonie-Orchester Graunke
Robert Heger (Elec)
[ASD2630   SME91759]   Sep 1968

92. Alexander Ritter
1. Primula Veris
Aribert Reimann (Elec)
[C065 02 674]   Mar 1974

93. Johann Rosenmüller
1. *Cantata*
Von den himmlischen Freuden.
Edith Picht-Axenfeld, Harpsichord
Georg Donderer, Cello
Hans Nowak, Bass (Elec)
[IC063 02 258]   Aug 1969

94. Gioacchino Rossini
1. *Wilhelm Tell*
Tell's aria
Radio-Sinfonieorchester, Berlin
Ferenc Fricsay (DG)
[LPM 18700   138700]   Apr 1961

2. *Wilhelm Tell*
Orchestra conducted by
Mario Rossi (Live) (CETRA)
[MRF 691–693]   Apr 1956

3. *Petite Messe Solenelle*
Kari Lövaas
Brigitte Fassbaender
Peter Schreier
Wolfgang Sawallisch (Eurodisc)
[SER 5693/94   86 321 XGK]

                       Jul 1972

95. Anton Rubinstein
1. Es blinkt der Tau op 72 no. 1
Aribert Reimann (Elec)
[C065–02 673]   Mar 1974

96. Camille Saint-Saens
1. *Duet*
Pastorale
Victoria de Los Angeles
Gerald Moore (Elec)
[E91098]   Dec 1960

97. Alessandro Scarlatti
1. *Infirmata vulnerata* (Cantata)
Aurèle Nicolet, Flute
Helmut Heller, Violin
Edith Picht-Axenfeld, Harpsichord
Irmgard Poppen, Cello (Elec)
[FALP PM 30544
ASDF PM130544]   Feb 1963

98. Johann Hermann Schein
1. *Duet*
Christe, der Du bist Tag und Licht. Gott der
Vater, wohn uns bei.
Janet Baker
Kenneth Heath, Cello
George Malcolm, Organ and Harpsichord (Elec)
[ASD 2710]   Live Feb 1970

99. Max von Schillings
1. Freude soll in deinen Werken sein op 16 no. 1
Aribert Reimann (Elec)
[C065–2 674]   Mar 1974

100. Othmar Schoeck
1. *Aus 'Ein Tagewerk'*
1. Vom Lager stand ich mit dem Frühlicht auf.
2. Aber ein kleiner goldener Stern. Frühgesicht.
Reisephantasie. Am Ende des Festes. Nachruf.
Jugendgedanken. Peregrina II. Auf ein Kind.
Dämm'rung senkte sich von oben. Ach, wie
schön ist Nacht und Dämmerschein.
Nachklang. Höre den Rat. Venezianisches
Epigramm. Jetzt rede du.
Margit Weber (DG)
[18511]   Apr 1958

2. 14 Gesänge from 'Lebendig begraben' von
Gottfried Keller, op. 40
Radio-Symphonie-Orchester, Berlin
Fritz Rieger (DG)
[138 821]   Mar 1962
3. *Notturno* op. 4 /
Juilliard-Quartet (CBS)
[72687   KS7131]   Apr 1967

4. *Lieder* op. 17. No. 4
Peregrina
Hermann Reutter (Elec)
[C065–02 676]   May 1970

5. Abendwolken op. 20 No. 6
Reiselied op. 12 No. 1
Aribert Reimann (Elec)
[C065–02 675]   Nov 1971

6. *Hesse-Lieder*
Karl Engel (DG)
[2530 877]   Mar 1977

101. Arnold Schoenberg
1. *Lieder*
Aribert Reimann (DG)
[2530 107]   Sep 1970

2. Warnung op 3 No. 3
Traumleben op 6 No. 1
Aribert Reimann (Elec)
[C065–02 677]   Mar 1974

102. Franz Schreker
1. Die Dunkelheit sinkt schwer wie Blei.
Aribert Reimann (Elec)
[C065–02 675]   Nov 1971

103. Christian Friedrich Daniel Schubart
1. Weihnachtslied der Hirten
Jörg Demus (DG)
                         1971

104. Franz Schubert
1. *6 Heine Lieder*
Der Atlas. Ihr Bild.** Das Fischermädchen.
**Die Stadt. *Am Meer. *Der Doppelgänger.
Du bist die Ruh. Erlkönig. Nacht und Träume.
Ständchen.
Gerald Moore (Elec)
*[DB 2182   WCLP 602
*DB 21517   *DB 21586
           **DA2045   Oct 1951

2. *Die schöne Müllerin* (D.795)
Gerald Moore (Elec)
[DB 21388/95   ALP 1913
ASD 481   ALP 1036/7
C 065–00202]   Oct 1951

3. *Die schöne Müllerin*
(With the prologue and epilogue of Wilhelm
Müller)
Gerald Moore (Elec)
[SME 91187/8]   Dec 1961

4. *Winterreise* (D.911)
Gerald Moore (Elec)
[SME 91239/40   LM–6036
7 ERW 5029   (RCA Victor)
ALP 1503/4   ALP 1298/9
*DA 5529   SLS 840
*DB 11594]   Jan 1955
* ** These indicate separate recordings of one or
more of the Lieder

5. *Winterreise*
Gerald Moore (Elec)
[ALPS 2001   ASDS551/ASD552
ALP 2002]   Nov 1962

6. *Winterreise*
and Das Weinen. Schiffers Scheidelied. Der
Kreuzzug. Vor meiner Wiege.
Frühlingslied.Jägers Liebeslied.
Jörg Demus (DG)
[39201/2   139201/2
2707028   2726058]
                                         May 1965

7. *Winterreise*
Daniel Barenboim (DG)
[2707 118
Tape 3301 237]   Jan 1979

8. *Lieder Recital I*
Der Wanderer. An den Mond. Über
Wildemann. Der Einsame. Auflösung. Der
Kreuzzug. Totengräbers Heimweh. Nachtviolen.
Frühlingssehnsucht. Geheimes. Rastlose Liebe.
Liebesbotschaft. Im Abendrot. Abschied.
Gerald Moore (Elec)
[ALP 1295   WALP 1295
7 RW 569]   May 1955

9. *Lieder Recital II*
Dem Unendlichen. Die Sterne. An die Musik.
Wehmut. Kriegers Ahnung. Der Zwerg. Der
Wanderer. Frühlingsglaube. Die Taubenpost.
An Sylvia. Im Frühling. Auf der Bruck.
Gerald Moore (Elec)
[ALP 532   WALP 532
XLP 30095   ERW 5344]   Sep 1957

10. *Lieder Recital III*
Ständchen. Alinde. Nähe des Geliebten.
Normans Gesang. In der Ferne. Aufenthalt. Lied
des gefangenen Jägers. Greisengesang. Erlkönig.
Nachtstück.
Gerald Moore (Elec)
[ALP 1827   WALP 535
E90 921   *DB21350]   May 1958

11. *Lieder to poems by Schiller (Recital IV)*
Gruppe aus dem Tartarus. Die Götter
Griechenlands. Die Erwartung. Sehnsucht. Der
Taucher.
Karl Engel (Elec)
[ALP 1767   WALP 540
ASDW 9023]   Jan 1959

12. *Lieder Recital V*
Der Sänger. Die Bürgschaft. Der Fischer. Die
Einsamkeit.
Karl Engel (Elec)
[ALP 1845   WALP 551
ASDW 9031]   Jan 1958

13. *Lieder Recital VI*
Am Strome. Der Alpenjäger. Erlafsee. Wie
Ulfru fischt. Beim Winde. Trost. Auf der Donau.
Abendstern. Liedesend. Sehnsucht. Heliopolis.

Zum Punsche. Der Sieg. An die Freunde.
Karl Engel (Elec)
[E91 024   ALP 1850
WALP 552   ASDW 9032]   Jun 1959

14. *Ein Schubert-Goethe Liederabend*
Wandrers Nachtlied. Ein Gleiches. Ganymed.
Jägers Abendlied. An Schwager Kronos.
Meeresstille. Prometheus. Gesänge des Harfners.
An den Mond. Auf dem See. Erster Verlust. Der
Musensohn.
Jörg Demus (DG)
[LPM 18 617   138 117
2535 104]   Sep 1959

15. *Duet (Mignon und der Harfner)* (Nur wer die
Sehnsucht kennt)
Victoria de Los Angeles
Gerald Moore (Elec)
[E 91098]   Dec 1960

16. *Schubert-Lieder (Im Spiegel der Antike)*
Die zürnende Diana. An die Leier. Memnon.
Lied eines Schiffers an die Dioskuren. Aus
Heliopolis. Freiwilliges Versinken. Fragment aus
dem Aeschylus. Fahrt zum Hades. Orpheus.
Philoktet. Orest auf Tauris. Der entsühnte
Orest.
Jörg Demus (DG)
[18 715   138 715]   Nov 1961

17. *Lieder Recital VII*
Der Atlas. Ihr Bild. Das Fischermädchen. Die
Stadt. Am Meer. Der Doppelgänger. Lachen
und Weinen. Dass sie hier gewesen. Sei mir
gegrüsst. Du bist die Ruh. Waldesnacht.
Gerald Moore (Elec)
[WALP 582   STE 91204
*DB 2045   *DB 21586
**DB 21349]   1962
***indicates separate recordings of one or more of
the Lieder.

18. *Dietrich Fischer-Dieskau sings popular Schubert
songs (Recital VIII)*
An die Laute. Auf der Riesenkoppe. Dass sie
hier gewesen. Der Jüngling an der Quelle. Des
Fischers Liebesglück. Die Forelle. Du bist die
Ruh. Fischerweise. Heidenröslein. Lachen und
Weinen. Sei mir gegrüsst. Seligkeit. Ständchen.
Waldesnacht.
Gerald Moore (Elec)
[SME 91418   ASD 2263
1C 063–00   *DB 21349]   Feb 1965

19. *Dietrich Fischer-Dieskau sings (Recital IX)*
An die Entfernte. Auf dem Wasser zu singen.
Das Heimweh. Der Jüngling und der Tod. Das
Lied im Grünen. Litanei auf das Fest
Allerseelen. Nachtgesang. Der Schiffer. Der
Strom. Der Tod und das Mädchen. Der
Wanderer. Der Winterabend. Das
Zügenglöcklein. Der zürnende Barde.
Gerald Moore (Elec)
[SME 91 419   ASD 2273]   Feb 1965

20. *Schwanengesang* (D.957)
Gerald Moore (Elec)
[ALP 1993   ASD 544
SME 91222   1C 063–00 222
ALP 1066   †DA 2045
*DA 2049   **DB 21586]
                                    Sep 1962
* ** † These indicate separate recordings of one
or more of the Lieder.

21. *6 Lieder aus dem Jahre der 'Winterreise'*
Das Weinen. Schiffers Scheidelied. Der
Kreuzzug. Vor meiner Wiege. Frühlingslied.
Jägers Liebeslied.
Jörg Demus (DG)
[139201–2   2726 058]   1965

22. *Lieder*
Vol. I (12 LPs) & II (13 LPs)
[2720 006   2720 022]
                    Recorded between Dec 1966 &
                                    Mar 1969
23. *Vol. III*
Winterreise   Aug 1971
Die schöne Müllerin   Dec 1971
Schwanengesang   Mar 1972
Gerald Moore (DG)
[2720 059]

24. *Songs by Franz Schubert* (Gerald Moore's
Farewell Concert)
Der Einsame. Nachtviolen. Abschied. Im
Abendrot.
Gerald Moore (Elec)
[SB 3697]   Feb 1967

25. *Duets*
Hermann und Thusnelda. Antigone und
Oedipus. Cronnan. Singübungen. Selma und
Selmar. Licht und Liebe. Hektors Abschied.
Mignon und der Harfner. Szene aus Goethes
'Faust'.
Janet Baker
Members of RIAS-Chamber Choir
Gerald Moore
[2530 328]   Mar 1972

26. *Trios*
Der Hochzeitsbraten. Die Advocaten.
Punschlied. Cantate zum Geburtstag des
Sängers Johann Michael Vogl. Cantate zur
fünfzigjährigen Jubelfeier Salieri's.
Verschwunden sind die Schmerzen.
Elly Ameling
Peter Schreier
Horst Laubenthal
Gerald Moore (DG)
[2530 361]   Apr 1972

·27. *Quartets*
Der Tanz. Des Tages Weihe. Hymne an den
Unendlichen. An die Sonne. Begräbnislied. Gott
im Ungewitter. Gott der Weltschöpfer.
Lebenslust. Gebet.
Elly Ameling
Janet Baker

Peter Schreier
Gerald Moore (DG)
[2530 409]   Apr 1972

28. *Symphony No. 5 in B flat major* (D485)
Symphony No. 8 in B minor (D759) ('The
Unfinished')
New Philharmonia Orchestra
Conductor–Dietrich Fischer-Dieskau (Elec)
[ASD 2942]   Feb 1973

29. *Die Zwillingsbrüder* (D.647)
Helen Donath
Nicolai Gedda
Kurt Moll
Bayrische Staatsoper München
Wolfgang Sawallisch (Elec)
[IC065–28 833Q   ASD 3300]
                                    Jan 1975

30. *Der vierjährige Posten* (D.190)
Helen Donath
Peter Schreier
Friedrich Lenz
Willi Brockmeier
Fritz Strassner
Choir of Bavarian Radio
Munich Radio Orchestra
Heinz Wallberg (Elec)
[IC 065–30 742Q]   Aug 1977

31. *Lieder*
Des Sängers Habe. Wehmut. Der Strom. Das
Zügenglöcklein. Abendbilder. Auf der Donau.
Der Schiffer. Totengräbers Heimweh. Am
Fenster. Die Sterne. Fischerweise.
Liebeslauschen. Der Wanderer. Auf der Bruck.
Im Frühling. Aus 'Heliopolis' II.
Sviatoslav Richter (live from the Touraine Music
Festival) (DG)
[DG 2530 988]   Jul 1977

32. *Alfonso und Estrella* (D.732)
Hermann Prey
Edith Mathis
Theo Adam
Peter Schreier
Berlin Radio Choir
Berlin State Orchestra
Otmar Suitner (Elec)
[IC157 30816–8]   1979

105. Robert Schumann
1. Mondnacht. Lotosblume. Du bist wie eine
Blume. Die beiden Grenadiere.
Gerald Moore (Elec)
[DB21350   *DB21517]   Oct 1951

2. *Liederkreis* op 24
Morgens steh' ich auf und frage. Es treibt mich
hin. Ich wandle unter den Bäumen. Lieb
Liebchen, leg's Händchen. Schöne Wiege
meiner Leiden. Warte, warte, wilder
Schiffsmann. Berg und Burgen schau'n herunter.
Anfangs wollt ich fast verzagen. Mit Myrten und
Rosen. Du bist wie eine Blume. Tragödie I–II.

Der arme Peter I–III. Mein Wagen rollet
langsam. Wir sassen am Fischerhause. Oben auf
des Berges Spitze. Die Mitternacht zog näher
schon.
Hertha Klust (Elec)
[C053–01340M   WALP525
7ERW 5334EP]   Sep 1956

3. *Dietrich Fischer-Dieskau singt Schumann*
Freisinn. Schneeglöckchen. Ständchen (Komm
in die stille Nacht). Venezianisches Lied (Leis'
rudern hier). Venezianisches Lied (Wenn durch
die Piazetta).
Des Sennen Abschied. Talismane.
Zwölf Gedichte op. 35 (by Justinus Kerner) Lust
der Sturmnacht. Stirb, Lieb und Freud.
Wanderlied. Erstes Grün. Sehnsucht nach der
Waldgegend. Auf das Trinkglas eines
verstorbenen Freundes. Wanderung. Stille Liebe.
Frage. Stille Tränen. Wer machte dich so
krank? Alte Laute.
Günther Weissenborn (DG)
[18380]   Jan 1957

4. *Dichterliebe* op. 48
Jörg Demus (DG)
[18370]   Feb 1957
*This indicates a separate recording of one of the
Lieder

5. *Dichterliebe*
Jörg Demus (DG)
[139109]   May 1965

6. *Dichterliebe*
Vladimir Horowitz (CBS)
Live at Carnegie Hall
[SQ 79200]   May 1976

7. *Lieder aus dem Spanischen und aus 'Myrten'*
Der Kontrabandiste. Zigeunerliedchen No. 1 und
2. Tief im Herzen trag ich Pein. Melancholie.
Sehnsucht. Geständnis. Oh, wie lieblich ist das
Mädchen. Weh, wie zornig ist das Mädchen.
Der Hidalgo. Romanze: Ebro caudaloso.
Widmung. Der Nussbaum. Lieder aus dem
'Schenkenbuch im Divan' Nos. 1 und 2. Die
Lotosblume. Aus den hebräischen Gesängen.
Zum Schluss. Mein schöner Stern.
Jörg Demus (DG)
[18655]   Apr 1960

8. *Lieder to poems by Eichendorff*
Liederkreis to poems by Eichendorff op. 39 Nos.
1–12.
In der Fremde. Intermezzo. Waldesgespräch.
Die Stille. Mondnacht. Schöne Fremde. Auf
einer Burg. In der Fremde. Wehmut. Zwielicht.
Im Walde. Frühlingsnacht. Der frohe
Wandersmann. Der Schatzgräber.
Frühlingsfahrt. Der Einsiedler.
Gerald Moore (Elec)
[IC 063–00 274   ALP 2103
ASD 650   LM 6036
WBLP 1068   SME 91351
7RW569   *DB 21517]
                                           Mar 1964

9. *Liederkreis* op. 24 (to poems by Heinrich
Heine)
Jörg Demus (DG)
[139109]   May 1965
*This indicates a separate recording of one of the
Lieder

10. *Lieder to poems by Heinrich Heine*
Die Lotosblume ängstigt. Lehn deine Wang' an
meine Wang'. Du bist wie eine Blume. Tragödie
I und II. Dein Angesicht ist lieb und schön. Der
arme Peter I, II, III. Es leuchtet meine Liebe.
Was will die einsame Träne. Belsazar. Die
feindlichen Brüder. Abends am Strand. Die
beiden Grenadiere. Mein Wagen rollet langsam.
Jörg Demus (DG)
[139110]   May 1965

11. *Duets* (Gerald Moore's Farewell Concert)
Er und sie. Ich denk dein. In der Nacht.
Tanzlied.
Elisabeth Schwarzkopf
Gerald Moore (Elec)
[SB 3697]   Feb 1967

12. *Lieder from 1840*
Liebesbotschaft. Nichts Schöneres. An den
Sonnenschein. Sonntags am Rhein. Dichters
Genesung. Was soll ich sagen. Die Löwenbraut.
Der Knabe mit dem Wunderhorn. Der Page.
Rätsel. Zwei Venezianische Lieder. Sag an, o
lieber Vogel mein. Jasminstrauch. Aus den
östlichen Rosen. Nur ein lächelnder Blick. Dem
roten Röslein gleicht mein Lieb. Niemand.
Hochländers Abschied. Hauptmanns Weib.
Freisinn. Talismane.
Jörg Demus (DG)
[139326]   Jun 1967

13. *Duets*
Er und sie. Herbstlied. Ich bin dein Baum.
Schön ist das Fest des Lenzes. Tanzlied.
Wiegenlied.
Janet Baker
Daniel Barenboim (Elec)
[ASD 2553]   Aug 1969

14. *Faust* (Scenes from Goethe's Faust)
(Faust & Dr. Marianus)
Elizabeth Harwood
John Shirley-Quirk
Peter Pears
Jennifer Vyvyan
Felicity Palmer
Meriel Dickinson
Aldeburgh Festival Singers
Wandsworth School Choir
English Chamber Orchestra
Benjamin Britten (Decca)
[SET 567–8]   Sep 1972

15. *Liederkreis* op. 24. From *Myrten* op. 25
Widmung. Freisinn. Der Nussbaum. Sitz ich
allein. Setze mir nicht, du Grobian. Die
Lotosblume. Talismane. Hochländers Abschied.
Aus den hebräischen Gesängen. Zwei

Venezianische Lieder. Hauptmanns Weib. Was
soll die einsame Träne. Niemand. Du bist wie
eine Blume. Ich sende einen Gruss wie Duft der
Rosen. Zum Schluss.
Christoph Eschenbach (DG)
[2530 543]   Jan 1974

16. *Piano Concerto in A minor, op 54.*
Introduction and Allegro appassionato in G major (op.
92)
Daniel Barenboim
London Philharmonic Orchestra
Conductor – Dietrich Fischer-Dieskau (Elec)
[ASD 3053   C065–02530]   Jun 1974

17. *Lieder Vol I*

Lieder Vol II
Poems by Heine, Geibel, Goethe, Immermann,
Kerner, L'Égru, Lorenz, Mörike, Rückert,
Schiller and Seidl.

Lieder Vol III
Poems by Buddeus, Byron, Candidus, Eichendorff, Ekert, Geibel, Goethe, Hebbel, Heine, Jacobi, Kerner, Kinkel, Lenau, Mörike, Pfarrius,
Platen, Rückert, Schiller, Shelley, Uhland, von
der Neun.
Christoph Eschenbach (DG)
[2740 167]   Apr 1975
                                    Apr/May 1976
                                           1977

18. *Symphony No. 2 in C* (op. 61)
Bamberger Symphoniker
Conductor – Dietrich Fischer-Dieskau (BASF)
[DC 227049]   Sep/Oct 1975

19. *Symphony No. 3 in E flat* (op. 97)
Overture *Manfred*
Bamberger Symphoniker
Conductor – Dietrich Fischer-Dieskau (BASF)
[DC 227049]   Sep/Oct 1975

20. *Genoveva* (Siegfried)
Edda Moser
Peter Schreier
Siegfried Lorenz
Siegfried Vogel
Gisela Schroeter
Karl-Heinz Strycek
Wolfgang Hellmich
Berliner Rundfunkchor
Gewandhaus Leipzig Orchestra
Kurt Masur (Elec)
[IC 157–02 914/16Q]   Oct 1976

21. *Vocal Duets*
Julia Varady
Peter Schreier
Christoph Eschenbach (DG)
[2531 204]   Dec 1977

106. Heinrich Schütz
1. *St Matthew Passion*
Johannes Richter
Wolf Zeddies

Harry Dschitzki
Hugo-Distler-Chor.
Klaus Fischer-Dieskau (DG)
[198 174]   Feb 1961

2. *Duets*
Der Herr schauet vom Himmel SWV.292
Cerbum caro factum est SWV.314
Janet Baker
Kenneth Heath, Cello
George Malcolm, Organ (Elec)
[ASD 2710]   Live Feb 1970

107. Reinhard Schwarz-Schilling
1. *Lieder to poems by Eichendorff*
Aribert Reimann (Elec)
[E 90189]   Nov 1961

2. *Eichendorff Lieder*
Todeslust. Marienlied. Kurze Fahrt.
Gerald Moore (Elec)
                                        Mar 1965

108. Siegmund von Seckendorff
1. *Goethe-Lieder*
Romanze aus 'Claudine von Villa Bella'
Jörg Demus (DG)
[2533 149]   Sep 1972

109. Gottfried-Heinrich Stölzel
1. Aus der Tiefe rufe ich dir (Cantata)
Festival Strings, Lucerne
Rudolf Baumgartner (DG)
[18969   138969]   Aug 1963

110. Johann Strauss
1. *Die Fledermaus* (Falke)
Anneliese Rothenberger
Brigitte Fassbaender
Renata Holm
Nicolai Gedda
Walter Berry
Chor der Wiener Staatsoper in der Volksoper
Wiener Symphoniker
Willi Boskovsky (Elec)
[SLS 964   ASD 2891
(Tape) TC ASD2891]   Dec 1971

111. Richard Strauss
1. *Lieder*
Traum durch die Dämmerung. Ständchen.
Morgen. Wozu noch, Mädchen. Freundliche
Vision. O wärst du mein. Befreit. Herr Lenz.
Die Nacht. Ach weh mir, unglückhaftem Mann.
All mein' Gedanken. Heimliche Aufforderung.
Nachtgang. Ich liebe dich. Ruhe, meine Seele.
Zueignung.
Gerald Moore (Elec)
[90 007   ALP 516
SME 91666   7ERW 5311 EP]
                                        Jan 1956

2. *Capriccio* (Olivier)
Elisabeth Schwarzkopf
Eberhard Wächter

Nicolai Gedda
Hans Hotter
Christa Ludwig
Rudolf Christ
Anna Moffo
Philharmonia Orchestra, London
Wolfgang Sawallisch (Elec)
[OC230–2   23CX1600–2
C80695]   Sep 1957

3. *Capriccio* (Count)
Gundula Janowitz
Peter Schreier
Hermann Prey
Karl Ridderbusch
Tatiàna Troyanos
Arleen Auger
Karl Christian Kohn
Symphony Orchestra of Bavarian Radio
Karl Böhm (DG)
[2530 202–4   2709 038]   Apr 1971

4. *Der Rosenkavalier* (Faninal)
Marianne Schech
Irmgard Seefried
Rita Streich
Ilona Steingruber
Sieglinde Wagner
Rudolf Franci
Kurt Böhme
Chor der Staatsoper Dresden
Sächsische Staatskapelle
Karl Böhm (DG)
[18570–3   136410
2537013   2711001
18656]   Dec 1958

5. *The three Lieder from the Bücher des Unmuts des
Randsch Nameh* (West-östlicher Divan) (Goethe)
1. Wer wird von der Welt verlangen
2. Hab' ich euch denn je geraten
3. Wanderers Gemütsruhe.
Karl Engel (DG)
[18590   138058]   Jun 1959

6. *Elektra* (Orest)
Jean Madeira
Inge Borkh
Marianne Schech
Fritz Uhl
Chor der Staatsoper Dresden
Sächsische Staatskapelle Dresden
Karl Böhm (DG)
[18690–1   270701
136 234]   Oct 1960

7. *Arabella* (Mandryka)
Lisa della Casa
Ira Malaniuk
Anneliese Rothenberger
Georg Paskuda
Karl-Christian Kohn
Carl Hoppe
Horst Günter
Bayrischer Staatsopernchor.

Bayrisches Staatsorchester
Joseph Keilberth (DG)
[138883–5   2709 013
135127   136 419]
                                             Aug 1963

8. *Die Frau ohne Schatten* (Barak)
Inge Borkh
Ingrid Bjoner
Martha Mödl
Hertha Töpper
Jess Thomas
Hans Hotter
Chor der Bayrischen Staatsoper
Bayrisches Staatsorchester.
Joseph Keilberth (DG)
[18911–14   138911–14
2711 005]   Nov 1963

9. Gefunden. Das Rosenband. Einerlei.
Winterweihe. Stiller Gang. Der Arbeitsmann.
Blindenklage. Heimkehr.
Jörg Demus (DG)
                                             Mar 1964

10. *Krämerspiegel* op. 66
Jörg Demus (DG)
[18916   138916
Archiv 43059]   Mar 1964

11. Enoch Arden op. 38 (Tennyson)
Jörg Demus (DG)
[18916   43059]   Mar 1964

12. *Das Liedschaffen*
Acht Gedichte op 10 aus *Letzte Blätter* von
Hermann Gilm. Fünf Lieder op. 15. Sechs
Lieder op. 17. Sechs Lieder. op 19. Schlichte
Weisen op 21. Zwei Lieder op 26.
Mädchenblumen op 22. Vier Lieder op 27.
Lieder op 29 nos 1 & 3. Drei Lieder op 31. Fünf
Lieder op 32. Lieder op 36 nos. 1 & 4. Lieder op
37 no. 1–3 & 5 & 6. Sechs Lieder op 56.
Krämerspiegel op 66. Lieder op 67 nos 4–6.
Lieder op 68 nos 1 & 4. Fünf kleine Lieder op
69. Gesänge des Orients op 77. Gesänge op 87
nos. 3 & 4. Lieder op. 88 nos. 1 & 2. Lieder
ohne Opuszahl
Gerald Moore (Elec)
[ASD 2399   ASD 2622/27
SLS 792]   1967–1970

13. *Ariadne auf Naxos* (Musiklehrer)
Reri Grist
Hildegard Hillebrecht
Arleen Auger
Trudeliese Schmidt
Tatiana Troyanos
Jess Thomas
Friedrich Lenz
Gerhard Unger
Symphonie-Orchester des Bayerischen
Rundfunks
Karl Böhm (DG)
[2709 033]   Sep 1969

14. *Salome* (Jokanaan)
Richard Cassilly
Mignon Dunn
Gwyneth Jones
Wieslaw Ochmann
Ursula Boese
Orchester der Hamburgischen Staatsoper
Karl Böhm (DG)
[2530 129–30   2707 052(2 LP's)]
                                Nov 1970

15. Wer hat's getan. op. posth.
Aribert Reimann (Elec)
[C065–02 675]   Nov 1971

16. *Intermezzo* (Storch)
Lucia Popp
Adolf Dallapozza
Kurt Moll
Sinfonieorchester des Bayrischen Rundfunks
Wolfgang Sawallisch (Elec)
[C065–02 675   SLS 5204 (3LP's)
TC 525 5204]   Jan 1980

112. Theodor Streicher
1. Ist dir ein getreues, liebesvolles Kind beschert.
Aribert Reimann (Elec)
[C065–02 674]   Mar 1974

113. Georg Philipp Telemann
1. Die Hoffnung ist mein Leben (Cantata)
Helmut Heller, Violin
Edith Picht-Axenfeld, Harpsichord
Irmgard Poppen, Cello (Elec)
[FALP PM30544]   Mar 1962

2. *Kanarienvogel Cantata*
Helmut Heller, Violin
Heinz Kirchner, Viola
Lothar Koch, Oboe
Edith Picht-Axenfeld, Harpsichord
Irmgard Poppen, Cello (Elec)
[ASD 534   IC063–28]   Mar 1962

3. *7 Lieder*
Die Einsamkeit. Glück. Das Frauenzimmer.
Seltenes Glück. Die vergessene Phillis.
Falschheit. Lob des Weins.
Edith Picht-Axenfeld, Harpsichord
Irmgard Poppen, Cello (Elec)
[E 50594]   Mar 1962

4. *Erquicktes Herz sei voller Freuden.* (Cantata)
Koji Toyoda, Violin
Edith Picht-Axenfeld, Harpsichord
Georg Donderer, Cello
Hans Nowak, Bass (Elec)
[IC063–02 258]   Aug 1969

5. *Ihr Völker, hört (Cantata)*
Jean-Pierre Rampal, Flute
Robert Veyron-Lacroix, Harpsichord
Jacques Neilz, Cello (Elec)
[ASD 2903]   Oct/Nov 1971

114. Heinz Tiessen
1. Vöglein Schwermut op. 23 No. 3
Aribert Reimann (Elec)
[C065–02 675]   Nov 1971

115. Peter Tchaikovsky
1. *Duet*
Schottische Ballade
Edward op. 46 No. 2
Victoria de Los Angeles
Gerald Moore (Elec)
[91 098]   Dec 1960

2. *Eugen Onegin* (Highlights – Title Rôle) (in German)
Evelyn Lear
Brigitte Fassbaender
Fritz Wunderlich
Martti Talvela
Chorus and Orchestra of the Staatsoper München
Otto Gerdes (DG)
[136 430   2537 005]   Jul 1966

116. Giuseppe Verdi
1. *Verdi Operatic Arias* (In Italian)
Il balen del suo sorriso (*Il Trovatore*)
Pari siamo (Act 1) (Rigoletto)
Cortigiani, vil razza dannata (Act 2) (*Rigoletto*)
In braccia alle dovizie (*I vespri siciliani*)
Per me giunto (*Don Carlos*)
Alla vita che t'arride (Act 1)
Eri tu che macchiavi (Act 3) (*Un ballo in maschera*)
Ehi! paggio (Act 1)
Ehi! Taverniere! (Act 3) (*Falstaff*)
Berlin Philharmonic Orchestra
Alberto Erede (Elec)
[ALP 1825   ASD 407
STE 91 005   **E50549
*E 50542]   Jun 1959

2. Scenes from *Falstaff* (Ford) (in German)
3rd Scene
Josef Metternich
RIAS Symphoniker
Ferenc Fricsay
[36016/17 LV (78 rpm)
E 50542]   1951

* ** This indicates a separate recording of one or more of the arias.

3. *Falstaff* (Title Rôle) (in Italian)
Rolando Panerai
Juan Oncina
Gerhard Stolze
Murray Dickie
Erich Kunz
Ilva Ligabue
Graziella Sciutti
Regina Resnik
Hilde Rössl-Majdan
Vienna Philharmonic Orchestra
Leonard Bernstein (CBS)
[BRG 72493–5   SBRG 72493–5
A73120   77392]   Mar 1966

4. *Ein Maskenball (Un ballo in maschera)* (René)
(in German)
Lorenz Fehenberger
Walburga Wegner
Martha Mödl
Anny Schlemm
Cologne Radio Choir and Orchestra
Fritz Busch (Live) Gebr. Busch Gesellschaft)
[12 PAL 4779–80]   1951

5. *Ein Maskenball* (Highlights) (René) (in
German)
Inge Borkh
Evelyn Lear
Sieglinde Wagner
Jess Thomas
Chorus and Orchestra of the Deutsche Oper,
Berlin
Giuseppe Patané (DG)
[19420]   Nov 1963

6. *Die Macht des Schicksals (La Forza del destino)* (in
German)
(Don Carlo's aria)
La Traviata (Germont's aria)
Radio Symphony Orchestra, Berlin
Ferenc Fricsay (DG)
[LPM 18700   138700
2705 001]   Apr 1961

7. *Rigoletto* (Highlights – Title Rôle) (in
German)
Ernst Kozub
Gisela Vivarelli
Chorus of the Deutsche Oper Berlin
Berlin Philharmonic Orchestra
Horst Stein (DG)
[136412   2537 006]   Apr 1962

8. *Rigoletto* (Title Rôle – in Italian)
Renata Scotto
Carlo Bergonzi
Ivo Vinco
Fiorenza Cossotto
Chorus and Orchestra of La Scala, Milan
Rafael Kubelik (DG)
[136280   2709014
135008   135145
(Tape)3371 001]   Jul 1964

9. *Die Macht des Schicksals* (Highlights – Don
Carlos) (in German)
Stefania Weytowicz
Jess Thomas
Georg Stern
Cvetka Ahlin
RIAS-Kammerchor
Radio Symphony-Orchestra, Berlin
Hans Löwlein (DG)
[19416]   Oct 1962

10. *Don Carlos* (Marquis Posa) (in Italian)
Renata Tebaldi
Grace Bumbry
Nicolai Ghiaurov
Carlo Bergonzi
Martti Talvela

Chorus and Orchestra of the Royal Opera
House, Covent Garden
Georg Solti (Decca)
[SET 3058   353(Highlights)
(Duets DPA517]   Jun/Jul 1965

11. *Don Carlos* (Highlights) (in German)
Edda Moser
Nicolai Gedda
Giuseppe Patané (Elec).
[C063–28 960]   Sep 1973

12. *La Traviata* (Highlights-Germont) (in
German)
Hilde Güden
Claudia Hellman
Fritz Wunderlich
Friedrich Lenz
Chorus and Symphony-Orchestra of Bavarian
Radio
Bruno Bartoletti (DG)
[136 431   2537 022]
[135 008]   Sep 1966

13. *La Traviata* (Germont) (in Italian)
Pilar Lorengar
Sergio Fiorentino
Virgilio Carbonari
Giacomo Aragal
Chorus and Orchestra of the Deutsche Oper
Berlin
Lorin Maazel (Decca)
[SET 401–2   QSET 483]
[GOSC 667]   Jun 1968

14. *Otello* (Highlights – Iago) (in German)
Wolfgang Windgassen
Teresa Stratas
Friedrich Lenz
Chorus of the Bavarian State Opera
Bavarian State Orchestra
Otto Gerdes (DG)
[136 434 2537 017]   Jun 1967

15. *Otello* (Iago) (in Italian)
James McCracken
Gwyneth Jones
Anna di Stasio
Piero de Palma
The Ambrosian Opera Chorus
The New Philharmonia Orchestra
Sir John Barbirolli (Elec)
[SLS 940 IC 065–01 928–30]
                                                Aug 1968

16. *Macbeth* (Title Rôle) (in Italian)
Elena Souliotis
Nicolai Ghiaurov
Luciano Pavarotti
Ricaro Cassinelli
Members of Wandsworth School Boys Choir
Ambrosian Opera Chorus
London Philharmonic Orchestra
Lamberto Gardelli (Decca)
[SET B 510–2   SET 539]
[6. 41854 AN   DPA 555]
                                                Aug 1970

117. Richard Wagner

1. *Tristan und Isolde* (Kurwenal)
Ludwig Suthaus
Kirsten Flagstad
Blanche Thebom
Josef Greindl
Rudolf Schock
Covent Garden Chorus
Philharmonia Orchestra London
Wilhelm Furtwängler (Elec)
(ALP 1030–35   SME 91 170–174]
[RLS 684]   Jun 1952

2. *Der fliegende Holländer* (Title Rôle)
Gottlob Frick
Marianne Schech
Rudolf Schock
Sieglinde Wagner
Fritz Wunderlich
Chor und Orchester der Deutschen Staatsoper,
Berlin
Franz Konwitschny (Elec)
[ASD 385–387   SME 91 056/58]
[ALP 2006   IC 063–28 169]
                                             Feb 1960

3. *Tannhäuser*
3 scenes (Wolfram)
Philharmonia Orchestra
Wilhelm Schüchter (Elec)
[E 50041]   1956

4. *Tannhäuser* (Wolfram)
Elisabeth Grümmer
Hans Hopf
Gottlob Frick
Chorus and Orchestra of the Deutsche
Staatsoper, Berlin
Franz Konwitschny (Elec)
[ASD 445–8   ALP 1876–9]
SME 91 087–90   Angel 3620
C063–28512   SME 80638
SLS 775   Oct 1960

5. *Tannhäuser* (Wolfram)
Birgit Nilsson
Wolfgang Windgassen
Horst Laubenthal
Friedrich Lenz
Theo Adam
Chorus and Orchestra of the Deutsche Oper,
Berlin
Otto Gerdes (DG)
[139284–7   2740 142]
[2911 108   2537 016][2721 112]   Dec 1968

6. *Lohengrin* (Telramund)
Jess Thomas
Elisabeth Grümmer
Christa Ludwig
Gottlob Frick
Chorus of the Vienna State Opera
Vienna Philharmonic Orchestra
Rudolf Kempe (Elec)
[SAN 121–5   STA 91 299–803]
[SLS 5071   SME 80853]
[(Tape) TC SLS 5071]   Nov/Dec 1962

7. *Lohengrin* (Telramund)
Wolfgang Windgassen
Birgit Nilsson
Theo Adam
Astrid Varnay
Eugen Jochum – (Live from Bayreuth)
(CETRA)
(CETRA L077(4)]   1954

8. *Götterdämmerung* (Gunther)
Birgit Nilsson
Wolfgang Windgassen
Gottlob Frick
Claire Watson
Christa Ludwig
Gustav Neidlinger
Helen Watts
Horst Hoffmann
Anita Valkki
Lucia Popp
Gwyneth Jones
Maureen Guy
Chorus of the Vienna State Opera
Vienna Philharmonic Orchestra
Georg Solti (Decca)
[SET 292–7   (Tape) K4W 32]
SXL 6220   SXL 20549 B]
KSXC 6220   Oct/Nov 1964

9. *Rheingold* (Wotan)
Josephine Veasey
Oralia Dominguez
Helen Donath
Edda Moser
Anna Reynolds
Donald Grobe
Zoltan Kelemen
Gerhard Stolze
Karl Ridderbusch
Martti Talvela
Berlin Philharmonic Orchestra
Herbert von Karajan (DG)
[SLPM 104966–8   2561 192–4]
[2740 145   2709 023]
[136 437   2537 027]
                             Dec 1967/Jan 1968

10. *Parsifal* (Amfortas)
Christa Ludwig
René Kollo
Gottlob Frick
Vienna Philharmonic Orchestra
Georg Solti (Decca)
[SET 550–4   SET 574]
                                             Dec 1971

11. *Parsifal* (Amfortas)
Ramón Vinay
Martha Mödl
Josef Greindl
Hans Hotter
Hans Knappertsbusch.
Live from Bayreuth (CETRA)
[L079(5)]   1956

12. *Goethe Lieder*
Lied des Mephistopheles. Brandners Lied.
Jörg Demus
[2533 149]   Sep 1972

13. Der Tannenbaum
Aribert Reimann (Elec)
[IC 065–02674]   Mar 1974

14. *Die Meistersinger von Nürnberg* (Hans Sachs)
Catarina Ligendza
Christa Ludwig
Placido Domingo
Roland Hermann
Horst Laubenthal
Gerd Feldhoff
Peter Lagger
Chorus and Orchestra of the Deutsche Oper,
Berlin
Eugen Jochum (DG)
[2740 149 (SLPs)   2537 041]
[(Tape) 3306 041   Mar/Apr 1976

15. *Fischer-Dieskau singt Wagner*
Der fliegende Holländer – Die Frist ist um
Parsifal – Nein, lasst ihn unenthüllt
       – Ja, Wehe! Wehe!
Die Walküre – Leb wohl, du kühnes,
          herrliches Kind
Symphony Orchestra of Bavarian Radio
Rafael Kubelik (Elec)
(IC 063–02 969 Q]   1977

118. Bruno Walter
1. *3 Lieder to poems of Eichendorff*
Musikantengruss. Der junge Ehemann.
Der Soldat.
Jörg Demus (DG)
[138 946]   May 1964

119. Carl Maria von Weber
2. *Scottish songs and folk-songs*
Helmut Heller, Violin
Irmgard Poppen, Cello
Aurèle Nicolet, Flute
Karl Engel (DG)
[138 706 2720 017]   Feb 1961

120. Anton von Webern
1. *Lieder*
Vorfrühling. Gefunden. Bild der Liebe.
Am Ufer. Dies ist ein Lied. An Bachesranft.
Noch zwingt mich Trauer. So ich traurig bin.
Ihr tratet zu dem Herde.
Aribert Reimann (DG)
[2530 107]   Sep 1970

2. *Vier Lieder*
Aribert Reimann (Elec)
[C065–02 677]   Mar 1974

121. Felix Paul von Weingartner
1. Liebes Feuer
Aribert Reimann (Elec)
[C065–02 674]   Mar 1974

122. Wilhelm Weismann
1. Schlaf wohl, du Himmelsknabe du (nach
Schubart)
Der heilige Nikolaus
Jörg Demus (DG)
[2530 219]   Nov 1970

123. Justus Hermann Wetzel
1. An meine Mutter op 3 No. 5
Der Kehraus
Aribert Reimann
[C065–002 675]   Mar 1974

124. Hugo Wolf
1. *From the Italianisches Liederbuch*
Nos. 4, 5, 7, 8, 13, 14, 17, 18, 22, 23, 33, 34, 35,
37, 41, 42
Hertha Klust (DG)
[18005]
[LM68455–58   S36401–2]
                           Apr 1950/Jan 1951
2. *Italienisches Liederbuch from poems by Paul Heyse*
Irmgard Seefried
Jörg Demus
Erik Werba (DG)
[18568–9   138 035–36][2705–118]   Oct 1958
3. *Italienisches Liederbuch*
Elisabeth Schwarzkopf
Gerald Moore (Elec)
[SAN 210–211   SMA 91546–7]
                             Jan/Feb 1966

4. *Italienisches Liederbuch*
Christa Ludwig
Daniel Barenboim (DG)
[2707 114]   1979

5. Goethe Lieder *and* Fussreise. Lebewohl.
Verschwiegene Liebe. Alle gingen.
Wer sein holdes Lieb verloren.
Gerald Moore (Elec)
                             Oct 1952

6. Der Tambour. Der Feuerreiter.
Storchenbotschaft.
Gerald Moore (Elec)
[7er 5044]   Jan 1955

7. *Mörike-Lieder I:*
Der Genesene an die Hoffnung. In der
Frühe. Fussreise. Gebet.
Im Frühling. Karwoche. Auf einer Wanderung.
Denk' es, o Seele.
Die Geister am Mummelsee. Begegnung.

Zitronenfalter im April. Der Gärtner.
Nimmersatte Liebe. Heimweh. Der Jäger.
Storchenbotschaft.
Gerald Moore (Elec).
[ALP 1617–8 WALP 529]   Sep 1957

8. *Mörike-Lieder II;*
Jägerlied. An die Geliebte. Peregrina I–II
Lebe wohl. Um Mitternacht.
Der Feuerreiter. Seufzer. Wo find' ich
Trost. Neue Liebe. Auf eine
Christblume I–II. Auf ein altes Bild.
Schlafendes Jesuskind.
Gerald Moore (Elec)
(ALP 1618–9 WALP 580 (1953)]
     Sep 1957

9. *Mörike-Lieder III:*
An den Schlaf. Verborgenheit. Gesang Weylas.
Lied eines Verliebten. Zur Warnung. Der
Tambour. Auftrag.
Bei einer Trauung. Selbstgeständnis.
Abschied.
Gerald Moore (Elec)
[ALP 1619 WALPS 531]   Sep 1957

10. From the *Spanisches Liederbuch*
Elisabeth Schwarzkopf
Gerald Moore (DG)
[SLPM 139329/30]   Dec 1966

11. *Eichendorff-Lieder*
Der Freund. Der Musikant.
Verschwiegene Liebe. Das Ständchen.
Der Soldat. I u. II Nachtzauber.
Der Schreckenberger. Der Glücksritter.
Lieber alles. Heimweh. Der Scholar.
Der verzweifelte Liebhaber. Unfall.
Liebesglück. Seemanns Abschied.
In der Fremde. I. Erwartung. Die Nacht.
Nachtruf.
Gerald Moore (Elec)
(ALP 1778 ASD 356]   Apr 1959

12. *Lieder to poems by various poets*
Gerald Moore (Elec)
[E91002 ASD 362]
[ALP 1783]   Apr 1959

13. *Goethe-Lieder I:*
Gerald Moore (Elec)
[ALP 1852 ASD 424]   Apr 1960

14. *Goethe-Lieder II:*
Gerald Moore (Elec)
(ASLP 1853 ASD 425]   Apr 1960

15. *Lieder*
Gesegnet sei, durch den die Welt entstund.
Der Mond hat eine schwere Klag erhoben.
Und willst du deinen Liebsten sterben sehn.
Nun lass uns Frieden schliessen.
Benedeit die sel'ge Mutter.
Jörg Demus (DG)
[109 108B *135 026]   Apr 1960

16. *Lieder to poems by Eduard Mörike.*
Der Genesene an die Hoffnung. In der Frühe.
Fussreise. Neue Liebe. Der Feuerreiter.
Jägerlied. Storchenbotschaft.
Verborgenheit. Im Frühling.
Auf einer Wanderung. An die Geliebte.
Peregrina I/II. Lebe wohl. Begegnung.
Der Jäger. Bei einer Trauung.
Sviatoslav Richter (DG)
Live recording from Innsbruck
[2530 584]   Oct 1973

17. *Lieder* Vol I
Poems by Eduard Mörike

Lieder Vol II
Poems by Johann Wolfgang von Goethe,
Heinrich Heine and Nikolaus Lenau

Lieder Vol III
Poems by Eichendorff, Michelangelo,
von Fallersleben, Reinick, Byron,
Shakespeare
Daniel Barenboim 'DG)
[2740 113 2740 156]   Dec 1972
[2740 162]   June 1973
     Jan/Feb 1974
     Oct/Nov 1974
     Nov 1976

125. Carl Friedrich Zelter
1. *Goethe-Lieder*
Rastlose Liebe. Um Mitternacht.
Gleich und gleich. Wo geht's Liebchen.
Jörg Demus (DG)
[2533 149]   Sep 1972

*This indicates a separate recording of one or
more of the Lieder.